Relators and Linkers

Linguistic Inquiry Monographs
Samuel Jay Keyser, general editor

6. *Some Concepts and Consequences of the Theory of Government and Binding*, Noam Chomsky
10. *On the Nature of Grammatical Relations*, Alec Marantz
12. *Logical Form: Its Structure and Derivation*, Robert May
13. *Barriers*, Noam Chomsky
15. *Japanese Tone Structure*, Janet Pierrehumbert and Mary Beckman
16. *Relativized Minimality*, Luigi Rizzi
18. *Argument Structure*, Jane Grimshaw
19. *Locality: A Theory and Some of Its Empirical Consequences*, Maria Rita Manzini
20. *Indefinites*, Molly Diesing
21. *Syntax of Scope*, Joseph Aoun and Yen-hui Audrey Li
22. *Morphology by Itself: Stems and Inflectional Classes*, Mark Aronoff
23. *Thematic Structure in Syntax*, Edwin Williams
24. *Indices and Identity*, Robert Fiengo and Robert May
25. *The Antisymmetry of Syntax*, Richard S. Kayne
26. *Unaccusativity: At the Syntax–Lexical Semantics Interface*, Beth Levin and Malka Rappaport Hovav
27. *Lexico-Logical Form: A Radically Minimalist Theory*, Michael Brody
28. *The Architecture of the Language Faculty*, Ray Jackendoff
29. *Local Economy*, Chris Collins
30. *Surface Structure and Interpretation*, Mark Steedman
31. *Elementary Operations and Optimal Derivations*, Hisatsugu Kitahara
32. *The Syntax of Nonfinite Complementation: An Economy Approach*, Željko Bošković
33. *Prosody, Focus, and Word Order*, Maria Luisa Zubizarreta
34. *The Dependencies of Objects*, Esther Torrego
35. *Economy and Semantic Interpretation*, Danny Fox
36. *What Counts: Focus and Quantification*, Elena Herburger
37. *Phrasal Movement and Its Kin*, David Pesetsky
38. *Dynamic Antisymmetry*, Andrea Moro
39. *Prolegomenon to a Theory of Argument Structure*, Ken Hale and Samuel Jay Keyser
40. *Essays on the Representational and Derivational Nature of Grammar: The Diversity of* Wh-*Constructions*, Joseph Aoun and Yen-hui Audrey Li
41. *Japanese Morphophonemics: Markedness and Word Structure*, Junko Ito and Armin Mester
42. *Restriction and Saturation*, Sandra Chung and William A. Ladusaw
43. *The Linearization of Chains and Sideward Movement*, Jairo Nunes
44. *The Syntax of (In) Dependence*, Ken Safir
45. *Interface Strategies*, Tanya Reinhart
46. *Asymmetry in Morphology*, Anna Maria Di Sciullo
47. *Relators and Linkers: The Syntax of Predication, Predicate Inversion, and Copulas*, Marcel den Dikken

Relators and Linkers

The Syntax of Predication, Predicate Inversion, and Copulas

Marcel den Dikken

A Bradford Book
The MIT Press
Cambridge, Massachusetts
London, England

MIT Press books may be purchased at special quantity discounts for business or sales promotional use. For information, please e-mail special_sales@mitpress.mit .edu or write to Special Sales Department, The MIT Press, 55 Hayward Street, Cambridge, MA 02142.

This book was set in Times New Roman on 3B2 by Asco Typesetters, Hong Kong. Printed and bound in the United States of America.

Library of Congress Cataloging-in-Publication Data

Dikken, Marcel den, 1965–
Relators and linkers : the syntax of prediction, predicate inversion, and copulas / Marcel den Dikken
    p.   cm.—(Linguistic inquiry monographs ; 47)
"Bradford book."
Includes bibliographical references and index.
ISBN 978-0-262-04231-4 (hc. : alk. paper)—978-0-262-54186-2 (pb. : alk. paper)
1. Grammar, Comparative and general—Verb phrase. I. Title. II. Series.
P281.D55   2006
415—dc22   2005050460

10 9 8 7 6 5 4 3 2

Contents

Acknowledgments   ix

Chapter 1

Introduction   1

Chapter 2

The Syntactic Configuration of Predication   7

2.1   The Meaning of Predication   8

2.2   The Syntax of Predication   11

2.3   A Brief Historical Interlude on Internal Subjects   17

2.4   On the Nature of Lexical Heads   20

2.5   On the Nature of the RELATOR   22

2.6   Adjectival and Adverbial Modification as Predication   29

2.7   Predication Alternations   43

2.8   Reverse Predications as Primary Predications   47

2.9   Concluding Remarks on the Syntactic Configuration of Predication   55

Chapter 3

Small Clauses and Copular Sentences
57

3.1   Small Clauses   58

3.2   Copular Sentences   64

3.3   Conclusions and Prospects   79

Chapter 4

Predicate Inversion: Why and How?
81

4.1   Predicate Inversion as
A-Movement   82

4.2   Predicate Inversion: Why?   87

4.3   Predicate Inversion: How?   110

4.4   Predicate Inversion and the
Postverbal Subject   117

4.5   Predicate Inversion and the
Distribution of the LINKER   143

4.6   Concluding Remarks   151

Appendix: On the Limited
Distribution of Copular Inversion
152

Chapter 5

**Predication and Predicate Inversion
inside the Nominal Phrase**   161

5.1   Qualitative Binominal Noun
Phrases and the Nondirectionality of
Predication   162

5.2   Attributive QBNPs: A Predicate-
Specifier Structure   165

5.3   Comparative QBNPs: An
Inverted Predicate-Complement
Structure   172

5.4   Quantification in Qualitative
Binominal Noun Phrases   186

Contents

5.5   Real and "Spurious" Articles in Qualitative Binominal Noun Phrases
198

5.6   The Nominal Copula   212

5.7   Other Cases of Predication and Predicate Inversion inside the Nominal Phrase   222

5.8   Concluding Remarks   245

Chapter 6

Predication, RELATORS, and LINKERS
247

Notes   251

References   311

Index   331

Acknowledgments

This book has had a rather long gestation period. Some of the ideas reported in these pages go back to my undergraduate years at Leiden University (see Den Dikken 1987), others stem from my graduate research at the same institution (see Den Dikken 1991, 1995c—the latter being the published version of my 1992 doctoral dissertation), but the core of this study was conceived in 1994 and 1995 while I was at the Vrije Universiteit Amsterdam, where I first applied the newly unveiled minimalist locality theory (with "equidistance" as one of its key ingredients) to the distribution of the copula (see Den Dikken 1994, 1995a). My "Copulas" paper, presented at the GLOW Colloquium in Tromsø in 1995, was never published—I never submitted it for publication at the time because I felt it needed more work. I did indeed continue to work on the project, which resulted in a few spin-off publications along the way (Den Dikken 1998b, 1999), but the core of the analysis remained the unpublished 1995 paper. When, in the fall of 2001, I taught an Advanced Syntax seminar at the CUNY Graduate Center (my home base since 1998) on the syntax of predication and Predicate Inversion, I returned to the original material as well as its spin-offs in an effort to unfold a unified and updated perspective on the variety of empirical material I had been grappling with over a nearly ten-year period. That class led to some new insights and also to a couple of excellent student papers (which I will have occasion to draw on in what follows), and overall rekindled the desire to get this material written up and published. In the summer of 2002 I started the process, but I had to put it to rest during the academic year that followed. Thanks in part to the lack of summery distractions in one of the meteorologically most depressing summers in New York City's history (see (28j) in chapter 5), I managed to finish the manuscript in August 2003. The text was subsequently reviewed by three readers, each providing invaluable feedback on the manuscript, for which I am deeply grateful. In July 2004 I completed the final revisions.

The outcome is rather different, in both fundamental and more superficial ways, from the original 1995 manuscript, in part as a consequence of developments in the theory within which this work is embedded and in part as a result of an exercise in rethinking the original material such that it would bring forth a fully integrated and internally consistent perspective on the syntax of predication in general and that of Predicate Inversion in particular.

I could easily fill the next page just listing the names of people who have inspired or helped me during the decade in which the ideas laid out in this book were developed. Many of these people will find their names in the notes or bibliography. But I want to make an exception for just a few people whose influence on this work has been particularly significant. First, I would like to acknowledge some key collaborations: with Hans Bennis and Norbert Corver on DP-internal predication and inversion in Dutch; with Anikó Lipták on some fascinating Hungarian cases of DP-internal predication; with Pornsiri Singhapreecha on Thai and sundry other Asian languages; with André Meinunger and Chris Wilder on pseudoclefts; and, early on, with Alma Næss on Locative Inversion in Norwegian. The fruits of all these collaborations are available in print (see the references); they will also be drawn on in what follows. I would like to take this opportunity to thank all these colleagues for such inspiring and productive collaborations.

Thanks are due as well to the colleagues, students, and staff at the various institutions that supported me in the course of the development of the ideas reported herein—the Vrije Universiteit Amsterdam, the Zentrum für Allgemeine Sprachwissenschaft (ZAS) in Berlin, the University of California at Los Angeles (UCLA), Tilburg University, and The Graduate Center of The City University of New York. In addition, I would like to gratefully acknowledge the written comments on parts of earlier drafts of this book provided by Péter Antonyi, Ana Longenecker, and Elena Rudnitskaya.

Apart from the obvious influence on this work of Noam Chomsky, Richard Kayne, Tim Stowell, and others, four colleagues deserve special mention. Jacqueline Guéron is one of the most original thinkers in the field, and a wonderful source of inspiration. It is impossible not to be struck by her ideas, yet it is often quite difficult to incorporate them into mainstream work. I think I have done a reasonable job on embedding her analysis of inverse copular sentences into an overall outlook on the syntax of predication and Predicate Inversion—but I am sure I could have taken better heed of her advice and more advantage of her many thought-provoking ideas and insights.

Caroline Heycock and I started working on copular sentences roughly at the same time, entirely independently of one another. But our paths have since intersected on many occasions. Though we have never managed to strike much of a common ground when it comes to the specifics of our analyses or even several of the fundamental questions lying beneath them, our general lines of approach have always been conducive to very fruitful interaction. Heycock's criticisms of my analyses, always entirely to the point and clever, have led to myriad improvements on my part. While we are continuing to agree to disagree on many points, I hope the discussions in these pages (many based on or in direct response to her work) will prove as meaningful to her as her work has been to me.

Andrea Moro is the next person to whom I owe a tremendous intellectual debt. His groundbreaking work on copular sentences and the raising of predicates is, as the numerous references to it in what follows will acknowledge at every point along the way, the original inspiration for almost every ingredient of the analysis. From its very earliest stages, Moro has always been a strong supporter of my work on the syntax of predication and Predicate Inversion. And though we ended up taking rather different avenues in our more recent work (the contrast between Moro 2000 and the present work could hardly be greater when it comes to the representation of nominal predication and the motivation for Copular Inversion), I trust that he will read this book with interest.

Finally, there is one person that played the single most important role in my development as a linguist and in the shaping of the ideas reported in this book. His seminal work and phenomenal classes on predication, small clauses, Locative Inversion, argument-structure alternations, and syntactic theory in general are an everlasting source of inspiration. The standard by which he judged people's work has always made me try just a little harder to iron out some of the remaining wrinkles and to find answers to some of the questions raised by the analysis. I hope that this work will, at least to some extent, have succeeded in meeting his standard. But unfortunately, I will never know for certain. Though he saw the beginnings of this work and strongly encouraged me to pursue it, he died long before I could complete it. This book is dedicated to the memory of this outstanding linguist, Teun Hoekstra.

New York City, July 2004

Chapter 1

Introduction

These are by no means the first words ever written about predication. In the Western philosophical tradition, predication was among the first topics to appear on the scene. Nor are these at all likely to be the final words on predication. There are doubtless many ways in which the ideas expounded in these pages will be found to be in need of revision, or simply wrong. What, then, justifies this new study of predication? My answer is that its raison d'être lies in the specific avenue toward predication taken here—an avenue that puts great emphasis on meaningless elements (meaningless in the sense of having no semantic load) that play an essential role in the establishment and syntactic manipulation of predication relationships. So rather than focusing on the meaningful parts of predication structures, this study gives pride of place to what I call RELATORS and LINKERS. The former mediate the relationship between a predicate and its subject in the base representation of predication structures; the latter connect the raised predicate to the small clause harboring its subject in so-called Predicate Inversion constructions, in which—as the name suggests—the predicate inverts with the subject.[1]

I first started studying LINKERS in the early 1990s (see Den Dikken 1994 for an initial report), when I tried to make sense of the obligatoriness of the copula *to be* in sentences of the type in (1b) (see Moro 1990, 1997 for the original observation), which alternate with constructions like (1a) in which no copula is needed.

(1) a. Imogen considers Brian (to be) the best candidate.

    b. Imogen considers the best candidate *(to be) Brian.

I found out that an analysis of what Moro (1997) calls "inverse" copular sentences in terms of A-movement of *the best candidate* into subject position could derive the obligatoriness of the copula from the locality theory just proposed in Chomsky's (1995, chap. 3) minimalist program, in terms of domain-extending head movement and equidistance. That analysis, lending strong support to the movement analysis of inverse copular sentences (which, in the generative literature, goes back at least to Blom and Daalder 1977; see also Heggie 1988; Heycock 1991, 1994; Hoekstra and Mulder 1990; and especially Moro 1997), identified the copula as a syntactic aid to the inversion of the predicate around the subject: the copula as the reflex of locality–theoretically forced movement of the functional head of the small clause to a higher head. This view of the copula as a "pivot" for Predicate Inversion was found, in subsequent work (see Den Dikken 1995a; Bennis, Corver, and Den Dikken 1998), to extend naturally into the nominal domain, where the LINKER element *van* rears its head in Dutch examples like (2b), which alternate with uninverted constructions such as (2a).

(2) a. een vent als   een beer (Dutch)
       a   bloke as/like a   bear
    b. een beer van een vent
       a   bear of a   bloke

A wide variety of constructions (in clauses as well as nominal phrases) were identified to support the generalization that inversion of a predicate around its subject gives rise to a LINKER element as a result of syntactic constraints imposed on the inversion process. The syntax, then, was seen to be entirely responsible for the distribution of copular elements in such contexts as (1b) and (2b).

Uninverted predications, however, may also feature meaningless elements between the two relata (subject and predicate). Thus, in (1a), although *to be* is by no means obligatory, whenever the matrix verb selects a *to*-infinitival complement, *be* must be included (*Imogen considers Brian to *(be) the best candidate*). And similarly, in (2a) the element *als*, the Dutch cognate of English *as*, is inomissible. These meaningless pieces are not there to facilitate inversion of the predicate around its subject, for in the a-examples there has been no such inversion. These, therefore, are lexicalizations of a different functional head in the structure—one that mediates the syntactic relationship between the predicate and its subject in the base. I call elements that perform this mediating function RELATORS. They originate in the functional head of small clauses, the RELATOR-head.

It is the responsibility of the RELATOR to establish the relationship between the predicate and its subject in the syntactic structure. In the examples in (1a) and (2a), that relationship is established in such a way that the subject is the specifier of the RELATOR-head and the predicate is its complement (see (3a)). This state of affairs is indeed the most common way the connection between the predicate and its subject is syntactically created. But there is no reason to think, a priori, that it is the only one. What if the predicate were base-generated as the specifier of the RELATOR and the subject as its complement? Does the structure in (3b) serve any purpose? Are there constructions that instantiate it? I will argue in chapter 2 that indeed there are several such constructions, and that, therefore, predication relationships, while always hierarchically asymmetrical, are fundamentally nondirectional.

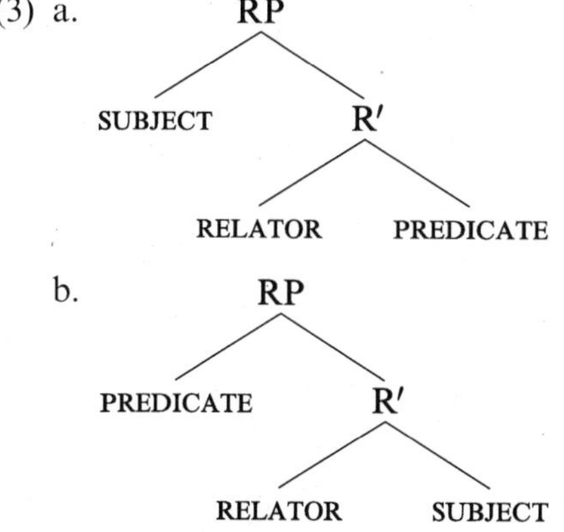

This study is organized into four substantive chapters, sandwiched between this introduction and the brief summary presented in chapter 6 of the major results of this study of predication and Predicate Inversion. Chapters 2 and 3 develop the hypothesis that *all* subject-predicate relationships are syntactically mediated by a RELATOR and that subject-predicate relationships in syntax are configurational and fundamentally nondirectional (chapter 2), and will explicitly refute claims to the effect that "bare" small clauses (subject-predicate structures lacking any internal functional structure) exist (chapter 3). In the course of the discussion in chapter 3, a typology of copular sentences is presented that leaves room for just two types (Moro's "canonical" and "inverse" copular sentences). In chapter 4, the focus will be on inversion of the predicate around its subject and the distribution of LINKER elements surfacing between the inverted predicate and the subject. Presenting an in-depth analysis of the syntax of Predicate Inversion, chapter 4 shows that inverse copular sentences, and Predicate Inversion constructions in general, involve A-movement of a null-headed small-clause predicate around the subject, the null-headedness of the predicate holding the key to the distribution of Predicate Inversion. Chapter 4 also takes care to distinguish between two types of Predicate Inversion constructions: those whose well-formedness is dependent on the projection in the tree of a LINKER element (such as the cases in (1b) and (2b), specimens of Copular Inversion) and those in which no LINKER is needed because the head of the predicate raises to the RELATOR-head of the small clause.

While chapters 2 through 4 concern themselves primarily with cases of predication inside finite and infinitival clauses, chapter 5 is a study (building on Den Dikken 1995a) of predication and Predicate Inversion in the nominal domain. Here, qualitative binominal noun phrases such as (2b) are examined in detail. The discussion will show that all qualitative binominal noun phrases share the fact that they involve two noun phrases entertaining a predication relationship, with the first noun phrase serving as the predicate of the second. In a case study of the central hypothesis that there are two ways, in principle, in which a predication relationship can be projected in the underlying representation (see (3a, b)), it will be shown in chapter 5 that qualitative binominal noun phrases come in two types, one employing the predicate-specifier structure in (3b) and base-generating the surface order of predicate and subject, and the other featuring the predicate-complement structure in (3a) and deriving the surface order of constituents via Predicate Inversion. Both types of qualitative binominal noun phrase give rise to a "nominal copula" (Dutch *van*, English *of*) between the predicate and the subject: in the predicate-specifier type, this copula is the lexicalization of the RELATOR, while in the predicate-complement type, whose derivation involves Predicate Inversion, the nominal copula is a spell-out of the LINKER. The case study of qualitative binominal noun phrases in chapter 5 thus lends support to the configurationality and fundamental nondirectionality of predication, and by identifying a copular element inside the nominal phrase and analyzing its distribution, it both furthers the parallelism between clauses and nominal phrases and vindicates the view that copular elements are meaningless spell-outs of functional heads inside or immediately outside small clauses (RELATORS and LINKERS).

After establishing the analysis of qualitative binominal noun phrases, chapter 5 proceeds to a brief discussion of other instances of noun-phrase internal predication and Predicate Inversion, reviewing *wh*-interrogative and *wh*-exclamative DPs, cases of DP-internal adjectival predication, possessed noun phrases and relative-clause constructions, and drawing on a variety of languages to illustrate its claims. Overall, the study of predication and Predicate Inversion in the complex noun phrase at the same time highlights the pervasiveness of predication and Predicate Inversion in the grammar, confirms the conclusions reached on the basis of the investigation of clause-internal Predicate Inversion in chapter 4, and provides us with a new window on the internal structure of the nominal phrase.

My general objective in this work is to present a syntax of predication and the inversion of the predicate around its subject. The analysis will be cast in the mold of the principles-and-parameters theory of generative grammar—specifically, its recent "minimalist" incarnation (Chomsky 1995 and later work). Of particular importance in the technical discussions will be the ingredients of the *locality* theory, including the minimal domain and the phase. Though prior knowledge of these ingredients will definitely expedite the reader's progress through these discussions, I have made a concerted effort to introduce the key concepts at the points at which they become relevant. Though the bulk of the discussion should be accessible (and of interest) to readers with only a general knowledge of generative syntax, there are some parts—particularly in chapter 4 (see especially section 4.3)—where the discussion is of a rather technical nature. Those not interested in the theoretical nitty-gritty may want to concentrate on the more empirically oriented portions of this study.

Chapter 2

The Syntactic Configuration
of Predication

In this chapter I will lay the theoretical foundations for the investigations that fill the rest of these pages. I will consider the question of how the semantic relationship of *predication* is projected in the syntactic tree, and what a syntactic predicate comes down to. To properly lay these foundations, I will need to go through some of the discussion in the philosophical and logicosemantic literature concerning the complicated notion of predication, singling out Aristotle and Frege as the two key players in the debate, and I will also need to make a number of syntactic decisions. Because of the plethora of syntactic and semantic approaches to predication and the lack of a consensus on fundamental questions in the linguistic representation of predication, I cannot simply pick one particularly attractive fruit from the tree laden with approaches to predication; instead, it will be necessary to carve out a consistent framework within which to set the syntactic analyses of predication and copular constructions in the later chapters.

In section 2.2, I develop a syntactic representation of predication relationships in which the relationship between the predicate and the subject is established by a connective, a RELATOR, in a functional structure in which there is an asymmetrical c-command relationship between the predicate and the subject, with either constituent being eligible in principle for the hierarchically superior position. In the remainder of the chapter, this structural representation of the predication is subsequently applied to a variety of constructions involving predication, including topicalization, focalization, and adverbial and adjectival modification. Chapter 3 then proceeds to an investigation of small-clause constructions against the background of the central hypothesis, arguing that all small clauses include a projection of a functional head and rejecting proposals to the effect that "bare" small clauses exist. A discussion of the syntax of copular sentences, which takes up the bulk of chapter 3, will strengthen this conclusion and will firmly establish the fundamental asymmetry of subject-predicate relationships in syntax.

2.1   The Meaning of Predication

In the Western philosophical tradition, Plato's *Sophist* is the first work to define the sentence as a conjunction of a subject and a predicate, an idea subsequently picked up by Aristotle (especially in his *Perì Hermēneías/De Interpretatione*), where the subject-predicate distinction plays a key role on both the grammatical and the logical planes.[1] On the predicate side of the dichotomy, with the *rhêma* 'rheme' (variably translated as "verb" or "predicate," the latter arguably being the superior rendition) being the "sign of what holds ... of a subject" (*De Interpretatione* 3, 16b, 7), Aristotle introduces a further terminological distinction between grammatical and logical notions, using the term *kategoroúmenon* to designate the syntactic constituent denoting the property assigned to the subject (grammatical predicate), and the term *symbebekós* for the property denoted by the predicate (logical predicate). Unfortunately, however, Aristotle failed to make a similar bifurcation on the subject side, using his term *hypokeímenon* ("subject" in the familiar Latin translation) to refer to that which the sentence is about (the logical subject, the counterpart to the *symbebekós*) but introducing no terminological counterpart to the *kategoroúmenon*. As Ackrill (1963, 120) puts it bluntly, "Aristotle's failure to clearly distinguish between grammatical and logical analysis" is "the root of the trouble"—the trouble, that is, of knowing what people mean when they use the terms *subject* and *predicate*. The trouble is aggravated further by the fact that the Latin translation of Aristotle's work does not distinguish between the *kategoroúmenon* and the *symbebekós*, collapsing the two into the single term *praedicatum*, our "predicate."

This in and of itself does not mean that we should abandon the distinction between subject and predicate, however. Terminological confusion does not jeopardize Aristotle's notion that a declarative sentence can be teased apart into something that ascribes a certain property to something else and the entity to which this property is ascribed (or "that which the sentence is about"). To argue against that notion one would have to show either that it is useless or that it is wrong. Frege (1879) found it useless. Noting that active *Imogen kissed Brian* (in which *Imogen* is the subject and *kissed Brian* the predicate) and passive *Brian was kissed by Imogen* (where *Brian* is the subject and *kissed by Imogen* the predicate) have the same semantic content ("begrifflicher Inhalt"), and stating that this is really the only thing that matters to his analysis, he concludes that no distinction need be made between any sentences whose semantic content is the same. The subject position is just that position in the sentence in which one typically expresses the topic; it does not have any formal significance.

What really matters for Frege is the *function-argument* structure, which is often deemed the ancestor of modern Theta Theory. And indeed, via the development of Frege's thoughts into a theory of *n*-ary predicates, grammatical theory did ultimately arrive at Theta Theory this way. But in Frege's (1879) own work, things are not quite that simple. For Frege, the function is that part of the expression that is invariant, the argument being the replaceable or exchangeable part. Thus, in the pair of sentences *Carbon dioxide is heavier than hydrogen* and *Carbon dioxide is heavier than oxygen* (Frege's examples on p. 16), we are dealing with the same function with different arguments, where *hydrogen* and *oxygen* are the arguments; the function is that part of the expression that does not change. Similarly, in a sentence like *Cato killed Cato*, if we consider the first instance of *Cato* to be the replaceable part, that will be the argument and "to kill Cato" the function; if, on the other hand, we take the second instance of *Cato* to be the exchangeable part, then that is the argument and "to be killed by Cato" the function; finally, if we assume *Cato* to be replaceable in both positions, the function we are dealing with is "to kill oneself."

What Frege's exercise in function-argument structure should make clear is that there is no obvious linguistic sense in which his notions of "function" and "argument" correspond to constituents of the syntactic structure, or elements of the lexicon. In his first example, with what follows *than* being the argument, that leaves *Carbon dioxide (is) heavier than* as the function, not a lexical category or syntactic constituent by any standard. And in the third subcase of his second example, where both instances of *Cato* are arguments, the function is the reflexive "to kill oneself," once again neither an identifiable syntactic constituent nor a lexical element.

To the extent that a correspondence can indeed be established between "function" and something in the grammar, it actually seems to be the Aristotelean "predicate." Thus, in the first two subcases of the *Cato killed Cato* example the function is "to kill Cato" or "to be killed by Cato," both predicates in Aristotle's sense, with Frege's "argument" paralleling Aristotle's "subject" in the sense of "that which the sentence is about." But now notice that that particular interpretation of the notion "subject," in turn, will not correspond to a fixed constituent in the grammatical structure of the sentence: the "logical subject" (or "topic") can be either in the syntactic subject position or in the object position.

In present-day linguistic theory, what we have is a notion of *n*-ary predicates (ultimately based on Frege), expressed in terms of θ-grids, in conjunction with the Fregean notion of "saturation," as well as both interpretations of Aristotle's confusing subject-predicate dichotomy: the logical one and the grammatical one. A lexical item with a θ-grid is called a predicate, and so, usually, is the combination of the predicate head and its internal argument(s)—that is, the syntactic constituent that is predicated of the subject. Not surprisingly, beginning students of linguistics have a hard time figuring out what a predicate might be.

My aim in this work, as stated in the introduction, is to present a syntax of predication and the inversion of the predicate around its subject. From this statement of purpose it will be evident that I will be using the term *predicate* as equivalent to the *syntactic constituent* that denotes the property ascribed to the subject—that is, I am using the term *predicate* as essentially equivalent to Aristotle's *kategoroúmenon*. I will have no business with the *symbebekós*, which is not a syntactic notion. As for the meaning of the term *subject*, it should be clear that my use of this term can be characterized as referring to the syntactic constituent of which the predicate is predicated. This interpretation of the term *subject* is not equivalent to the term *external argument* familiar from Williams's (1980) work: thus, unaccusative predicates like *fall* or *die*, which have no external argument, do have a subject (they are, after all, property-denoting expressions). Nor does my notion of "subject" correspond to "grammatical subject" in the sense of the constituent that is in the subject position of the sentence: in a noun phrase like *a beautiful flower*, *flower* is the subject of *beautiful* but it is not a grammatical subject; similarly, on a ("functional") perspective on Topic-Comment structures as predicational structures, the Topic is the subject (the "logical subject" or "theme," some would say) of the Comment, which is the predicate (the "rheme"), but of course the Topic does not have to be the grammatical subject.

The preceding paragraphs have served the purpose of making my position in the realm of predication explicit. To repeat, the predicate is the syntactic constituent that expresses a property ascribed to the subject. The remainder of this work will be aimed at two things:

1. Developing a syntactic representation of the subject-predicate relationship—one in which predication is always mediated by a RELATOR, a functional category that takes the subject and the predicate as its dependents

2. Implementing this syntactic theory of predication in analyses of syntactic processes that syntactic predicates undergo—in particular, *inversion* of the predicate around its subject, in so-called *Predicate Inversion* constructions

In the end, I hope this work will show that "predicate" has a fundamental role to play in syntax (alongside the role that it plays in the interpretation of linguistic expressions), and that a proper understanding of the syntax of predication and Predicate Inversion sheds important light on such time-honored questions as the distribution of copular elements and (the parallels between) the structures of sentences and noun phrases.

2.2   The Syntax of Predication

2.2.1   The Syntactic Configuration and Locality of Predication

The cornerstone of the present exercise in the syntax of predication and Predicate Inversion is the hypothesis that all predication relationships are syntactically represented in terms of a structure in which the constituents denoting the predicate and the subject are dependents of a connective or RELATOR that establishes the connection—both the syntactic link and the semantic one—between the two constituents.[2] Thus, all predication relationships are syntactically represented as in (1).

(1) *The syntactic configuration of predication*

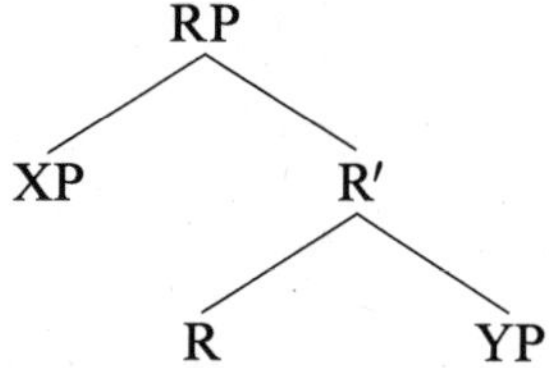

This representation is hardly revolutionary in and of itself. The idea that (1) embodies is that all predication relationships are mediated by a RELATOR—much as in Arnauld and Lancelot's (1660) *Grammaire générale et raisonnée* but without requiring the postulation of abstract copulas for all noncopular sentences. Arnauld and Lancelot split up a proposition such as *The earth is round* into a subject, *the earth*, and a predicate, *round*, connected to each other by the copula *is*. And by the same token, they represented a proposition such as *John walks* in terms of a subject, *John*, and a predicate, *walk*, connected by a RELATOR—which, once again, is taken to be the copula *be*: for Arnauld and Lancelot take the role of establishing the connection between the two terms of a proposition (the mental operation of "judgment") to be played systematically by the copula (see Arnauld and Lancelot 1660, 91; Harris and Taylor 1997, 96, 103). By taking the copula to be the quintessential RELATOR, they are forced to represent all noncopular sentences underlyingly as copular constructions—an abstraction that is of course an artifact of the hypothesis that the RELATOR role is unique to the copula. Once we abandon this specific claim and take the RELATOR to be an abstract functional connective (which can certainly be realized by the copula when it is present), as in (1), we can do away with the cumbersome representation of verbal predications as copular sentences that Arnauld and Lancelot were led to, while preserving the general insight underlying Arnauld and Lancelot's approach to predication as mediated by a connective, a RELATOR.

With the RELATOR providing the connection between the predicate and its subject, the approach in (1) gives syntactic, configurational expression to perspectives on syntactic predication that appeal to "predicate linking" (Rothstein 1983; also Heycock 1991): the idea that "predicates appear in positions where they can be linked to their subjects" (Heycock 1991, 21) translates into a statement to the effect that the predicate must be one of the two dependents of the RELATOR in the configuration in (1), with the subject being the RELATOR's other dependent. With (1) in place, the *locality* of predication relationships can be stated as in (2).[3]

(2) *The locality of predication*
    The RELATOR accommodates the predicate and the subject in its
    MINIMAL DOMAIN.

The statement in (2) is my alternative to Williams's (1980) classic approach to the locality of predication, which had it that subject and predicate must entertain a relationship of mutual c-command, as accomplished in ternary-branching (hence, nonantisymmetrical) representations of the structure of the sentence in vogue at the time.

2.2.2 The Nondirectionality of Predication

By requiring simply that the RELATOR accommodate the predicate and its subject in its minimal domain, (2) superimposes no directionality on predication relationships. While predication relations in syntax are configurational (see (1)), the theory of predication espoused in this work makes them fundamentally nondirectional. That is, the structure in (1), with its indeterminate labels "XP" and "YP" for the specifier and complement of the RELATOR, factors out into two separate subcases—each perfectly compatible with the idea that predication relationships are asymmetrical and need to be mediated by a RELATOR. These two subcases of (1) are spelled out in (3).

(3) a. [RP [XP SUBJECT] [R′ RELATOR [YP PREDICATE]]]
$$\hspace{6cm}\text{(Predicate-complement structure)}$$
    b. [RP [XP PREDICATE] [R′ RELATOR [YP SUBJECT]]]
$$\hspace{6cm}\text{(Predicate-specifier structure)}$$

The case in (3a), to which I will refer as the "predicate-complement" structure or as "straight/canonical predication," is the familiar one, with the subject in the specifier position and the predicate in the complement of the RELATOR. But the geometric inverse of (3a), the "predicate-specifier" or "reverse-predication" structure in (3b), is also structurally well formed.[4] We will see later in this chapter (especially in section 2.6) that the structure in (3b) plays an essential role in the syntax of nominal, adjectival, and adverbial predication.

Rothstein (1983, 27), who explicitly includes a directionality clause in her "predicate linking rule" in (4), stipulates that in English the predicate must follow the subject: "linking is from right to left."

(4) *Rule of Predicate Linking* (for English) (Rothstein 1983)
    a. Every non-θ-marked XP must be linked at S-structure to an argument which it immediately c-commands and which immediately c-commands it.
    b. Linking is from right to left.

She goes on to note that this is presumably a language-particular issue, and since she takes her rule of predicate linking to be an S-structure rule in any case (see (4a)), the directionality clause in (4b) is unlikely to have any fundamental import. Déchaine (1993, 13) goes further and stipulates in her definition of the "⊓-relation" (i.e., predication) that "α is ⊓-related to β iff β precedes α (...)"—but she never actually addresses directionality directly. So we cannot take these remarks about directionality to lead the way.

From the perspective of the syntactic definition of predication in (1), there is in fact absolutely no reason to expect there to be any directionality requirement on predication relationships in the base. Both (3a) and (3b) are perfectly well formed as far as syntax is concerned. And since both also feed straightforwardly into a semantics of predication in terms of property ascription (which, while asymmetrical, is of course not directional in any way), there is nothing that would favor either one of these representations over the other, all else equal:

(5) Predication is *nondirectional*.

With (5) replacing Rothstein's (4b), the alternation in (3) opens up a broader perspective on the ways a predicate can be connected to its subject than traditional approaches within the principles-and-parameters framework, which have typically subscribed to the (often tacit, sometimes explicit) assumption that the subject precedes its predicate underlyingly.

Before proceeding, I should add a note on the relationship between (3)/(5) and Baker's (1988) Uniformity of Theta-Assignment Hypothesis (UTAH), reproduced in (6).

(6) *Uniformity of Theta-Assignment Hypothesis* (UTAH)
    Identical thematic relationships between items are represented by
    identical structural relationships between those items at the level of
    D-structure.

With the subject interpreted as, say, the Agent of the event denoted by a VP-predicate, UTAH would appear to ban any kind of alternation between (3a) and (3b): the Agent would have to be projected either as the specifier of the RELATOR phrase or as the RELATOR's complement; one could not have it both ways. Two theoretical considerations lead one to question the idea that UTAH has jurisdiction over (3), however. First, important work by Hale and Keyser (1993) (to be reviewed in sections 2.3 and 2.4) has recast most of Baker's UTAH in structural terms in the form of "l-syntactic" hierarchical representations: thus, the Theme role, for instance, is systematically projected in "l-syntactic" representations as a VP-specifier. But the Agent is not covered by Hale and Keyser's structural rendition of UTAH: the "external argument" of a verbal predicate is truly external in the sense that it is projected *outside* "l-syntactic" structure, in "s-syntax." With "l-syntactic" structural configurations as the successors to Baker's UTAH, this then puts the "external argument" squarely outside UTAH's reach. Second, while "internal arguments" are typically the recipients of a θ-role assigned by some lexical head, for "external arguments" or subjects of predication one cannot make a statement to the same effect. From the realm of *tough*-movement constructions, we are familiar with subjects that do not, on standard assumptions, receive a θ-role from any lexical head: in *John is easy to please*, it is plain that *John* serves as the subject of *easy to please*, its predicate; but there is no lexical head in the structure of this sentence that could be held responsible for the assignment of an "external θ-role" to *John* (*easy* is not a θ-role assigner in this context, as is evident from the fact that expletive *it* can be its subject in *It is easy to please John*; and *please* assigns an *internal* θ-role to a null operator ultimately bound by *John*). The predication relationship between *easy to please* and *John* is therefore not recastable in terms of "external θ-role assignment" in any straightforward manner. Predication more generally does not seem to be recastable this way (among other works, see also Heycock 1994b; Déchaine 1993). This in turn entails that predication relationships are beyond the reach of UTAH. For these theoretical reasons, therefore, it would be wrong to cast the alternation in (3a, b) aside based on considerations of configurational uniformity of θ-role assignment.

2.2.3 The RELATOR as an Abstraction

The approach to the syntax of predication advanced in this work, summed up by (1), is structurally parallel to Bowers's (1993) outlook on predication. Bowers represents the syntax of predication in terms of a structure identical with (1) and has the functional head of (1) perform precisely the same syntactic and semantic functions that I am ascribing to the RELATOR. But the present proposal differs fundamentally from Bowers's approach, not just in its emphasis on the asymmetrical yet *nondirectional* nature of the predication relationship in syntax but when it comes to the nature of the RELATOR as well. Bowers is explicit in recognizing the mediator head as "a new functional category" (Bowers 1993, 593). He gives it the category label "Pr," "a mnemonic for predication" (Bowers 1993, 595), and makes it clear that Pr is present in the syntactic representation of all predication constructions and is never to be identified with any of the extant functional or lexical categories.

Here Bowers and I part ways. For me, the RELATOR in the structure of predicational relationships in (1) is an *abstract* functional head—not a novel lexical category, not even a specific functional element (like T or D or some such), but a placeholder for *any* functional head in the structure that mediates a predication relation between two terms, in conformity with (2). That head can be the copula (as in *The earth must <u>be</u> round*) or a prepositional element (as in *They take him _for_ a fool* or *They regard him _as_ a strong president*; see also Aarts 1992; Bowers 1993; Starke 1995; Bailyn 2004),[5] but it can also be T (or Infl), as in *John walks*, or indeed any head that relates a predicate to its subject, including functional heads in the A′-domain of the sentence (such as Topic and Focus). I will return to this issue in more detail in section 2.5. For now, what is important to bear in mind throughout the discussion to follow is that "R" is not a designated category; the RP structure in (1) represents a *syntactic configuration* rather than a claim about the lexicon.[6]

2.2.4 Predication, Coordination, and Semantics

With the role of RELATOR performed by Infl, and with XP being the subject and YP the verbal predicate, (1) delivers (8a), equivalent to the outlook on the structure of sentences presented in *Barriers* (Chomsky 1986), reproduced in (8b).[7] Thus, (8) is the follow-up, from the present perspective, to the early transformational approach to the structure of the sentence (still subscribed to in Chomsky 1981), according to which it is a flat, ternary-branching structure, as in (7).

(7) [$_S$ [$_{NP}$ SUBJECT] Aux/Infl [$_{VP}$ PREDICATE]]

(8) a. [$_{RP}$ [$_{NP}$ SUBJECT] [$_{R'}$ RELATOR=Infl [$_{VP}$ PREDICATE]]]
    b. [$_{IP}$ [$_{NP}$ SUBJECT] [$_{I'}$ Infl [$_{VP}$ PREDICATE]]]

The move from (7) to (8), taken in the 1980s, was followed a decade later by a parallel development of the syntactic representation of coordination. Coordination used to be commonly represented in the syntax in terms of a ternary-branching structure, with the conjunction on the middle branch in languages such as English. Thus, the classic approach to coordination is as in (9), where the syntactic role of the conjunction is really minimal: it does not define a projection of its own and it does not determine the category of the coordination; the coordination is simply given the label of the two conjoined constituents.[8]

(9)

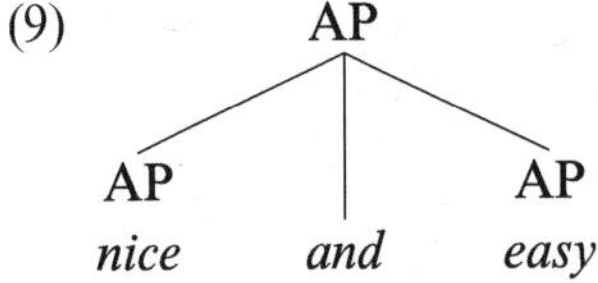

More recently, however, the syntax of coordination has been recast in terms of a binary-branching structure, headed by the conjunction, as in

(10) (see Kayne 1994, Johannessen 1998, and so on; for an overview of the various approaches to the syntax of coordination, see Progovac 2003).

(10)

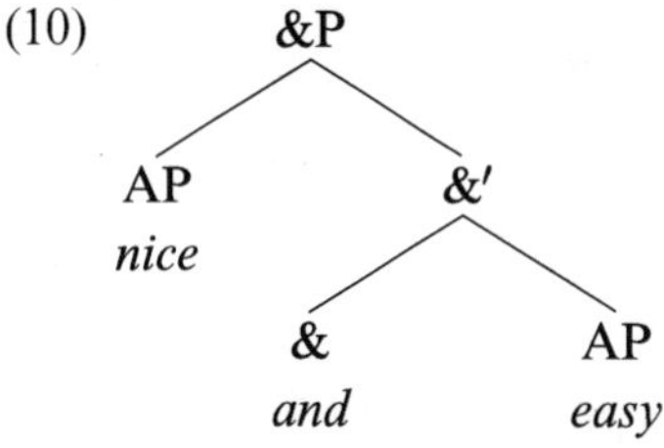

The structure in (10) not only brings coordination in line with the conclusion that all branching is binary (Kayne 1984) because phrase structure obeys antisymmetry (Kayne 1994), it also gives a straightforward reflection of the semantics of coordination, with the coordinator represented as a connective that takes one set-denoting linguistic expression and relates it to another set-denoting expression, delivering the intersection ($\cap$) of the two sets. Let us then take (10) to give us a general format for the expression of set intersection in syntax. With (10) being an instantiation of (1), this presents the possibility that the RELATOR in (1) might uniformly be the logical operator "$\cap$," with predication being semantically represented as set intersection.[9]

Set intersection is plainly not all there is to the semantics of predication, however: as I pointed out in section 2.1, there is an asymmetrical relationship between a predicate and its subject, with the predicate *ascribing* a property to its subject—a predicate is a function (in simple cases, such as *Imogen sneezed*, from individuals to truth values), the subject its argument. Though much more can be and has been said about the semantics of predication, for our purposes in this study, which, as its subtitle reveals, focuses on the *syntax* of predication, it will be sufficient to think of the semantics of predication as an intersective relationship between two sets, one (corresponding to the function) denoting a property ascribed to the other (the argument).

2.3 A Brief Historical Interlude on Internal Subjects

Returning now to syntax, let us take a closer look at (8), the structure of the clause as presented in Chomsky 1986. At the time that *Barriers* was published, (8) was in a way the old-fashioned approach to the base generation of the subject. For with the advent of small clauses (Williams 1975;

Stowell 1981), the notion that the predicate head accommodates the subject *inside* its maximal projection—the *LP–Internal Subject Hypothesis*, as I will call it here[10]—had started to gain more and more ground in the early and mid-1980s (see Manzini 1983; Fukui and Speas 1986; Kuroda 1988; Koopman and Sportiche 1990; Huang 1993; and so on). Several incarnations of the LP–Internal Subject Hypothesis are available in the literature (see (11)).

(11) a. $[_{IP} [_{NP}$ SUBJECT$]_i [_{I'}$ Infl $[_{VP} t_i [_{V'}$ PREDICATE$]]]$

     b. $[_{IP} [_{NP}$ SUBJECT$]_i [_{I'}$ Infl $[_{VP} t_i [_{VP}$ PREDICATE$]]]$

     c. $[_{IP} [_{NP}$ SUBJECT$]_i [_{I'}$ Infl $[_{VP*} t_i [_{VP}$ Spec $[_{V'}$ PREDICATE$]]]]$

These variations on the theme of LP-internal base generation of the subject diverge primarily on the question of whether the base position of the external argument is taken to be a *specifier* position (daughter of XP, sister of X′; Stowell 1981) or an *adjunction* position (daughter of XP, sister of XP; Manzini 1983; Fukui and Speas 1986); a third variant, pursued by Koopman and Sportiche (1990), is to base-generate the subject in a position that is neither a garden-variety specifier nor an adjunct, as in (11c).[11]

Though the matter is not discussed in any detail in *Barriers*, Chomsky (1986) could not adopt (11a). Base-generating the subject of the clause in SpecVP would make it radically impossible for adjuncts to ever extract long-distance: the V′ of the matrix clause would form a minimality barrier breaking the adjunct's chain.[12] So (8b) was adopted, and the status of the SpecVP position was left open.

While *Barriers* assigned specifiers to all maximal projections, including VPs that serve as complements to causative and perception verbs (as in *Imogen made/saw Brian sing a song*—cases of small-clause complementation, with small clauses represented in *Barriers* as projections of the predicate head, as in Stowell 1981), the VP in the complement of Infl apparently had no use for a specifier position. This hybrid system led some (in particular, Kuroda 1988) to adopt the structure in (11a), according to which the subject *systematically* originates in the predicate's specifier position. This then commits one to the point of view that, whenever a predicate is being extracted, what is being moved is a constituent containing a *trace* of the predicate's subject (on the standard assumption that only maximal projections are eligible for movement)—a consequence that, according to Huang (1993), finds support in the binding facts of predicate fronting constructions: the fact that, while (12a) is ambiguous when it comes to the binder of *himself*, the VP-fronting case in (12b) allows only the *Bill*-reading readily follows from Principle A of the Binding Theory if there is a subject trace inside the VP.

(12) a. [pictures of himself$_{i/j}$]$_k$, John$_j$ thinks Bill$_i$ would never buy t_k
     b. [t_i admire himself$_{i/*j}$]$_k$, John$_j$ thinks Bill$_i$ never would t_k
     c. [t_i buy pictures of himself$_{i/j}$]$_k$, John$_j$ thinks Bill$_i$ never would t_k

But the fact that (12b) is unambiguous does not seem to have anything to do with the presence of a VP-internal trace of the subject—in (12c) that trace will, by parity of reasoning, be present as well, yet the *John*-reading is as available here as it is in (12a). What seems to set (12b) and similar cases apart from (12a) and (12c) is that, in (12b), *himself* and *Bill* are coarguments—something that, by Reinhart and Reuland's (1993) theory of binding, will straightforwardly guarantee that the only thing that will ever be able to bind *himself* in (12b) is *Bill*, entirely irrespective of whether there is a VP-internal trace of the subject or not (see Heycock 1995). We do not seem to need a VP-internal subject trace, therefore, to come to terms with the binding facts.

On the contrary, postulating an LP-internal subject, as in (11), incurs problems of its own—a nontrivial one being the fact (noted by many researchers pondering the question of the base generation of the subject; see, e.g., Bowers 1993, 593) that it provides no obvious analysis for sentences such as *I consider John my best friend*, where *my* is the specifier of the predicate nominal. Sentences of this type are perhaps the most immediate empirical motivation for base-generating the subject outside the maximal projection of the predicate.

In more recent years, the idea that the subject originates outside the maximal projection of the predicate has regained canonicity under the impetus of an assumption made in Chomsky 1995, chap. 4, introduced by Larson (1988), Hale and Keyser (1993), and Kratzer (1996)—the idea that the VP predicate is associated with its external argument via a light verb v (a "Voice" head for Kratzer), which takes the lexical VP as its complement and introduces the external argument in its specifier, as in (13).

(13) [$_{IP}$ [$_{NP}$ SUBJECT]$_i$ [$_{I'}$ I [$_{vP}$ t_i [$_{v'}$ v [$_{VP}$ PREDICATE]]]]]

Though it was not intended as such, (13) is in a way a compromise between (8) and (11): the external argument is base-generated outside the maximal projection of the VP-predicate, but it is still not "as external" as it is in (8), where it originates in SpecIP.

The structure in (13) also resolves the conundrum that the *Barriers* approach in (8) presented when it comes to the distribution of specifiers of lexical categories. What is needed is an account that ensures that lexical projections will have specifiers only if some argument can be base-generated in them, not otherwise. On the assumption (which (13) expresses) that the V-head's own external argument is not projected in SpecVP, this means that no property of V itself will ever give VP a specifier. For Hale and Keyser (1993), whose ideas Chomsky (1995) adopts in their essentials, VP will only have a specifier if V's complement happens to be a predicate that needs to be saturated. In other words, VPs (and lexical projections more generally) will only have specifiers if their complements are unsaturated predicates. Hale and Keyser (1993) take sentences like (14) to instantiate such cases, with *to Imogen*, *on the shelf*, and *yellow* serving as complements of V (*put, paint*) in a Larsonian "VP-shell" structure, predicated of *the book*, which is base-generated in SpecVP (see (15)). The verbal head, originating in the lower V-position in (15), raises up to the higher V-position (the head of the outer "VP-shell") in overt syntax, thus ending up to the left of *the book*.[13]

(14) a. Brian gave the book to Imogen.
    b. Imogen put the book on the shelf.
    c. Brian painted the book yellow.

(15) a. [VP [V *ec*] [VP [the book] [V' give [PP to Imogen]]]]]
    b. [VP [V *ec*] [VP [the book] [V' put [PP on the shelf]]]]]
    c. [VP [V *ec*] [VP [the book] [V' paint [AP yellow]]]]]

2.4 On the Nature of Lexical Heads

Why do Larson (1988) and Hale and Keyser (1993) call the mediator of the predication relationships in (15) a V, and then go into the business of erecting these "VP-shell" structures with mysterious empty-headed VPs? The answer seems to be that by calling the mediator "V" they can have their cake and eat it, too—that is, they can have the complement of V function as a predicate of the NP in SpecVP while at the same time allowing V's complement to receive a θ-role from the verb. For what is the point of calling the mediator V? There is none unless this mediator is *also* supposed to have a *thematic* function. If the mediator had no θ-assigning role to play, there would be no reason to insist on calling it a *V*—as opposed to some functional category, that is. But since both Larson and Hale and Keyser seek to syntactically express the traditional view that verbs like *give* and *put* have three θ-roles to assign, they are committed to the claim that the relationship between the complement and the specifier is mediated by a *lexical* head (a *verb*), not by some functional category.

Without entering into a detailed discussion of why it would be mistaken to think of verbs like *give* or *put* as three-place lexical heads (that discussion has been conducted in extensive detail already, for instance in Hoekstra 1988, Mulder 1992, and Den Dikken 1995c), I will set aside the idea that the relationship between the secondary predicates and their subjects is mediated by a verb, as in (15), on the following basis. It is hardly controversial that the PP/AP following *the book* in (14) is a predicate of *the book*. And it has also been argued convincingly (especially in Hoekstra 1988) that *the book* is not an argument of the verb in any sentence of the type in (14): instead, it is uniquely the subject of the secondary predicate. When we add these two things together, we reach the conclusion that the verb in fact has nothing at all to do with the relationship between *the book* and the PP/AP that follows it: it has no thematic relationship with either.

This now leads to the conclusion that the structures in (15) are flawed in taking the predication relationship between the PP/AP and *the book* to be mediated by a lexical verb, on the hypothesis that lexical heads must assign their complements a θ-role.

(16) A LEXICAL HEAD must assign a θ-role to its complement.

Rothstein's (1983) argument to the effect that a constituent serving as a predicate cannot be assigned a θ-role guarantees, once it is agreed that the PP/AP following *the book* in (14) is a predicate, that the PP/AP cannot be θ-marked. So V cannot be involved in the assignment of a θ-role to the PP/AP in (15). And although *the book* is definitely a θ-role bearer, it does not receive its θ-role from the verb but exclusively from the secondary predicate (PP/AP). The fact that V in (15) does not assign θ-roles to either of its dependents thus tells us that it has no right to exist as a lexical category—and that in turn tells us that the structures in (15) are illegitimate.

They are not far off the mark, though. They can easily be "converted" into perfectly legitimate structures by abandoning the "VP-shell" idea and base-generating the lexical verb in the position corresponding to the outer V-head in (14), and by having the relationship between the secondary predicates and their subjects mediated by a *functional* RELATOR, as in (17).

(17) a. [$_{VP}$ give [$_{RP}$ [the book] [$_{R'}$ RELATOR [$_{PP}$ to Imogen]]]]]
        b. [$_{VP}$ put [$_{RP}$ [the book] [$_{R'}$ RELATOR [$_{PP}$ on the shelf]]]]]
        c. [$_{VP}$ paint [$_{RP}$ [the book] [$_{R'}$ RELATOR [$_{AP}$ yellow]]]]]

This is the familiar "small-clause" structure of secondary predication, with "RP" corresponding to a small clause, and "R" being the syntactic *head* of the small clause.[14] Small clauses, then, are not projections of the predicate head (as Stowell 1981, 1983 had it) but instead projections of a RELATOR-head.[15]

2.5   On the Nature of the RELATOR

2.5.1   A Functional Head

What is the nature of this RELATOR-head? One thing that should be immediately obvious from what I said about lexical heads in the previous section is that RELATOR-heads are *never* lexical heads:

(18) a. A RELATOR is not a θ-role assigner, hence
        b. A RELATOR is a *functional* head.

The rationale behind the combination of (16) and (18) is the idea that a head H is a θ-assigner or a mediator of predication but never both at the same time—an approach, in other words, that strictly divides the labor of θ-assignment and mediation of predication relationships. From the perspective outlined in this work, no lexical projection ever has a specifier,[16] while every RELATOR must have a specifier.

2.5.2   The RELATOR and the Generalized "Light Verb"

The fact that RELATORs are functional categories has an immediate advantage in comparison to Chomsky's (1995, chap. 4) approach to external θ-role assignment in the *v*P configuration in (13). For Chomsky, the light verb *v* is a bit of a hybrid element: it is lexical in taking part in the assignment of the external θ-role, but at the same time, the strength of its morphological features (especially its Case feature) is parametrically variable (i.e., some languages perform Object Shift in the overt syntax, others do it covertly),[17] and since Chomsky, following Borer (1984), confines all parametric variation to nonlexical or functional heads, that means that *v* cannot be a strictly lexical element. Chomsky (1995, 368) ends up calling it a "nonsubstantive" category, something of a crossbreed of purely functional and purely lexical categories. From the perspective on predication relationships unfolded here, no such move is necessary. The RELATOR of the predication relation between VP and its subject is a genuinely nonlexical category: it is not involved in the assignment of any θ-roles; it creates a syntactic configuration within which predication is possible. The RELATOR head does not need to be lexical in any way—nor, in fact, *could* it be lexical.[18]

If Chomsky's (1995) light verb *v* is an instantiation of the RELATOR, and if for transitive constructions we have a structure of the type in (13) (with *v* as our RELATOR), does this mean that we also need some sort of light verb in unaccusative sentences like *Imogen fell*? The question is of considerable interest because the literature to date has not managed to reach a verdict on this issue.

Chomsky (1995) initially introduced his light verb *v* as a causative or transitivizing element, intrinsically introducing both the external θ-role and an accusative Case feature. But in his more recent writings, Chomsky (2001) has generalized *v* across all VPs, not necessarily transitivized ones (with the transitivizing light verb now being annotated as *v**).' The question that we need to ask, from the point of view of the present enterprise, is whether recourse to a light verb is necessary in unaccusative constructions.

One way of approaching this question is from the perspective of the semantics of a sentence like *Imogen fell*. For transitive sentences like *Imogen kissed Brian* we have assumed (see section 2.2.4) a semantic representation in terms of the intersection of two sets, one denoted by the subject (*Imogen*) and one by the predicate (*kissed Brian*). For unaccusative constructions we would want to say the same thing: we are dealing with two sets, one denoted by the surface subject (*Imogen*) and one by the predicate (*fell*); the set denoted by the predicate ascribes a property to the subject. By this line of thought, therefore, we arrive at the conclusion that there is indeed a predication relationship to be mediated in unaccusatives.

This, in turn, leads to the conclusion that there is a need for a mediator of the connection between *Imogen* and *fell*. But there is no need to introduce a light verb *v* to mediate the predicational relationship between *fell* and *Imogen* because that relation can be established perfectly well by the Tense-head of the sentence. The T-head is the optimal candidate for serving as the RELATOR of the subject and the predicate and its subject in an unaccusative construction.[19] Confronted with the choice between (19a) and (19b), which both converge, the former is selected because it introduces no additional structure that is unmotivated.[20]

(19) a. $[_{TP} [Imogen]_i [_{T'} T=$RELATOR $[_{VP} fell\ t_i]]]$
      b. $[_{TP} [Imogen]_i [_{T'} T [_{vP} t_i [_{v'} v=$RELATOR $[_{VP} fell\ t_i]]]]]$

Returning now to the transitive sentence *Imogen kissed Brian*, we need to ask why, in this case, the relationship between the VP and the subject does have to be mediated by a light verb *v*. In other words, why do we need (13) (reproduced here as (20b))? Why can't we content ourselves with the *Barriers* representation in (10) (reproduced in a trivially modified form as (20a)), in which T serves as the RELATOR?

(20) a. $^*[_{TP} [Imogen]_i [_{T'} T=$RELATOR $[_{VP} kissed\ Brian]]]$
      b. $[_{TP} [Imogen]_i [_{T'} T [_{vP} t_i [_{v'} v=$RELATOR $[_{VP} kissed\ Brian]]]]]$

There are reasons extraneous to the predication relationship between *kissed Brian* and *Imogen* that force the introduction of additional functional structure—a projection of a light verb *v*, in particular. For in (20) the object of the verb *kissed* needs to get its uninterpretable Case feature checked, and this Case checking will fail in (20a): T cannot entertain a Case checking relationship with more than one noun phrase (English has no multiple nominative constructions), and since it is already committed to checking *Imogen*'s Case feature, it cannot enter into a Case checking relationship with *Brian*.[21] This leaves the latter's Case feature unchecked, causing the derivation to crash. In (20b), by contrast, the light verb *v* comes with a Case feature of its own, which is straightforwardly checked against *Brian*'s Case feature. Hence (20b) converges.

We find, then, that in transitive sentences the fact that the predication relationship between the VP and its subject is mediated by *v* rather than T is ultimately the consequence of something that lies outside the realm of predication—Case. Since that motive for the inclusion of a *v*P does not present itself in unaccusative constructions (which, as their name suggests, lack an accusative Case-marked object), it follows by Occam's razor that if there are no other reasons for including a *v*P (see the second paragraph of note 20), no *v*P is projected in the structure of unaccusative constructions, the predication relationship between the VP and the surface subject being mediated in this case by the T-head.

This exercise should bring home once again the point that "RELATOR" does not stand for a particular functional category—anything can be a RELATOR, as long as it is a functional element that finds itself in between the predicate and its subject, in a structure of the type in (1). The choice between candidates for the RELATOR function will often be made on the basis of factors extraneous to the predication relationship to be established.

2.5.3 Topicalization, "Logical Subjects," and the RELATOR

While in (19) and (20) the position of the subject of the predication is unquestionably an A-position (or L-related position, in the sense of Chomsky 1995), predication relationships can also be established between a predicate and a subject sitting in an A′-position. The obvious case in point is the topicalization construction: in (21), the topic is in an A′-position but it serves as the "logical subject" of the sentence.

(21) [$_{Topic}$ Brian]$_i$, [$_{TP}$ Imogen really adores ec_i]

In section 2.1 I commented on the confusion in logic and grammar when it comes to the interpretation of the term *subject*, stemming from Aristotle's failure to pair his distinction between the *kategoroúmenon* (the grammatical predicate) and the *symbebekós* (the logical predicate) to a similar dichotomy in the subject domain and his concomitant use of the term *hypokeímenon* ('subject') ambiguously. There are at least three different notions of "subject" in linguistic theory: (i) *thematic* subject (the external argument, *Imogen* in (22a, b, d)), (ii) *grammatical* subject (the constituent in the subject position; see the italicized noun phrases in (22a–c) but not (22d)), and (iii) *logical* subject (that which the sentence is about—that is, the "topic" or "theme," *Brian* in (22d)). Setting the circumscription "the constituent in subject position" aside for subjects in the sense of (ii), my use of the term *subject* in this work as the syntactic constituent that the predicate is predicated of includes (i) (for predicates that are unergative/transitive) but also (iii).

(22) a. *Imogen* kissed Brian.
    b. *Brian* was kissed by Imogen.
    c. *Imogen* fell.
    d. *Brian*, Imogen really adores.

There is no particular reason to set (iii) aside. In some languages, the relationship between a topic and the comment is mediated by exactly the same element that also mediates perhaps less controversial subject-predicate relationships. I mention the distribution of the Rotuman linker *ne* as a case in point here. Churchward (1940), in his grammar of

Rotuman (an Oceanic language spoken on Rotuma, Fiji, and in the dia-spora), calls *ne* a "predicative sign" in topic-comment constructions of the type in (23a, b), and he notes that *ne* also rears its head in a variety of other constructions, all arguably involving a relationship of predica-tion between the constituents separated by *ne*.

(23) a. fā   ta   *ne* popot pau ?e ?on ?i? (Rotuman)
         man SG.DEF NE busy   very at present
         'The man is very busy at present.'
      b. itu?   ta   *ne* fā   ta   rē ...
         district SG.DEF NE man SG.DEF do
         'the district, the man did ...'
      c. tē   *ne* ?ofat
         thing NE joy.SG
         'a matter of joy'
      d. vak   *ne* ?otou le?   ta
         canoe NE my   child SG.DEF
         'the canoe of my child, my child's canoe'
      e. fāat   *ne* leum ?e asa
         man.SG NE come yesterday.DEF
         'the man who came yesterday'

Thus, (23c) is arguably a case of noun-phrase internal nominal predica-tion (see English *the City of London*), and so is the example in (23d), on an analysis of possession that has it that the possessum is the subject of a small-clause predicate that harbors the possessor (see Den Dikken 1995c, chap. 3, and also the discussion in section 5.7.3). The use of *ne* in relative-clause constructions (23e) goes along with this line of thought as well, the relative clause being a predicate of the "head" of the relative clause (see section 5.7.4). If, then, all of the cases in (23c–e) involve subject-predicate relationships, there is something about the distribution of *ne* that is tied to predication. Indeed, Den Dikken (2003b) argues that *ne* is strictly a linker of predication relationships.[22] If this is right, it suggests that (23a, b) also involve predication, with *ne* as the RELATOR, sitting in the functional head that has the topic in its specifier, commonly referred to as "Top^0." For (23b), this gives us the structure in (24a). By the same token, (21)=(22d) can be structurally represented as in (24b).[23]

(24) a. [$_{TopP}$ [*itu? ta*]$_i$ [$_{Top'}$ Top=RELATOR (*ne*) [$_{TP}$ *fā ta rē* (...) *ec*$_i$]]]
      b. [$_{TopP}$ [*Brian*]$_i$ [$_{Top'}$ Top=RELATOR ($\emptyset$) [$_{TP}$ *Imogen really adores ec*$_i$]]]

With the constituent in SpecTopP looked upon as the (logical) subject of the topicalization construction, the rest of the sentence (the TP, representing the "comment" or "rheme") serves as its predicate. The relationship between the logical subject and its predicate is established in the syntax in the familiar way, via a RELATOR—the Top-head in (24). Thus, by taking the relationship between the topic and the comment to instantiate a predication relationship (along the lines of Aristotle's interpretation of the *hypokeímenon* or *subject* as "that which the sentence is about"), we arrive at the conclusion that topicalization constructions must involve a functional projection whose head takes the topic as its specifier and the predicate (TP in (24)) as its complement, thereby rejecting an adjunction approach to topicalization.

The label "TopP" is immaterial as far as the *relation* established inside it is concerned. The Italian "cartographers" (Rizzi, Cinque, and others) have recently unfolded a densely structured grammar of the left periphery of the sentence, including TopP as one of its members. The present discussion supports this approach insofar as it supports the need for a RELATOR of the topic and the comment. But it does not thereby support the "cartographic" enterprise per se, since it explicitly confines its endorsement of left-periphery functional heads to those that perform the role of a RELATOR. Nor does the present approach to topic-comment structures support the labeling of the projection. The relationship between the topic and the comment is not established by a dedicated functional head "Top." On a neutral reading of the examples in (22a c) (one in which the italicized noun phrases are not focally stressed), the grammatical subjects of these sentences are their topics. An analysis that insists on placing topics in the specifier position of a dedicated functional projection TopP would be committed to analyzing (22a–c), on their neutral (topic-comment) readings, in terms of string-vacuous topicalization of the subject to SpecTopP. But as is well known, the subject of (22a–c) does not behave like a nonsubject topic: the comma intonation familiar from (22d) is necessarily absent in (22a–c), and subextraction, while marginally possible from nonsubject topics (see (25a)), is entirely impossible from subjects, whether they are topics or not (see (25b); the contrast in (25) was noted by Lasnik and Saito 1990).

(25) a. (?)?*Who* does Brian think that [pictures of *t*], Imogen would
          never buy?

     b.   **Who* does Brian think that [pictures of *t*] appeal to Imogen?

The present approach to topic-comment constructions avoids these problems by having the T-head serve as the RELATOR of the topic and the comment in subject topic constructions of the type in (22a–c): the same functional head that relates the predicate to its subject also relates the comment to the topic in such constructions. In nonsubject topic constructions, by contrast, an additional functional head (call it "Top"[24]) is called on to relate the comment (TP) to the topic. Throughout, all that is needed is a RELATOR of some sort to connect topic and comment; whenever the T-head can perform this function, it will—no additional functional structure is called on in such cases, and hence, by general economy considerations, such additional structure will be ungrammatical.

2.5.4 Focalization and the RELATOR

Focus particles (*only, even*) can be thought of as ternary functions, taking the focus, the presupposition, and the "alternative set" (Rooth's 1985 "p-set") as their arguments. But we have already seen in our brief discussion of ditransitive constructions in sections 2.3 and 2.4 that there can be no such thing as a triadic predicate in syntax: a predicate has a single subject and the predicate head can take at most one complement. It will be impossible, therefore, to represent focus particles as triadic predicates in syntax. But we can still incorporate the key insight that focus particles serve to establish the relationship between the focus and the presupposition, by following up on Kayne's (1998) approach to the syntactic representation of focus particles.

Kayne (1998) proposes that focus particles like *only* originate in a functional head (let us call it "Foc") fairly high up the tree, and that they attract the focused constituent up into their specifier position in overt syntax, with subsequent movement of the focus particle to a functional head (which Kayne labels "W") immediately above FocP and remnant movement of the complement of the Foc-head into the specifier position of WP. For a sentence such as (26a), this translates into the derivation in (26b).

(26) a. Imogen eats only biscuits.

   b. [$_{TP}$ *Imogen eats biscuits*]

   → merger of Foc=*only*; attraction of *biscuits* to SpecFocP →

   [$_{FocP}$ *biscuits*$_i$ [*only* [$_{TP}$ *Imogen eats t*$_i$]]]

   → merger of W; raising of *only* to W and attraction of remnant TP to SpecWP →

   [$_{WP}$ [$_{TP}$ *Imogen eats t*$_i$]$_k$ [*only*$_j$ [$_{FocP}$ *biscuits*$_i$ [*t*$_j$ *t*$_k$]]]]

It is the first step in this derivation—that is, the merger of Foc=*only* and the attraction of the focus to its specifier—that results in the predication relationship between the focus and the presupposition, with the focus particle serving as the RELATOR of the two. Focus particles, then, are instantiations of the RELATOR on this outlook on focus constructions.

2.5.5 Conclusion

The preceding subsections have argued that the RELATOR is a general-purpose connective between predicates and their subjects, not a particular functional or lexical category, and not confined to the A-domain. A particular RELATOR can certainly have a highly specific bundle of features of its own, but those features are a reflex of its syntactic environment (for instance, v has tense, ϕ-, and Case features because it is selected by T, licenses or identifies (see note 20) a V, and Case-checks a ϕ-agreeing noun phrase in its complement), not the inherent baggage of a RELATOR category.

Any semantic relationship of predication can in principle be translated into a syntactic configuration of the type in (1). As we have seen, the syntax generally benefits from representing such semantic predication relationships in terms of (1); by doing so, we find natural homes for elements that it would otherwise be hard to accommodate in the syntactic tree, elements that, given (1), can be looked on as lexicalizations of the RELATOR.

2.6   Adjectival and Adverbial Modification as Predication

A difficult area when it comes to predication relationships is that of adjectival and adverbial modification. There is no doubt, of course, that adjectives can be predicative—in simple copular sentences such as (27), that is precisely what the adjective *beautiful* is. And it goes without saying that sentences of this type are readily accommodated by the approach to the syntax of predication relationships taken here: the AP projected by *beautiful* serves as the complement of the RELATOR, and *Imogen* in (27a) or *Imogen's dancing* in (27b) originates in the specifier position of the RELATOR's projection.

(27) a. Imogen is beautiful.

       [$_{RP}$ [*Imogen*] [RELATOR=*be* [*beautiful*]]]

    b. Imogen's dancing is beautiful.

       [$_{RP}$ [*Imogen's dancing*] [RELATOR=*be* [*beautiful*]]]

But things rapidly become more complicated when we start to consider examples such as (28). It would appear that for (28a), an analysis that treats *beautiful* as a predicate will, if predication involves set intersection, commit the analyst to an intersective interpretation for *Imogen is a beautiful dancer* paraphrasable as *Imogen is beautiful and Imogen is a dancer*— but as is well known, such an intersective interpretation is not the only one available for sentences of the type in (28a): one may also take (28a) to mean that Imogen dances beautifully, as in (28b).

(28) a. Imogen is a beautiful dancer.
      b. Imogen dances beautifully.

There does not seem to be any obvious way, however, in which we can intersect the set denoted by *beautiful* with a set of dancing events instigated by Imogen—one might perhaps be inclined to face the problem posed by (28a) by postulating a verbal base for *dancer*, but it is clear that such a strategy will not take care of the problem as a whole, given cases like *a just king* (Vendler 1967; Hoekstra, Van der Hulst, and Van der Putten 1988, 311–312; Larson 1998), which, like deverbal *a just ruler*, supports what one might call the adverbial reading of the attributive modifier. Besides, (28b) is troublesome enough by itself: its paraphrase relation with (27b) should somehow be captured, and the fact that it features the adverbial suffix *-ly* (obligatorily absent from (27) and (28a)) needs to be explained as well.

2.6.1 Manner Adverbials as Predicates of Propositions Rather Than Predicate Modifiers

Let me start with (28b), then, and find a way of capturing the paraphrase relationship with (27b) and a home for the adverbial suffix. Taking the structure underneath (27b) to correctly represent the underlying syntax of this copular sentence, let us assume that (28b) is underlain by an entirely parallel structure, once again featuring *beautiful* as the predicate in the complement of the RELATOR and the proposition constituted by the predication *Imogen dances* as its subject, as in (29a).[25]

(29) a. Imogen dances beautifully.
          [RP [*Imogen dances*] [RELATOR=*-ly* [*beautiful*]]]
      b. Imogen dances like a beauty.
          [RP [*Imogen dances*] [RELATOR=*like* [*a beauty*]]]

This structure of course captures the parallelism between (27b) and (28b) straightforwardly. It moreover accommodates the adverbial suffix *-ly* by treating it as the lexicalization of the RELATOR (with *beautiful* raising up to *-ly* in the course of the syntactic derivation[26]). By doing so, it elevates *-ly* to the status of a syntactically autonomous marker—a RELATOR of subject-predicate relations similar to *like* in (29b). Thus the analysis captures the historical relationship between *-ly* and *like*, by generating them in the same structural position and giving them the same syntactic function: that of relating a predicate to its subject.[27]

Notice that the structures in (29) place adverbial modifiers like *beautifully* and *like a beauty* in a low position in the tree. Thus the present analysis mirrors Larson's (1988) approach to adverbial modifiers as "innermost complements"—though not of the verb but instead of a RELATOR head that establishes the predication relationship between the modifier and its modifiee. Notice also that the structures in (29) take the modifiee of the manner adverbial to be the entire proposition (*Imogen dances*), not just the VP of *dance*. This is an immediate consequence of taking the parallelism between (28b) and (27b) seriously.

2.6.2 Intersective and Apparently Nonintersective Adjectival Modifiers as Predicates (I): Semantics

If it is indeed the case that *Imogen is a beautiful dancer* (28a), on its "adverbial" interpretation, is equivalent to *Imogen dances beautifully* (28b), can we represent this structurally in a syntactic analysis of (28a)? The point of Larson's (1998) discussion of (28a) is precisely to establish such a structural relationship. Assuming, in line with Larson 1988, that in (28b) *beautifully* is the "innermost complement" of the verb *dances* (see (30a)), he presents an analysis of (28a) in which *beautiful* is similarly the complement of the noun *dancer*, as in (30b), with the event-related interpretation of the adjective resulting by applying the adjective to the *event role* of the noun *dancer*.

(30) a. [$_{VP}$ *Imogen* [$_{V'}$ *dances* [$_{AP}$ *beautifully*]]]
     b. [$_{NP}$ *Imogen* [$_{N'}$ *dancer* [$_{AP}$ *beautiful*]]]

Of course (30b) as it stands does not yield the desired surface word order, so Larson (1998) proposes that the AP preposes to a position to the left of *dancer*.

This analysis is of interest primarily because it takes the apparently nonintersective reading of *beautiful* in (28a) to be genuinely intersective, with the adjective predicated, not of the individual denoted by *dancer*, but instead of the event role borne by *dancer*, exactly like the adverb *beautifully* is predicated of the event role borne by *dances*. Larson's analysis suffers, however, from the general problems surrounding "VP-shell" structures of the type proposed in Larson 1988 (which have been discussed in other contexts; see, e.g., Den Dikken 1995c, section 3.2), and his particular approach to (30b) has the specific drawback that it needs to have the AP front to a position to the left of *dancer* and that it does not have any obvious place to put the determiner introducing the predicate nominal (*a* in *a beautiful dancer*). These are nontrivial problems that, combined with the fact that Larsonian shells do not fit into the general approach taken here, lead me to pursue a different analysis.

What is worth preserving from Larson's analysis of the apparently nonintersective reading of *a beautiful dancer* is the idea that it *is* in fact intersective, as well as the idea that the adjective is treated as a *predicate*, not as a predicate modifier.[28] In both respects, Larson's analysis matches that of Szabó (2001). But Szabó rejects Larson's idea that *beautiful* in the apparently nonintersective interpretation of (28a) is predicated of the event variable of *dancer*. Instead, he proposes that *beautiful* is a one-place predicate that is incomplete in the sense that it bears a variable R that stands for a certain "role" in which the property denoted by the adjective can hold of an individual. And he takes the set denoted by this incomplete one-place predicate to intersect with the set denoted by *dancer* (see (31)). Simply put, then, (28a) can be paraphrased as follows: 'Imogen is a dancer and she is beautiful (in her role) as a dancer.'

(31) *dancer*(*Imogen*) $\wedge$ (*beautiful*(R))(*Imogen*)

2.6.3   Intersective and Apparently Nonintersective Adjectival Modifiers as Predicates (II): Syntax

Szabó's (2001) discussion of (28a) and its ilk confines itself entirely to the semantics of these kinds of sentences. Assuming that his semantics of (28a) is basically right, how do we go about translating it into a syntactic representation of this sentence? I would like to propose that the translation of (31) into syntax is (32).[29]

(32) Imogen is a beautiful dancer.
   [$_{RP}$ *Imogen* [RELATOR=*be* [$_{DP}$ *a* [$_{RP}$ [$_{AP}$ *beautiful*] [RELATOR [$_{NP}$ *dancer*]]]]]]

That is, *Imogen* is the subject of a predicate nominal (DP) whose D-head (*a*) embeds a predication (RP) of which the AP of *beautiful* is the predicate and the NP of *dancer* is the subject—but, interestingly, with the predicate projected in the *specifier* position of the RELATOR phrase and the subject in the RELATOR's complement. By projecting the predicate and its subject in this manner, we obtain simultaneously the desired predicative relationship between *beautiful* and *dancer* and the restrictive function played by the NP of *dancer*. In fact, a minimal variant of (32) that has a full-fledged DP rather than a bare NP in the complement of the RELATOR (given in (33)) expresses precisely what the second conjunct of Szabó's paraphrase of (28a) expresses: 'Imogen is beautiful as a dancer,' with *as* (see *like* in (29b)) lexicalizing the RELATOR.

(33) Imogen is beautiful as a dancer.
 [RP *Imogen* [RELATOR=*be* [RP [AP *beautiful*] [RELATOR=*as* [DP *a* [NP *dancer*]]]]]]

I propose, therefore, that the restrictive function of *(a) dancer* in *beautiful as a dancer* and the apparently nonintersective reading of *a beautiful dancer* is the result of *a dancer*'s originating in the complement of the RELATOR. Thus, there is a two-way relationship between *beautiful* and *(a) dancer* in (32) and (33): the AP is predicated of the (extended) noun phrase thanks to the fact that it is connected to the (extended) noun phrase by the RELATOR, and at the same time the (extended) noun phrase restricts the adjectival predicate thanks to the fact that the (extended) noun phrase is the complement of the RELATOR head. In garden-variety predicational structures in which the predicate is the *complement* of the RELATOR, the predicative and restrictive functions coincide in the predicate, but in the reverse structures in (32) and (33), the two functions rest on the shoulders of different constituents.

So far we have concentrated on Szabó's variable R in (31) and given a syntactic translation of it in terms of a structure in which *dancer* (the value of the variable R in the case at hand) is projected as the complement of the RELATOR, thereby functioning both as the subject of the AP and as a restrictor of the AP. But the structure below (32) also gives expression to the fact that, for (32) to be true, Imogen not only has to dance beautifully, she also has to be a dancer—that is, *dancer* must be predicated of *Imogen*, as expressed in the first conjunct of (31). This is guaranteed by the fact that the container of the RP dominating *beautiful* and *dancer*, the DP headed by the indefinite article *a*, is a predicate nominal whose semantic head is *dancer* and whose subject is *Imogen*.[30]

2.6.4 Spelling out the RELATOR-head

Apparently tied to the fact that in the structure of (32) the RP representing Szabó's *beautiful*(R) is contained in a predicate nominal (DP), while in (33) this RP serves as the primary predicate of the copular sentence by itself, is the fact that the RELATOR in (32) remains silent while in (33) it is spelled out as *as*. Things have to be that way, apparently: the sentences in (34) are ungrammatical.

(34) a. *Imogen is a beautiful as dancer.
     b. *Imogen is beautiful a dancer.

In light of the structures of (32) and (33), this difference between the two constructions is characterizable in terms of selection: when the RELATOR takes a bare nominal complement, it must be silent; on the other hand, when R takes an extended nominal complement (DP), it is spelled out as *as*.[31]

The *as* that lexicalizes the RELATOR-head in (33) is exactly the same *as* that we find in, for instance, (35a–c), for which Aarts (1992) and Bowers (1993), among others, have argued that it spells out the functional head of the small clause in the complement of the verb—a head that Bowers calls "Pr" and that corresponds to my RELATOR.

(35) a. Imogen regards Brian *(as) a nice guy.
        Imogen regards Brian *(as) nice.
     b. Imogen views Brian *(as) a nice guy.
     c. Imogen considers Brian (as) a nice guy.
     d. Imogen finds Brian (*as) a nice guy.

The question of whether the RELATOR-head of the small clause is spelled out overtly (as *as*) turns out not to be solely a function of the categorial status (NP *vs* DP) of the complement of the RELATOR: the verb selecting the small clause has a hand in it as well. This, too, can be expressed in terms of selection: the verb, after all, takes the projection of the RELATOR as its complement.

Selection by the verb is not just a matter of taking or not taking an overt spell-out of the RELATOR. It also determines the precise choice of spell-out of the RELATOR. While *regard, view,* and *consider* want (or at least allow) *as* to lexicalize the RELATOR-head of their small-clause complements, the verb *treat* can take *like* (which we already saw in action as the RELATOR in (29b)), and *take* selects *for* as the realization of the RELATOR.

(36) a. Imogen treats Brian like a fool.
     b. Imogen takes Brian for a fool.
         Imogen takes these things for granted.

2.6.5 "Autonymous θ-Marking" as Reverse Predication

One reason I decided to bring up the case of *take* with a *for*-headed small-clause complement in this context is that it forms a natural bridge to a brief discussion of sentences of the type in (37).

(37) a. This butterfly is big for a butterfly.
     b. This is a big butterfly.
     c. This butterfly is big.

Higginbotham (1985, 564) calls the *for*-phrase in (37a) the *attribute*, and claims (without discussion) that it is "an argument of the adjective." Basing himself on this claim, he then proceeds to present a structure of noun phrases like *a big butterfly* in which the adjective's external θ-role is θ-*identified* with the head noun's θ-role, and in which the adjective's second θ-role (the one realized by the attribute in (37a)) is assigned "to the very noun itself" via what he calls "*autonymous θ-marking*." But the invention of "autonymous θ-marking" extends the already quite substantial inventory of thematic relations in Higginbotham's (1985) theory, and any form of θ-marking of a lexical head (N^0 in Higginbotham's account) should raise suspicion. What is more, it is unlikely that the attribute could indeed be accommodated as a θ-dependent of the adjective: it certainly could not be its internal argument, in light of examples such as (38), where *at math* serves as the adjective's internal argument already.

(38) Imogen is good at math for a five-year-old.

There is little to be gained in pursuing the "autonymous θ-marking" approach to attributes, therefore. An alternative is called for. In light of our discussion of (33) in the foregoing, (37a) can readily be accommodated with the aid of the structure in (39)—a "reverse predication" in the sense of section 2.2.2.

(39) [RP *this butterfly* [RELATOR=*be* [RP [AP *big*] [R′ RELATOR=*for* [DP *a butterfly*]]]]]

In this structure, the AP is predicated of the DP across the RELATOR, and the DP in its turn restricts the denotation of the AP headed by *big*.

Higginbotham (1985) notes that (37a) and (37b) have the same meaning, differing as a pair from (37c). Only (37a, b) force "grading with respect to the attribute given in N" (Higginbotham 1985, 563) as part of their meaning: "We judge that [(37a)] is true if the object indicated is big for a butterfly [see (37b)], but that [(37c)] is more open-ended; since even big butterflies are not big creatures, [(37c)] can count as false with respect to an object for which [(37a)] counts as true." Let us take it, then, that (37a, b) are semantically equivalent when it comes to the relationship between *big* and *butterfly*. With the analysis in (39) (which is identical to the structure below (33)) in place as the representation of sentences of the type in (37a), this then leads us right back to a structure for attributive adjectival modification that matches the structure underneath (32), in which, once again, the AP is generated as a predicate in the specifier position of the RELATOR phrase.[32]

2.6.6 Reverse Nominal and Prepositional Predication

Prepositions like *as*, *for*, and *like*[33] can serve as lexicalizations of the RELATOR in straight predications involving adjectival and nominal predicates, as we saw in (35) and (36). We have also seen them lexicalize the RELATOR in reverse predications featuring adjectival predicates, as in (37a). Naturally, we would expect them to show up as RELATORs in reverse nominal predications as well—an expectation that is indeed fulfilled. Thus, consider the bracketed parts of the examples in (40):

(40) a. Imogen regards [the president as a fool].
          Imogen takes [the president for a fool].
      b. We have [a fool as our president].
          We have [a fool for a president].

In the b-sentences, the nominal predicate *a fool* appears in a reverse predication (a "predicate-specifier" structure of the type in (3b)), with *as/for* lexicalizing the RELATOR-head. Similarly, in the b-examples in (41) and (42) we find nominal predicate-specifier constructions with *for* serving as the lexicalization of the RELATOR. Example (42c) shows that prepositional predicates are possible here, too.

(41) a. This butterfly is big for a butterfly.
      b. This butterfly is a big creature for a butterfly.

(42) a. Brian is skinny for an American.
  b. Brian is a skinny guy for an American.
  c. Brian is in good physical shape for an American.

But while *big for a butterfly* alternates with *a big butterfly*, and *skinny for an American* with *a skinny American*, the reverse nominal predications in (41b) and (42b) cannot be embedded inside a noun phrase: (43a, b), which have the structures given in (44) (see (32)), are ungrammatical.

(43) a. *This (butterfly) is a big creature butterfly.
  b. *Brian is a skinny guy American.

(44) a. *[RP *this butterfly* [RELATOR=*be* [DP *a* [RP [NP *big creature*]
       [RELATOR [NP *butterfly*]]]]]]
  b. *[RP *Brian* [RELATOR=*be* [DP *a* [RP [NP *skinny guy*] [RELATOR [NP
       American]]]]]]

The roots of the ill-formedness (44) may lie in the fact that the predicate nominals in these structures, embedded as they are inside a larger DP, are bare NPs. The distribution of bare-NP predicates is extremely limited, particularly in languages like English, where things like *George is president (of the United States)* are just about the only instances of bare predicate nominals. There are cases, though, in which near-minimal pairs of DP-external and DP-internal reverse nominal predication *can* be found. They are not hugely numerous—but the pairs in (45) and (46) are illustrative of a grammatical pattern (see also Matushansky 2002 for discussion).[34]

(45) a. We have an idiot for a doctor.
       [RP [DP *an idiot*] [R′ RELATOR=*for* [DP *a doctor*]]]
  b. We have an idiot doctor.
       [DP *an* [RP [NP *idiot*] [RELATOR=∅ [NP *doctor*]]]]

(46) a. He is a madman as a driver.
       [RP [DP *a madman*] [R′ RELATOR=*as* [DP *a driver*]]]
  b. He is a madman driver.
       [DP *a* [RP [NP *madman*] [RELATOR=∅ [NP *driver*]]]]

I will return to constructions of the type in (45b) and (46b) in chapter 5 (especially section 5.2), as part of the discussion of noun-phrase internal Predicate Inversion. For now, suffice it to say that, with nominal predicates as with adjectival ones, reverse predication is possible both inside and outside the complex noun phrase.

2.6.7 Reverse Predication versus Adverbial Modification

With (42a), repeated here as (47a), straightforwardly assimilable to (39), we should ask whether this analysis should carry over to (47b) as well.

(47) a. Brian is skinny for an American. (= (42a))
      b. Brian is skinny for/by American standards.

At first blush, the two sentences in (47a) and (47b) seem to be semantically equivalent. But closer scrutiny reveals that it is unlikely that (47b) has a structure of the type in (39). Whereas the AP projected by *skinny* can of course be taken to be a predicate of *an American* in (47a), it seems entirely implausible to have *skinny* be predicated of *American standards*— we are not claiming, of course, that American standards are skinny; it is hard to even imagine how they could be such. Also, (47a) claims that Brian is an American—something that fits in with Kamp's (1975) and Siegel's (1976) argument to the effect that both the noun phrase following *for* and the AP preceding it are predicates in sentences of the type in (37a) and (47a), with the AP serving as a function from predicates (properties) to predicates (properties). But the noun phrase *American standards* in (47b) is not, of course, predicated of *Brian*: we are not claiming that Brian is American standards, whatever that might mean. Nor, even, is (47b) making any necessary claims about Brian's citizenship, it seems to me: (47b) can be true even if Brian is not an American, but just happens to be skinny for American standards.

   What seems to tie in with the fact that the noun phrase following *for/by* in (47b) is not the complement of the RELATOR-head in the structure in (39) is the fact that *for/by American standards* combines readily with a *for*-phrase that does arguably instantiate the R′ of (39), as in (48b), whereas combining *for an American* with another *for*-phrase of the same type is ungrammatical (see (48a)).

(48) a. *Brian is skinny for a twelve-year-old for an American.
      b.   Brian is skinny for a twelve-year-old for/by American standards.

   Traditionally, what one would say about *for/by American standards* is that it is an adjunct, presumably at the level of the small clause (i.e., the top RP in (39)), modifying *skinny for a twelve-year-old*. Updating this to the "modification is predication is mediated by a RELATOR" approach taken in these pages, what we have to say is that the phrase *for/by American standards* is a subconstituent of an RP in which it serves as the predicate of the other *for*-headed RP, *skinny for a twelve-year-old*—with the predicate (which, after all, follows its modifiee) occupying the complement of the RELATOR. The entire constituent [[*skinny for a twelve-year-old*] *for/by American standards*] (which qualifies as a predicate by virtue of the fact that the predicate nominal *a twelve-year-old* is still unsaturated) is finally predicated of *Brian*, with the copula *be* as the RELATOR. This is depicted in (49).

(49) [$_{RP_1}$ *Brian* [RELATOR=*be* [$_{RP_2}$ [$_{RP_3}$ [$_{AP}$ *skinny*] [$_{R'}$ RELATOR=*for* [$_{DP}$ *a twelve-year-old*]]] [RELATOR=*for/by* [$_{DP}$ *American standards*]]]]]

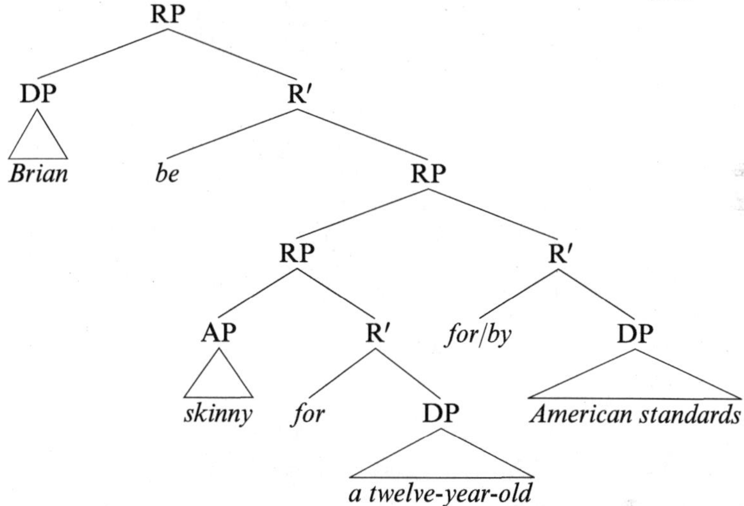

2.6.8 Back to Adverbial Modification: Word Order and Scope Issues

There are two ways, in principle, in which the structure in (49) can come about: either (i) the entire RP dominating *skinny for a twelve-year-old* is merged directly in the specifier position of the larger RP, or (ii) the former RP is moved into the specifier position of the larger RP, with the larger RP base-generated on a left branch. There is no particular reason to assume, for the specific case of (48b), that the movement derivation in (ii) should be selected. But there are contexts in the domain of adverbial modification in which we arguably do have to select the movement scenario. To see this, let me turn to manner adverbials and ask how the word-order alternation in pairs of the type in (50) should be accounted for.

(50) a. Imogen kissed Brian gently.
      b. Imogen gently kissed Brian.

Cinque (1999)—like me but not for the same reasons—starts out from the assumption that all adverbial modifiers are associated with their modifiees via functional categories (of which Cinque, in the "cartographic" line, presents a sizable inventory of candidates; the labels do not matter for our purposes here). His work is a representative of a movement approach to word-order alternations of the type in (50). In particular, he takes the word order in (50b) to be basic and the one in (50a) is derived from it via leftward movement (of the VP). In other words, he takes adverbials to be systematically base-generated in *specifier* positions of functional projections, and in agreement with Kayne's (1994) antisymmetry, he takes those specifiers to be systematically on the left. When the constituent modified by the adverbial surfaces to the adverbial's left, that means that there has been leftward phrasal movement of that constituent in the overt-syntactic derivation. And since subconstituents of that constituent could in principle be removed from it prior to its leftward movement, remnant movement should be able to give rise to a surface word order in which one part of the modified constituent shows up to the left of the adverbial and the other (the "remnant") to its right—producing "straddling" word orders such as those in (51), where the clause-final PPs are the remnants.

(51) a. Imogen kissed Brian gently on the head.
      b. Imogen thanked Brian profusely for his help.

If rightward movement and right-adjunction are universally prohibited (by Kayne's 1994 Linear Correspondence Axiom), word orders of the type in (51) can only result from leftward movement of a subpart of the modified (extended) projection of the verb, around the adverbial modifier's base position.[35]

It must be possible, therefore, to base-generate adverbial modifiers to the left of their modifiees, on a left branch, and to move their modifiees around them. On the assumption—made explicitly in Barbiers 1995—that the motivation for leftward movement of the modifiee actually lies in the need to establish a predication relationship between the adverbial modifier and the (extended) projection of the verb, this entails that movement of the (extended) projection of the verb into the specifier position of a RELATOR-head that takes the adverbial modifier as its complement should be possible—concretely, then, (52a) should exist.[36]

(52) a. [$_{RP}$ [$_{vP}$ DP [$_{v}$ VP]] [$_{RELATOR}$ AdvP]] (...) [$_{vP}$ ~~DP [$_{v}$ VP]~~]

b. [$_{RP}$ [$_{vP}$ DP [$_{v}$ VP]] [$_{RELATOR}$ AdvP]]
c. [$_{RP}$ AdvP [$_{RELATOR}$ [$_{vP}$ DP [$_{v}$ VP]]]]

But (52b) and (52c) are logical possibilities as well. The structure in (52b) is identical with (52a) except for the fact that the VP does not end up in SpecRP via movement but is merged there in the base, and (52c) is identical to (52b) except that it reverses the hierarchical relationship between the adverbial modifier and the modifiee, with R still establishing the predication relationship between the two.

It will be clear that, since neither (52b) nor (52c) involves movement of the VP, neither structure can give rise to "straddling" word orders of the type in (51). In fact, for (52b) and (52c), what you see is basically what you get, with (52b) producing an output in which the adverbial follows the entire VP and (52c) giving rise to a word order featuring the adverbial to the left of the VP. It will also be clear that (52b) and (52c), while both featuring a predication relationship between the AdvP and the VP, have different consequences in the domain of scope—a quantificational adverbial inserted in the position of AdvP in (52c) will scope over the VP; no such scopal relationship is establishable on the basis of (52b) (on the assumption that adverbials do not move). For (52a), predictions regarding scope are less categorical: while AdvP does not itself c-command any copy of the VP, the RP of which the adverb is the lexical head does asymmetrically c-command the lower copy of the VP. I will assume that this state of affairs gives rise to ambiguity: a quantificational adverbial in the position of AdvP in (52a) has the option of scoping over the VP but is not obliged to do so.

When we now take a look at a concrete case of a quantificational adverbial modifier, we find that the facts indicate that (52a) cannot be the sole underlier of adverbial-modification constructions: (52b) and (52c) must exist as well.[37] Of the triplet in (53), (53a) is perfectly ambiguous between a reading in which there is a single event of giving two knocks on the door, and an interpretation in which there are two events of knocking on the door (see Cinque 1999, 26). This ambiguity falls out from the fact that (53a) has two different derivations, one built on (52a) and one built on (52b). The latter delivers a single-event interpretation only, due to the fact that the adverb *twice* cannot take scope over the event role for lack of c-command. The former, while supporting a single-event reading, can give rise to a multiple-event interpretation as well, with RP asymmetrically c-commanding the lower copy of the VP. The "straddling" word order in (53b) is derivable on the basis of (52a) as well, hence is expected to allow both a single-event and a multievent interpretation. This is correct—though perhaps the single-event reading is more prominent in (53b) than it is in (53a) (for reasons I do not fully understand[38]), both sentences are ambiguous. By contrast, (53c) is unambiguous. The fact that the VP in (53c) surfaces to the right of *twice* makes it compatible with the structure in (52c) only: it is plain that (52a) and (52b) will not do, and that, therefore, a single-event interpretation is unsupportable in the case of (53c).

(53) a. Imogen knocked on the door twice.
      b. Imogen knocked twice on the door.
      c. Imogen twice knocked on the door.

These conclusions are confirmed by the behavior of the examples in (54), which differ from (53) in featuring an additional instance of *twice* in preverbal position.

(54) a. Imogen twice knocked on the door twice.
      b. Imogen twice knocked twice on the door.
      c. *Imogen twice twice knocked on the door.

Preverbal *twice*, which occupies the SpecRP position in the structure in (52c), always takes scope over the VP, hence systematically delivers a multiple-event interpretation. That makes it incompatible with another instance of preverbal *twice*, as in (54c). On the other hand, the "straddling" word order, which is derived via (52a) and is ambiguous between a multievent and a single-event reading, is readily compatible with an additional *twice* in preverbal position, as in (54b), and so is (54a). As Cinque (1999, 27) notes, (54a, b) have preverbal *twice* scoping over the event: it occupies the SpecRP position in (52c) and hence delivers a multiple-event interpretation. The second instance of *twice* in (54a, b) is compatible with a single-event reading, while the fact that the second preverbal *twice* in (54c) is forced to take scope over the event filters this example out, as desired.

The discussion of (53) and (54) thus supports the conclusion that, alongside a structure in which the adverbial phrase (the modifier or predicate) sits in the complement position of the RELATOR (as in (52a) and (52b)), we also find adverbial-modification constructions involving a structure of the type in (52c), with the predicate base-generated in SpecRP and its subject (the modified (extended) projection of the verb) occupying the RELATOR's complement position—a conclusion that we had already found substantial evidence for in the discussion of adjectival modification.

2.7 Predication Alternations

The discussion in section 2.6 lends support for the conclusion, drawn in section 2.2.2, that predication relationships in syntax are configurational yet fundamentally nondirectional—(3a) and (3b), repeated here, are in principle available alongside one another.

(3) a. [$_{RP}$ [$_{XP}$ SUBJECT] [$_{R'}$ RELATOR [$_{YP}$ PREDICATE]]]

$\qquad\qquad\qquad\qquad\qquad$ (Predicate-complement structure)

$\qquad$ b. [$_{RP}$ [$_{XP}$ PREDICATE] [$_{R'}$ RELATOR [$_{YP}$ SUBJECT]]]

$\qquad\qquad\qquad\qquad\qquad\quad$ (Predicate-specifier structure)

In this section, I will explore a number of further consequences of the nondirectionality of predication.

2.7.1 The Active/Passive Diathesis Alternation and the Perfect

One immediate result of introducing two ways of linking a predicate to its subject is that it provides a straightforward perspective on the active/passive diathesis alternation, and on auxiliary selection in periphrastic perfective constructions.[39] Though it is customary to take the passive construction to be derived from its active counterpart (either via a lexical operation or via a syntactic transformation), the precise details of the way the erstwhile agent is "shunted" to *chômeur* status (to use the Relational Grammar term) and, concomitantly, the precise structural position of the *by*-phrase and the way it is connected to the agent θ-role, have never become perfectly clear. What one typically finds in discussions of the passive is a considerable amount of hand-waving when it comes to these matters.[40]

On other hand, if one takes the claim seriously that the predicate and its subject can be related to each other in either of the two ways in (3), the account of the active/passive diathesis alternation becomes almost trivial: the active in (55a) employs the structure in (3a), while the passive in (55b) avails itself of (3b).

(55) a. Imogen kissed Brian.

      [$_{v}$P [$_{DP}$ *Imogen*] [$_{v'}$ [$_v$ $\varnothing$] (=RELATOR) [$_{VP}$ *kissed Brian*]]]

    b. Brian was kissed by Imogen.

      [$_{RP}$ [$_{VP}$ *kissed Brian*] [$_{R'}$ [$_P$ *by*] (=RELATOR) [$_{DP}$ *Imogen*]]]

The RELATOR in (55a) is Chomsky's (inaudible) light verb *v*, while in (55b) the connection between the event and the agent is established by a relational *preposition*, the *by* of the *by*-phrase.

From the structure beside (55a) one gets to the surface output by merging the *v*P with T and raising the agent *Imogen* to SpecTP, to satisfy T's EPP-property. The V-head raises to *v* and, depending on the properties of T, the complex thus created either raises further up to T or enters into an Agree relationship with T without moving any further—whichever derivation ensues, the [tense] feature of T will be appropriately checked.[41]

For (58b) things are slightly more complicated because of the lack of a verbal head that could raise to T to check the latter's [tense] feature: the participle *kissed* cannot take care of this since it lacks a [tense] feature itself.[42] To get the [tense] feature on T checked, therefore, a dummy bearer of a [tense] feature is called upon. This leads to the emergence in the structure of a form of the copula *be*, a familiar ingredient of the periphrastic passive construction. Finally, to satisfy T's EPP-property, the complement of the participle, *Brian* (rather than *Imogen*, which is "frozen" inside the *by*-PP,[43] getting all its features checked there), is raised to SpecTP, and the derivation is complete. The result is depicted in (55c).

(55) c. [$_{TP}$ *Brian*$_i$ [$_{T'}$ *was* [$_{RP}$ [$_{VP}$ *kissed t$_i$*] [$_{R'}$ [$_P$ *by*] (=RELATOR) [$_{DP}$
      Imogen]]]

If, instead, we raised the prepositional RELATOR up to the PP-external copula, leaving everything else in (55b) the same, we would end up with a copular element with a P incorporated into it—a *be* + P composite that, by Benveniste's (1966) adage in (56), is realized on the surface as a form of *have*.[44]

(56) "*Avoir* n'est rien autre qu'un *être à* inversé."

(Benveniste 1966, 197)

With P incorporated into the copula, that leaves the complement of P with no source to check its Case feature within the PP. The derivation will converge with *Imogen* raising to SpecTP checking nominative Case and *Brian* entering in an Agree relationship with the transitivized copula (now in possession of an accusative Case feature thanks to the incorporation of P, which is lexically equipped with a Case feature), checking

accusative Case via this route. This derivation yields the periphrastic
have-perfect in (57).

(57) Imogen has kissed Brian.
  be [$_{PP}$ [$_{VP}$ *kissed Brian*] [$_{PP}$ [$_P$ ∅] (=RELATOR) [$_{DP}$ *Imogen*]]] →
  [$_{DP}$ *Imogen*]$_j$ [*be*+P$_i$=*have* [$_{RP}$ [$_{VP}$ *kissed Brian*] [$_{R'}$ t_i t_j]]]

2.7.2 Romance Causatives

The syntax of Romance causative constructions is another interesting domain in which the alternation between the predicate-complement structure in (3a) and the predicate-specifier structure in (3b) brings forth an
account of recalcitrant facts. The alternation, for French *laisser* 'let' and
for Spanish *hacer* 'make', for instance, between sentences of the type in
(58a) and their counterparts in (58b) has given rise to an avalanche of
discussion in the generative literature at least since Kayne 1975. And
though there is a general consensus that (58a) is transparently the French
equivalent of its English ECM translation, it has proved very difficult
to find a satisfactory account of the syntax of (58b), the *faire*-infinitive
construction.

(58) a. je laisse/*fais Imogen embrasser Brian (French)
          I let/make   Imogen kiss   Brian
      b. je laisse/fais embrasser Brian à   Imogen
          I let/make kiss   Brian to Imogen
          'I let/make Imogen kiss Brian.'

From the perspective of (3), the alternation between (58a, b) is basically
straightforward: (58a) represents (3a), with the subject of the infinitive
(the "causee") surfacing as a DP-subject of a *v*P embedded in the complement of *laisser*, while (58b) realizes (3b), with the subject of the lower VP
base-generated as the complement of a dative P, *à*, which serves as the
RELATOR, its projection being the complement *laisser*.

Digging a little deeper into the pair in (58), let us start out from the fact
that the light verb *v* and the VP must be adjacent—there can be no projection in between *v* and the root-VP. This is explicitly assumed, but not
derived, in Chomsky 1995, chap. 4; on my assumptions it falls out from
(2), the locality condition on predication. As a result, the light verb *v*
must take a *bare* VP as its complement. The verbal head of that root-VP
needs to incorporate into *v* in order to be licensed. And the *v*–V composite resulting from V-incorporation into *v* in turn depends on T for its
licensing. Put differently, approaching the issue from the other direction:

(59) T identifies the RELATOR in (55a) as a light verb v.

In order, therefore, to legitimate the inclusion of the substructure in (55a), with RELATOR=v, in the complement of *laisser*, we need to ensure that *laisser*'s complement includes a TP. The presence of the embedded T licenses the embedded v, and at the same time makes temporal adverbial modification and negation available inside the causative complement, as desired (see (60a)).

(60) a. je laisse Imogen (ne   pas) embrasser Brian (demain) (French)
         I let   Imogen NEG not kiss   Brian tomorrow

   b. je laisse (*ne   pas) embrasser Brian (*demain)   à Imogen
         I let   NEG not kiss   Brian   tomorrow to Imogen

The matrix T in its turn licenses another v, responsible for the introduction of the causer and capable of licensing another root-VP in its complement: the projection of the causative matrix verb *laisser*. Putting all this together, we arrive at the structure in (61a) for the "*laisser*-ECM" construction in (58a).

(61) a. $[_{vP_2}$ $[_{DP}$ CAUSER $[_{vP}$ $v2$ $[_{VP}$ V$_{CAUS}$ $[_{TP}$ $[_{DP}$ CAUSEE$]_i$ T $[_{vP_1}$ t_i $[_{vP}$ $v1$ $[_{VP_1}$ V1_{Inf} OB$]]]]]]]]$

   b. $[_{vP}$ $[_{DP}$ CAUSER $[_{v'}$ v $[_{VP_2}$ V$_{CAUS}$ $[_{RP}$ $[_{VP_1}$ V1_{Inf} OB$]$ $[_{R'}$ RELATOR=P($à$) $[_{DP}$ CAUSEE$]]]]]]]$

While in (60a) negation and temporal adverbial modification of the caused event are grammatical thanks to the presence of an embedded TP, in (60b) negation and temporal adverbial modification of the caused event are impossible. This reliably indicates that there is no TP present in the complement of *laisser* in (58/60b). The entire causative construction in (58b) has precisely one TP—and, concomitantly, since every v has to be licensed by its own T, there is exactly one vP as well. This means that the causee of the causative construction in (58b) cannot be introduced by a light verb: the single light verb present in the structure introduces the causer. Instead, the causativized event (denoted by the VP projected by the causativized verb) is linked to its instigator via the other route: with the aid of a *prepositional* RELATOR, as in (58b). This prepositionally headed RELATOR phrase serves as the complement to *laisser*, which is itself embedded in the familiar light-verb environment, as depicted in (61b), the structure of constructions of the type in (58b).[45]

The important thing to note when it comes to (58b) is that the empirical fact that no temporal adverbial modification or negation is possible in the causativized VP tells us that there is no TP present in the complement of *laisser* here, and that this, in turn, excludes the selection of the predicate-complement structure in (3a) with a T-dependent light verb v as *laisser*'s complement and forces us down the other route, that of the predicate-specifier structure in (3b). In transitive causative constructions of the type in (58b), the RELATOR-head of this structure is lexicalized by the dative preposition *à*, a spell-out of the RELATOR that, thanks to its being a preposition, can check the Case feature of the causee in its complement under Agree. The RELATOR in (61b) *has to* be spelled out by a Case-checking preposition to help out the causee since, with v already engaged in a Case-checking Agree relationship with the causativized verb's object (OB in (61b)), it will be impossible for the causee of a transitive causative to check its Case feature against the matrix "light verb" v.[46]

In unergative-based causative constructions, by contrast, the causativized verb does not take an object. We therefore expect such causatives, which have the same gross structure as (61b), not to feature a prepositional spell-out of the RELATOR: the causee now has no competitor when it comes to Case, hence it is expected to check accusative Case against v. And indeed, in unergative-based *faire*-infinitive constructions such as (62a), analyzed as in (62b), we see the causee show up to the right of the infinitive in a "bare" form, not preceded by the dative preposition *à*.

(62) a. Imogen laisse/fait rire   (*à) Brian (French)
        Imogen lets/makes laugh   to Brian
        'Imogen lets/makes Brian laugh.'
     b. [$_{v}$P [$_{DP}$ CAUSER [$_{v'}$ v [$_{VP_2}$ V$_{CAUS}$ [$_{RP}$ [$_{VP_1}$ V1$_{Inf}$] [$_{R'}$ RELATOR=$\varnothing$ [$_{DP}$
        CAUSEE]]]]]]]

In this way, the approach to *faire*-infinitive causatives captures in an entirely straightforward fashion the difference in Case marking of the causee between transitive and unergative-based causatives. The overall structures of the two constructions are entirely parallel, the difference between the two lying solely in whether the RELATOR that connects the causativized VP to its subject (the causee) is spelled out as a preposition or not.[47]

2.8 Reverse Predications as Primary Predications

The discussion in the preceding sections suggests that the relationship between a predicate and its subject is establishable in either of two directions, with the predicate either being the complement of the RELATOR or its specifier, as in (3a) and (3b) (repeated below), respectively.

(3) a. [$_{RP}$ [$_{XP}$ SUBJECT] [$_{R'}$ RELATOR [$_{YP}$ PREDICATE]]]
                                   (Predicate-complement structure)
     b. [$_{RP}$ [$_{XP}$ PREDICATE] [$_{R'}$ RELATOR [$_{YP}$ SUBJECT]]]
                                   (Predicate-specifier structure)

We have seen that these structures both yield grammatical outputs. In the foregoing discussion, we have come across three different instances of the predicate-specifier structure in (3b), reproduced below in a format that abstracts away from individual lexical items.[48]

(63) a. [$_{RP}$ AP/DP/NP/PP   [$_{R'}$ RELATOR DP/NP]]]
                                      (cf. (39), (41), (42), (45), (46))
      b. [$_{RP}$ VP   [$_{R'}$ RELATOR DP]]]
                                           (cf. (55b), (61b), (62b))
      c. [$_{RP}$ AdvP   [$_{R'}$ RELATOR vP]]]   (cf. (52c))

I will close this chapter by briefly considering the syntactic distribution of the structures in (63), with particular reference to the question of whether any of the reverse predications in (63) can serve as a *primary* predication—with *primary predication* defined as in (64) (see also Napoli 1989, 88).

(64) The *primary predication* is the main, tensed subject-predicate
      relationship of the clause.

2.8.1 Adjectival, Nominal, and Prepositional Predicates

We have seen (63a) instantiated by sentences such as *Brian is skinny/a skinny guy/in good physical shape for an American*, where the RELATOR-head is lexicalized by the preposition *for*, checking Case against the DP in its complement and "freezing" that DP inside the RP. For obvious reasons, it is impossible to embed this RP under T and raise either one of the constituents of (63a) to SpecTP to satisfy the EPP. With DP "frozen in place," it cannot A-move to SpecTP (see (65a)); and raising the predicate specifier to SpecTP, while presumably satisfying the EPP, will not get T's uninterpretable Case feature checked (since predicates do not have structural Case features).[49]

(65) a. *a butterfly is big for   a'.   a butterfly is big
      b. *big is for a butterfly   b'. *big is a butterfly

Of course (65a′) is grammatical (regardless of its veracity), and straightforwardly derived from a predicate-complement structure of the type in (3a). But could (65a′) also be derived from the predicate-specifier structure in (3b), with raising of the *null* RELATOR's complement (which is not Case-licensed in situ this time, unlike in *big for a butterfly*) across the predicate in specifier position? This would, in effect, be the structural counterpart to Predicate Inversion in a predicate-complement structure of the type in (3a), where likewise the RELATOR's complement raises around its specifier (as shown in chapters 4 and 5). And indeed, with the AP of *big* serving as a function from predicates (properties) to predicates (properties) in *big for a butterfly* (see Kamp 1975, Siegel 1976, and section 2.6.7), the RELATOR's complement in the predicate-specifier structure is itself a predicate. It is there, in fact, that the answer to the question of whether (65a′) can be derived from a predicate-specifier structure is to be found. *Given that* the AP serves as a function from predicates to predicates, it follows that the RP in (63a) must either be embedded in another RP whose specifier can serve as the subject of the RP in (63a), as in (66a), or be generated as the complement of D, as in (66b).[50]

(66) a. This butterfly is big for a butterfly.
      [RP *this butterfly* [RELATOR=*be* [RP [AP *big*] [RELATOR=*for* [DP *a* [NP *butterfly*]]]]]]
   b. This is a big butterfly.
      [RP *this butterfly* [RELATOR=*be* [DP *a* [RP [AP *big*] [RELATOR [NP *butterfly*]]]]]]

Failure to embed the RP in (63a) in another RP or under D, on the other hand, will deliver an ungrammatical output: the noun phrase in the RELATOR's complement cannot be saturated. That is why (65a′) *cannot* be derived from (3b) via raising of the RELATOR's complement, and why (65b′) (an attempt at having T, lexicalized by the copula, serve as the RELATOR of AP and DP in (63a)) is ungrammatical as well.

While successful in ruling out (65b′) and a (3b)-based derivation for (65a′) and ruling in (66), this account begs a major question—a question that I already anticipated by italicizing "given that" in the last sentence above (66). Why are adjectival (as well as nominal and prepositional) predicate-specifiers functions from predicates (properties) to predicates (properties)—why can't they serve as functions that take individuals as arguments to yield truth values, as they can in predicate-complement structures? Why, put differently, must the complement of the RELATOR in adjectival (nominal, prepositional) predicate-specifier structures apparently always be interpreted as what Higginbotham (1985) called an *attribute*? At this time, I do not know what the deep answer to this question is. While recognizing that this is a major open end, I will lay down (67) as what appears to be a fact about the interpretation of predicate-specifier structures of the type in (63a).[51]

(67) Predicate-specifier structures with adjectival, nominal, and
      prepositional predicates receive an *attributive* interpretation.

It is (67) (or rather, whatever the roots of (67) may turn out to be) that is responsible for the impossibility of deriving (65a′) from a predicate-specifier structure.

The spectrum of syntactic manipulations of the predicate-specifier structure in (63a) is thus severely restricted. The predicate in RP's specifier position cannot raise up to SpecTP (see (65b, b′)), nor can the RELATOR's complement raise out (see (65a′)). Basically, then, predicate-specifier structures of the type in (63a) are "frozen" as far as the two major constituents, the subject and the predicate, are concerned. For predicate-complement constructions, by contrast, we face no such restrictions. We have already seen plenty of cases in which, in a (3a)-type structure, the subject raises out. And in chapters 4 and 5 I will illustrate and discuss in detail derivations featuring raising of the predicate from the RELATOR's complement to a higher, RP-external A-position: instances of Predicate Inversion.

2.8.2 Verbal Predicates

Two of the three instances of (63b) that we encountered in the foregoing, like the instantiations of (63a), have a preposition lexicalizing the RELATOR—*by* in the passive, and a dative preposition in instances of the Romance *faire*-infinitive construction built on a transitive base verb. In unergative-based *faire*-infinitive causatives, we saw that the RELATOR-head of the reverse verbal predication structure remains empty. The Italian examples in (68) illustrate all three cases.[52]

(68) a. Imogen fa   telefonare Brian (Italian)
          Imogen makes phone   Brian
          [$_{v}$P *Imogen* [RELATOR=v [VP *fa* [RP [VP *telefonare*] [RELATOR=∅
          [DP *Brian*]]]]]]

    b. Imogen fa   mangiare le mele a Brian
       Imogen makes eat   the apples to Brian
       $[_{vP}$ *Imogen* $[$RELATOR$=v$ $[_{VP}$ *fa* $[_{RP}$ $[_{VP}$ *mangiare le mele*$]$
       $[$RELATOR$=da$ $[_{DP}$ *Brian*$]]]]]]$
    c. Imogen fa   mangiare le mele da Brian
       Imogen makes eat   the apples by Brian
       $[_{vP}$ *Imogen* $[$RELATOR$=v$ $[_{VP}$ *fa* $[_{AspP}$ Asp $[_{RP}$ $[_{VP}$ *mangiare le mele*$]$
       $[$RELATOR$=da$ $[_{DP}$ *Brian*$]]]]]]]$

In (63b), the DP in the complement of the RELATOR is not an "attribute" in the sense of Higginbotham (1985); hence, (63b) is not governed by (67), and we should expect there to be no particular impediment to having T serve as the RELATOR of a reverse VP predicate and its subject. What could be the output of a structure of the type in (69)?

(69) $[_{TP}$ VP $[_{T'}$ T DP$]]$

  For languages allowing postverbal subjects with unergative verbs, such as Italian, (69) opens up an interesting perspective on the syntax of "free-inversion" constructions with unergative verbs of the type in (70b).

(70) Q: che cosa è successo? (Italian)
          what thing is happened
          'What happened?'
   A1:   ha telefonato Brian
          has phoned Brian
          'Brian called.'
   A2: #ha mangiato le mele Brian
          has eaten   the apples Brian
          'Brian has eaten the apples.'

These kinds of sentences have given rise in the literature to a variety of accounts, many involving right-adjunction of the subject (Rizzi 1982; Burzio 1986; Belletti 1988), some featuring a right-peripheral SpecVP (see Bonet 1989; Rosen 1989; Koopman and Sportiche 1990; Giorgi and Longobardi 1991; Friedeman 1992; Guasti 1993).[53] But base-generating the subject in a right-peripheral adjunction or specifier position, apart from being incompatible with the LCA (Kayne 1994), fails to shed light on why placement of the subject to the right of the predicate does not generalize to nonverbal predicates, and why, in wide-focus contexts such as the answer to a "What happened?" type question, the possibility of placing the subject to the right of the predicate does not even generalize to transitive VPs, as seen in (70.A2).[54]

With (70.A1) analyzed along the lines of (69), as in (71a), the fact that (70.A2) is unacceptable (in the wide-focus context in which it is presented here, in answer to (70.Q)) follows straightforwardly: there is no way for the direct object *le mele* to check its uninterpretable Case feature.

(71) a. [$_{TP}$ [$_{VP}$ *telefonare*] [T [$_{DP}$ *Brian*]]]
    b. *[$_{TP}$ [$_{VP}$ *mangiare le mele*] [T [$_{DP}$ *Brian*]]]
    c. *[$_{TP}$ [$_{vP}$ *v* [$_{VP}$ *mangiare le mele*]] [T [$_{DP}$ *Brian*]]]

By the time that VP is merged in SpecTP, T has already checked its Case feature against the DP in its complement (i.e., the postverbal subject); and there is no "light verb" *v* present in the structure—nor could there be: if the VP in SpecTP in (71b) were extended up to *v*P, as in (71c), so that accusative Case would become available, the *v*-head would fail to serve as a RELATOR, in violation of its quintessential function.[55]

Notice that the Case problem for the object of V would evaporate if the structure in (63b), rather than having the RELATOR *identified* as T, *merged* with T. On that scenario, V's object would be the first available candidate to check T's uninterpretable Case feature (and it would raise to SpecTP to satisfy the EPP if necessary). With V realized as a past participle, the result is a *passive*, as depicted in (72) (which elaborates (55b)), where a Case-checking RELATOR of VP and the subject is required to satisfy the Case needs of the subject (which, with V's object checking Case against T, cannot check nominative Case)—and of course insertion of a preposition under the RELATOR-head (English *by*, Italian *da*) fits the bill perfectly.

(72) a. (le mele) sono mangiate   (le mele) da Brian (Italian)
       the apples are   eaten-3F.PL the apples by Brian
    b. [$_{TP}$ DP$_i$ [$_{T'}$ *be*=RELATOR [$_{AspP}$ Asp [$_{RP}$ [$_{VP}$ V$_{PPTC}$ *t*$_i$] [$_{R'}$ *by*=RELATOR DP]]]]]

Note that embedding the RP [$_{RP}$ [$_{VP}$ *mangiare le mele*] [RELATOR=*a* [$_{DP}$ *Brian*]]] in (68b) under T, with T lexicalized as the copula, does not yield a grammatical output—sentences like **le mele sono mangiare a Brian* 'the apples are eat to Brian' are bad. A well-formed sentence results only once the infinitive *mangiare* is replaced with the past participle *mangiato*, with *da* but not *a* as the RELATOR. The obligatoriness of a past participle in (72a) arguably translates into the obligatory presence of an AspP outside the RELATOR's projection in the structure of the passive: Asp^0 is required to check the features of the past participle (*mangiate* in (72a)). This in turn will then guarantee, on the assumption that Asp selects *da* but not *a* as the lexicalization of the RELATOR (see Den Dikken and Longenecker 2004, section 4.2, and note 52, above), that, while there is a choice of RELATOR in the causative (see (68b, c)), only *da* can be chosen in (72).

It seems, then, that (63b) exists as a primary predication—in two surface guises, one in which the RELATOR is itself T (as in (69)), and one in which the RELATOR is a preposition and RP serves as the complement of an Asp-head whose projection is merged with a T that entertains an Agree relationship with the object of V and (for EPP reasons, whenever applicable) attracts this DP to its specifier (as in (72)). The latter is instantiated by the familiar passive construction, which has a wide (though by no means universal[56]) crosslinguistic distribution. The former's distribution is quite restricted, on the other hand: Italian allows it but English does not. The answer to the question of what determines the distribution of (69) across languages seems to lie in the EPP: in line with Alexiadou and Anagnostopoulou (1998), we can say that only languages that allow *verbs* to check the EPP (whether by raising to T or by heading a VP in SpecTP) admit the structure in (69).[57]

2.8.3 Adverbial Predicates

Finally, let us consider (63c), involving adverbial predication. We have seen (63c) attested in sentences such as *Brian twice knocked on the door* (see section 2.6.8), where *twice* takes scope over the event and delivers an interpretation of the sentence according to which there were two separate "knocking on the door" events. In sentences such as these, the RP in (63c) clearly does not function as the primary predication—*Brian* occupies SpecTP and the RP in (63c) is only the predicate of the primary predication, not itself the primary predication. So let us ask whether the RELATOR in (63c) could ever be T itself.

Though the answer to this question is less than straightforward given that our understanding of adverbial modification is still quite imperfect, it seems to me that it will at the very least be worth our while to consider the possibility that sentences of the type in (73a) involve a structure of the type in (63c) in which T serves as the RELATOR.

(73) a. Imogen thinks that for all intents and purposes Brian won the race.
b. Who does Imogen think that *(for all intents and purposes) *t* won the race?

To account for the fact that the presence of adverbial modifiers between the complementizer and the subject lifts the ban on extraction of the subject across the local complementizer (the "*that*-trace effect"), Culicover (1993) resorts to an additional functional projection ("FP") between C and TP, with the adverbial sitting in its specifier. A simple alternative, afforded by the approach to subject-predicate relationships taken in this work, is to assume that the adverbial modifier is actually occupying SpecTP itself, with the *v*P containing the subject of the embedded clause sitting in the complement of T. The subject can then extract via intermediate adjunction to TP.

(74) [$_{TP}$ [$_{PP}$ *for all intents and purposes*] [$_{T'}$ T=RELATOR [$_{vP}$ *t* [$_{v'}$
       v=RELATOR VP]]]]

I would like to present (74) as a possible approach to the lifting of the "*that*-trace effect" seen in (73b).[58] If it holds up to further scrutiny, it will stand as an instantiation of reverse adverbial predication serving as the primary predication.

2.8.4 Conclusion

In the preceding subsections, I briefly examined the vicissitudes of the reverse-predication structures in (63a–c) as *primary* predications. While (63a) is entirely unable to function as a primary predication (with (67) being the descriptive generalisation covering the facts), we have found that (63b) and (63c) both seem to occur as primary predications, with T serving as the RELATOR or taking the RP as its complement and establishing an Agree relationship with a subconstituent of the predicate-specifier. The distribution of predicate-specifier structures is severely restricted. They can be primary predicates only if T can get its formal requirements satisfied (i.e., can get its uninterpretable features checked). If they cannot be primary predicates, however, they are still excellent candidates for being *secondary* predicates or (in the particular case of (63a) with a bare NP in the RELATOR's complement) as complements of D.

The distribution of reverse-predication structures follows by and large[59] from the principles and parameters of the theory of grammar. Admitting the predicate-specifier structure in (3b) as a legitimate predication structure alongside the familiar predicate-complement structure in (3a) does not lead to massive overgeneration of bizarre predication constructions, therefore: the syntactic distribution of (3b) is accurately curbed by the theory.

In chapters 3 and 4, our attention will largely be confined to (3a), the predicate-complement structure, which serves as the input to the Predicate Inversion operation—the central theme of chapter 4 of this study. But (3b) will return to the stage in chapter 5, in the discussion of predication in nominal phrases.

2.9 Concluding Remarks on the Syntactic Configuration of Predication

I started in this chapter, which lays the foundations for what is to come, by presenting a syntactic perspective on predication relationships in terms of the general structure in (1), repeated below. In this structure, the relationship between the predicate and the subject is mediated by a RELATOR, a cover for a *functional* element that (*pace* Bowers 1993) can be realized by a variety of categories. These categories include Chomsky's (1995) light verb *v* (which is now identified as purely functional, a clear advance over Chomsky's own hybrid approach) as well as Tense, the head of TP, and also the "Top" head of what is commonly known as TopP, and the heads of a variety of functional categories identified by the "cartographers" (see, e.g., Cinque 1999), both inside the clause (for adverbial modifiers) and within the complex noun phrase (for attributive adjectives).

(1) *The syntactic configuration of predication*

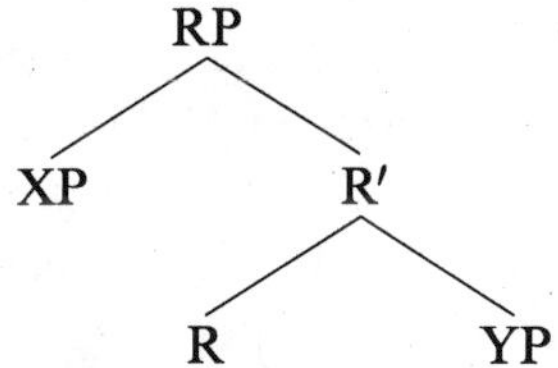

The structure in (1) structurally assimilates predication and coordination, both featuring a hierarchically asymmetrical structure and both quite possibly involving set intersection as well. While hierarchically asymmetrical, coordination is linearly permutable—*Brian and Imogen* is equivalent to *Imogen and Brian*. As I showed in detail in this chapter, the parallel between coordination and predication in fact extends to this fundamental nondirectionality: predication relationships, too, can be established with either of the major constituents of RP (i.e., XP and YP) taking the specifier position of the RELATOR phrase, with the other major constituent occupying the RELATOR's complement. Sentences representing the predicate-complement structure in (3a), in which the predicate sits in the complement of the RELATOR, are of course familiar. But while such straight predications do indeed make up the bulk of primary predications, there are a few cases of primary predication that involve the predicate-specifier structure in (3b), and outside the realm of primary predication (in secondary predication contexts and in DP-internal predication), (3b) is by no means uncommon, as we have seen.

(3) a. [$_{RP}$ [$_{XP}$ SUBJECT] [$_{R'}$ RELATOR [$_{YP}$ PREDICATE]]]

(Predicate-complement structure)

   b. [$_{RP}$ [$_{XP}$ PREDICATE] [$_{R'}$ RELATOR [$_{YP}$ SUBJECT]]]

(Predicate-specifier structure)

In both representations in (3), the "external argument" or subject is fully external to the predicate, the projection denoting the property ascribed to the subject. And in (3a) it is also external to the X′-projection of the RELATOR. So in (3a) the "external argument" is truly external. But in (3b), the "external argument" is projected as the *complement* of the RELATOR, hence actually an *internal* argument in X′-theoretic terms. Thus, when it comes to the question of how external the external argument actually is (see Den Dikken 1996), the answer is that it is systematically external to its predicate but it may be internal to the RELATOR's X′.

A significant ingredient of this chapter has been an exercise in the nondirectionality of predication, making the case for a hierarchically asymmetrical but linearly nondirectional syntactic representation of predication relationships. Reverse predications of the type in (3b) will now be put on the back burner for a while, until they resurface in chapter 5. In the upcoming two chapters, my focus will be on straight predications of the type in (3a), in which the subject originates in the specifier position of the RELATOR phrase.

In the next chapter, I will narrow in on instantiations of the predicate-complement structure in (3a) that lack tense—structures commonly known in the literature by the name of "small clauses." Arguing that small clauses must always include a functional head (the RELATOR that links the predicate to its subject), I reject the existence of what some have called "bare" small clauses: symmetrical subject-predicate structures that lack internal functional structure. With that conclusion in place, I then proceed to the analysis of copular sentences, reducing the typology of copular sentences to a mere two types: canonical and inverse copular sentences.

Chapter 3

Small Clauses and Copular Sentences

In the previous chapter, I laid out the basic syntactic configuration of predication—an asymmetrical structure in which the relationship between a predicate and its subject is established via a RELATOR, a functional head that takes the predicate and its subject as its dependents, with one sitting in the specifier position of the RELATOR phrase and the other occupying the RELATOR's complement position. A substantial portion of the discussion in chapter 2 was devoted to demonstrating the fundamental nondirectionality of predication by establishing the existence of what I called *straight* and *reverse* predications. In this chapter, I will start working my way toward the conclusion—to be defended and developed in much greater detail in chapters 4 and 5—that *straight* predications can undergo a syntactic process by which the predicate, which originates to the right of the subject, ends up to its left. This process, called *Predicate Inversion*, gives rise to so-called *inverse* or *inverted* predications—with inversion resulting from syntactic A-movement of the predicate around its subject. There are two ways, therefore, in which a predicate may surface in an A-position to the left of its subject: it may either be *merged* there, as in *reverse*-predication constructions (or predicate-specifier structures, with the predicate originating in the specifier position of the RELATOR phrase), or it may be *moved* across the subject into a higher A-position, as in *inverse/inverted* predication constructions.[1]

I will work toward the conclusion that there are two ways a predicate may surface in an A-position higher than its subject by first examining the structure of straight predications lacking tense—so-called small-clause constructions. The central hypothesis of this study that all predication relationships are fundamentally asymmetrical in the base leads to the conclusion that small clauses always include a functional head (a RELATOR), a conclusion I will defend in the face of recent claims to the effect that "bare," symmetrical small clauses exist. Arguing first against the existence of equative structures in which neither of the major constituents is a predicate, I then proceed to an investigation of the typology of copular sentences, reducing that typology to just two members: *canonical* and *inverse* copular sentences. The resulting typology of copular sentences will subsequently serve as the input to a detailed investigation of Copular Inversion in chapter 4.

3.1 Small Clauses

3.1.1 Secondary Predication and Small Clauses

Subject-predicate structures come in a variety of guises, as we have seen in chapter 2. Some of these are fully clausal, including tense. These represent what I referred to in chapter 2 as *primary* predications. But plenty of subject-predicate structures occur in tenseless environments. One such environment is the complement of verbs—epistemic verbs, positional verbs, or dynamic verbs.

(1) a. Brian considers Imogen smart.
     b. Brian hung his shirt on the line.
     c. Brian's shirt was hanging on the line.
     d. Brian hammered the metal flat.
     e. Brian ran the pavement thin.

There has been a tremendous amount of discussion in the generative literature regarding the syntactic representation of sentences of the type in (1)—so-called *secondary* predication constructions. Most approaches assign all sentences in (1) a parallel structure, but analysts disagree on the nature of that structure. Williams (1980) gives these sentences a flat structure of the type in (2a), Neeleman (1994) and also Johnson (1991) assign them a structure in which the verb and the secondary predicate form a unit in the underlying representation (see (2b), going back to Chomsky [1955] 1975), and on the small-clause analysis (represented by Kayne 1984, Hoekstra 1988, and many others) the secondary predicate and its subject are put together under a single node (cf. (2c)). In addition to analyses that treat all of (1a–e) on a par, there are hybrid approaches that assign different structures to the various members of the quintuplet in (1) (see, e.g., Carrier and Randall 1992).

(2) a. [$_{VP}$ V DP Pred]

   b. [$_{VP}$ [$_V$ V Pred] DP]

   c. [$_{VP}$ V [DP Pred]]

It seems to me plain that flat structures of the type in (2a) have little to recommend them—especially, of course, if one believes in the antisymmetry of syntax (Kayne 1994), but even without the LCA, a theory that assumes *n*-ary branching is less restrictive than one that restricts phrase structure to binary branching configurations, and from a learnability perspective the latter is therefore to be preferred. Analyses that start out from (2b) will have little trouble accommodating sentences such as *Brian looked up the number* and *Brian hammered flat the metal* but struggle to grapple with the word order represented by (1), with the secondary predicate following its subject. By contrast, (2c) base-generates this word order. It will need to find a way of deriving the verb-predicate-subject order instantiated by things like *Brian looked up the number*; there is no shortage in the theory of mechanisms by which this word order can be procured.[2]

But apart from the word-order issue that sets (2b) and (2c) apart, there is a more profound way in which these approaches to secondary predication constructions of the type in (1) differ: they make fundamentally different claims about the way the secondary predicate is connected to its subject. While (2c) is perfectly compatible with the idea that subject-predicate relationships are represented in syntax in the form of a constituent dominating the predicate and its subject as its only dependents, the structure in (2b) is not. More specifically, whereas (2c) can be brought in line with the overarching hypothesis of this study concerning the syntactic representation of subject-predicate relations in terms of a RELATOR phrase, (2b) cannot.

Mindful of what I argued in the previous chapter, therefore, I am led to set (2b) aside as an underlying representation of secondary predication. With (2a) rejected on the grounds of its symmetrical organization, we thus end up with (2c) as our global outlook on secondary predication constructions. In this structure, the verb selects a constituent as its complement that comprises the secondary predicate and its subject—a constituent that is customarily referred to in the literature as a SMALL CLAUSE (a term going back to Williams 1975). The standard definition of a small clause reads as in (3), a definition that covers all the examples in (1).

(3) A SMALL CLAUSE is a subject-predicate structure lacking tense.

In line with the general theory outlined in the foregoing, I will assume here that all secondary predication constructions involve a small-clause structure.

3.1.2   Small Clauses and Directionality

The definition of a small clause in (3), in combination with the perspective on the syntactic representation of subject-predicate relationships outlined in chapter 2, lets in a wider variety of things than the unidirectional approach to predication relations that is typically taken in the literature. Thus, recall from the discussion in sections 2.7.2 and 2.8.2 that in Romance *faire*-infinitive causative constructions, the causative verb arguably takes as its complement a RELATOR phrase whose specifier is the VP-predicate, with the causee (the subject of the causativized VP) sitting in the RELATOR's complement position, as in (4).

(4) a. Imogen fa   ridere Brian (Italian)
       Imogen makes laugh Brian
       [$_{\nu P}$ *Imogen* [RELATOR=ν [$_{VP}$ *fa* [$_{RP}$ [$_{VP}$ *ridere*] [RELATOR=∅
       [$_{DP}$ *Brian*]]]]]]

    b. Imogen fa   mangiare le mele   a Brian
       Imogen makes eat   the apples to Brian
       [$_{\nu P}$ *Imogen* [RELATOR=ν [$_{VP}$ *fa* [$_{RP}$ [$_{VP}$ *mangiare le mele*]
       [RELATOR=*a* [$_{DP}$ *Brian*]]]]]]

Since it has been amply demonstrated in the literature (see, e.g., Guasti 1993 for detailed discussion) that the complement of the causative verb in *faire*-infinitive constructions is T-less (as is apparent from the impossibility of including temporal adverbials or sentential negation in the causativized constituent), and since the RPs embedded under *fa* in (4) are, by definition, subject-predicate structures, they are identified, by (3), as small clauses.

This is a perfectly desirable result. Just as the small clauses in (1) turn into well-formed copular sentences when they are taken out of the complement of their selecting verbs and placed in a tensed environment (see (5)), so also can the embedded RP in (4a) survive perfectly well on its own, as we saw in the discussion of "free-inversion" constructions in section 2.8.2 (cf. (6a)). And although (6b), an attempt at turning the RP in (4b) into a primary predication, is ungrammatical, the *structure* is not ill-formed as such, qua primary predication, as is clear from the fact that replacing the infinitive with a past participle (*mangiato*) and lexicalizing the RELATOR as *da* 'by' delivers a well-formed passive (cf. (6c)).

(5) a. Imogen is smart.
   b. Brian's shirt is on the line.
   c. The metal is flat.
   d. The pavement is thin.

(6) a. ha   riso   Brian (Italian)
       has laughed Brian
   b. *sono mangiare le   mele   a/da Brian
        are   eat   the apples to/by Brian
   c. sono mangiate le   mele   *a/da Brian
        are   eaten   the apples to/by Brian

The cause of the ungrammaticality of (6b) is in all likelihood entirely orthogonal to the question of whether the RP in (4b) can survive as a primary predication, having to do with the distribution of "naked" infinitives. While "naked" infinitives cannot be licensed in the complement of *essere* "be" (for reasons that need not concern us here), past participles can; concomitantly, (6c) is perfectly fine.[3]

I conclude, then, that tenseless *reverse* predications (i.e., predicate-specifier structures) deserve the title "small clause" just as much as do tenseless *straight* predications (the familiar predicate-complement structures). This is what one would expect. It would, in fact, require brute force to exclude the RPs in (4) from the set of small clauses: to do so, one would have to make explicit reference to directionality in one's definition of small clauses (by insisting that only *subject-initial* RPs lacking tense qualify as small clauses—that is, by taking "subject-predicate structure" in (3) to make reference to linear order, with the subject coming first). There is obviously very little merit in doing this, in light of the discussion in chapter 2, where predication relationships were shown to be fundamentally nondirectional. The null hypothesis is that small clauses, like predication relationships in general, are nondirectional. I will assume so, strengthened by the fact that declaring the reverse RPs in (4) small clauses has no negative consequences whatsoever.[4] The definition of a small clause that I will adopt in this work thus reads as in (7).

(7) A SMALL CLAUSE is a tenseless RP.

3.1.3 Small Clauses and Functional Structure

Moro (2000, 46) argues that the copula *be* takes "bare" small-clause complements—small clauses that lack internal functional structure and hence make no space available for elements like *as* and *for*. Pereltsvaig (2001), while taking a different route toward a similar conclusion, claims that "bare" copular sentences exist. We will take a look at their arguments in the next section. But before we turn to these, let us consult the theory to evaluate the viability of "bare" small clauses.

It should be clear that from the perspective of the syntactic representation of predication outlined in this study, the postulation of "bare" small clauses is an anomaly. After all, with the term *small clause* standing for a tenseless subject-predicate structure, it is strictly impossible for a small clause not to have a predicate, but any constituent containing a predicate must have that predicate locally connected to its subject via a RELATOR, a functional category of sorts. In other words:

(8) *All* SMALL CLAUSES are projections of a functional head.

This is a necessary outcome of the general assumptions about predication relationships that I laid out in chapter 2.[5] Those assumptions could be wrong, of course, but as I have already begun to show and as I will continue to argue throughout this work, it seems to me that the RELATOR phrase as the syntactic representation of predication is robustly supported.[6]

3.1.4 RELATORS and Copulas

For Moro (2000, 46), what triggered his conclusion that the copula *be* takes "bare" small-clause complements is the fact that sentences of the type in (9) are systematically ungrammatical with *as/for* included, not just in English but in other languages as well (Moro's examples being Italian sentences with *come* 'as/like').

(9) a. Brian is (*as) a singer.
     b. Imogen is (*for) a woman.

If *be* takes a "bare" small-clause complement, so the argument goes, it will be ensured that it is impossible for *as* or *for* (which, after all, are lexicalizations of a functional head) to show up in between *be* and the small-clause predicate.

The argument does not go through, however. For as we know from the discussion in chapter 2 of sentences of the type in (10), there *are* indeed sentences in which *as* and *for* show up in the complement of the copula *be*. Sentences of the type in (10) are analyzed along the lines of (11) (for the specific case of (10a)). In this structure, the copula *be* lexicalizes the outer RELATOR$_2$ and *as* and *for* are lexicalizations of the inner RELATOR$_1$.

(10) a. This butterfly is [big for a butterfly].
     b. Brian is [skinny for an American].
     c. Imogen is [popular as a singer].

(11) [$_{RP_2}$ [$_{DP}$ *this butterfly*] [$_{R'}$ *is*=RELATOR$_2$ [$_{RP_1}$ [$_{AP}$ *big*] [$_{R'}$ *for*=RELATOR$_1$ [$_{DP}$ *a butterfly*]]]]]

If this is right, then it is apparently possible for *as* and *for* to show up in copular sentences. But in simpler sentences such as (9), *as* and *for* are barred from surfacing. What is it that makes (10) grammatical while declaring (9) ill-formed?

In (10) we need to establish *two* predication relations: one between the (predicative) AP and the (predicative) nominal across *as/for* (recall that the AP is a function from predicates (properties) to predicates (properties); Kamp 1975, Siegel 1976), and one between the entire bracketed constituents and the subject of the sentence. So we need two RELATORS. One of these, the higher one, can and will be realized as the copula in a tensed context: something is needed to check T's [tense] feature, and in the absence of a lexical verb that carries tense features, the only option is to lexically realize the outer RELATOR$_2$ as an inflected form of the copula, basically for tense-support reasons.[7]

In (9), on the other hand, we are dealing with just one predication relationship: that between the predicate nominal and its subject. There is need for just a single RELATOR, therefore. In fact, there is no chance of including more than one RELATOR in the structure:[8] there is a one-to-one relationship between RELATORS and predication relationships; it is impossible to generate scores of RELATORS "just for the hell of it." This in and of itself is sufficient to rule out (9) as they stand. And confronted with the choice of spelling the single RELATOR out as *as/for* or as an inflected form of the copula, the fact that (9a, b) are tensed sentences settles the issue in favor of the latter option.

Of course, in the tenseless small-clause complement of a verb, choosing the finite copula will not do: there is nothing that the copula could check its [tense] feature against in that case. Instead, the RELATOR then either remains empty or is lexicalized by *as, for,* or *like*—something that is entirely dependent on the lexical specifications of the selecting verb: *treat* likes *like* (12a), *take* demands an overt RELATOR but is not "picky" when it comes to its form (both *for* and *as* being possible, depending, it seems, on the nature of the embedded predication; see (12b, c)), *regard* wants *as* as the lexicalization of the RELATOR in its complement (12d), and *consider* is happy to let the RELATOR be null, although it also allows the RELATOR to be realized as *as* (see (12e)).

(12) a. Imogen treats him *(*like*) a fool.
    b. Imogen takes him *(*for*) a fool.
    c. Imogen takes this *(*as*) a sign of economic recovery.
    d. Imogen regards him *(*as*) a fool.
    e. Imogen considers him (*as*) a fool.

The choice between *as*, *for*, *like*, and $\emptyset$ as the realization of the RELATOR in small-clause complements to verbs is ultimately a matter of lexical selection. The only interesting thing about (12) is that it shows that small clauses have functional heads and that the particular incarnation of that functional head is determined by selection. More interesting is the contrast between (9) and (10). That contrast is a direct reflection of the number of RELATORS present in the structure—and the number of RELATORS is, in its turn, a direct reflection of the number of predication relationships: two in (10), one in (9).

That said, it should be clear that the ungrammaticality of (9) is not an argument in favor of the postulation of "bare" small clauses. I conclude this discussion of the structure of small clauses, therefore, by reiterating the conclusion to which the approach to the syntactic representation of subject-predicate relationships taken in this study leads incontrovertibly: that small clauses, like all predication relations, *must* include a functional category, a RELATOR establishing the connection between the predicate and its subject.

3.2 Copular Sentences

3.2.1 "Bare" Copular Sentences

While Moro (2000) seized on (9) to make a case for the existence of "bare," symmetrical small clauses, a case that has been found wanting, Pereltsvaig (2001, 182ff.) arrives at the conclusion that "bare" copular sentences exist via an entirely different route, on the basis of a discussion of copular sentences such as those in (13).

(13) a. Brian is the culprit.
     b. Imogen is the best cook in town.
     c. Ivan is the bravest soldier.

To sentences of this type, Pereltsvaig assigns the structure in (14).

(14)

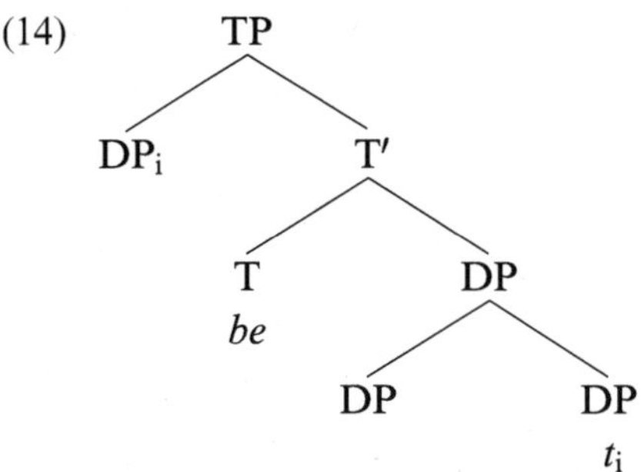

Pereltsvaig calls sentences like (13) "bare" copular sentences, and notes explicitly that a structure of the type in (14) cannot involve a *predication* relationship between the two DPs. That is certainly right: it could not possibly involve predication, given the fundamentally asymmetrical structure of predication relationships in syntax argued for in chapter 2. So the DP dominating the two lower DPs in (14) cannot be called a small clause, not even a "bare" one. The question is what it *would* be, and whether there is in fact any need for (14).

3.2.1.1 "Bare" Copular Sentences and the Theory Chomsky (1995, 244) points out that when merging two constituents α and β into a node γ, the label of γ could be determined in any of three ways, a priori: the label of γ could be (i) the intersection or (ii) the union of α and β, or (iii) the label of one of its two dependents. He goes on to note that, in the normal case, in which α and β have different features, (i) and (ii) are straightforwardly out of the question, so we derive the result that, in the normal case, one of the two dependents must project its label to the complex node created via Merge. Rethinking Moro's (2000) reevaluation of Chomsky's (1995) discussion of projection, Pereltsvaig (2001, 103) notes that in the "abnormal" case in which two merged constituents α and β have fully identical sets of features, the output of merger of the two constituents into a complex node γ will be the same regardless of how we take Merge to proceed: whether it proceeds via intersection, union, or projection, the result will always be that γ has the features of both of its dependents.[9] From this, Pereltsvaig concludes that, in such an "abnormal" case, structures of the type in (14) can be projected.

Assuming further that referential indices are to be thought of as *features* of lexical categories, Pereltsvaig goes on to conclude that the obligatory identity of the feature bundles of the two constituent DPs in (14) derives the fact that they are coindexed in syntax, hence coreferential. In this, Pereltsvaig goes beyond Fiengo and May's (1994) discussion of sentences of the type in (13), where it is crucially assumed that the two noun phrases, while coreferential, are not coindexed. The reason for Fiengo and May's assumption should be obvious: coindexing the two noun phrases in sentences such as (13) should lead to a violation of Principle C of the Binding Theory. Pereltsvaig notes that her move to derive the coreferentiality of the two constituent DPs in (14) from forcing their coindexation in syntax incurs a binding-theoretic problem (see also Moro 1988, 1997). She stipulates it away in a revised definition of binding (see p. 191), which basically says that all bets are off in cases in which the coindexed elements are in a relationship of mutual c-command in the base. It should be clear that Pereltsvaig's way of deriving the coreference of the two DPs in (13) from the symmetrical structure in (14) will not serve as a strong motive for adopting (14).

3.2.1.2 "Bare" Copular Sentences and the Facts (I): Russian What are the empirical reasons for believing that in sentences of the type in (13) the underlying relationship between the two noun phrases is a symmetrical one? Here, the substantive part of Pereltsvaig's discussion concerns itself with the alternation in Russian between nominative-marked and instrumental-marked predicates in copular sentences—that is, with the difference between sentences such as (15a) and (15b).

(15) a. Ivan byl xrabryj   soldat (Russian)
        Ivan was brave.NOM soldier.NOM
     b. Ivan byl xrabrym   soldatom
        Ivan was brave.INST soldier.INST
        Both: 'Ivan was a brabe soldier.'

For Pereltsvaig, (15a), with its nominative marking on the predicate nominal, instantiates the symmetrical structure in (14), while (15b) is a specimen of an asymmetrical structure of the type that has been at the forefront throughout the discussion in this chapter so far—we may plausibly take the instrumental case marker to represent the RELATOR.[10] Now, the interesting thing about pairs such as (15a, b) is that their members are not semantically equivalent. Speakers report with reference to (15a) that "for this sentence to be used felicitously, Ivan must be dead" (Pereltsvaig 2001, 198)—that is, not only Ivan's brave soldierhood must be a thing of the past, Ivan himself must also be a thing of the past. There is no way, in (15a), for Ivan's brave soldierhood to be a thing of the past without Ivan himself being dead as well. Pereltsvaig takes this to follow from the coindexation of the two DPs in (14), as a result of which they are necessarily coreferential, denoting the same individual: "By uttering this sentence, the speaker asserts that in some past situation there existed a unique Ivan and a unique brave soldier and that these two were one and the same person" (Pereltsvaig 2001, 199). Not so in (15b), which is a garden-variety predicational copular sentence.

Pereltsvaig thus derives the peculiar interpretation of (15a) from her analysis in (14) by capitalizing on the symmetry of the structure, necessarily leading to coindexation of the constituent noun phrases—which is interesting. But she also says explicitly (in the course of a discussion that eventually culminates in (15)) that "under the analysis proposed here sentences with the NOM-NOM pattern [such as (15a)] have an equative interpretation" (p. 194)—which is false. No matter how one wants to describe the interpretation of sentences like *Ivan was a brave soldier*, there is simply no sense in which they are equative. By Pereltsvaig's (2001, 199) own paraphrase of (15a), reproduced at the end of the previous paragraph, Ivan would have to have been the *one and only* brave soldier in the universe of discourse (see (13c), where there is indeed such a uniqueness entailment), and we know that this by no means has to be the case. Here, by using an indefinite postcopular noun phrase in what cannot, on standard assumptions, be called an equative sentence, Pereltsvaig actually shows that whatever lies beneath the difference in interpretation of copular sentences with nominative and instrumental postcopular noun phrases, it is definitely not equativity. But if that is the case, then that shows that it will be wrong to assign sentences of the type in (15a) a structure of the type in (14)—for, as Pereltsvaig shows, (14) effectively *forces* an equative interpretation: neither of the two constituent noun phrases is a predicate, and the two are necessarily coindexed in syntax, hence interpreted as coreferential.

This line of thought leads to the conclusion, therefore, that the structure in (14) is not the appropriate vehicle with which to approach the peculiar interpretive properties of Russian NOM-NOM copular sentences of the type in (15a).[11]

3.2.1.3 "Bare" Copular Sentences and the Facts (II): Celtic The symmetrical structure in (14) might still be of use for the analysis of copular sentences such as those in (13), repeated below, where the postcopular noun phrase is a definite noun phrase.

(13) a. Brian is the culprit.
      b. Imogen is the best cook in town.
      c. Ivan is the bravest soldier.

On the assumption that definite noun phrases are always fully internally saturated (but see below), these should be unable to serve as small-clause predicates—so perhaps these should be analyzed as in (14)?

   The facts of Celtic are instructive when it comes to answering this question. For it turns out that copular sentences like (13) are untranslatable into Celtic in the form of garden-variety copular sentences—Scottish Gaelic (16a) and Irish Gaelic (17a) are ungrammatical. Instead, Celtic resorts in these cases to constructions of the type in (16b) and (17b), which feature a special form of *be* called the "defective copula" and an element *e/é*, called a "pronominal augment."[12]

(16) a. *tha   Calum an tidsear (Scottish Gaelic)
              be-PRES Calum the teacher
      b. 's   e   Calum an tidsear
          COP 3SG Calum the teacher
          'Calum is the teacher.'

(17) a. *tá   Seán an dochtúir (Irish Gaelic)
              be-PRES Seán the doctor
      b. is   é   Seán an dochtúir
          COP 3SG.M.ACC Seán the doctor
          'Seán is the doctor.'

Of these two elements, the defective copula also occurs in inverse copular sentences in Scottish Gaelic—sentences in which the relative order of subject and predicate is inverted, such as the ones in (18).

(18) a. is   mòr an   duine sin (Scottish Gaelic)
          COP big   that man
      b. is   le   Calum an cù
          COP with Calum the dog (i.e., the dog belongs to Calum)

As for the pronominal augment (*e/é*), Doherty (1996) points out that it is an accusative pronoun agreeing in number with the subject noun phrase (see (19)), and he also notes that it is used in cleft sentences, such as the one in (20).

(19) a. is   iad   na sagairt an trioblóid (Irish)
        COP 3PL.ACC the priests the trouble
        'The priests are the trouble.'
    b. *is   iad   an triobloid na sagairt
        COP 3PL.ACC the trouble   the priests
        'The trouble is the priests.'

(20) is   é   Tadhg a   bhuaidh an duais (Irish)
    COP 3SG.ACC Tadhg that.PAST won   the prize
    'It was Tadhg who won the prize.'

The occurrence of the pronominal augment in clefts makes it likely that it is the counterpart, in Celtic, of the English *it* surfacing in sentences of the type in (21).

(21) a. It's that Imogen left.
        be [RP [CP *that Imogen left*] [RELATOR [*it*]]]
    b. It seems that Imogen left.
        seem [RP [CP *that Imogen left*] [RELATOR [*it*]]]
    c. It is Imogen that left.
        be [RP [*Imogen*] [RELATOR [*it*]]] [CP *that left*]

For the *it* of (21a, b), Moro (1997, 174ff.) argues that it starts out underlyingly as the predicate of a small clause, predicated of the CP (cf. the structures to the right of (21a, b)). An analysis of this type extends naturally to the cleft sentence in (21c), as shown to the right of the example (where the exact insertion position of the relative CP is left open). So let us take the *it* of (21) to be an underlying predicate. Then the fact that the pronominal augment of Celtic is used in clefts lends support to Adger and Ramchand's (2003) claim that in sentences of the type in (16b), *e* (the pronominal augment) is an underlying predicate, with *Calum* as its subject, and *an tidsear* in an adjunction position, loosely construed with the subject (like the relative clause in (21c)).

It seems, then, that what we have on our hands in these Celtic copular constructions is a structure corresponding to that of an English *it*-cleft—a structure, on an analysis based on Moro 1997, in which we *are* in fact dealing with a predicational structure in the underlying representation:

the predicate of the small clause is the pro-predicate *it*, which inverts with its subject (the focus) in the course of the syntactic derivation.[13] An analysis along these lines (following in the footsteps of Adger and Ramchand 2003) gives us a straightforward account of the pronominal augment. And with the pronominal augment analyzed as a small-clause *predicate* (à la Moro 1997), these Celtic sentences lead us to reject a symmetrical structure of the type in (14) for such copular sentences—at least for Celtic.

For Celtic, a cleftlike analysis of copular sentences of the type in (16b) and (17b) is forced, according to Adger and Ramchand (2003), because noun phrases introduced by the definite article are necessarily as large as a full-fledged DP, hence ineligible as predicates. For English, on the other hand, Zamparelli (2000) has argued that the definite article is not necessarily in the highest head position in the complex noun phrase. So noun phrases introduced by *the* are not necessarily full DPs. And that means that an analysis of English copular sentences of the type in (13) in which the definite noun phrase originates as the predicate of a small clause is readily available. In English, then, no recourse to a cleft is necessary in such copular sentences. But crucially, it will not be necessary to resort to a symmetrical structure of the type in (14) in these cases either—for the postcopular noun phrase is in fact eligible for predicatehood in these English sentences.[14]

3.2.1.4 "Bare" Copular Sentences: Conclusion   Let us draw this discussion of "bare" copular sentences to a conclusion. We have seen that (14) is not needed for the analysis of English copular sentences such as (13)— and I will go on to show in what follows that it be would in fact be wrong to assume a symmetrical structure for these constructions. We have also seen that (14) is not used in the corresponding Celtic copular sentences either. As a matter of fact, if (14) *were* a legitimate structure, we would entirely fail to understand the ungrammaticality of the examples in (16a) and (17a), the word-for-word counterparts of the grammatical English sentences below the b-examples. The conclusion, then, is simple and plain: (14) is not a legitimate structure of UG.

3.2.2 Equative Copular Sentences

3.2.2.1 What Equative Copular Sentences Are Not   If (14) is not a grammatical structure, that means that so-called equative copular sentences, illustrated in (22), cannot be analyzed in these terms either.

(22) a. Cicero is Tully.
      b. The Morning Star is the Evening Star.
      c. Your attitude toward Jones is my attitude toward Davies.

For these constructions, the case for an asymmetrical small clause would seem very weak indeed. First of all, as Heycock and Kroch (1999) note, the fact that each of the two noun phrases in an equative copular sentence can be modified by a nonrestrictive relative clause (see (23)) is a sure sign that both noun phrases are referential.

(23) Your attitude toward Jones, which you got from your parents, is
      my attitude toward Davies, which I got from mine.

The fact that both noun phrases are referential entails, of course, that neither noun phrase is itself a predicate. And not only are the noun phrases not predicative, there does not seem to be any other obvious candidate for predicatehood in the sentences in (22)—except perhaps the copula itself. It is not surprising, therefore, that many scholars over the centuries have given in to the temptation of calling the copula in (22) a transitive verb, assigning two θ-roles, one to each of the two noun phrases (see, e.g., Bowers 1991).[15]

But it is easy to show that sentences like (22) do not behave like garden-variety transitive sentences at all.[16] Apart from the fact that the copula *never* behaves like a θ-assigning verb in English when it comes to verb raising (as is evident from the fact that the copula will systematically raise to T, across negation, and on to C in interrogative contexts, regardless of the type of copular sentence we are dealing with), particularly strong evidence to the effect that (22a–c) are not simple transitive sentences comes from the fact that neither of the two noun phrases can be *wh*-extracted, as pointed out by Heycock and Kroch (1999, 377):

(24) a. *Whose attitude toward Davies would you say your attitude
          toward Jones is *t*?
      b. *Whose attitude toward Jones would you say *t* is my attitude
          toward Davies?

In this regard, equative copular sentences behave exactly like what Moro (1997) calls inverse copular sentences—specificational copular sentences that have the inverse word order of those in (13).[17] Thus, consider the behavior of (25b) under *wh*-extraction, illustrated in (27).

(25) a. Brian's arrest was the biggest upset.
      b. The biggest upset was Brian's arrest.

(26) a. Whose arrest do you think *t* was the biggest upset?

    b. How big an upset do you think Brian's arrest was *t*?

(27) a. *Whose arrest do you think the biggest upset was *t*?

    b. *How big an upset do you think *t* was Brian's arrest?

For Heycock and Kroch (1999), this parallel behavior occasioned an analysis of Moro's inverse copular sentences (like (25b)) parallel to that of equative copular sentences, not involving Predicate Inversion at all. One of the major objectives of this study is to show, however, that Predicate Inversion *is* indeed involved in the derivation of constructions like (25b). And I will show in chapter 4 that a Predicate Inversion analysis accounts for all the extraction facts, doing better in this regard than Heycock and Kroch's analysis. (Heycock and Kroch decline to pursue the matter altogether;[18] it seems unlikely that an analysis in terms of an equative predicate will have anything to contribute toward the solution of the *wh*-extraction puzzle.)

3.2.2.2 What Equative Copular Sentences Are: Inverse Copular Sentences

Let us not pursue an "equative predicate" approach to equative copular sentences, therefore—whether the "equative predicate" is the copula itself (as in most approaches of this kind; see note 15) or an abstract small-clause head (as on Heycock and Kroch's assumptions[19]). Instead, let us sketch the outlines of an analysis of equative copular sentences that can capture their properties while starting out from a predicative small-clause structure.

The particular structure I have in mind is one that runs parallel in its essentials to that of the Celtic specificational copular sentence: an analysis in which the predicate of the small clause is a pro-predicate—something like *it*, except that the pro-predicate is itself null, and associated with a reduced relative clause, the two of them together forming a *free relative*.

(28) [PRO-PREDICATE$_\varnothing$ [$_{CP}$ Op_i [C$_\varnothing$ [$_{RP}$ *Cicero* [RELATOR$_\varnothing$ t_i]]]]]

This reduced free relative (cf. *what Cicero is*[20]) as a whole serves as the predicate of a small clause whose subject is the other noun phrase (*Tully* in the example in (22a)). For reasons that will be addressed in detail in chapter 4, the entire constituent depicted in (28) must invert with its subject and raise to SpecTP via *Predicate Inversion*. This is sketched out in (29), which delivers the desired word order and in addition assimilates equative sentences to inverse specificational copular sentences of the type in (25b), hence correctly predicts their parallel behavior under *wh*-extraction.[21]

(29) a. [$_{RP}$ *Tully* [RELATOR [$_{Pred}$ PRO-PREDICATE$_\varnothing$ [$_{CP}$ *Op*$_i$ [C$_\varnothing$ [$_{RP}$ *Cicero* [RELATOR$_\varnothing$ *t*$_i$]]]]]]]]

    → merging T and applying Predicate Inversion to the reduced free relative →

  b. [$_{TP}$ [$_{Pred}$ PRO-PREDICATE$_\varnothing$ [$_{CP}$ *Op*$_i$ [C$_\varnothing$ [$_{RP}$ *Cicero* [RELATOR$_\varnothing$ *t*$_i$]]]]]]$_j$ [T+RELATOR$_k$=*be* [$_{RP}$ *Tully* [*t*$_k$ *t*$_j$]]]

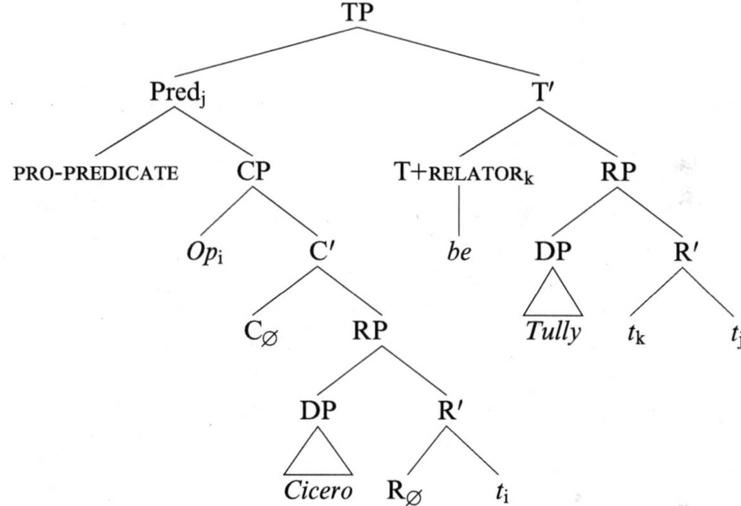

This analysis of equative copular sentences likens them to specificational pseudoclefts—particularly, pseudoclefts of Type B in Den Dikken, Meinunger, and Wilder's (2000) typology (see also the appendix to chapter 4). These constructions are exemplified by English (30) (from Akmajian 1979; see Higgins 1979 for detailed discussion of specificational pseudoclefts, and Den Dikken 2005 for an overview of the literature on these constructions). In these specificational pseudoclefts, the *wh*-constituent is a free relative (see Heggie 1988).

(30) a. What Brian said is that he likes Imogen.

    b. That he likes Imogen is what Brian said.

While specificational pseudoclefts and equative copular sentences share their free invertibility (cf. (30a, b) with the fact that the noun phrases in the examples in (13) freely change places),[22] there are two major differences between garden-variety specificational pseudoclefts of the type in

(30) and equative copular sentences—two differences that, I would like to argue, are correlated.

What immediately catches the eye, of course, is that, while specificational pseudoclefts have a full-fledged free relative as one of their major constituents (*what Brian said* in (30)), equative copular sentences such as the ones in (13) do not. I do nonetheless analyze equatives in the same terms as specificational pseudoclefts, assigning them a structure of the type in (29), where the surface-precopular constituent is a *reduced* rather than a full free relative (recall also note 20). To this difference between specificational pseudoclefts and equative copular sentences I believe is related the fact that the free relative must invert with its subject in the latter, while it does not have to in the former. That no inversion is necessary in specificational pseudoclefts is of course plain from the fact that (30) exhibits a word-order alternation. It is not immediately obvious that equative copular sentences do not allow the reduced free relative to stay in situ—as I pointed out in the previous paragraph, they, too, allow the two major constituents to change places. But the fact that equative copular sentences completely ban all A′-extraction (recall (24), repeated below), whereas extraction of the precopular noun phrase in (30b) is grammatical, suggests that equative copular sentences systematically have the profile of the inverted specificational pseudocleft in (30a), which—like equatives—blocks A′-extraction of the postcopular constituent (see (31a)).

(24) a. *Whose attitude toward Davies would you say your attitude
        toward Jones is *t*?
     b. *Whose attitude toward Jones would you say *t* is my attitude
        toward Davies?

(31) a. *Which of these things do you think what Brian said is *t*?
     b. Which of these things do you think *t* is what Brian said?

Though we will manage to put our finger on exactly what causes sentences such as (31a) to be ill-formed only in the course of the discussion in chapter 4, for now we can take the deviance of (31a) as an indication that in specificational pseudoclefts in which the free relative is in precopular position, A′-extraction of the postcopular constituent fails. The fact that, with respect to A′-extraction, *both* word-order variants of equative copular sentences behave like (31a) then serves as an empirical argument to the effect that equative copular sentences systematically feature the reduced free relative in the structure in (28) in precopular position on the surface, as in (29b). So the free relative in (28) *must* invert with its subject in equatives—and as I intimated before, I believe this is related to the fact that it is a *reduced* free relative: its being headed by a null pro-predicate forces the reduced free relative to front to SpecTP in order to get the pro-predicate formally licensed.

I will return to this at much greater length in chapter 4. But for now, the thing to note is that the two differences between specificational pseudoclefts and equative copular sentences that we discovered in this section do not jeopardize an analysis of the latter in terms of an underlying small-clause structure in which the predicate is a reduced free relative, as in (28). On the strength of the fact that this structure (i) assigns a well-formed, properly asymmetrical underlying representation to equatives and (ii) explains their extraction properties in (24), I submit (28) and the derivation in (29) as the analysis of the syntax of equative copular sentences.

3.2.2.3 On the Distribution of Equative Copular Sentences in Celtic

With this said, let us ask why it is that Scottish Gaelic does not have equative copular sentences, not even with the "defective copula" and the pronominal augment that we encountered in Celtic specificational copular sentences in section 3.2.1.3.[23]

(32) a. *'s   e   Cicero Tully (Scottish Gaelic)
         COP 3SG Cicero Tully
     b. 's   e   Cicero agus Tully an aon   duine
         COP 3SG Cicero and Tully the same person
         'Cicero and Tully are the same person.'

Recall that Celtic constructions with the "defective copula" and the pronominal augment are cleft constructions, but the analysis in (28) and (29) likens equative sentences to specificational *pseudo*clefts, with the constituent in precopular position being a reduced free relative.[24] Interestingly, now, Scottish Gaelic lacks specificational pseudoclefts, as David Adger (personal communication) informs me. With equative copular sentences analyzed as reduced specificational pseudoclefts, and with Scottish Gaelic lacking specificational pseudoclefts, it follows as a matter of course that Scottish Gaelic cannot have true equatives—as desired.

It will now be interesting to take a quick look at Welsh, which seems to confirm a parallel between the presence of a null pronominal augment in specificational sentences and the presence of specificational pseudoclefts. Welsh differs from Irish and Scottish Gaelic in having a null pronominal augment: there is no overt pronoun in a Welsh specificational copular sentence (see (33), from Rouveret 1996).[25]

(33) fi yw/*ydw 'r   brenin (Welsh)
     I is/am   the king
     '*I* am the king'; French 'le roi, c'est moi.'

Concomitantly, Welsh also differs from Irish and Scottish Gaelic in having specificational pseudoclefts (cf. Zaring's 1996 example in (34)).

(34) [beth ydy Sión] ydy niwsans
     what is   Sión is   nuisance
     'What Sión is is a nuisance.'[26]

Adding these things together, we now expect Welsh to differ from Irish and Scottish Gaelic in a third way as well: it should have true equative sentences like (22).[27] And indeed, as Alain Rouveret (personal communication) tells me, equative copular sentences do exist in Welsh. Two examples are given in (35).

(35) a. Rhodri yw Mr. Morgan
        Rhodri is Mr. Morgan
        'Mr. Morgan is Rhodri.'
     b. brawd Mair yw tad   John
        brother Mair is   father John
        'John's father is Mair's brother.'

   This microscopic difference within the Celtic language family seems to me to lend striking support to the approach to equative copular sentences as hidden specificational pseudoclefts.

3.2.2.4 Equative Copular Sentences: Conclusion I present this brief sketch of an analysis of equative copular sentences here for the benefit of future research. It is not my intention to develop the details of this analysis beyond the remarks made in the foregoing since the aim of this study lies elsewhere, outside the realm of equative copular sentences. Its only function in the context of this work is to demonstrate that an analysis of equative sentences is constructible that is compatible with the idea that copulas are never lexical, θ-role assigning elements but instead serve as lexicalizations of a functional head mediating between the predicate and its subject, and—most pertinent to the topic of this chapter—with the claim laid down in (8), repeated here.

(8) *All* SMALL CLAUSES are projections of a functional head.

3.2.3   The Typology of Copular Sentences

3.2.3.1   All Copular Sentences Involve a Small Clause   With even so-called equative copular sentences (the least obviously predicational type of copular sentences) being underlyingly predicational, one is led to suspect that *all* copular sentences feature a small clause in their underlying syntactic structure.[28] This conclusion, if tenable, drastically reduces the typology of copular sentence types: underlyingly, there is just one type of copular sentence—not the four types recognized in Higgins's (1979) classic typology, reproduced in (36).[29]

(36) a. Brian is a clever guy.   (Predicational)
     b. Brian is the culprit.   The culprit is Brian.
                                                      (Specificational)
     c. Brian is that man over there.   That man over there is Brian.
                                                      (Identificational)
     d. Cicero is Tully.   Tully is Cicero.   (Equative)

If all copular sentences are underlyingly predicational hence all include a small clause in their syntactic structure, the fact that all small clauses include a functional head (8) then leads to the conclusion that copular sentences of all types should feature a RELATOR. In (12), repeated here as (37), I showed that this RELATOR can get an overt phonetic realization in the form of connectives like *as*, *for*, and *like* (see Aarts 1992; Bowers 1993).

(37) a. Imogen treats him *(*like*) a fool. (= (12))
     b. Imogen takes him *(*for*) a fool.
     c. Imogen takes this *(*as*) a sign of economic recovery.
     d. Imogen regards him *(*as*) a fool.
     e. Imogen considers him (*as*) a fool.

What we now expect, at least in principle, is that small-clause constructions of all types can have their RELATOR head realized overtly. The paradigms in (38) and (39) show that this is indeed the case.

(38) a. Imogen described Brian *as* a clever guy.   (Predicational)
     b. Imogen described Brian *as* the culprit.   (Specificational)

    c. Imogen described Brian *as* that man over there.

                                         (Identificational)

    d. Imogen described/identified the Morning Star *as* the Evening Star.

                                           (Equative)

(39) a. Imogen took this *for* a fact.   (Predicational)

       b. Imogen took this *for* the root of the problem.   (Specificational)

       c. Imogen mistook this *for* that thing over there.   (Identificational)

       d. Imogen mistook the Morning Star *for* the Evening Star.

                                         (Equative[30])

3.2.3.2 What Is Left of the Typology: Canonical versus Inverse Copular Sentences

If, then, all types of copular sentences behave the same way when it comes to their underlying structure, all involving a small clause, there is no deep sense in which there is a typology of copular sentences—copular sentences are all fundamentally of the same type in the sense of involving a predication structure represented in terms of a small clause. There is nonetheless a residual typology when it comes to the *surface* syntax of copular constructions—a distinction between *canonical* and *inverse* copular sentences.

(40) *Two types of copular sentences*

      a. **Canonical** copular sentences   SUBJECT–*BE*–PREDICATE

      b. **Inverse** copular sentences   PREDICATE–*BE*–SUBJECT

For equative copular sentences, I argued in section 3.2.2.2 that they systematically instantiate inverse copular sentences, derived from their base structures via Predicate Inversion—the instance of Move/Attract that I will have much more to say about in chapter 4. Predicational copular sentences cannot invert, but specificational and identificational copular sentences oscillate between (40a) and (40b).

In advocating a two-way surface typology of copular sentences derived from a unique underlier, I follow a line of research initiated by Blom and Daalder (1977), and pursued in detail in Moro 1988, 1997, Heggie 1988, and Verheugd 1990. To my knowledge, Blom and Daalder were the first in the generative framework to claim explicitly that there are just two surface types of copular sentence (the predicational and specificational types) and that as far as the underlying relationship between two NPs in predicational and specificational copular sentences is concerned there is no difference between the two sentence types: in both, one of the two NPs is the predicate of the other. Underlyingly, then, both types of copular construction are predicational.[31] Blom and Daalder (1977) (who express their indebtedness to Den Hertog 1903; see also Jespersen 1924) are perhaps the most rigid and explicit champions of the idea that all copular sentences are underlyingly represented as predications, with one of the two NPs functioning as the HYPERONYM (Lyons's 1977 "superordinate"; cf. "predicate") of the other (the HYPONYM).[32]

Blom and Daalder (1977) even extend their hyponym/hyperonym (or subject/predicate) approach to so-called equative sentences, saying that the postcopular noun phrase in such constructions is the hyponym of the precopular NP and claiming hence that of the two NPs in (36d) only the precopular one is referential. This is demonstrably false, however. For one thing, as we saw in our brief discussion of Celtic in section 3.2.2.3, equative copular sentences clearly behave differently from predicational and specificational copular constructions. And moreover, as Heycock and Kroch (1999) note, each of the two noun phrases in an equative copular sentence can be modified by a nonrestrictive relative clause (see (23), repeated below)—a clear indication that both noun phrases are in fact referential.

(23) Your attitude toward Jones, which you got from your parents, is
      my attitude toward Davies, which I got from mine.

But though Blom and Daalder's specific approach to equatives is not on the right track, we have already seen that there is an alternative approach to these constructions that fits them neatly into the simple typology of copular sentences in (40)—the analysis sketched out in section 3.2.2.2, which treats equatives as inverse copular sentences featuring a reduced free relative as the predicate of the small clause and thereby puts them in the same ballpark as specificational pseudoclefts with initial *wh*-clauses. This analysis also accounts for the fact that, as far as their syntactic properties are concerned, equatives have more in common with inverse specificational copular sentences than with their predicational brethren (see section 3.2.2.2, as well as Heycock and Kroch 1999 and Guéron 2001).

3.3 Conclusions and Prospects

Against the background of the general recipe for the syntactic projection of predication relationships unveiled in chapter 2, I argued in section 3.1 of this chapter for a representation of small clauses as RELATOR phrases, an analysis that leads to the incontrovertible conclusion that, since RPs are projections of a RELATOR, all small clauses include a functional head (8)—a conclusion I defended at length in the face of arguments in the recent literature (Moro 2000; Pereltsvaig 2001) for "bare" small clauses and "bare" copular sentences, symmetrical structures that I showed are supported neither by the theory nor by the facts they are supposed to take care of.

Having ascertained that all small clauses are asymmetrical, I subsequently proceeded to show, in section 3.2, that all copular sentences have an asymmetrical structure as well—not just predicational copular sentences but the Higginsian specificational and equative constructions, too. The structure underlying specificational and equative copular sentences is in fact the same as that of predicational copular constructions: a predicate-complement structure, with the predicate in the complement of the RELATOR. What makes specificational and equative copular sentences special, in comparison with their predicational counterparts, is that their syntactic derivation may or, in the case of equatives, must involve *Predicate Inversion*—the promotion of the underlying predicate to subject. Inversion is forced in the case of equative copular sentences because of the fact that their predicate is a reduced free relative whose pro-predicate head must be formally licensed in the domain of inflection, something I will return to at length in chapter 4.

We have now made our way toward the discussion of the syntax of Predicate Inversion and the distribution of LINKER elements, which forms the backbone of chapter 4. There, I will lay out the technicalities of the syntax of Predicate Inversion in detail, introducing the notion of a LINKER as the manifestation of a syntactic aid to inversion. In chapter 5, I will then move over into the realm of complex noun phrases, discussing a variety of instances of predication and Predicate Inversion inside the noun phrase (including things like *a jewel of a village, an idiot of a doctor, how big of a problem, the question of what to do next,* relative-clause constructions, and possessed noun phrases).

Chapter 4

Predicate Inversion: Why and How?

This chapter is concerned with the key issues in the syntax of Predicate Inversion—in particular, with (i) its trigger, (ii) the locality constraints imposed on the process, and (iii) the extraction restrictions it exhibits. I will be looking at two instantiations of Predicate Inversion in detail in the discussion to follow: Copular Inversion (illustrated in (1b)) and Locative Inversion (see (2b)).[1]

(1) a. Brian is the best candidate.
    b. The best candidate is Brian.

(2) a. A picture of Imogen hung on the wall.
    b. On the wall hung a picture of Imogen.

At their core, these two incarnations of Predicate Inversion share the fact that both involve A-movement of the predicate to subject position in the course of their derivation. In section 4.1, I will make the case for an analysis of both types of Predicate Inversion as involving A-movement. Establishing this immediately raises two important questions: (i) why would the predicate want to invert with its subject at all, and (ii) how does it manage to cross over its subject in keeping with the locality restrictions on movement? Section 4.2 addresses the question of what triggers Predicate Inversion. The answer to this question that I will present and defend is that licensing the emptiness of (the head of) the predicate is the key to inversion of the predicate around its subject. With the answer to the question of why the predicate must invert with its subject when it does in place, section 4.3 subsequently investigates the legitimacy of the inversion process from the point of view of locality, and section 4.4 addresses the vicissitudes of the postverbal subject of Predicate Inversion constructions. In the course of this discussion, I will introduce the second type of element figuring in the main title of this book: the LINKER. The distribution of this LINKER and its surface realization are the topic of section 4.5. In the appendix, I will finally comment on the limited distribution of Predicate Inversion.

4.1   Predicate Inversion as A-Movement

4.1.1   Predicate Inversion and Interpretation

What all Predicate Inversion constructions have in common is the fact that the postcopular/postverbal constituent is a FOCUS—a *presentational* focus in Locative Inversion constructions (see Hetzron 1971 for a typological study of Locative Inversion that was the first to reach this conclusion; see also Penhallurick 1984, as well as Bresnan 1994 on English) and in Copular Inversion constructions in which the preposed predicate nominal is indefinite (such as *An example of this is World War II*), and an *identificational/exhaustive* focus in Copular Inversion sentences with definite predicate nominals like (1b) (see, e.g., Higgins 1979, 234–236, Partee 2000, and Mikkelsen 2002b on focus in Copular Inversion constructions). This is evident both as regards the postverbal noun phrase's intonational properties (it receives heavy stress: *The best candidate is* BRIAN[2]) and with respect to its interpretation (it is being introduced on the scene, or it is the one and only entity, in the universe of discourse, for which the property denoted by the predicate holds; see Birner 1994 for a more detailed investigation of the information-structural profile of Predicate Inversion constructions, broadly fitting the present analysis). Intonationally, Predicate Inversion constructions are actually no different from garden-variety transitive sentences, which, in languages like English, typically feature focal stress on the final element in the VP, which, in simple transitives, is the direct object (cf. *Imogen kissed* BRIAN)—as Bresnan (1994, 90) puts it, "The object is the focussable syntactic function *par excellence*." But interpretationwise there is an important difference. In uninverted predications a heavy stress on the last element may propagate up to higher nodes in the syntactic tree, via focus projection (see Selkirk 1995), as illustrated in (3). Predicate Inversion constructions, on the other hand, always have a narrow focus, strictly confined to the stressed postcopular/postverbal noun phrase (see Guéron 1992). That is, in (4), only the postcopular constituent *Brian* is the focus.

(3) Imogen considers Brian to be the best CANDIDATE.
   a. She does not consider him to be the best [MAGISTRATE].
   b. She does not consider him to be the [DEVIL INCARNATE].

    c. She does not consider him to [have the brains to GRADUATE].
    d. She does not consider [the country to need another WATERGATE].
    e. She does not [think that the test results would be easy to REPLICATE].

(4) Imogen considers the best candidate to be BRIAN.
    a. She does not consider the best candidate to be [RYAN].
    b. *She does not consider the best candidate to [have been LYING].
    c. *She does not consider [this pilot to be particularly good at FLYING].
    d. *She does not [think those allegations about her sex life are worth DENYING].

Predicate Inversion, then, is a syntactic device that leads to the assignment of focal stress and narrow-focus interpretation to the subject of the inverted predicate. The postcopular/postverbal subject's focal stress is the consequence of its finality in the sentence; the fact that focus does not project beyond the subject seems to be a reflex of the fact that the subject noun phrase of a Predicate Inversion construction is basically "frozen" in the syntax.

4.1.2 Predicate Inversion as Movement Rather Than Base Generation

The "frozenness" of the subject of a Predicate Inversion construction manifests itself in a variety of other ways as well. I will address these manifestations of "freezing" in more detail in section 4.4, but for present purposes it will be useful to highlight the fact that A′-extraction of the postverbal subject of a Copular Inversion construction such as (5a) or a Locative Inversion case like (6a) fails entirely, as the ill-formedness of the b-examples shows.

(5) a. I think the best candidate is this man.
    b. *_Which man_ do you think the best candidate is _t_?

(6) a. I said that on this wall hung a picture of Imogen.
    b. *_Whose picture_ did you say that on this wall hung _t_?

This ban on extraction of the postverbal subject of Predicate Inversion constructions can be exploited to argue against a variety of approaches to Predicate Inversion.

Confronted with alternations like those in (1)–(2), a question that arises immediately is whether they are the result of movement or not. The answer to this question is by no means obvious, for two reasons. First, one may debate the equivalence of the two members of pairs like (1), and/or the predicativity of the constituent in precopular position in (1b). Thus, while Moro (1997) and Hoekstra and Mulder (1990) defend a movement account on the basis of the hypothesis that *the best candidate* is an inverted predicate, Heycock and Kroch (1999) fervently oppose such an approach, arguing instead for base generation and treating specificational copular sentences as equative constructions. While it is true that inverse copular sentences of the type in (1b) share with equative constructions the ban on A′-extraction of the postcopular noun phrase (recall the ungrammaticality of things like **Whose opinion of Smith do you think your opinion of Jones is?*), reducing (1b) to the class of equative copular sentences does little to *explain* this extraction restriction (as I pointed out at the end of section 3.2.2.1, Heycock and Kroch (1999) actually decline to present an account for this fact). This, in conjunction with the argument presented in chapter 3 to the effect that equative constructions do not exist as an underlying type of copular sentences (equative constructions must be underlyingly represented as predicative constructions, and are themselves derived via Predicate Inversion), leads me to set aside Heycock and Kroch's (1999) plea for base generation of (1b) as an equative construction—an approach that, of course, would entirely fail to carry over to (2b) and hence would miss an important generalization in light of the fact (to be amply illustrated in what follows) that the b-sentences in (1)–(2) share a significant portion of their syntactic derivations.

An alternative base-generation approach to the predicate-subject order of Predicate Inversion constructions would start out from the hypothesis that these instantiate what I have called the "predicate-specifier structure"—a structure in which the specifier of the RELATOR corresponds to the predicate, with its subject being the RELATOR's complement. In chapter 3, we have encountered a variety of instantiations of the predicate-specifier structure—instances of "reverse predication" such as (7a–d) (with *by*, *as*, and *for* lexicalizing the RELATOR-head).

(7) a. Brian is [$_{RP}$ [$_{VP}$ loved *t*] [RELATOR=*by* [$_{DP}$ Imogen]

    b. Brian is [$_{RP}$ [$_{AP}$ clever] [RELATOR=*for* [$_{DP}$ a five-year-old]

    c. Brian is [$_{RP}$ [$_{DP}$ a real disgrace] [RELATOR=*as/for* [$_{DP}$ a heavyweight champion]

    d. Brian is [$_{RP}$ [$_{PP}$ in excellent physical shape] [RELATOR=*for* [$_{DP}$ an American teenager]

The predicates of these reverse predications can be of all categorial types —including noun phrases and PPs. One might envision, therefore, that examples such as (1b) and (2b) could be treated in a way similar to (7c) and (7d), with the nominal or prepositional predicate base-generated in the specifier position of the RELATOR phrase.

(8) a. be [RP [DP the best candidate] [RELATOR [DP Brian]
    b. hang [RP [PP on the wall] [RELATOR [DP a picture of Imogen]

Would (8) be a viable approach to Predicate Inversion constructions such as (1b) and (2b)?

The answer to this question is negative. One clear empirical indication to this effect is the fact that predicate-specifier constructions of the type discussed in chapter 2 behave quite differently from Predicate Inversion constructions when it comes to extraction. In (5b) and (6b), we saw that A′-extraction of the postverbal subject of the latter type of construction fails miserably. But as the sentences in (9), based on predicate-specifier constructions of the type in (7), show, extraction of the subject in predicate-specifier structures is grammatical.[3]

(9) a. Who do you think Brian is loved by *t*?
    b. ?A five-year-old, Brian would actually be clever for *t* (but
        unfortunately, he is twelve already).
    c. ?I can't figure out what I'm looking at—a butterfly, this creature is
        too small for *t*; but a dragonfly, I think it would be too big for *t*.
    d. ?A baseball player, he would be in fine physical shape for *t*; but
        he wants to be a real athlete.

To this we might add the fact that, while the postcopular subject of a Copular Inversion construction cannot project focus up the tree (as we saw in (4)), the subject in the complement of the RELATOR in predicate-specifier constructions supports focus projection perfectly happily.

(10) Imogen said Brian is clever for a FIVE-YEAR-OLD.
    a. She did not say he's clever for [a NINE-YEAR-OLD].
    b. She did not say he's [ugly for a CENTERFOLD].
    c. She did not say he [smelled like a MARIGOLD].
    d. She did not say [the United States has the world in a
        STRANGLEHOLD].

There are solid empirical grounds, therefore, for believing that Predicate Inversion constructions of the type in (1b)–(2b) are not base-generated as predicate-specifier structures. In fact, in section 2.8.1, I had already ruled out primary predications of the type in (8) (see the generalization in (67) given there, the roots of which remain as yet obscure). A movement derivation, with the predicate literally inverting around its subject, thus remains as the only alternative.

4.1.3 Predicate Inversion as A-Movement of the Predicate to SpecTP

Not only would the sharp ungrammaticality of the b-examples in (5) and (6) be entirely unexpected if the predicate-subject order of Predicate Inversion constructions were base-generated, it would also be surprising if the predicate fronted around its subject via A′-movement. For as the relatively benign subjacency effects in (11) and (12) show, extraction of the subject across its A′-moved predicate does not result in as strong a degradation as the one seen in (5b) and (6b).

(11) a.   I called [$_{RP}$ him [RELATOR$_\varnothing$ [an idiot]]]
     b.   I don't know what to call him.
     c.   ?*Who* don't you know what to call *t*?

(12) a.   I hung [$_{RP}$ this picture [RELATOR$_\varnothing$ [on that wall]]]
     b.   I don't know on which wall to hang this picture.
     c.   ?*Which picture* don't you know on which wall to hang *t*?

This suggests, therefore, that, while Predicate Inversion involves movement, it is not a case of A′-movement.

There is, in addition, positive evidence in favor of an analysis of Predicate Inversion in terms of A-movement: both Copular Inversion and Locative Inversion are legitimate long-distance, in raising constructions (as Bresnan 1977 first noted for Locative Inversion).

(13) a.   It was claimed that the best candidate was Brian.
     b.   The best candidate was claimed to be Brian.

(14) a.   It was claimed that on this wall hung a picture of Imogen.
     b.   On this wall was claimed to have hung a picture of Imogen.

It seems to me that this argument for an A-movement derivation of Predicate Inversion, via (at the very least) the SpecTP position of the embedded infinitival clause, has never been successfully countered in the literature.[4] The support that these kinds of sentences give to the A-movement account is robust.[5]

In what follows I will develop the A-movement analysis of Predicate Inversion in detail, addressing the extraction restrictions on these con-

structions as well as the effect of Predicate Inversion on the distribution of
the copula. I will approach the account from the perspective of a particularly burning question: that of the *trigger* of inversion of the predicate
around its subject. With the answer to that question in place, I will subsequently turn to the legitimacy of such inversion, from the point of view of
the theory of locality, and to the restrictions imposed on the postverbal
subject of inversion constructions.

4.2 Predicate Inversion: Why?

Copular Inversion constructions like (1b) and Locative Inversion cases
such as (2b) raise a variety of questions. The most pressing ones are these:

- *Why* does the predicate invert with its subject?
- *How* can it invert (i.e., A-move around its subject) at all?

Any analysis of Predicate Inversion will need to address these questions,
of which the first is a particularly difficult one. So let me start out by
providing a motive or *trigger* for Predicate Inversion, moving on subsequently (in section 4.3) to the technical implementation of the *how* of
Predicate inversion.

4.2.1 Two Failed Rationales

4.2.1.1 Information Structure Bresnan's (1994) important paper on
Locative Inversion in English and Chicheŵa has an entire section (section
5) devoted to the question of why Locative Inversion occurs. Her answer
to this question capitalizes on the information-structural profile of the
phenomenon, something I already drew attention to in section 4.1.1. In a
nutshell, for Bresnan the fact that the theme of a Locative Inversion
construction is in focus is the motivation for inversion. For a ⟨*theme,
location*⟩ argument structure, the default syntactic realization would feature the theme in subject position. But since the subject is the unmarked
discourse topic, presentational focus on the theme is an incentive to make
the locative the subject and realize the theme as an object—"the focussable syntactic function *par excellence*" (Bresnan 1994, 90).

    The trouble with exploiting focus as the rationale for Locative Inver-
sion, however, is that, as Bresnan herself points out, Locative Inversion
is by no means "the only syntactic means available to meet the functional requirements of presentational focus" (p. 20): one may also exploit

expletives to keep the theme low; and in languages like English, it is not even impossible to realize the presentational focus as a subject, by exploiting intonation (as Guéron (1980, 659) noted already; see also note 29 of chapter 3, above). The triplet in (15) illustrates the range of options.

(15) a. The case was judged, and then a LAWYER appeared in the courtroom.
 b. The case was judged, and then in the courtroom appeared a LAWYER.
 c. The case was judged, and then there appeared a LAWYER in the courtroom.

While the possibility of realizing the presentational focus in subject position (as in (15a)) is restricted, the fact that it is possible in the presence of a locative complement (*in the courtroom*) seems to defeat any attempt to hold presentational focus responsible for the application of Locative Inversion. There is no denying, obviously, that presentational focus plays a role in the analysis of Locative Inversion—but it would seem plain that focus on the theme is not the *trigger* for the inversion, precisely because there are other ways to allow the theme to be focused.

The case against focus as a rationale for Locative Inversion can be broadened by a quick look at languages that are often taken to exploit focus as a trigger for syntactic displacement—Hungarian being perhaps the most famous case in point. In Hungarian, foci generally appear in a designated syntactic slot in the left periphery, to the immediate left of the finite verb (see (16a)). But as (16b) shows, foci per se are by no means illegitimate in nonpreposed positions: as Horvath (2000, 201) points out, "any time the assertion involves exhaustive identification, only the (overtly) preposed version can be used," as in (16a); but "when it is not intended to be an exhaustive identification of the proper subset of contextually relevant entities involved," a nonpreposed focus is perfectly fine, as in (16b), where "for example" and "among others" highlight nonexhaustivity.[6]

(16) a. JÁNOST   hívták   meg (Hungarian)
        János-ACC invited-3PL.DEF PRT
        'They invited JÁNOS (and nobody else).'
 b. meghívták   például/   többek között JÁNOST
        invited-3PL.DEF for-example others among János-ACC
        'They invited JÁNOS, for example/among others.'

It appears, then, that it is *exhaustivity* (a quantificational property), not *focus*, that drives syntactic displacement. It would be wrong to take focus to be responsible for the word order in (16a). This conclusion is reinforced by the fact that "focus movement" can pied-pipe large constituents that cannot otherwise be pied-piped, for instance by *wh*-fronting in relative clauses, which is known to be readily amenable to pied-piping.

(17) a. [BARACKPÁLINKÁT   követelő   vendégektől] fél   a
          apricot-brandy-ACC demanding guests-from   fears the
          pincér (Hungarian)
          waiter
          'It is customers demanding APRICOT BRANDY that the waiter is
          afraid of.'
     b. *az ital [amit követelő   vendégektől] fél   a   pincér ...
          the drink which demanding guests-from   fears the waiter

Since the [+wh] feature on the relative pronoun in (17b) is ostensibly incapable of pied-piping the bracketed constituent, it is unlikely that the fronting of the bracketed phrase in (17a) is triggered by a [+focus] feature on *barackpálinkát*, as Horvath (2000, 197–198) (to whom the examples in (17) are due) rightly points out. This, combined with the conclusion drawn from (16), makes it clear that focus per se is not a driving force for syntactic displacement, not even in languages such as Hungarian. While in her recent repartee of Horvath 2000, Szendrői (2003) takes focal stress to be the key trigger for leftward displacement of focused constituents in Hungarian, she agrees with the conclusion just reached that information structure cannot drive syntactic movement: "Pragmatic considerations may drive syntactic operations ... only *indirectly* ... if they themselves are formally encoded in LF or PF notions present in the core grammar" (p. 75).

The notion that information-structural properties of sentence constituents could be *responsible* for movement operations taking place within the sentences of which they are a part would in fact have far-reaching repercussions (see also Fiengo 2002 for related discussion). Topics and foci, in their pragmatic sense, can only be determined at the level of the discourse: knowing whether some part of a given sentence is "old" or "new" information presupposes knowledge of the discourse that the sentence in question is uttered in. In general, the pragmatic functions of sentence constituents cannot be determined until the level of discourse analysis. Syntactic movement can certainly create the requisite configuration for a particular pragmatic construal of a constituent, and in this respect the use of pragmatically flavored projections such as FocP and TopP in syntax is not in and of itself an anomaly. But only if one were prepared to demand that discourse analysis be *prior to* syntactic analysis could one exploit pragmatic functions in one's syntactic analysis as *triggers* for movement and say that a constituent's desire to be interpreted as a topic or a focus in discourse is what *drives* movement (either of the constituent itself or of some other syntactic phrase) in syntax.

I take the above to be sufficient discouragement for an attempt at deriving the rationale for Locative Inversion (and Predicate Inversion more generally) from information-structural notions such as focus and topic.

4.2.1.2 Breaking Symmetry Moro (2000) presents a very simple rationale for Copular Inversion. He postulates a structure of predicate nominal constructions in which the copula takes a "bare" small clause as its complement, one of the type in (18), in which there is a symmetrical relationship between the two constituent noun phrases. The symmetry inside the SC in (18), while admissible (for Moro) in the initial phrase-structure representation, must be broken in the course of the derivation, in order that the output will comply with Kayne's (1994) Linear Correspondence Axiom (LCA). So since (18) cannot survive as it stands, one of the two NPs must raise out of the small clause, to a higher specifier position. SpecTP is the obvious candidate. With the left-hand NP raising to SpecTP, we derive the familiar "canonical" copular sentence in (1a), while raising of the right-hand NP to SpecTP yields an "inverse" copular sentence of the type in (1b). Either NP can raise, and raising of either NP will break the symmetry. The trigger for raising is the resolution of symmetry; Copular Inversion, therefore, is driven by the very same trigger that drives the production of "canonical" copular sentences.

(18) [be [$_{SC}$ NP NP]]

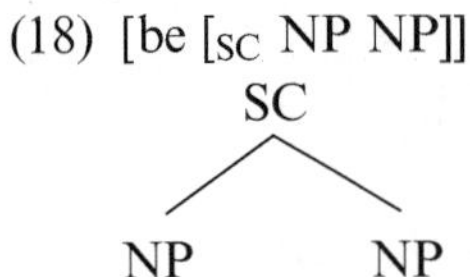

I already pointed out in chapter 2 that structures of the type in (18) have no legitimacy in the framework that I am adopting—one in which symmetrical structures like these are quite simply meaningless, no relationship being establishable between the two constituents of the small clause. And since (18) is unavailable, Moro's "dynamic antisymmetry" approach to Copular Inversion will be, too.

A nontrivial empirical question raised by Moro's "dynamic antisymmetry" approach to pairs like (1) is why Copular Inversion is not perfectly general. In the realm of predicate nominal constructions, only specificational and equative copular sentences are candidates for inversion, and copular sentences with an adjectival predicate generally seem to resist Copular Inversion (in the technical sense in which this term is employed here; see especially Heycock 1991, 1998a, and also the appendix to this chapter). Thus, the b-examples in (19) are ungrammatical.

(19) a.   Imogen is {a girl/beautiful}.
     b. *{A girl/beautiful} is Imogen.

The restriction operative here does not seem to be one that is formulable in terms of a definite versus indefinite dichotomy—for (20a) and (21a) do support Copular Inversion.[7]

(20) a. Brian is an excellent doctor.
     b. An excellent doctor is Brian.

(21) a. The Vietnam War and the Gulf War are examples of this.
     b. Examples of this are the Vietnam War and the Gulf War.

The key difference between (19) on the one hand, and (20) and (21) on the other, seems to be that (20b) and (21b) are *specificational* copular sentences whereas (19b) cannot be so construed. As Higgins (1979) points out, a defining characteristic of specificational copular sentences that sets them apart from their predicational cousins is that they involve the specification of a value for a variable, something that is similar to enumerating items on a list. Thus, in (21b), *examples of this* defines a list that has several items on it, and the specificational copular sentence gives a (partial) enumeration of the items on that list. Quite generally, inverse specificational copular sentences with indefinite precopular noun phrases can be read as though they had a colon to the right of the copula; one may typically insert *for instance/example* to the right of the copula as well (cf. *An excellent doctor is, for instance, Brian* or *Examples of this are, for instance, the Vietnam War and the Gulf War*; inserting a colon or *for instance/example* is clearly infelicitous in (19b)). By this criterion, the examples in (20b) and (21b) are specificational copular constructions; the one in (19b) clearly is not.

4.2.2 The Alternative: Licensing the Empty-Headed Predicate

4.2.2.1 Copular Inversion   Of the members of the Higgins/Declerck typology of copular sentences, we have seen in section 3.2.3 that specificational and equative copular sentences support inversion.[8] For the latter, chapter 3 has presented an analysis in which the precopular constituent is a reduced free relative. Thus, my analysis of an equative copular sentence such as (22) runs as in (23) (which repeats chapter 3's (29), which also provides an arboreal rendition of the resulting b-structure).

(22) Cicero is Tully.

(23) a. [PRO-PREDICATE$_\varnothing$ [$_{CP}$ Op_i [$C_\varnothing$ [$_{RP}$ *Cicero* [RELATOR$_\varnothing$ t_i]]]]]
    $\rightarrow$ merging the RELATOR and the subject, *Tully*

  b. [$_{RP}$ *Tully* [RELATOR [$_{Pred}$ PRO-PREDICATE$_\varnothing$ [$_{CP}$ Op_i [$C_\varnothing$ [$_{RP}$ *Cicero* [RELATOR$_\varnothing$ t_i]]]]]]]
    $\rightarrow$ merging T and applying Predicate Inversion to the reduced free relative $\rightarrow$

  c. [$_{TP}$ [$_{Pred}$ PRO-PREDICATE$_\varnothing$ [$_{CP}$ Op_i [$C_\varnothing$ [$_{RP}$ *Cicero* [RELATOR$_\varnothing$ t_i]]]]]$_j$ [T+RELATOR$_k$=*be* [$_{RP}$ *Tully* [t_k t_j]]]

Predicate Inversion here applies to a reduced free relative, and it applies to it obligatorily—all so-called equative copular sentences have the properties of inverse copular sentences: obligatoriness of a copula under *consider*, as well as severe restrictions on A′-extraction (see Heycock and Kroch 1999).[9]

(24) a. I consider your opinion of New York *(to be) my opinion of Amsterdam.

  b. I consider my opinion of Amsterdam *(to be) your opinion of New York.

(25) I think your opinion of New York is my opinion of Amsterdam.

  a. *Whose opinion of Amsterdam* do you think your opinion of New York is *t*?

  b. *Whose opinion of New York* do you think *t* is my opinion of Amsterdam?

  c. *What city* do you think your opinion of New York is my opinion of *t*?

(26) I think my opinion of Amsterdam is your opinion of New York.
   a. *_Whose opinion of New York_ do you think my opinion of
      Amsterdam is _t_?
   b. *_Whose opinion of Amsterdam_ do you think _t_ is your opinion of
      New York?
   c. *_What city_ do you think my opinion of Amsterdam is your
      opinion of _t_?

I have taken the need for inversion to indicate that a reduced free relative
is not licensed to stay in the predicate position of a small clause: it must
raise to SpecTP in order to be properly licensed. More specifically, the
null head of the reduced free relative must raise to SpecTP to be formally
licensed and content-licensed—behaving like _pro_ in this regard (see Rizzi's
1986 theory of _pro_-licensing).[10]

(27) A reduced free relative predicate inverts with its subject and raises
     to SpecTP to be licensed.

With this in mind, let us return to copular sentences of the type in (1)
and (20)–(21). Inversion in (1) and (20)–(21) is not obligatory: these copular sentences exhibit the quintessential alternation that has given rise to
so much discussion in the literature on copular constructions: the alternation between a "canonical" and an "inverse" construction, each with different properties when it comes to the distribution of the copula and
restrictions on A′-extraction.[11]

(28) a. I consider Imogen's article about Brian (to be) my key example
        of good journalism.
     b. I consider my key example of good journalism *(to be) Imogen's
        article about Brian.

(29) I think Imogen's article about Brian is my key example of good
     journalism.
   a. _Whose key example of good journalism_ do you think Imogen's
      article about Brian is _t_?
   b. _Whose article about Brian_ do you think _t_ is my key example of
      good journalism?
   c. ?_Which genre of writing_ do you think Imogen's article about
      Brian is my key example of _t_?

(30) I think my key example of good journalism is Imogen's article
     about Brian.

   a. *Whose article about Brian* do you think my key example of
      good journalism is *t*?

   b. *Whose key example of good journalism* do you think *t* is
      Imogen's article about Brian?

   c. *Which person* do you think my key example of good journalism
      is Imogen's article about *t*?

Of the two word-order possibilities in (1), therefore, only the latter involves inversion of the predicate around its subject; (1a) reflects the base word order.

For equative copular sentences such as (22), I forced Predicate Inversion regardless of the surface word order on the assumption that the predicate of the small clause is a reduced free relative in all equatives. This follows quite simply from the fact that *referential* noun phrases cannot be predicates—in equative sentences, both noun phrases are referential expressions (as is evident from the fact that both can be modified by a nonrestrictive relative clause; see Heycock and Kroch 1999), hence neither qualifies as a predicate. But since the underlying representation of equative copular sentences does involve predication (see chapter 3 for discussion), we systematically need one of the two noun phrases to be embedded inside a reduced free relative that can serve as a small-clause predicate. And since that reduced free relative *must* invert with its subject (by (27)), we derive the fact that all equative copular sentences, regardless of their surface word order, give rise to the copula and extraction restrictions characteristic of inverse copular sentences.

In pairs like (1), on the other hand, we find these copula and extraction restrictions only for the b-cases, not for the a-cases. The a-cases actually behave like garden-variety *predicational* copular sentences, while the b-cases have the characteristics of *equative* copular constructions. So it should be clear what we want to say when it comes to the syntactic analysis of pairs like (1): the a-member of the pair represents a copular sentence in which the postcopular noun phrase is *itself* the predicate nominal (see Zamparelli 2000 on the possibility for English definite noun phrases to function as predicates), while the b-member is a copular sentence in which the *inverted* predicate of the small clause is a reduced free relative *containing* the precopular noun phrase, either as its subject (à la (23)) or as its predicate (as in (32); see Higgins 1979 on the parallel between *the cause of the riot was Bush's speech* and specificational pseudoclefts such as *what caused the riot was Bush's speech*, with *what caused the riot* in the latter being a predicate).

(31) The best candidate is Brian.

(32) a. [NULL PRO-PREDICATE [$_{CP}$ Op_i [$C_\varnothing$ [$_{RP}$ t_i [RELATOR$_\varnothing$ *the best candidate*]]]]]]
       → merging the RELATOR and the subject, *Brian*

   b. [$_{RP}$ *Brian* [RELATOR [$_{Pred}$ NULL PRO-PREDICATE [$_{CP}$ Op_i [$C_\varnothing$ [$_{RP}$ t_i [RELATOR$_\varnothing$ *the best candidate*]]]]]]]]
       → merging T and applying Predicate Inversion to the reduced free relative →

   c. [$_{TP}$ [$_{Pred}$ NULL PRO-PREDICATE [$_{CP}$ Op_i [$C_\varnothing$ [$_{RP}$ t_i [RELATOR$_\varnothing$ *the best candidate*]]]]]]$_j$ [T+RELATOR$_k$=*be* [$_{RP}$ *Brian* [t_k t_j]]]

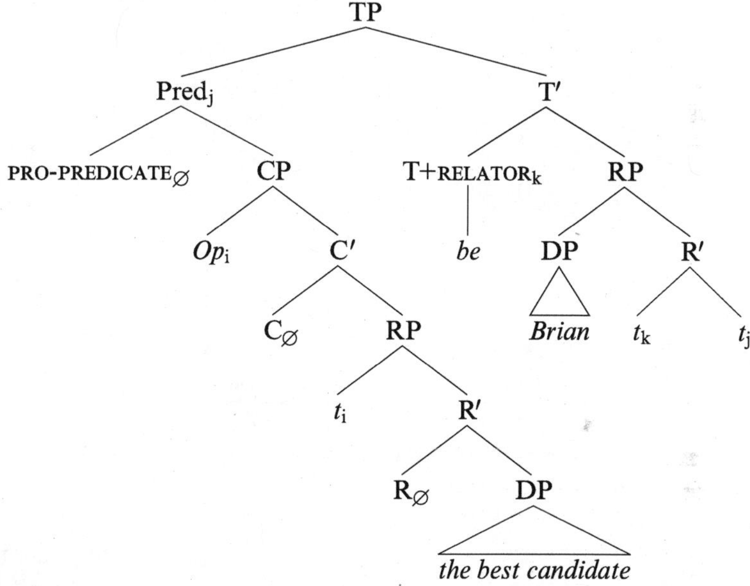

With the inverse copular sentence in (1b) represented as in (32), in both (1a) and (1b) *the best candidate* is the predicate of a small clause—the difference between the two lying in the question of *which* small clause it is the predicate of: the matrix small clause or one embedded inside a reduced free relative. In "canonical" specificational copular sentences, the postcopular noun phrase is itself the predicate of the one and only small clause present in the structure, the one that takes the precopular noun phrase as its subject; in "inverse" specificational copular sentences, the precopular noun phrase is the predicate of a small clause embedded in a reduced free relative that serves as the predicate of the postcopular subject. The reduced free relative in (32) must invert with its subject for

precisely the same reasons that it must in all equative copular sentences—
for licensing purposes (see (27)).

This reduced free relative approach to specificational copular sentences
of the type in (1b) has an interesting spin-off in the domain of agreement.
A well-known fact about English inverse copular sentences of the type
in (1b) is that the precopular noun phrase must trigger agreement on the
finite verb—this becomes clear in constructions in which the inverted
predicate and its subject disagree in number, as in (33). In Dutch, by contrast, specificational copular sentences of this type feature obligatory
agreement with the postcopular subject, not the inverted predicate, as
seen in (34).[12]

(33) a. I believe that the children {are/*is} the biggest problem.
     b. I believe that the biggest problem {is/*are} the children.

(34) a. ik geloof dat de kinderen het grootste probleem
        I believe that the children the biggest problem
        {zijn/*is} (Dutch)
         are/is
     b. ik geloof dat het grootste probleem de kinderen {zijn/*is}
        I believe that the biggest problem the children   are/is

This difference between English and Dutch has proved elusive. Moro
(1997) discusses in some detail the difference between English and Italian
in the domain of agreement in specificational copular sentences of the type
in (33b), but as I show in detail in Den Dikken 1998a, his account—
couched in terms of *pro*-drop—fails to carry over to the contrast between
English and Dutch illustrated above. It is interesting, then, to note that
the reduced free relative approach to inverse copular sentences assimilates
this contrast to the one found in specificational pseudoclefts of the type in
(35) and (36). As Declerck (1988, 80) notes, English (35a), with singular
is, is specificational (*What you have bought is the following: fake jewels*)
while (35b), with plural *are*, is predicational, with *fake jewels* serving as
the predicate of the copular sentence.[13] In Dutch, on the other hand,
(36a) is ambiguous between a predicational and a specificational reading
and (36b) is ungrammatical.

(35) a. I believe that what you have bought is fake jewels.

                                                      (Specificational)
     b. I believe that what you have bought are fake jewels.

                                                      (Predicational)

(36) a.   ik geloof dat wat jij   hebt gekocht valse juwelen
          I believe that what you have bought fake jewels
          zijn (Ambiguous) (Dutch)
          are
     b. *ik geloof dat wat jij   hebt gekocht valse juwelen is
          I believe that what you have bought fake jewels   is

Specificational pseudoclefts are inverse copular sentences whose precopular constituents are *physically* free relatives. The fact, then, that specificational pseudoclefts pattern exactly with inverse copular sentences whose precopular constituent, on the surface, is a noun phrase, when it comes to agreement with the copula, can be construed as an argument in favor of an account of inverse copular sentences according to which the constituent in precopular position is *systematically* a free relative—full or reduced.[14]

The result that inverse specificational copular sentences feature a reduced free relative in the subject position of the sentence (SpecTP) converges in an interesting way with the analysis that Guéron (1992, 1994) arrives at for these constructions. She, too, ends up with a representation in which the precopular noun phrase is a subconstituent of a reduced free relative. But she does not base-generate it that way. That is, she does not assume that the precopular noun phrase is *born* as a subconstituent of a reduced free relative. Instead, she raises it into the free relative, which is itself base-generated in SpecTP. And she takes the establishment of the reduced free relative structure in (32c) to happen at a point in the derivation that does not belong to the syntax proper.[15] I am convinced, however, that both equative and inverse specificational copular sentences are derived via garden-variety syntactic operations (in particular, A-movement to SpecTP of the predicate of the small clause)—a view for which I present a variety of syntactic evidence in these pages. I will not, therefore, adopt Guéron's specific way of deriving the structure in (32c). Instead, I base-generate the reduced free relative as a constituent in the small-clause predicate position and invert it with its subject, obligatorily (by (27)).

What we have now arrived at is the conclusion that all inverse copular sentences (i.e., all equatives and all inverse specificationals) have in common the fact that their structure features a small clause whose predicate is a *reduced free relative* of the type in (23a) or (32a), a constituent that, due to the licensing restrictions imposed on its null head, must raise to

SpecTP. The claim in (27), then, is my answer to the question of what triggers inversion in copular sentences.

(27) A reduced free relative predicate inverts with its subject and raises to SpecTP to be licensed.

Since the licensing requirement that drives fronting to SpecTP is imposed by the pro-predicate heading the reduced free relative, we can broaden the formulation of the trigger for inversion by making reference to the licensing of the empty predicate head rather than specifically to reduced free relatives, as in (37).

(37) Predicate Inversion involves A-movement to subject position triggered by the need to license an empty predicate head.

I submit (37) as the overarching syntactic rationale for Predicate Inversion.

4.2.2.2 Locative Inversion   If indeed (37) is the general trigger for Predicate Inversion, how does it extend to Locative Inversion constructions? It would appear that Locative Inversion does not involve an empty predicate at all: a full-fledged PP appears to be fronted to subject position, roughly as in (38).

(38) [$_{TP}$ [$_{PP}$ *on the wall*]$_i$ [T [$_{VP}$ *hung* [$_{RP}$ [*a picture of Imogen*] [RELATOR t_i]]]]]

There is ample reason to believe, however, that (38) as it stands is inaccurate as an analysis of Locative Inversion in languages such as English.

An immediate indication to this effect comes from a comparison of Locative Inversion and Copular Inversion in ECM contexts. While Copular Inversion is perfectly legitimate in the infinitival complement of ECM-verbs such as *expect*, Locative Inversion within the infinitival clause is possible only if the locative PP does not actually surface there but instead shows up in topic position in the matrix clause. Of course, topicalization is possible in (39) as well, but the point is that in these Copular Inversion constructions it is by no means forced while in the Locative Inversion cases in (40), it is (see Bresnan 1994, 108).[16]

(39) a. Imogen expects the best candidate to be Brian.
      b. The best candidate Imogen expects to be Brian.

(40) a. *Imogen expects on this wall to be hung a portrait of Brian.
      b.   On this wall Imogen expects to be hung a portrait of Brian.

If (38) were right, there would be no reason to expect there to be anything amiss with (40a): if the SpecTP of a finite clause can be occupied by a fronted locative PP, it should also be possible for the SpecTP of an infinitival clause to have a fronted locative PP in it. The fact, then, that (40a) is ungrammatical spells doom for (38).

The reader might still be inclined at this point to quibble with the conclusion based on (39) and (40)—it might be, after all, that there is some difference between finite and infinitival TPs that prevents locative PPs from landing in the specifier position of the latter while still allowing them to settle down in the SpecTP of a finite clause. But there is evidence that even in finite clauses, the fronted locative PP must be topicalized. The evidence comes from two sources. One is the fact that, in contrast to Copular Inversion, Locative Inversion totally resists subject-auxiliary inversion: whereas (41b) is perfect, (42b) crashes dramatically.

(41) a. The best candidate seems to be Brian.
     b. Does the best candidate seem to be Brian (or Imogen)?

(42) a.   On this wall seems to have hung a picture of Brian.
     b. *Does on this wall seem to have hung a picture of Brian (or Imogen)?

With respect to subject-auxiliary inversion, therefore, the fronted predicate nominal in Copular Inversion constructions behaves like a genuine subject occupying SpecTP, but the preposed locative PP in Locative Inversion constructions clearly does not. Instead, it patterns with topics, which likewise resist inversion with the finite auxiliary.

(43) a.   To Imogen, Brian never gives presents.
     b. *Does to Imogen, Brian ever give presents?

The topiclike behavior of the fronted locative in Locative Inversion constructions is further confirmed by the fact that Locative Inversion constructions are systematically islands for all extraction—not just extraction of the postverbal subject (which is generally impossible in Predicate Inversion constructions across the board; see (44b) and (45b)) but extraction of other material as well (which is fine in Copular Inversion constructions; contrast (44c, d) and (45c, d)).[17]

(44) a. The best candidate was claimed by Imogen at the party to be Brian.
     b. *This is the guy *who* the best candidate was claimed by Imogen at the party to be.

    c.   This is the girl *by whom* the best candidate was claimed at the party to be Brian.

    d.   This is the party *at which* the best candidate was claimed by Imogen to be Brian.

(45) a.   On this wall was claimed by Imogen at the party to have hung a portrait of Brian.

    b.   *This is the portrait *which* on this wall was claimed by Imogen at the party to have hung.

    c.   *This is the girl *by whom* on this wall was claimed at the party to have hung a portrait of Brian.

    d.   *This is the party *at which* on this wall was claimed by Imogen to have hung a portrait of Brian.

The conclusion, first drawn by Bresnan (1990) (Coopmans (1989, 735) also takes the fronted PP to be topicalized), that the fronted locative PP in Locative Inversion constructions of the English type must be *topicalized* still leaves room for a number of competing analyses. On one, the locative PP physically fronts to SpecTP and subsequently raises on to the topic position (see (46a)); on an alternative approach, the locative PP is base-generated in topic position and is associated with a *pro*-PP that originates as the predicate of the locative small clause, and inverts with its subject by raising to subject position (see (46b)).

(46) a. [$_{\text{TopP}}$ [$_{\text{PP}}$ P DP]$_i$ [$_{\text{TP}}$ t_i [T [$_{\text{VP}}$ V [$_{\text{RP}}$ DP [RELATOR t_i]]]]]]

    b. [$_{\text{TopP}}$ [$_{\text{PP}}$ P DP]$_i$ [$_{\text{TP}}$ [$_{\text{PP}}$ NULL PRO-PREDICATE]$_i$ [T [$_{\text{VP}}$ V [$_{\text{RP}}$ DP [RELATOR t_i]]]]]]

The derivation in (46a) involves movement from SpecTP to SpecTopP, a case of vacuous topicalization. The status of vacuous movement is generally tenuous in any event (see Chomsky 1986), but the case for vacuous topicalization it is especially weak. As Lasnik and Saito (1990) point out, subextraction from topics gives rise to relatively mild deviations in English (cf. (47a)); see also Torrego's (1985) cases of subextraction from constituents, including subjects, in SpecCP in Spanish, referred to in Chomsky 1986, 25–26. Now, if vacuous topicalization of the subject were legitimate, Lasnik and Saito argue, the status of subextraction from the subject should match that of subextraction from topics (see (47a)). But as is well known, subextraction from the subject of a finite clause is entirely impossible (see (47b)). This then tells us, so the argument goes, that vacuous topicalization of the subject is prohibited. As a matter of fact, since SpecTP is the unmarked discourse topic position, there is no reasonable motive for raising from SpecTP to SpecTopP to begin with (see also the discussion in section 2.5.3). This makes the step from SpecTP to SpecTopP in (46a) highly dubious.

(47) a. ??*Who*$_j$ do you think that [pictures of t_j]$_i$, Imogen would never
          buy t_i?
      b. *Who*$_j$ do you think that [pictures of t_j] would never be bought
          by Imogen?

But the alternative in (46b) seems to have problems of its own. Observing that A$'$-dependencies between a fronted PP and a gap inside an island (see (48b)) are more seriously degraded than A$'$-dependencies between a fronted DP and an island-contained gap (see (48a)), Cinque (1990) denies that a null resumptive strategy—which he exploits in his account of (48a)—could ever be used for A$'$-dependencies involving PPs. And if anything, establishing a long-distance dependency in the Locative Inversion construction in (48c) is in fact even worse than it is in (48b). It seems that the analysis in (46b) would leave it obscure why (48c) should be so severely degraded.

(48) a. ?That room, I wonder whether anyone would be able to
          appreciate/occupy for more than a day.
      b. ?*In that room, I wonder whether anyone would be able to work
          for more than a day.
      c. *In that room, I wonder whether ever hung a portrait of Brian.

But as a matter of fact, as Culicover and Levine (2001, 301–302) emphasize (taking issue with Bresnan's work on this point), *all* long-distance dependencies involving the fronted locative fail in genuine Locative Inversion constructions—including dependencies not involving any islands at all. Thus, (49a) is ill-formed.[18] Even short-distance dependencies involving the *wh*-word *where* crash in genuine Locative Inversion constructions, as the ill-formedness of (49b) (adapted from Culicover and Levine 2001, 304) shows.[19]

(49) a. *Into the room I claim/believe walked/will walk Brian.
      b. *This is the city where lives Brian.

What this demonstrates, it seems to me, is that the locative PP in genuine Locative Inversion constructions is base-generated in a topic position *strictly local to the pro-predicate* in SpecTP. That is, the base position of the topic-PP must be the SpecTopP immediately outside the TP whose specifier serves as the landing site of the A-movement operation affecting the locative pro-predicate. It is impossible for the topic-PP to be base-generated in the topic position of a higher clause or in SpecCP; nor can the topic-PP raise from its base position local to the pro-predicate to a higher position (whether it be a SpecCP or a higher SpecTopP position): movement from SpecTopP is impossible.[20]

The analysis of Locative Inversion in (46b) actually allows us to explain why it is impossible for the topic-PP to be base-generated in a topic position that is not local to (i.e., in the same clause as) the landing site of the fronted pro-predicate. On the standard assumption that nonexpletive *pro* is in need of both formal licensing and content licensing (Rizzi 1986), this follows readily: T is capable only of formal licensing of the pro-predicate; for content licensing, it is dependent on a local identifier, and that identifier is the topic-PP coindexed with the pro-predicate.[21] For reasons of content licensing, therefore, it is essential that the topic-PP originate in the same clause as the pro-predicate that it identifies. As a consequence, the topic-PP will be strictly confined to the clause in whose SpecTP the pro-predicate lands. This explains all of the facts in (48c) and (49a, b).

Far from jeopardizing it, the facts in (48c) and (49a, b) thus reinforce the pro-predicate approach to Locative Inversion in (46b), which I will therefore adopt, assuming henceforth that the locative PP in Germanic-style Locative Inversion constructions originates as a Topic and is linked to a null PP that inverts with its subject, raising to SpecTP.[22] With this conclusion in mind, we may now return to the question of how (37), repeated here, could carry over to Locative Inversion.

(37) Predicate Inversion involves A-movement to subject position
     triggered by the need to license an empty predicate head.

With (46b) in place as the analysis of Germanic-style Locative Inversion, the answer is of course plain: the locative predicate raising to subject position in a Locative Inversion construction is a pro-predicate, in need of licensing.

4.2.2.3 "Beheaded" Locative Inversion and Dative Shift An interesting variation on the theme of Locative Inversion is a construction type that, on the surface, does not in fact look like Locative Inversion at all. Though in English this type of construction has a very restricted distribution, (50c) may serve as an initial illustration thereof.[23]

(50) a. Little attention has been paid to this issue in the literature.
  b. To this issue has been paid little attention in the literature.
  c. This issue has been paid little attention to in the literature.

Whereas (50b) is a garden-variety case of Locative Inversion, (50c) looks more like a pseudopassive—except, of course, that in familiar pseudopassives (such as *This bed has been slept in by Napoléon*) we never find an argumental noun phrase to the immediate right of the verb (*little attention in* (50c)). One peculiar thing about this noun phrase is the fact that it can sit there at all; another is that it seems to be completely frozen in place: any movement of this noun phrase, including A′-extraction, is blocked. In this respect, (50c) behaves exactly like the Locative Inversion construction in (50b), which likewise resists extraction of the postverbal noun phrase.[24]

(51) a. How much attention has been paid to this issue in the literature?
  b. *How much attention has to this issue been paid in the literature?
  c. *How much attention has this issue been paid to in the literature?

The reader may not be impressed with these observations about English (50) (after all, (50c) is indeed of very limited distribution in English). But Norwegian allows us to strengthen our case for a "beheaded Locative Inversion" approach to (50c). In Norwegian, sentences of this type are by no means rare, being constructible for a wide variety of verb-plus-preposition combinations (see especially Taraldsen 1979; Lødrup 1991).[25]

(52) a. frimerker ble klistret på brevet (Norwegian)
    stamps   be pasted on letter-the
  b. på brevet   ble klistret frimerker
    on letter-the be pasted stamps
  c. brevet   ble klistret frimerker på
    letter-the be pasted stamps   on
    All (approx.): 'There were stamps pasted on the letter.'

Den Dikken and Næss (1993) make a detailed case for an analysis of (52c) that assimilates it in key respects to the Locative Inversion construction in (52b) (which, in Norwegian, is stylistically highly marked, perhaps more so than in English; (52c), on the other hand, is entirely natural). Despite appearances, what is fronted in (52c) is the entire locative PP, but the head of this PP is extracted from it prior to the PP's fronting. Just as in the case of English (50c), this analysis is supported by the fact that extraction of the postverbal subject is impossible in (52c) (see (53c)), just as in garden-variety Locative Inversion constructions (see (53b)).

(53) a.   hvor mange frimerker tror   du   at   ble klistret på brevet?
             how many stamps   think you that be pasted on letter-the
      b. *hvor mange frimerker tror   du   at   på brevet   ble klistret?
             how many stamps   think you that on letter-the be pasted
      c. *hvor mange frimerker tror   du   at   brevet   ble klistret på?
             how many stamps   think you that letter-the be pasted on

   Another reliable indicator of the fact that (52c) is derived via (remnant) PP fronting comes from the parallel between (54b) and (55b).

(54) a. They sent ⟨out⟩ a schedule ⟨out⟩ to the stockholders.
      b. To whom did they send ⟨out⟩ a schedule ⟨*out⟩?
      c. Who did they send ⟨out⟩ a schedule ⟨out⟩ to?

(55) a. de   sendte ⟨ut⟩ møteprogrammet ⟨ut⟩ til aksjonærene
             they sent   out schedule-the   out to stockholders-the
      b. aksjonærene   ble sendt ⟨?ut⟩ møteprogrammet ⟨*ut⟩ til
             stockholders-the be sent   out schedule-the   out to

Den Dikken (1995c) observes that, while complex particle constructions of the type in (54a) normally allow placement of the particle on either side of the Theme noun phrase, extraction of the PP secondary predicate forces the particle to be placed in verb-adjacent position (see (54b)). Extraction of just the complement of the preposition, on the other hand, does not force the "inner-particle" construction (see (54c))—in fact, if anything, placement of the particle to the right of the Theme is the preferred option in this case. Interestingly, now, Norwegian constructions of the type in (52c) pattern with the English PP-extraction case, not with the P-stranding one: (55b) is acceptable only with verb-adjacent particle placement, just like (54b).

   I take these data to constitute evidence that the Norwegian constructions in (52c) involve fronting of the PP, via "beheaded" Locative Inversion. "Beheaded" Locative Inversion involves A-movement of the beheaded PP predicate to subject position—a paradigm case of Predicate Inversion. Den Dikken and Næss's (1993) analysis of "beheaded" Locative Inversion constructions presents a structural implementation of this conclusion. It has the head of the PP predicate raise to the functional head position of the locative small clause (my RELATOR), the remnant PP being fronted across its subject via Predicate Inversion (i.e., A-movement to subject position), as depicted in (56).[26]

(56) a. [RP [*frimerker*] [RELATOR [PP *på brevet*]]]
           → raising P=*på* to RELATOR →

      b. [RP [*frimerker*] [RELATOR+*på*$_i$ [PP t_i *brevet*]]]
           → merging V and T; raising remnant PP to SpecTP →

      c. [TP [PP t_i *brevet*]$_j$ [T=*ble*$_k$ [VP t_k *klistret* [RP [*frimerker*]
          [RELATOR+*på*$_i$ t_j]]]]]]

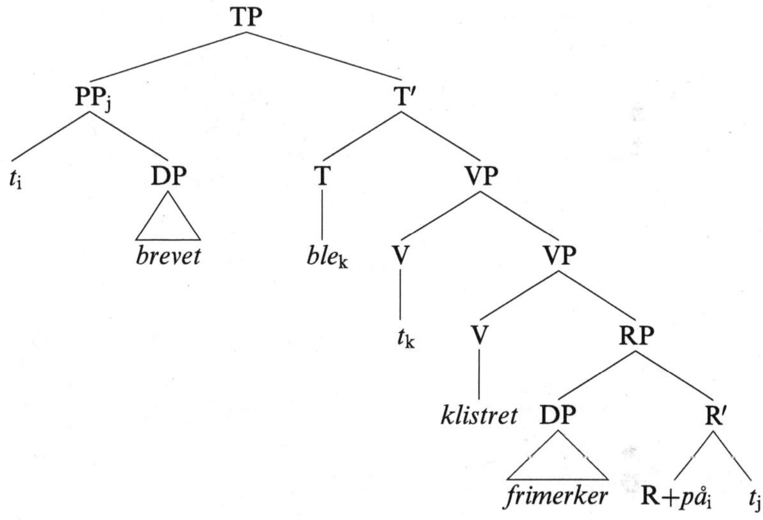

Locative Inversion in some of the Bantu languages exhibits something similar to Norwegian (52c) and English (50c), alongside garden-variety Locative Inversion involving fronting of the entire locative phrase. In the OluTsootso dialect of Luhya, studied in Dalgish 1976, 2002, the non-inverted sentence in (57a) alternates with two similar yet crucially distinct inversion cases, given in (57b) and (57c).

(57) a. aBa-xasi Ba-tsiits-aanga ha-mu-chela (Luhya)
          2-woman SM.2-go-TNS   LOC-3-river
          'The women go near the river.'

      b. ha-mu-chela ha-tsii-Buungwa-ho   neende aBa-xasi
          LOC-3-river SM.LOC-go-PASS.TNS-LOCSFX by   2-woman
          (Approx.) 'Near the river is gone by the woman.'

   c. omu-chela ku-tsii-Buungwa-ho   neende aBa-xasi
      3-river   SM.3-go-PASS.TNS-LOCSFX   by   2-woman
      (Approx.) 'The river is gone near by the woman.'

Luhya (57c), with what is apparently a simple DP fronted to SpecTP and with its locative suffix *ho* attached to the verb, should presumably be analyzed along the same lines as Norwegian (52c) and English (50c)—except that P raises one step further in the overt syntax, not just to the RELATOR but all the way up to V, being realized as a locative suffix (*ho*) on the verb (a case of P-incorporation, well attested throughout Bantu; see Baker's 1988 analysis of applicative constructions, and references cited there).[27]

The cross-Bantu distribution of this "beheaded" Locative Inversion construction in Bantu appears to be quite restricted: it is not found in Chicheŵa, for instance (see Bresnan and Kanerva 1989 for detailed discussion of Locative Inversion in Chicheŵa). The more familiar pattern in (57b), featuring locative agreement on the verb, is widespread in Bantu. Yet even here, Luhya is different from Chicheŵa in featuring a locative suffix on the verb (just as in (57c)). For comparison, consider the Chicheŵa pair in (58) (from Bresnan and Kanerva 1989).

(58) a. a-lendô-wo   a-na-bwér-á   ku-mu-dzi (Chicheŵa)
      2-visitor-2those SM.2-RECPST-come-IND 17-3-village
      'Those visitors came to the village.'
   b. ku-mu-dzi   ku-na-bwér-á   a-lendô-wo
      17-3-village SM.17-RECPST-come-IND 2-visitor-2those
      'To the village came those visitors.'

It seems that Luhya always combines Locative Inversion with overt P-incorporation, resulting in the presence of a locative suffix on the verb (which I analyze as the spell-out of an incorporated preposition, analogously to Baker's treatment of applicative morphemes[28]). In a real sense, therefore, Locative Inversion in Luhya seems to always be "beheaded" Locative Inversion: P always raises out of the fronted PP prior to PP-fronting. But a copy of the incorporated P can be spelled out in its base position, inside the fronted PP—and when it is, we get (57b), with P lexicalized both inside the inverted PP and as a locative suffix on the verb.[29]

With the locative suffix in (57b, c) analyzed as an incorporated preposition, it is but a small step from these examples to applicative constructions, which, as I have pointed out, Baker (1988) analyzes in terms of

P-incorporation. The pair in (59) illustrates the applicative alternation for Chicheŵa (examples taken from Baker 1988; see this work for the origin of these examples).

(59) a. ndi-na-tumiz-a   chipanda cha mowa kwa
     SM.1SG-PST-send-ASP calabash of   beer   to
     mfumu (Chicheŵa)
     chief
     'I sent a calabash of beer to the chief.'
  b. ndi-na-tumiz-ir-a   mfumu chipanda cha mowa
     SM.1SG-PST-send-APPL-ASP chief   calabash of   beer
     'I sent the chief a calabash of beer.'

This pair mimics the "beheaded" Locative Inversion alternation in Luhya (57a, c) to a significant degree: the relative order of the major constituents in the complement of the verb is inverted, the erstwhile P-marked noun phrase is no longer accompanied by a preposition, and a suffixal marker surfaces on the verb. In Den Dikken's (1995c) analysis of the dative/applicative alternation, all these properties fall out from the fact that the derivation of the applicative (or double-object) construction involves "beheaded" Predicate Inversion: P raises up, and the remnant dative PP inverts with its subject, the theme. The structures in (60) give a general impression of the Dative Shift alternation on the approach taken in Den Dikken 1995c.

(60) a. V [$_{RP}$ THEME [RELATOR [$_{PP}$ P$_{DAT}$ GOAL/RECIPIENT]]]
   b. V+P$_{DAT}$ [$_{PP}$ t_P GOAL/RECIPIENT]$_i$ [$_{RP}$ THEME [RELATOR t_i]]]

This analysis extends straightforwardly to Dative Shift constructions of the Germanic type, the only difference with Bantu-type applicatives being that there is no overt reflex of P-incorporation in the Germanic languages: the incorporated dative preposition is null.

As Den Dikken (1995c) shows, the "beheaded" Locative Inversion approach to Dative Shift is supported by a variety of empirical facts. One such piece of evidence is the fact that, just as in constructions in which the dative PP is raised via A'-extraction, it is impossible to modify a particle in the double-object construction (see Oehrle 1976, 192; Carlson and Roeper 1980, 150, note 12; Kayne 1985, 126–127).

(61) a. To whom did Brian send (*right) out a schedule?
   b. Brian sent the stockholders (*right) out a schedule.

This suggests that the entire dative PP in the complement of the particle undergoes movement in the derivation of the double-object construction, such movement being contingent on reanalysis of the verb and the particle, which in turn renders particle modification impossible. What tallies with this conclusion is that all and only those particles that are allowed to reanalyze with the verb and, as a result, end up in verb-adjacent position in the prepositional dative construction are the ones that can be used in the double-object construction (as noted by Oehrle 1976, 230–234).

(62) a. Brian read ⟨*back*⟩ the figures ⟨*back*⟩ to me.
     b. Brian read ⟨*off*⟩ the figures ⟨*off*⟩ to the crowd.
     c. Brian read ⟨*out*⟩ the figures ⟨*out*⟩ to the audience.
     d. Brian read ⟨**down*⟩ the announcement ⟨*down*⟩ to the crowd.
     e. Brian read ⟨**in*⟩ the figures ⟨*in*⟩ to the secretary.
     f. Brian read ⟨**through*⟩ the figures ⟨*in*⟩ to the audience.
     g. Brian read ⟨**up*⟩ the figures ⟨*up*⟩ to the guest (on the second floor).

(63) a. Brian read me *back* the figures.
     b. Brian read the crowd *off* the figures.
     c. Brian read the audience *out* the figures.
     d. *Brian read the crowd *down* the announcement.
     e. *Brian read the secretary *in* the figures.
     f. *Brian read the audience *through* the figures.
     g. *Brian read the guest (on the second floor) *up* the figures.

Finally, as Stowell (1981, 342) reports, in double-object constructions with a verbal particle (such as the ones in (63a–d)), it is impossible for the theme to undergo *wh*-extraction—(64b) is ungrammatical.[30]

(64) a. The board sent the members out an announcement.
     b. *This is the announcement which the board sent the members out.

This of course recalls the general ban on A′-extraction of the subject of an inverted predicate, illustrated for both garden-variety and "beheaded" Locative Inversion constructions in (51) and (53). Thus, though "beheaded" Locative Inversion constructions of the type in (50c) are quite limited in distribution in English, the language nonetheless features "beheaded" Locative Inversion productively in the syntax of Dative Shift.

    Having established that "beheaded" Locative Inversion exists and behaves significantly like Copular Inversion, we should now ask *why* it occurs. One thing is clear: once the P-head raises out of the PP, it becomes absolutely obligatory for the beheaded PP to move as well. Thus, there is no variant of Luhya (57a) in which there is a locative suffix on the verb but the PP (beheaded or with an overt head, *ha*; see (57b, c)) stays in situ, to the right of the verb: (57a′) is ungrammatical. Similarly, it is impossible in English to decapitate the dative PP while leaving the PP in situ, to the right of the theme (and the verbal particle, if present): (65c) is impossible.[31]

(57a′) *aBa-xasi Ba-tsiits-aanga-*ho* (ha-)mu-chela (Bantu: Luhya)
        2-woman SM.2-go-TNS-LOCSFX LOC-3-river

(65) a. Brian sent a letter (out) to his friends.
     b. Brian sent his friends (out) a letter.
     c. *Brian sent a letter (out) his friends.

So decapitation of PP is inextricably linked to inversion of the PP with its subject. I will argue in the paragraphs that follow that this can once again be understood from the perspective of licensing requirements—the umbrella generalization in (37), repeated here.

(37) Predicate Inversion involves A-movement to subject position
     triggered by the need to license an empty predicate head.

Suppose that, with the runaway P raising all the way up to V, the beheaded PP were to stay put in its base position. This derivation results in the representation in (66).

(66) $[_V \text{V} + [_R \text{RELATOR} + P_i]_j] (\ldots) [_{RP} \text{DP} [t_j [_{PP} t_i \text{DP}]]]$

In this representation, the trace of the raised preposition is not locally c-commanded by its antecedent—the trace of the RELATOR-head, which has a different index, is in the way. Chomsky (1995, 214, note 20) notes this with reference to an analogous successive-cyclic V-raising derivation. The fact that it is apparently innocuous in the case of verb raising leads Chomsky to conclude, in his chapter 3, that derivationalism is superior to representationalism: while in the final representation the HMC/ECP is violated, it is satisfied at each particular step along the derivation. In more recent work, however, Chomsky has abandoned the syntactic approach to verb raising, relegating all verb movement to PF. The status of the successive-cyclic V-raising argument as an argument for derivationalism then becomes unclear. Suppose, then, that it does matter whether a trace is local to its antecedent in the output representation. If so, (66) is an anomaly: the P-trace t_i cannot be licensed by its antecedent P_i, which is too far removed from it in this structure.

If (66) is ill-formed, a straightforward way of fixing it is to move the beheaded PP into a position which *is* local to the antecedent of the P-trace. And a straightforward way to do that is to apply Locative Inversion to the beheaded PP, resulting in something like (67):[32]

(67) $[_V \; V + [_R \; \text{RELATOR} + P_i]_j] \; [_{PP} \; t_i \; DP]_k \; (\ldots) \; [_{RP} \; DP \; [t_j \; t_k]]$

In this representation, the P-trace t_i is perfectly local to its antecedent P_i and can thus be licensed, as desired. Hence, with P raising to V, the beheaded PP must always undergo inversion with its subject in order to meet the licensing requirements on the empty head of the PP.[33]

I will leave the account of the trigger for "beheaded" Locative Inversion at this admittedly rather sketchy level. While the details of the analysis of "beheaded" Locative Inversion certainly merit much further attention, it seems to me that a reasonable case has been made for the claim that "beheaded" Locative Inversion, like garden-variety Locative Inversion and Copular Inversion, is driven by the need to license the empty head of the predicate of the small clause—a head that is radically empty in the case of Copular Inversion and Germanic-style Locative Inversion but that is a P-trace in need of a local antecedent in the case of "beheaded" Locative Inversion.[34]

4.3   Predicate Inversion: How?

Now that we have an integrated answer to the question of *why* Predicate Inversion happens, let us ask *how* it can come about in the first place. There are two major issues that need to be addressed in this context. First, of course, there is the fact that (1) and (2), repeated below, show an alternation between two word orders, each perfectly grammatical. The question that this poses is how such optionality can be accommodated in a theory, such as that of Chomsky (1995), which abides strictly by considerations of economy of derivation. This question receives an entirely straightforward answer in the analysis of Predicate Inversion constructions presented here, as I will show in section 4.3.1.

(1) a. Brian is the best candidate.
     b. The best candidate is Brian.

(2) a. A picture of Imogen hung on the wall.

    b. On the wall hung a picture of Imogen.

The second question that arises (section 4.3.2) is how the predicate, which after all is farther removed from T than its subject, can make it to SpecTP across the small-clause subject. The locality issues that such movement poses were a major ingredient of the account of the distribution of linker elements in Predicate Inversion constructions in Den Dikken 1995a. I will revisit and develop that account in section 4.5.

4.3.1 Economy

Pairs such as those in (1) and (2) seem, at first blush, to pose a major conundrum for a minimalist approach to syntactic derivation. If both members of the pairs in (1) and (2) are based on the same numeration (i.e., the same set of lexical and functional building blocks), then how could there ever be two surface outputs, given that, plainly, of the two major constituents of the small clause (RP) in (68), the subject is closer to T than the predicate?

(68) T ... [$_{RP}$ SUBJECT [RELATOR [PREDICATE]]]

Collins (1997) addresses this question in particular detail. He comes to the conclusion that Predicate Inversion constructions constitute an argument for *local* rather than *global* economy. Global economy would be unable to make the inverted examples in (1b) and (2b) come out grammatical since their derivation involves at least one more derivational step than that of the a-sentences (for Collins, the additional step is the covert raising of the formal features of the postverbal subject to T, for feature-checking purposes; in the a-cases this step does not ensue since here the subject undergoes category movement to SpecTP overtly). But both the canonical and the inverted word order are compatible with *local* economy: Collins shows that both meet the Last Resort and Minimality conditions, the only local economy conditions postulated.

I will not review Collins's attempt at bringing Predicate Inversion in line with economy—not because I find Collins's account uninteresting or internally flawed but because I believe a key premise on which it is based is incorrect: the assumption that the inverted and noninverted derivations are based on the same numeration.[35] In the foregoing, I have made it clear that Copular Inversion and Locative Inversion constructions differ fundamentally from their uninverted counterparts in featuring a propredicate in addition to the overt (nominal or prepositional) predicate.

(69) a. [TP T . . . [RP *Brian* [RELATOR [*the best candidate*]]]]

 b. [TP T . . . [RP *Brian* [RELATOR [NULL PRO-PREDICATE [CP Op_i [C$_\varnothing$
      [RP t_i [RELATOR [*the best candidate*]]]]]]]]] (cf. (32c))

(70) a. [TP T . . . [RP *a picture of Imogen* [RELATOR [*on the wall*]]]]

 b. [TP T . . . [RP *a picture of Imogen* [RELATOR [NULL PRO-
      PREDICATE] (cf. (46b))

With the structures of the a- and b-examples in (1) and (2) juxtaposed as
in (69) and (70), it will be clear that there is no competition between the
two forms: the predicates in the two members of each pair are different.
In the a-cases, raising of the subject to SpecTP to satisfy the EPP is the
only option because it is the most economical route toward a converging
derivation. In the b-structures, by contrast, there is a compelling need on
the part of the pro-predicate to be licensed, and this need overrides the
desire to settle for least effort (i.e., raising the subject of the small clause):
the predicate *has to* be raised to SpecTP since doing so is the only way to
get the pro-predicate licensed.

4.3.2 Locality

Though economy is not an issue in the sense discussed in the previous
subsection, we still need to ascertain that movement of the predicate to
SpecTP across its subject, which we know is *forced* in the b-structures in
(69) and (70), is actually *legitimate*. To check this, we should ask whether
T can establish an Agree relationship with the predicate (in the sense of
Chomsky 2000, 2001). In order for T to establish an Agree relationship
with the predicate, there must be no phase boundary in between T and
the predicate. And for raising of the predicate across its subject to be
allowed, the two phrases must moreover be equidistant. Both conditions
have to be met in order for Predicate Inversion to be successful. In the
subsections that follow, I will investigate in detail how these conditions
are satisfied in Copular and Locative Inversion constructions.

4.3.2.1 The Small Clause as a Phase   Let us start by asking whether
there are any phase boundaries between T and the predicate of the small
clause in the structures in (69b) and (70b). Given that Predicate Inversion
only occurs in intransitive constructions, we can safely assume that there
will be no *v*P phase between T and the small clause.[36] But the small clause
itself is arguably a phase in its own right: like *v*P (a strong phase that is
itself an instantiation of the RELATOR phrase), it is a Complete Functional

Complex;[37] on the assumption (made explicitly in Chomsky 2001) that (71) is the defining property of phases, small clauses would certainly seem to qualify as phases. Property (72), in conjunction with the Phase Impenetrability Condition in (73), entails that only constituents on the edge of the small clause will be accessible to outside probes.

(71) Phases (Φ) are propositional.

(72) Small clauses are phases.

(73) *Phase Impenetrability Condition* (Chomsky 2001)
In a phase α with head H, the domain of H is not accessible to operations outside α, but only H and its edge.

The effect of (73) is that operations cannot "look into" a phase α below its head H—in order for an outside probe to be able to establish a relationship with something inside a phase α, that something must be either the head of the phase or a constituent on the edge of the phase, where the edge of a phase basically consists of its specifier(s) and anything adjoined to it. In the specific case of a small-clause phase, the RELATOR-head is trivially visible to outside probes: it is the head of the phase. And the small-clause subject, too, should have no trouble establishing Agree relationships with functional heads outside the small clause: it is on the phase edge. But the predicate, it seems, is "trapped" inside the phase. If this is the end of the story, we are in trouble—for clearly, in order for (69b) and (70b) to become part of a converging derivation, the pro-predicate *must* establish an Agree relationship with T and raise up to SpecTP.

There are two ways, in principle, in which this problem can be averted. We can either (i) raise the head of the small-clause predicate up to the RELATOR-head (as in (74a)), or (ii) introduce a functional head outside the small clause and raise the RELATOR-head up to it (as depicted in (74b)).

(74) a. $[_{RP}$ DP $[$RELATOR$+$X$_j$ $[_{XP}$ t_j ...$]]]$
b. $[_{FP}$ Spec $[$F$+$RELATOR$_i$ $[_{RP}$ DP $[t_i$ $[_{XP}$ PREDICATE$]]]]]$

I will discuss each of these strategies in turn, in abstract terms. In subsequent sections, I will then illustrate each strategy with reference to concrete instances of Predicate Inversion.

4.3.2.2 Raising the Predicate Head Before we start, let us quickly remind ourselves of what both strategies in (74) should accomplish: they should (i) ensure the predicate is *visible* to a probe outside the small-clause phase, and (ii) render the predicate and its subject *equidistant*. In the specific case of (74a), raising of the predicate head up to the RELATOR should be the thing that brings both results about.

Let us start with the latter requirement: equidistance. What we want is for raising of the predicate head to the RELATOR to make the extraction site of the raised predicate and the base position of the subject equidistant, in keeping with Chomsky's (1995, 356–357) definition of "closeness":[38]

(75) β is *closer to* K than α unless β is in the same minimal domain as
   (a) τ or *(b)* α.

As Chomsky's own definitions stand, movement of the predicate head to the RELATOR will not actually manage to make the subject position of the small clause a member of the same minimal domain as the predicate's base position: the predicate is excluded as a member of the domain (hence also the minimal domain) of the chain (H, t) on account of the fact that the predicate contains a member of the chain (namely, the trace of the raised predicate head; see Chomsky 1995, 178, 299).[39]

(76) a. The *domain* δ(CH) of CH=(α, t) is the set of categories included
       in Max(α) that are distinct from and do not contain α or t.
   b. The *minimal domain* δ_{MIN}(CH) of CH=(α, t) is the largest subset
       S of δ(CH) such that none of S's members is dominated by any
       member of δ(CH).

A slight modification of the definition of the minimal domain of a head-movement chain, however, delivers the desired result that raising of the predicate head in (74a) makes the predicate's base position equidistant from the subject's: by (77), the minimal domain of the chain (α, t) includes the maximal projection of the raised head (which is included in the minimal domain of the host β of the raised head α).[40]

(77) The *minimal domain* δ_{MIN}(CH) of a chain resulting from head-adjunction of α to β is $\delta_{MIN}(\alpha) \cup \delta_{MIN}(\beta)$.

With the predicate and the subject rendered equidistant as a result of movement of the predicate head to the RELATOR, let us proceed to checking whether (74a) will also make the predicate *visible* to a probe outside the small clause (RP). This is indeed the case, thanks to the fact that raising of the predicate head to the head position of the small-clause phase makes the predicate's features visible on the *head* of the phase (the RELA-

TOR) by literally transferring the features of the predicate head right up to the head of the phase.

(78) Movement of the head H of a phrase HP embedded inside a phase Φ to the head of a phase makes both H and its maximal projection visible to probes outside the phase.

PROBE ... [$_{RP}$ R+H$_i$ [$_{HP}$ ... t_i ...]]
Φ

Movement of the head of a phrase trapped inside a phase to the head of the phase will make not just that head but also its associated maximal projection visible to an outside probe.

As a result of movement of the predicate's head to the RELATOR, therefore, the predicate is free to move past its subject into the domain of an outside probe: it is both equally close to the probe as its subject and not trapped inside the small-clause phase, thanks to the movement of the predicate head up to the head of the phase, the RELATOR.

4.3.2.3 Raising the RELATOR Having established that (74a) does indeed allow us to accomplish both of our goals, let us consider how (74b) manages to make the predicate and its subject equidistant, and how it meets the Phase Impenetrability Condition.

Introducing a functional head F outside the small clause (RP) is tantamount to introducing a landing site both for the RELATOR-head of the small clause and for a phrasal constituent of the small clause—after all, F brings with it the possibility of projecting a specifier. So suppose that we introduce such a functional head outside RP and have it attract the RELATOR-head overtly, as depicted in (74b).[41] On the analogy of Chomsky's (1995, chap. 3) notion of "domain-extending head movement," I will assume, as stated in (79), that movement of the RELATOR-head up to this outside functional head F extends the RP phase up to FP. This phase extension is depicted in (80b).

(79) Movement of the head of a phase to a higher head F *extends the phase* to FP.

(80) a. [$_{RP}$ SUBJECT [RELATOR [PREDICATE]]]
Φ

b. [$_{FP}$ F+R$_i$ [$_{RP}$ SUBJECT [t_i [PREDICATE]]]]
Φ←——————(Φ)

c. [$_{FP}$ PREDICATE$_j$ [F+R$_i$ [$_{RP}$ SUBJECT [t_i t_j]]]]
Φ

This already ensures that movement of the predicate to SpecFP will not illegitimately cross a phase boundary: movement of the RELATOR up to F shifts the phase up to FP, which dominates the first available landing site of the raised predicate. But we still need to contend with the minimality problem: how does the predicate manage to A-move across its subject, which is sitting in a c-commanding A-position? In my earlier work on the syntax of Predicate Inversion (see especially Den Dikken 1994, 1995a), I seized upon the Relativized Minimality problem posed by Predicate Inversion and exploited it to derive the distribution of copular elements in Copular Inversion constructions. In this section, I will reproduce the technical line of thought, built on Chomsky's (1995, chap. 3) original minimalist theory of locality. In the next section, I will then go on and address the empirical support for the account.

A-movement of the predicate across the subject would incur a minimality violation unless (on the assumptions of Chomsky 1995, chap. 3) there is some minimal domain in the structure such that it contains both the small-clause subject and the first available landing site for the moved small-clause predicate. Being members of the same minimal domain, those two positions would then be *equidistant*, so that movement of the predicate around its subject would actually comply with the Minimal Link Condition ("shortest move"). In the locality theory laid out in the original minimalist program, the requisite minimal domain results from domain-extending movement of the functional head of the small clause (the RELATOR) to some higher head position whose specifier serves as a landing site for movement of the inverted predicate. This higher head cannot be the matrix verb: V is a lexical head, and lexical heads (on the theory outlined in chapter 2) do not have specifier positions. So what we need is an additional *functional* head into to which the RELATOR can raise—the F-head in (80). In what follows, I will refer to this F-head as the "LINKER"—the head that provides the *link* between the raised predicate and the small clause that it came from. By having the RELATOR raise to the LINKER, we create a minimal domain that includes SpecFP and SpecRP, thereby enabling the predicate to raise to SpecFP in conformity with the minimalist locality theory.[42]

We have seen so far that movement of the RELATOR up to the LINKER does two things, technically: (i) it extends the RP phase up to the projection of the LINKER, thereby making the predicate visible to probes outside the small clause (including the LINKER itself), and (ii) it makes the predicate eligible for movement across the subject thanks to equidistance. As a matter of fact, the astute reader will have noticed that phase-extending movement of the RELATOR has one further consequence, for the subject of the inverted predicate. I will address this consequence in the next section, after which I will proceed, in section 4.5, to show that movement of the RELATOR up to the LINKER has a number of additional empirical consequences that strongly underpin the Predicate Inversion derivation built on (74b).

4.4 Predicate Inversion and the Postverbal Subject

4.4.1 The Postcopular Subject in Copular Inversion Constructions

While phase extension (as in (80b)) has a beneficial effect for the predicate, it seems to trap the subject of the small clause inside the newly extended phase. The subject of RP, while originally on the edge of the RP phase (see (80a)), ends up being embedded within a phase as a result of Predicate Inversion within FP (see (80c)). As a result, the subject will not be visible to any outside probes. What this means is that, as a consequence of Predicate Inversion inside FP, the subject becomes unable to establish any Agree relationships with outside probes.

This has desirable repercussions in the domain of feature checking and A-movement in Copular Inversion constructions (which are built on (74b): there is no movement of the predicate head up to the RELATOR in these constructions). First of all, the fact that the subject of the small clause is trapped inside a phase is responsible for the fact that, in English Copular Inversion constructions, the finite verb must agree with the inverted predicate, not with the in situ small-clause subject (see (81a))—the latter is simply invisible from T, hence T cannot establish an Agree relationship with the subject, hence cannot check nominative Case directly against T either, as a result of which it surfaces with default accusative case, as in (81b).[43]

(81) a. The biggest problem is/*are the children.
      b. The best candidate is me/her/him.

The fact that the in situ subject of the inverted predicate in (80c) is invisible to outside probes is also responsible for the fact that the subject cannot undergo A-movement across the inverted predicate. That is, after inversion of the order of subject and predicate as in (80c), a T-node outside FP cannot have its EPP property satisfied by attracting the small-clause subject to SpecTP, producing something like (82b).

(82) a. They consider the best candidate to be Brian.
     b. *Brian is considered the best candidate to be.

These effects are the simple corollary of the fact that, as a result of Predicate Inversion in (80c), the subject of the small clause ends up entrenched within a phase.

4.4.2 The Postverbal Subject in Locative Inversion Constructions

Things are different in (74a), the Predicate Inversion derivation built on raising of the predicate head up to the RELATOR. This time, there is no phase extension, hence the subject of the small clause continues to be on the edge of the RP phase. We predict, therefore, that, in the interim structure in (83), the probe T^{EPP} should be able to establish an Agree relationship with both the subject of the small clause (which is on the phase edge "by birth," so to speak) and its predicate (which becomes visible thanks to the fact that its head is raised up to the head of the phase).

(83) $T^{EPP} \ldots [_{RP}$ DP $[RELATOR+H_i [_{HP} t_i \ldots]]]$
          Φ

In principle, therefore, T should be free to attract the PP up to it to satisfy its EPP property but at the same time to establish a φ-feature and Case-checking relationship with the subject of the small clause.

  This is true for Germanic-type Locative Inversion constructions—the finite verb agrees with the postverbal subject here (recall note 34).

(84) a. On this wall hangs/*hang a picture of Imogen.
     b. On this wall hang/*hangs pictures of Imogen.

But for "beheaded" Locative Inversion constructions and for Locative Inversion cases of the Bantu type, it is false. The Luhya and Chicheŵa agreement facts in (57b, c) and (58b), as well as the fact that the preverbal plural in English (85a) triggers plural agreement and the fact that the pronoun in Norwegian (85b) checks nominative Case, tell us without a doubt that subject agreement is controlled in these constructions by the constituent in preverbal position, not by the postverbal subject. This suggests that, whenever T *can* establish all of its feature agreement relationships with one and the same constituent, it *must* do so—"promiscuity" (i.e., a situation in which T satisfies its EPP property by attracting a PP but establishes Agree relationships with a postverbal noun phrase to get its Case and agreement features checked, as in (84)) is allowed only as a last resort.[44]

(85) a. These issues have/*has been little attention to in the literature.
     b. hun/??henne   ble klistret en tøybit   på (Norwegian)
         she.NOM/her.OBL be pasted a patch of fabric onto

When it comes to A-movement of the subject of the inverted PP, the prediction that this should be possible is hard to test. But there is in fact one context in which this is testable: the double-object construction. In section 4.2.2.3, I argued (following the discussion in Den Dikken 1995c, chap. 3) that Dative Shift involves "beheaded" Locative Inversion. Specifically, Den Dikken (1995c, chap. 3) presents an analysis of Dative Shift that runs essentially along the lines of (86), with the (null) dative P raising up to the RELATOR-head of the small clause, and the beheaded PP-predicate raising to the specifier position of a higher particle phrase, inverting with the theme in the process.

(86) a. [$_{\text{PrtP}}$ Prt [$_{\text{RP}}$ THEME [RELATOR+P$_i$ [$_{\text{PP}}$ t_i GOAL]]]]
     b. [$_{\text{PrtP}}$ [$_{\text{PP}}$ t_i GOAL]$_j$ [Prt [$_{\text{RP}}$ THEME [RELATOR+P$_i$ t_j]]]]

Assuming that this is right, let us ask what happens when the triadic verb is passivized. In particular, let us ask which of the two noun phrases (the theme and the goal) T will end up establishing an Agree relationship with. Empirically, what we find is that there is crosslinguistic variation on this point. Within the Germanic language family (excluding Icelandic, Dutch, and German; see Den Dikken 1995c, chap. 4), Norwegian and some (mostly British[45]) varieties of English allow either of the two noun phrases to agree with T and raise to its specifier position (to satisfy T's EPP property). But in other varieties of English, as well as in Danish and Swedish, only the GOAL can be promoted to subject in a double-object passive.

(87)	English-A/Danish/ Swedish	English-B/ Norwegian
a. The boy was given the book.	✓	✓
b. The book was given the boy.	*	✓

The fact that (87b) is grammatical in varieties of English and in Norwegian suggests that it *is* indeed possible to have the subject of the small clause A-move in a "beheaded" Locative Inversion construction.

Clearly, though, such movement is not legitimate across the board. Why do we not find optionality of NP-movement in Standard English, Danish, or Swedish double-object passives? A suggestion that presents itself is that PrtP in (86b) may be a *phase* in certain languages/dialects while it is not a phase in others. In (mostly) British English varieties and in Norwegian, (empty-headed) PrtP is not a phase, hence either of the two constituents inside PrtP may check T's EPP property. But suppose that in Standard English, Danish, and Swedish, PrtP does have the status of a phase.[46] As a result, in these languages, the theme is invisible to T, and only the goal (more precisely, the PP harboring the goal) may check T's EPP property by raising to SpecTP.

(88) $[_{PrtP} [_{PP} t_i \text{ GOAL}]_j [Prt [_{RP} \text{THEME} [\text{RELATOR}+P_i t_j]]]]$
        (Φ) Φ
    a. PrtP$=\Phi$ English-A, Danish, Swedish, etc.
    b. PrtP$\neq\Phi$ English-B, Norwegian, etc.

It is not unreasonable to speculate that the phasehood of PrtP depends on whether Prt is construed as a lexical or a functional element. Particles are famously "in between" lexical and functional elements (see Van Riemsdijk 1990; Den Dikken 1995c), having properties of both. So languages presumably have a choice when it comes to pushing particles into the lexical or functional ballpark. On the further assumption that (89) holds, we may pin the variation among languages with respect to the phasehood of PrtP in (88) down on the question of whether they treat their particles as lexical or functional elements.

(89) Phases are (extended) projections of *lexical* heads.

What seems to go along with this is the fact that theme promotion to subject becomes ungrammatical in all varieties of English when there is an overt particle present under Prt.

(90) a. %The schedule was sent the stockholders.
     b. *The schedule was sent ⟨out⟩ the stockholders ⟨out⟩.

Thus, while in English-B a zero particle may count as nonlexical (hence a PrtP headed by a null particle is not a phase), an overt particle does give its maximal projection phasehood. In English-B, then, the phasehood of PrtP depends on properties of Prt itself, which suggests that Prt defines its own, independent projection in syntax. In English-A, by contrast, the overtness of the particle is inconsequential: here PrtP always counts as a phase, being analyzed as an extended projection of the predicate head, not as an autonomous projection.

4.4.3 The Postverbal Subject and A′-Extraction

While, as we have just seen, there are significant differences between the derivations in (74a) and (74b) in the realm of L-related phenomena (agreement, Case and A-movement), *all* Predicate Inversion constructions behave entirely alike when it comes to A′-extraction of the postverbal subject: it is impossible throughout. We have already had occasion to illustrate this in the foregoing—for A′-movement of the postverbal subject is in effect one of the key diagnostics of Predicate Inversion, as Moro (1997) was the first to stress. The examples in (91)–(94) give an overview of the extraction facts, for Copular Inversion, "true" Locative Inversion, "beheaded" Locative Inversion, and Dative Shift, respectively (see (25), (26), (30), (45), (51), (53), and (64) for other examples showing the same thing).[47]

(91) a. Imogen thinks that the best candidate is Brian.
    b. *Which guy does Imogen think that the best candidate is *t*?

(92) a. Imogen thinks that on this wall hung a picture of Brian.
    b. *Whose picture does Imogen think that on this wall hung *t*?

(93) a. Imogen tror   at   brevet   ble klistret frimerker
      Imogen thinks that letter-the be pasted stamps
      på (Norwegian)
      on
    b. *hvor mange frimerker tror   Imogen at   brevet   ble klistret
      how many   stamps   thinks Imogen that letter-the be pasted
      på?
      on

(94) a. Imogen thinks that Brian sent his friends out an invitation to his party.
    b. *What kind of invitation does Imogen think that Brian sent his friends out *t*?[48]

What we would like to be able to say in some technical way is that it is impossible to extract the subject over its own predicate—but only if that predicate lands in an A-position: for there is nothing seriously wrong (other than a subjacency violation) with A′-extraction of a subject across its own predicate when the latter occupies an A′-position.

(95) a. ??Which guy does Imogen wonder how good a candidate Brian
         considers t_{SU} to be t_{Pred}?
     b. ?Which book does Imogen wonder on which shelf she should
         put t_{SU} t_{Pred}?

The problem lies specifically in the extraction of the subject across its
predicate *in an A-position*. And the problem in question is also specific to
extraction *of* the subject—while the b-examples in (91)–(94) all behave on
a par, there is no uniformity among the various instances of Predicate Inversion in the domain of extraction *from* the postverbal subject.

(96) a. Imogen thinks that the best candidate is a friend of Brian.
     b. *Which guy does Imogen think that the best candidate is [a
         friend of *t*]?

(97) a. Imogen thinks that on this wall hung a picture of Brian.
     b. *Which guy does Imogen think that on this wall hung [a picture
         of *t*]?

(98) a. Imogen tror   at   brevet   ble klistret frimerker fra
         Imogen thinks that letter-the be pasted stamps   from
         Nederland   på (Norwegian)
         Netherlands on
     b. ?hvilket land   tror   Imogen at   brevet   ble klistret
         which country thinks Imogen that letter-the be pasted
         [frimerker fra *t*] på?
         stamps   from on

(99) a. Imogen thinks that Brian sent his friends out an invitation to his
         party.
     b. Which party does Imogen think that Brian sent his friends out
         [an invitation to *t*]?

Though extraction *from* the postverbal subject fails in Copular Inversion
(Moro 1997) and "true" Locative Inversion constructions (Hoekstra and
Mulder 1990; Den Dikken and Næss 1993), it succeeds perfectly well in
"beheaded" Locative Inversion and Dative Shift constructions.

In the case of (97b), the cause of ungrammaticality doubtless lies in the
fact that "true" Locative Inversion constructions in Germanic are topic
islands—the locative PP is base-generated in topic position (see above).
There is arguably nothing specific about movement across the raised
predicate that wreaks havoc in (97b).

The Copular Inversion case in (96b) is not dismissible this way, however. What I take to cause the ill-formedness of this example (following the spirit of Moro's 1997 subjacency analysis in its essentials) is that intermediate adjunction to the extended phase (necessary in order to extract constituents fully enveloped in a phase out of the phase[49]) is impossible in the substructure in (74b) (repeated below)—something that may follow from a general restriction on adjunction that can be formulated as in (100).

(74b) [$_{FP}$ Spec [F+RELATOR$_i$ [$_{RP}$ DP [t_i [$_{XP}$ PREDICATE]]]]]]

(100) Adjunction to meaningless categories is disallowed.

Since FP in the structure of (96b) is the projection of a meaningless LINKER element (the copula), this phrase is not available as an intermediate adjunction site for A′-extraction. This immediately rules out (96b)—and as a matter of fact, it captures the ill-formedness of (91b) as well, by precisely the same token.[50]

Moro (1997) similarly captures the ban on A′-extraction of and from the postcopular subject in Copular Inversion constructions in terms of barrierhood. Moro assumes that the copula is unable to L-mark its small-clause complement (because it is not lexical). As a result, this small clause is a barrier, which means, in turn, that all extraction of and from the subject violates subjacency, and in addition, the trace of an extracted subject fails to be properly governed, in violation of the ECP. But in Locative Inversion constructions, where the small clause is governed by a *lexical* verb, no subjacency or ECP problems are expected to manifest themselves. Moro's approach to (91b) and (96b) thus does not generalize to Locative Inversion constructions. Nor does an appeal to a condition like (100). This is actually a good result in light of the grammaticality of the b-examples in (98) and (99): if the account of the Locative Inversion and Dative Shift cases were to run along exactly the same lines as that of Copular Inversion, we would be at a loss to explain the legitimacy of sub-extraction *from* the postverbal subject in (98b) and (99b). But now we are left with the question of how to rule out extraction *of* the postverbal subject, as in the b-sentences in (92)–(94).

Hoekstra and Mulder (1990, 45–46), in accounting for the ban on extraction of the postverbal subject of Locative Inversion constructions, capitalize on the hypothesis that the subject is coindexed with its predicate, as a result of which A′-extraction of the subject across its coindexed predicate in a higher A-position constitutes a *Strong Crossover* effect (BT-C) of sorts, as depicted in (101).

(101) *[CP [*WH*-SUBJECT]$_i$ . . . [TP [XP PREDICATE]$_i$ . . . [RP t_i [RELATOR $t_{Pred/i}$]]]]

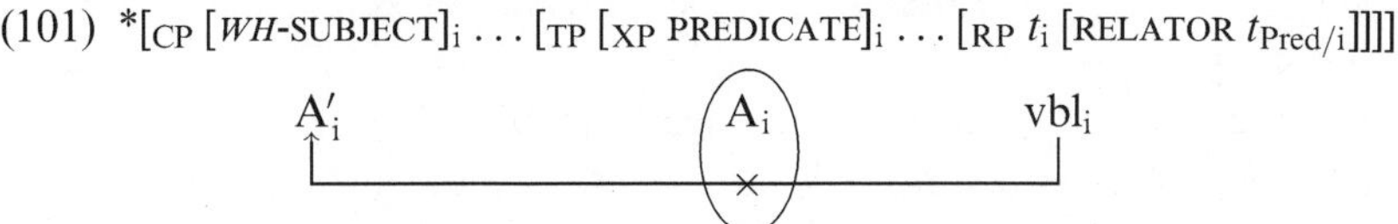

This account (which I adopted in my earlier work; see Den Dikken and Næss 1993 as well as Den Dikken 1995a) is technically sound for the cases for which it was designed (though it stretches the notion of "crossover" and the coverage of BT-C rather far beyond its original limits). But it raises the nontrivial question (first raised by Heycock 1994, 5, note 7) of how the base configuration in the small clause (with the subject asymmetrically c-commanding the predicate with which it is coindexed) escapes a BT-C violation (especially, of course, in predicate nominal constructions).[51] And it also encounters nontrivial trouble in the context of A′-extraction of the predicate across its subject in canonical predication constructions, which is empirically entirely unproblematic (cf., e.g., *How good a candidate do you think Brian really is?* or *On which shelf do you think I should put this book?*). One would presumably have to say (as in Den Dikken 1998b, 206, note 6) that traces left in predicate positions do not qualify as variables, hence do not incur the kind of crossover effect that (101) does. But if A′-extraction of a predicate does not leave a variable, it becomes difficult to make sense of it as A′-extraction to begin with, and it looks like the operator in SpecCP has no variable to bind, resulting in an egregious case of vacuous quantification. Moreover, the very fact that the account based on (101) needs to assume that the predicate is coindexed with its subject makes it fit rather poorly in a minimalist framework (see Chomsky's 1995 remarks about the role of indices in minimalist syntax).

There is, in fact, a much simpler account of the ban on extraction of the postverbal subject of Predicate Inversion constructions available— one that capitalizes on the fact (noted in section 4.1) that the subject of an inverted predicate is invariably a FOCUS.[52] Put differently, the position occupied by the postverbal/postcopular subject in a Predicate Inversion construction is a FOCUS position. And we know independently from languages that displace their (identificational/exhaustive) foci to a designated syntactic position (such as Hungarian) that long-distance displacement of a focus does not proceed successive-cyclically through lower focus positions. To see this, consider the fact that in Hungarian, fronting of the identificational focus triggers placement of the verb to its immediate right, leaving behind any particle-like elements that might accompany the verb. This is shown in (102a). Now, in (102b) (adapted from É. Kiss 2002, 250–251, 254), a construction in which the focus undergoes long-distance fronting into the *matrix* clause (something Hungarian allows freely so long as subjacency is respected), we see that the verb is not separated from its particle in the embedded clause, indicating that no focus movement has applied within the embedded clause.

(102) a. CSAK JÁNOST   hívtam   meg (Hungarian)
       only János-ACC invite-PST-1SG PRT
       'It was only János that I invited.'

     b. CSAK JÁNOST   engedte   [CP hogy meghívjam]
       only János-ACC allow-PST-3SG   that PRT-invite-SUBJUNC-1SG
       'It was only János that she or he allowed me to invite.'

Let us conclude from these data that focus is determined once and for all (recall also note 20, above). A constituent that ends up in a syntactic configuration that leads it to be interpreted as a focus will inevitably be interpreted as the focus of the clause that it is in, and will literally be frozen in place:[53] just as clauses have a unique focus (see É. Kiss 1987), so also is a focus the focus of a unique clause. Any syntactic chain that would lead a constituent to be construed as the focus of *multiple* clauses will be rejected in the pragmatic component. And of course any chain that would lead a constituent to have *contradictory* pragmatic functions is ruled out as well: an expression that is simultaneously a focus and a topic is a pragmatic anomaly. It is plain, therefore, that foci cannot serve as input to topicalization or relativization operations: that would result in an incoherent information-structural profile for the output sentence. We need spill no further ink, therefore, over the ill-formedness of sentences such as (103a) or (103b).

(103) a. *Brian, Imogen thinks the best candidate is.
     b. *Brian is the guy who Imogen thinks the best candidate is.
     c. *How good a candidate does Imogen think is Brian?
     d. The best candidate, Imogen thinks is Brian.

Pragmatic incoherence is also to blame for the ungrammaticality of (103c) (noted by Heycock and Kroch 1999, 377), featuring *wh*-extraction (i.e., focusing) of the inverted predicate of a Copular Inversion construction. The fact that the inverted predicate is and can only be a topic (after all, the postcopular subject, *Brian,* is the focus of the embedded clause, and there generally is a unique focus per clause; cf. É. Kiss 1987) renders it ineligible for focus. But Heycock and Kroch's categorical conclusion, based on (103b), that extraction of the precopular noun phrase in an inverse copular sentence is systematically impossible was clearly arrived at too hastily. For while *wh*-extraction predictably fails, topicalization of the inverted predicate to a position in the matrix clause is grammatical, as shown in (103c). The examples in (104) provide further illustration of the same points.

(104) a. *Brian, Imogen considers her best friend to be.
　　　b. *Whose best friend does Imogen consider to be Brian?
　　　c.   Her best friend, Imogen considers to be Brian.

The examples in (103d) and (104c) instantiate garden-variety syntactic topicalization of the occupant of the subject position (SpecTP) of an embedded clause. This is generally legitimate (cf. *Brian, Imogen thinks should get the award*). Note that *wh*-extraction of an embedded subject is of course fine as well (provided, in English, that the complementizer be dropped): *Who does Imogen think should get the award?* This does not contradict our earlier discussion of the sentences in (103c) and (104b), however. Although the subject position is the *canonical* topic position, it is not true that occupants of SpecTP *must* have the topic function (see Guéron's (1980) *The case was judged, and then a LAWYER appeared,* discussed in section 4.2.1.1). What makes Predicate Inversion constructions differ from garden-variety TPs is that, because of the fact that the postverbal subject takes on the focus function, the predicate in SpecTP cannot, and is thus basically condemned to being the topic, which renders it ineligible for *wh*-extraction.

The pragmatic functions of the inverted predicate and its postverbal subject thus help us make sense of a subset of the extraction restrictions on Predicate Inversion constructions. Most germane to the topic of the discussion in this subsection, we have found that[54]

(105) a. The subject of Predicate Inversion constructions is in a FOCUS
　　　　　position.
　　　b. A′-extraction of a constituent occupying a FOCUS position is
　　　　　impossible.

With this important conclusion in place, I will consider four batches of facts that apparently contradict the ban on movement of the postverbal subject of Predicate Inversion constructions.

4.4.4   Some Special Cases

4.4.4.1   Heavy NP Shift and the Postverbal Subject   From the perspective of the generalizations in (105), it may come as a bit of a surprise that the postverbal subject of a Predicate Inversion construction can be a heavy noun phrase in extraposed position. Thus, sentences such as those in (106a–c) are fine.[55]

(106) a. The best candidate turned out to be ____ after all the job talks had been delivered [the guy that nobody had given a chance at the start of the job search].
     b. On this wall used to hang ____ throughout my entire childhood [a beautiful picture of Brian].
     c. Brian sent his friends out ____ yesterday [a beautifully crafted invitation to his party].

If Heavy NP Shift involves movement, whether rightward (as in the traditional approach) or leftward (followed by remnant movement around the heavy noun phrase, as in Kayne's (1998) analysis; see also Den Dikken 1995b), the facts in (106) pose a serious problem. If, alternatively, Heavy NP Shift constructions involve base generation of the heavy noun phrase in a sentence-peripheral position, associated with a *pro* in the position where it is supposed to pick up its θ-role, there is no conflict between (105) and (106) whatsoever.

(107) ... [RP *pro*ᵢ [RELATOR [PREDICATE]]] ... [DP HEAVY NOUN PHRASE]ᵢ

In this section, I will present an argument in support of (107) as the core of the analysis of Heavy NP Shift, thereby eliminating the threat that the sentences in (106) apparently pose for (105).

Heavy NP Shift has a peculiar tangle of properties, inventoried in a particularly illuminating way in Takano 2003. The process is characterized by the following facts: (i) the heavy noun phrase in extraposed position can antecede an anaphor to its left, as in (108a); (ii) the heavy noun phrase can contain an R-expression coreferential with a pronoun that c-commands the θ-position of the heavy noun phrase (see (108b)); (iii) the heavy noun phrase, in the guise of a negative QP, fails to license a polarity item (here *any*) to its left (see (108c));[56] and (iv) the heavy noun phrase can license a parasitic gap to its left (see (108d)).

(108) a. Imogen wanted to meet ____ until each other$_i$'s trials [the men who had been accused of the crime]$_i$.

   b. Imogen had been requesting that he$_i$ return ____ ever since last Tuesday [the book that John$_i$ borrowed from her last year].

   c. *Imogen tells ____ with any gusto [none of the standard jokes about a duck in a bar].

   d. Imogen offended ____ by not recognizing *pg* immediately [her favorite uncle from Cleveland].

The trick is to reconcile all these facts with one's favorite analysis of Heavy NP Shift. And as Takano (2003) shows, this is by no means easy on a movement-based approach.

To capture (108a), a movement account would need to raise the heavy noun phrase into an A-position from which it can c-command the anaphor, in conformity with Principle A of the Binding Theory (BT-A)—an A-position that arguably needs to be situated in the *matrix* clause given that the *until*-adjunct is most plausibly interpreted as a modifier of *want*. And for (108b), what is needed on the movement approach is that the heavy noun phrase maneuver itself outside the c-command domain of the subject of the embedded clause, into a position that will not feed reconstruction, for otherwise this antireconstruction effect would still fail to fall out. The fact that the heavy noun phrase cannot license a polarity item to its left, whereas a negative adverbial base-generated in a right-peripheral position can (see note 56), shows, as Takano (2003) points out, that a rightward movement account of Heavy NP Shift that takes the heavy noun phrase into the same kind of position as the one occupied by the adverbial will not do. A leftward movement account that has the remnant VP (*tells with any gusto*) shift across the moved heavy noun phrase *will* be able to take care of (108c) on the assumption that polarity item licensing under reconstruction (of the remnant VP) is impossible. But even on this leftward-movement analysis, we still need to grapple with the grammaticality of (108d), which suggests that the heavy noun phrase entertains an A'-dependency with the gap in its θ-position—something hard to reconcile with the arguments based on (108a) and (108b), which both suggest, on the movement analysis, that the heavy noun phrase is raised to an *A*-position. While Postal's (1994) observations about apparent parasitic-gap constructions such as (108d) may call into question the claim that the gap marked by *pg* in (108d) is a genuine parasitic gap, the leftward A-movement analysis continues to raise problems. Thus, one wonders how the heavy noun phrase could A-move past the subject of the embedded clause in (108a, b) (given that A-movement past the subject of a finite clause is not otherwise attested). One also wonders how the heavy noun phrase could manage simultaneously to locally bind the anaphor inside a temporal modifier and to allow an R-expression contained in it to be coreferential with a pronoun in subject position, as in (109).

(109) He$_i$ met ____ during each other$_j$'s trials [the men who Brian$_i$ believed had committed the crime]$_j$.

Here, the lack of a BT-C effect demands that the heavy noun phrase not be reconstructed to a position anywhere in the c-command domain of the subject pronoun, but in order for the heavy noun phrase to be able to locally bind the anaphor *each other*, it would have to occupy an A-position below the subject (for otherwise the subject would be the closest potential A-binder for the anaphor). It seems that there is no way for the movement analysis to meet all the demands in (108)–(109) simultaneously.

By contrast, the base-generation account faces no trouble at all in dealing with these data. To see this, let me be specific first of all with respect to the position of the heavy noun phrase. This noun phrase is base-generated in a very high position in the tree, so high that it will never be c-commanded by the subject of the clause to which it belongs. In fact, one may safely assume that the heavy noun phrase itself is incapable of entertaining *any* relationships with any constituents of the clause to which it belongs: it is extraclausal, probably added in via something like Koster's (2000) "parallel construal," a case of asyndetic coordination.[57]

As a consequence of the fact that the heavy noun phrase originates in an extraclausal position, no R-expression contained in it will ever face the threat of a BT-C violation in the clause to which the heavy noun phrase belongs (see (108b)). By the same token, we correctly expect the heavy noun phrase to be unable to license a polarity item to its left (see (108c)). Its proxy inside the clause, the null pronoun occupying the θ-position, is likewise incapable of licensing the polarity item: there is no negative *pro*; put differently, the negative features of *pro*'s associate are not copiable onto the pronoun. But *pro* being a pronoun agreeing in φ-features with

its associate, it *will* of course be able to antecede an anaphor that it c-
commands. The grammaticality of (108a) is thus taken care of as well.[58]
And finally, the parasitic-gap facts in (108d) (to the extent that they are
a case of genuine parasitic gaps to begin with) can be accommodated
in the same way as Cinque's (1990) approach to island-escaping A′-
dependencies (e.g., ?*Which books are you wondering whether to return to
the library without reading?*) captures their *pg*-licensing capacity: the A′-
binding relationship between the noun phrase and its *pro*-associate is apparently sufficient to license a parasitic gap.

So we have seen that, in contradistinction to movement-based
accounts, a base-generation analysis of Heavy NP Shift constructions
along the lines of (107) takes care of the complicated tangle of properties
of these constructions without any trouble. And as an added bonus, this
analysis will also allow us to avert a collision with the generalizations in
(105) in the face of the grammaticality of the sentences in (106)—with
Heavy NP Shift not involving movement but base generation instead, it
is clear that (106) presents no challenge whatsoever for (105).

4.4.4.2 ***Wh*-in-Situ and the Postverbal Subject**   Having dealt with the
only potential threat to (105) I know of from the realm of overt movement processes, let me take a look now at a number of cases from the
area of LF-movement phenomena that may seem to compromise (105).
The first of these concerns *wh*-in-situ.

Bresnan and Kanerva (1989, 36) note that the postverbal subject of a
Chicheŵa Locative Inversion construction such as (110a) cannot be *wh*-
extracted in the cleft construction, as seen in (110b). This, of course, is
an instance of the generalizations in (105). But interestingly, Bresnan
and Kanerva go on to note that "questioning the inverted subject in place
is fine," as (110c) demonstrates.

(110) a.   pa-m-chenga p-a-im-a   nkhandwe (Chicheŵa)
           16-3-sand   SM:16-PERF-stand-IND 9fox
           'On the sand is standing the fox.'
      b. *n'chi-yâni chi-méné pa-m-cheng ap-á-ím-a?
           COP7-Q   7-REL   16-3-sand   SM:16REL-PERF-stand-IND
           Lit.: 'What is it that on the sand is standing?'
      c.   kodí pá-m-chenga p-a-im-a   chi-yâni?
           Q   16-3-sand   SM:16-PERF-stand-IND 7-what
           'On the sand is standing what?'

Although overt A′-extraction of the postverbal subject fails in Chicheŵa Locative Inversion constructions, it is perfectly possible to form a question via the *wh*-in-situ strategy.

In English, too, it turns out that an in situ [+WH] postverbal subject is grammatical in Predicate Inversion constructions. The multiple *wh*-question in (111b) is a case in point, contrasting robustly with (111a). Similarly, for English Locative Inversion, Coopmans (1989, 733) notes the grammaticality of (111c).

(111) a. *Which boy did this girl say that her greatest love was?
      b. Which girl said that her greatest love was which boy?
      c. Out of which barn ran which horse?

As a matter of fact, (111b, c) even allow a pair-list interpretation: (111b) can receive an answer such as "Imogen said her greatest love was Brian, Sue said greatest love was Bill, Mary said her greatest love was Robin, etc." We are dealing here, therefore, with run-of-the-mill multiple *wh*-questions.

From the point of view of the standard approach to multiple *wh*-questions, which postulates LF-movement of the in situ *wh*-phrase up to the SpecCP occupied by the overtly moved *wh*-phrase in order to form a pair of *wh*-constituents, the grammaticality of (111b, c) constitutes a direct collision with (105)—if, that is, (105) is to hold throughout, including LF. Since it refers to pragmatic functions, it is not immediately obvious that (105) does indeed hold at LF. But I will assume here that it does, in the absence of clear evidence to the contrary. On the assumption that (105) blocks *all* movement of the postverbal subject of Predicate Inversion constructions, including LF-movement, we are then led to the conclusion, in light of the examples in (110c) and (111b, c), that in situ *wh*-phrases do *not* undergo category movement at LF.

That conclusion still leaves room for the possibility that the *wh*-features of the in situ *wh*-phrase move at LF, via *feature movement* (Chomsky 1995). Indeed, there does not seem to be any indication that (105) blocks movement of (a subset of) the features of the focused constituent. LF feature movement thus suggests itself as a way of analyzing the facts in (110c) and (111b, c)—though other possibilities ("absorption" in the semantic component, for instance) present themselves as well.

4.4.4.3 Quantification and the Postverbal Subject Questions about the nature of LF-processes also arise in connection with quantifier scope interaction in Predicate Inversion constructions, which is another potential but merely apparent threat to (105). At first blush, the quantification facts actually appear to provide interesting *support* for (105). Moro (1990, 1997) presents the fact that Copular Inversion constructions, in contradistinction to their canonical counterparts, are scopally rigid as an argument in favor of the Predicate Inversion analysis. Thus, in (112b), the quantified postverbal subject cannot gain scope over a quantifier contained in the fronted predicate.[59] And likewise, as Kuno (1971, 366) has noted, in Locative Inversion constructions, the postverbal subject cannot scope over the raised predicate either, as shown in (113b).

(112) a.   Every boy is the problem in some school.   *some* >/< *every*
     b.   ?The problem in some school is every boy.   *some* >/*< *every*

(113) a.   Some letter was lying in every pigeonhole.   *some* >/< *every*
     b.   In some pigeonhole was lying every letter.   *some* >/*< *every*

But there is reason to believe that (112) and (113) should not be treated exactly on a par. As Heycock and Kroch (1999, 386–387) point out, (112b) is somewhat awkward and, more importantly, to the extent that it succeeds, it forces a nonquantificational group reading onto the postcopular QP. They go on to show that, in general, the second noun phrase in an inverse copular sentence "cannot function as a pure quantifier at all," a claim they support further by pointing out that postcopular noun phrases that are unambiguously quantificational yield ungrammatical results, as (114a) shows. By contrast, there is nothing particularly awkward about (113b), and concomitantly, using an unambiguously quantificational postverbal subject in a Locative Inversion construction is unproblematic: (114b) is fine, but of course it still accepts a only narrow-scope reading for the subject-QP.

(114) a.   ?*Every student's purchase was fewer than six novels.
     b.   In some pigeonhole were lying fewer than six letters.

When we look beyond Copular Inversion and "true," Germanic-style Locative Inversion, we find that in "beheaded" Locative Inversion constructions, the quantification facts are intriguingly subtle. In Norwegian, "true" Locative Inversion and "beheaded" Locative Inversion go their own separate ways, it seems, when it comes to quantifier scope interaction between the postverbal noun phrase and the noun phrase to the left of the finite verb: while (115b) is unambiguous (like English (113b)), (115c) seems to support a wide-scope reading for the existential quantifier in postverbal position.[60]

(115) a. et stempel   ble satt på hvert brev   *a >/< every*
         a postmark be put on every letter
      b. på hvert brev ble satt et stempel   *a *>/< every*
         on every letter be put a postmark
      c. hvert brev ble satt et stempel   på   *a >/< every*
         every letter be put a postmark on

This contrast, and especially the ambiguity of (115c), is worth noting especially in light of an observation made by Bruening (2001)—an observation whose similarity with the one just made will become apparent presently. From Larson's (1988) and Aoun and Li's (1989) work on the dative alternation, we are familiar with the fact that, unlike the prepositional dative construction, the double-object construction is scopally rigid when it comes to the quantifiers in the direct and indirect objects.

(116) a. Imogen gave some book to every boy.   *some >/< every*
      b. Imogen gave some boy every book.   *some >/*< every*

But as Bruening (2001) notes, notwithstanding the fact that the direct object cannot scope over the indirect object in the double-object construction, it *can* still take scope over the subject. Thus, (117b) has a reading that says that in every athletic event, at least two judges thought the athlete in question deserved the medal.

(117) a. I awarded at least two athletes every medal.

                                        at least two >/< every*
      b. At least two judges awarded the athlete every medal.

                                        at least two >/< every

These observations are germane to the topic under investigation because, as I argued above, double-object constructions are "beheaded" Locative Inversion constructions. And what we find in these constructions is that, though the subject of the small clause is unable to scope over a clause-internal QP (the indirect object in (116b) and (117a)), it *can* scope over the QP in SpecTP (see (115c) and (117b)).

In a nutshell, Bruening's analysis of the facts in (117a, b) runs as follows. He capitalizes on the fact that, in constructions like (117a), both objects need to undergo QR to get into a position in which they can be interpreted as quantifiers, while in (117b), the subject QP does not need to undergo QR at all: being in SpecTP is sufficient for the subject QP to be interpretable (see Heim and Kratzer 1998). So in (117b) there is no "QR competition"; but in the example in (117a), since there are two QPs that both need to undergo QR, a Superiority effect ensues: the higher of the two QPs will undergo QR first, the inferior one "tucking in" (Richards 1997) below the superior QP and being destined to have narrow scope vis-à-vis the superior QP. So the direct object QP in (117a) and (117b) does indeed move at LF: it undergoes QR and in so doing is able to gain scope over the subject QP in (117b), but it can never scope over the indirect object QP because it always "tucks in" below the QR-ed indirect object.

Bruening's (2001) analysis of the facts in (117) is couched in the QR-as-pied-piping-movement-at-LF approach to quantifier scope interaction. This is the standard approach, going back to May 1985, treating it in terms of LF-movement of the quantified noun phrases up to adjunction positions in the left periphery of the clause (typically, IP-adjoined positions). As Bobaljik (1995), Groat and O'Neil (1996), and Pesetsky (1998), among others, have shown, this LF-movement-of-the-entire-QP approach can be reanalyzed in terms of overt-syntactic QP-movement—the fact that no overt displacement is perceived then being due to the fact that the lower copy of the moved constituent is sent to PF.[61] Both these approaches share the assumption that quantifier scope interaction involves the raising of entire quantified noun phrases—and both are equally incompatible with the scope facts of Predicate Inversion constructions canvassed in the foregoing. For in Predicate Inversion constructions, movement of the entire small-clause subject is ruled out by (105). Taking (105) to hold throughout the derivation (including at LF), we are led to assume, in light of the fact that quantified small-clause subjects in Predicate Inversion constructions *can* scope out under certain circumstances, that quantifier scope interaction may come about via movement of just the quantifiers themselves, leaving the rest of the noun phrase behind (see Chomsky 1995 on the absence of pied-piping at LF).

While a pied-piping QP-raising approach would wrongly rule them out, a Q-raising approach (raising just the quantifier and not pied-piping its entire container) accommodates the grammaticality of (115c) and (117b) straightforwardly—nothing blocks raising of the quantifier associated with the small-clause subject because, in "beheaded" Locative Inversion constructions, *sub*extraction from the postverbal subject is generally possible (see above).[62] The lack of scope ambiguity in (116b) and (117a) falls out, without further ado, from Bruening's (2001) analysis, which I will adopt.[63] That "true" Locative Inversion constructions do not support quantifier scope interaction is quite simply the consequence of the fact that the PP in sentence-initial position is base-generated in the topic position, a position higher than the highest position that can be reached via QR. That then leaves us with the Copular Inversion facts with which we started the discussion. The question we face here is why the postcopular subject is not allowed to be a genuine quantified noun phrase at all.

The answer to this question should be: because raising the postcopular subject's quantifier up to a scope position at LF is impossible. And indeed, this is precisely what our earlier inventory of the properties of Copular Inversion constructions leads us to expect. For recall that Moro (1997) had found that in Copular Inversion constructions, neither extraction of nor subextraction from the postcopular noun phrase is legitimate.

(118) a.   I think that the cause of the riot was a picture of the wall.
      b. *_Which picture of the wall_ do you think that the cause of the riot was _t_?
      c. *_Which wall_ do you think that the cause of the riot was a picture of _t_?

So in Copular Inversion constructions, neither QP-raising (extraction of the entire postcopular subject) nor Q-raising (subextraction from it) will manage to maneuver the quantifier contained in the postcopular subject up into a scope position, which means that no genuine quantified noun phrases may serve as postcopular subjects in Copular Inversion constructions.

In the end, then, Moro's (1997) scope facts continue to serve as evidence for the predicate-raising approach to Copular Inversion constructions. But the analysis of the scope facts of Predicate Inversion turned out to be subtler than hitherto assumed. A careful analysis of these facts has led me to the conclusion that the analysis of Predicate Inversion does indeed capture the facts, but that these facts have no immediate bearing on the validity of (105). Quantifier scope ambiguity in "beheaded" Locative Inversion constructions such as (114c) and (116b) is the result, not of raising of the entire quantified noun phrase, but of raising of just the quantifier—a case of _sub_extraction from the postverbal subject, not subject to (105).

4.4.4.4 Antecedent-Contained Deletion and the Postverbal Subject In the previous subsection, we were led to adopt a Q-raising approach to quantifier scope interaction. The argument for the alternative approach, in terms of pied-piping movement of entire QPs, generally comes from Antecedent-Contained Deletion (ACD) phenomena, to which I turn now. These phenomena provide perhaps the most interesting challenge, especially when it comes to the reconstruction of the VP-gap.

Both Hornstein (1995, 76) and Bruening (2001) note that there are contexts in which quantified noun phrases seem to be frozen in place as far as their scope relative to other scope-bearing elements is concerned, but they are nonetheless capable of hosting a relative clause containing a VP-gap in the so-called ACD construction. Thus, Hornstein notes that while (119a)—in contradistinction to the ambiguous (119a′)—is scopally rigid (supporting only a narrow-scope reading for the universal), (119b) is perfectly fine even without *to be*.

(119) a.   Someone considers every congressman a fool.

some $>$/*$<$ *every*

a′. Someone considers every congressman to be a fool.

some $>$/$<$ *every*

b.   Someone considers [everyone you do [$_{VP}$ *ec*]] (to be) a fool.

And Bruening (2001) points out that while in double-object constructions, a quantified direct object cannot scope over the indirect object (see (120a); recall the discussion in the previous subsection), the ACD construction in (120b), with the VP-gap inside the direct object, is unobjectionable.

(120) a.   Imogen gave someone everything.   *some* $>$/*$<$ *every*

b.   Imogen gave someone [everything that Brian did [$_{VP}$ *ec*]].

These kinds of pairs present us with an interesting puzzle. On the one hand, the fact that the universal QP cannot gain scope over the existential QP suggests, on a Quantifier Raising approach to quantifier scope interaction, that QR of the universal QP is blocked. On the other, the grammaticality of the ACD examples in (119b) and (120b) suggests that the universal QP, which contains the VP-gap that is to be filled in at LF via reconstruction of the matrix VP, must be able to undergo movement—if the universal stayed put, we would seem to be presented with a case of infinite regress.[64] Bruening (2001), who has presented the most detailed account of these facts to date, concludes from this state of affairs that it must indeed be possible for the universal QP to undergo LF-movement.

He supports his conclusion on the basis of the fact that the inability of the direct object QP in (120a) to gain scope over the indirect object does not translate into a general incapacity on the part of the direct object to scope over higher QPs: as we saw in (117), repeated below, the direct object *can* gain scope over the subject.

(117) a. I awarded at least two athletes every medal.

at least two >/*< *every*

    b. At least two judges awarded the athlete every medal.

at least two >/< *every*

Bruening's analysis of these facts (which capitalizes on the fact that in (117b) the higher QP is in subject position, hence not in need of QR) reconciles them with LF-movement of the direct object QP, and thus makes averting infinite regress in the ACD example in (120b) entirely unproblematic. Bruening can quite simply follow the standard May 1985/Larson and May 1990 account of ACD resolution in terms of QR. It certainly stands out as a significant accomplishment of Bruening's (2001) analysis that it manages to reconcile (120a) with (120b).

But it should be clear that Bruening's (2001) approach to the contrast in (117) does not extend in any obvious way to the contrast Hornstein (1995) noted between (119a) and (119a'): the fact that the existential QP is the matrix subject in both these examples should exempt it from the need to QR, on Bruening's account. The fact, then, that wide scope for the universal QP is out of the question in (119a) must be due to something else. But if that something else is some general ban on LF-movement on the part of the small-clause subject in (119a), the grammaticality of (119b) without *to be* is once again up in the air—it cannot, in any event, be dealt with along the lines of the May 1985/Larson and May 1990 LF-movement account of ACD resolution.[65]

As it turns out, there is strong evidence that such an account cannot cover the entire spectrum of ACD cases at any rate. The evidence in question comes—not surprisingly, in the context of the discussion at hand—from Copular Inversion constructions, in particular cases whose postcopular subject is quantificational and harbors a VP-gap.[66] Consider first the examples in (121) and (122) (the latter modeled on an example from Heycock and Kroch 1999, 386, who discuss the quantificational properties of inverse copular sentences and specificational pseudoclefts in great detail). These are variations on the theme of Hornstein's examples in (119a'), which serve to set the case up.

(121) a. Someone will take every picture that you took to have been the
        cause of a riot. ∃ >/< ∀
     b. Someone will take [every picture that you do [$_{VP}$ *ec*]] to have
        been the cause of a riot.

(122) a. Someone considers every boy to be the problem in this school.
                                                              ∃ >/< ∀
     b. Someone considers [every boy you do [$_{VP}$ *ec*]] to be the problem
        in this school.

Infinitival clauses below *consider* are different from small clauses in this
context when it comes to quantifier scope interaction, as Hornstein
(1995) notes: while (119a) is scopally rigid, (119a′) and the structurally
similar (121a) allow the universal to scope over the existential quantifier
perfectly fine. The fact that (121b) and (122b) are grammatical is hardly
exciting, therefore. I presented these examples only to set up the case that
I am about to make on the basis of the Copular Inversion counterparts to
the examples in (121) and (122), given in (123) and (124).

(123) a. Someone will take the cause of a riot to have been every
        picture that you took. ∃ >/*< ∀
     b. Someone will take the cause of a riot to have been [every
        picture that you do [$_{VP}$ *ec*]].

(124) a. Someone considers the problem in this school to be every boy.
                                                              ∃ >/*< ∀
     b. Someone considers the problem in this school to be [every boy
        you do [$_{VP}$ *ec*]].

Here, what we find is that we get the same split between quantifier scope
interaction and ACD resolution: while (123a) and (124a) show that the
universal QP in postcopular position cannot gain scope over the existential QP in the matrix subject position (in fact, as I pointed out in the
previous subsection, it cannot be a true quantified expression at all; see
Heycock and Kroch 1999), the grammaticality of the b-sentences in
(123) and (124), and similar examples such as (125b), shows that ACD is
unobstructed in this context.

(125) a. I consider [all the boys that you do [$_{VP}$ *ec*]] to be the biggest
        troublemakers.
     b. I consider the biggest troublemakers to be [all the boys that
        you do [$_{VP}$ *ec*]].

Now note that the examples in (123), (124), and (125b) are Copular Inversion constructions and that, as I established in section 4.4.3, the postcopular subject in Copular Inversion constructions is entirely frozen—it can undergo neither A- nor A′-movement, and it disallows subextraction as well.

(126) a.   Imogen considers the best candidate to be a friend of Brian.
      b.   *A friend of Brian is considered the best candidate to be t.
      c.   *Which guy does Imogen consider the best candidate to be t?
      d.   *Which guy does Imogen consider the best candidate to be a friend of t?

On the standard assumption (adopted throughout) that what holds of overt-syntactic movement holds of LF-movement as well, there is no chance, therefore, of performing *any* movement operation on the postcopular subject or a subconstituent thereof in the examples in (123b), (124b), and (125b). Besides, the fact that the postcopular subject cannot be a genuine QP (see Heycock and Kroch 1999 and section 4.4.4.3) makes it unlikely that it would undergo Quantifier Raising to begin with. Thus, ACD resolution via LF-movement of the noun phrase containing the VP-gap seems entirely out of the question in these examples.

At this juncture, one possibility that presents itself is a partial return to a variant of Baltin's (1987) approach to the avoidance of infinite regress in ACD. Baltin argued that overt-syntactic extraposition of the relative clause is what allows the VP-gap to be filled in without the risk of infinite regress; a variant of this approach would have it that the entire noun phrase containing the relative clause is extraposed, via Heavy NP Shift. Both "extraposition" processes arguably involve base generation—presumably in the complement of an abstract functional head that takes the preceding part of the clause as its specifier (see Koster 2000 on the details of this asyndetic coordination approach to extraposition, adopted in section 4.4.4.1). And since neither involves movement, no collision with (105) presents itself.[67]

Concretely, then, one way of analyzing the ACD facts in (123b), (124b), and (125b) is by assimilating them to the likewise perfectly grammatical (albeit somewhat heavy-handed) examples in (127a–c), involving Heavy NP Shift performed on the subject of a canonical copular construction.

(127) a. Someone will take to have been the cause of a riot [every picture that you do [$_{VP}$ ec]].

b. Someone considers to be the problem in this school [every boy
   you do [$_{VP}$ *ec*]].
c. I consider to be the biggest troublemakers [all the boys that
   you do [$_{VP}$ *ec*]].

Here, infinite regress is not an issue, given that the extraposed heavy noun phrase is not a constituent of the matrix VP. Thus, for the specific example in (127c), we can simply copy the contents of the matrix VP, *consider to be the biggest troublemakers*, into the VP-gap in the relative clause, and the desired result comes out: *I consider to be the biggest troublemakers all the boys that you consider to be the biggest troublemakers.*

Now, assuming that the b-examples in (123), (124), and (125) likewise feature (string-vacuous) "extraposition" of the postcopular noun phrase, we can avert the infinite regress that would otherwise ensue without resorting to any kind of movement on the part of the postcopular subject—obviously a desirable result in light of (105). But the astute reader will have noticed that even with "extraposition" of the postcopular subject, our problems with (123b)–(125b) are not entirely over yet. For consider what we would get if we literally copied the content of the matrix VP (not containing the postcopular noun phrase) into the VP-gap inside the relative clause. In the particular case of (125b), that yields (128a)—which is unacceptable.

(128) a. *I consider the biggest troublemakers to be [all the boys that
         you [$_{VP}$ consider the biggest troublemakers to be]].
      b. I consider the biggest troublemakers to be [all the boys that
         you [$_{VP}$ consider to be the biggest troublemakers]].

The problem with (128a) is that it features relativization of the postcopular subject of an inverse copular sentence, something that is *never* possible—it violates (105). While we have now managed to avoid infinite regress without violating (105), we still have a violation of (105) on our hands. What we need to accomplish in one way or another is that the VP of the relative clause can be "rebuilt" as a *canonical* copular sentence— that is, we would like (128b) to come out rather than (128a).

Thus, in order to accommodate the b-examples in (123)–(125), what we need to reconstruct into the VP-gap is something that is not actually being provided in the overt syntax of the examples: a VP in which, in the complement of the ECM-verb, the predicate nominal has not inverted with its subject. The connection between the *actual*, physical VP and the copy reconstructed into the VP-gap thus needs to be looser than expected on a strict reconstruction approach.

Note that this is not the only context in which, for the desired result to come out in ACD constructions, one needs the relationship between the reconstructed VP and its syntactic antecedent to be less than strict. From Fiengo and May's (1994) work on ACD, we are familiar with sentences of the type in (129a), which are grammatical with *John* and *he* coindexed, as marked. As (129b) shows, reconstruction of the exact VP (without the preposition's object) into the VP-gap would result in a BT-C violation. To avert this, Fiengo and May resort to a mechanism they call "vehicle change"—we are allowed to substitute a pronoun for the R-expression *John* inside the reconstructed VP, as in (129c), which is of course perfectly well formed.

(129) a.   Imogen introduced Brian$_i$ to [everyone he$_i$ wanted her to [$_{VP}$ *ec*]].

     b.   *Imogen introduced Brian$_i$ to [everyone he$_i$ wanted her to [$_{VP}$ introduce Brian$_i$ to *t*]].

     c.   Imogen introduced Brian$_i$ to [everyone he$_i$ wanted her to [$_{VP}$ introduce him$_i$ to *t*]].

Returning now to our problem with (123b) and its ilk, what we would like to be able to do is something similar to what happens in (129c): with preservation of the semantics, we rebuild a subpart of the reconstructed VP such that a grammatical result ensues. In (129c) the rebuilding operation in question is pronominalization—semantically entirely neutral, but syntactically highly beneficial since it allows us to steer clear of the Binding Theory violation that looms large. In (123b)–(125b), the trick is to convert the inverse copular sentence of the model VP (the overt copy) back into a canonical copular sentence—that, too, is a semantically neutral operation;[68] and by changing our vehicle (i.e., the specific type of copular sentence) this way, we are awarded a perfectly grammatical output after reconstruction: the sentence in (128b) (for the specific case of (125b)).

I would like to make it absolutely clear that the way I avoided a collision with (105) (the ban on extraction of the subject of an inverse predication) in the *matrix* clause (to avoid infinite regress) is entirely independent of the way I avoided a collision with (105) in the *relative* clause. *Any* strategy that successfully "removes" the postcopular subject from the matrix VP will have to face the problem in (128a). The "vehicle-change" approach to this problem that I laid out in the preceding paragraphs is what I suggest here as a possible (and potentially quite interesting) way out of this problem.

The solution to the other problem—that is, *how* to "remove" the post-copular subject from the matrix VP—is not in any way contingent on that of the problem posed by (128a). I have suggested that an "extra-position" approach, inspired by Baltin (1987), has the desired effect of producing a VP that does not contain the postcopular subject *without moving that noun phrase*, thereby allowing us to meet the demands of (105). By invoking an "extraposition" approach to infinite regress avoid-ance for examples of the type in (125b), I am in no way committed to a wholesale adoption of a Baltin-type approach for ACD constructions in general—that is, an "extraposition" approach to (125b) and its ilk may be right while at the same time a QR-type analysis is correct for the more familiar cases. In the foregoing discussion, we have seen that (i) there are contexts in which Quantifier Raising is literally raising of *just* the quantifier (see section 4.4.4.3), and (ii) there are contexts in which in-finite regress avoidance in ACD constructions does not involve movement of the container of the relative clause harboring the VP-gap; but these conclusions leave entirely unaffected the possible existence of pied-piping movement (whether at LF or in the overt syntax) of quantified noun phrases ("QP-raising"). Nothing in the above is incompatible with QP-raising per se. We should be free, therefore, to continue to invoke it— and it seems likely that we do indeed need something like QP-raising in the analysis of ACD constructions of the type in (121b), (122b), and (125a): the surface position of the container of the VP-gap makes it clear that no account in terms of "extraposition" will do here.[69]

The message of the preceding discussion, then, is this: though QP-raising may very well exist and is presumably necessary in the account of, for instance, ACD constructions like (121b), it is not the one and only mechanism by which quantifier scope interaction and ACD are to be treated; alongside QP-raising, the grammar employs the independently motivated mechanisms of Q-raising (i.e., movement of the quantifier by itself, stranding the rest of the noun phrase) and "extraposition" (i.e., the base generation of constituents in clause-external positions).

4.4.5 Conclusion

With this message in place, I conclude this discussion of the vicissitudes of the small-clause subject of Predicate Inversion constructions by reiterating that extraction of this constituent is systematically forbidden, both in overt syntax and at LF—a conclusion that reconfirms Moro's (1997), and that can now be chalked up as a powerful diagnostic for Predicate Inversion.

4.5 Predicate Inversion and the Distribution of the LINKER

In section 4.3, I argued that there are two ways Predicate Inversion can be rendered compatible with locality: (74a) and (74b), repeated here.

(74) a. $[_{RP}$ DP $[\text{RELATOR}+X_j$ $[_{XP}$ t_j ... $]]]$
    b. $[_{FP}$ Spec $[F+\text{RELATOR}_i$ $[_{RP}$ DP $[t_i$ $[_{XP}$ PREDICATE$]]]]]$

We have already seen that the parallel existence of (74a, b) has a number of beneficial consequences. In this section, I will investigate another spin-off of the two analyses of Predicate Inversion constructions in (74a, b)—the predictions they make with respect to the distribution of copular elements.

4.5.1 Copular Inversion and the LINKER

On the assumption that the LINKER in (74b)/(80) is spelled out as the copula (the Latin word *copula* literally means "link(er)"), the derivation of Predicate Inversion via raising of the RELATOR makes interesting predictions with respect to the distribution of the copula, as was first shown in Den Dikken 1995a.

4.5.1.1 Copular Inversion and the Distribution of the Copula The alternation in (1) (repeated here) is customarily called the Copular Inversion alternation because, as its name suggests, it features the copula as the pivot in between the two noun phrases.

(1) a. Brian is the best candidate.
    b. The best candidate is Brian.

Even in contexts in which in the "canonical" construction (the a-case) there is no need for a copula, one finds a copula cropping up in the "inverse" case. Thus, while in (130a) the copula may be either present or absent (depending on whether *consider* selects a small clausal complement or a *to*-infinitive), in the Copular Inversion case in (130b) *to be* is inomissible (unless (130b) is given the intonation of a Heavy NP Shift construction, irrelevant here; recall section 4.4.4.1), as Moro (1990, 1997) first pointed out.

(130) a. Imogen considers Brian (to be) the best candidate.
      b. Imogen considers the best candidate *(to be) Brian.

One might be tempted to think that the copula is needed in (130b) because of some semantic property of the inverse copular sentence—its alleged "equative" nature, for instance. What seems to lend support to this kind of approach is that in typical equative copular sentences like *Your opinion of New York is my opinion of Amsterdam*, the copula is needed in the complement of *consider* regardless of the order in which the two noun phrases show up. This was first noted by Heycock and Kroch (1999).

(131) a. Imogen considers Brian's opinion of New York *(to be) her
         opinion of Amsterdam.
      b. Imogen considers her opinion of Amsterdam *(to be) Brian's
         opinion of New York.

But Heycock and Kroch (1999) are quick to point out that one cannot attribute the semantics of equation to the copula and ascribe the obligatoriness of *to be* in (130b) and (131b) to "equative" semantics (whatever that may be). For, as Heycock (1994) noted, in examples such as (132b), an inverse copular sentence of the same type as (130b), no copula is necessary at all. I agree with Heycock and Kroch (1999) (and, ultimately, Aristotle, in *De Interpretatione*), therefore, in denying the copula any semantic contribution: it is a meaningless element whose presence in the structure is forced by (morpho)syntactic constraints.

(132) a. If Bill has an alibi for 6 p.m., that makes John the murderer.
      b. If Bill has an alibi for 6 p.m., that makes the murderer John.

In the case of (130b), one might also be tempted to think that the syntactic constraint in question is the need for space—after all, if the predicate is to invert with its subject via A-movement, as I argued in section 4.1, then there had better be an A-position available that the predicate could land in. The fact that no A-specifier is available in between the small-clause subject position and the matrix verb *consider* will then straightforwardly rule out the variant of (130b) lacking *to be*: the inverted predicate simply has no place to land. In the variant of (130b) that does contain *to be*, on the other hand, there *is* a landing site available for the raised predicate, hence the derivation converges.

Moro (1997) takes an approach to the facts in (130) that basically runs along the lines just sketched. But it can easily be shown that the availability of space per se is not the issue when it comes to the distribution of the copula in Copular Inversion constructions.[70] For even when there *is* in fact space available for the predicate to move to, the copula is still obligatorily present, as Heycock (1994) points out.

(133) a. Brian is considered (to be) the best candidate.
     b. The best candidate is considered *(to be) Brian.

The obligatoriness of the copula in (133b) cannot this time be blamed on mere space considerations: regardless of the presence of *to be*, the SpecTP position of the *matrix* clause will serve as the landing site of the raised predicate. So space per se is not the issue either; there must be something else that is responsible for the obligatory presence of the copula in (133b).

That "something else" was made readily available by the discussion of phase-extending head movement in the previous section: on the assumption that the LINKER in (74b)/(80) is spelled out as the copula *be*, the obligatoriness of the copula in (130b) and (133b) can be tied to the fact that inversion of the predicate around its subject, in contexts in which the head of the predicate is not raised up to the RELATOR (as in all Copular Inversion cases), is dependent on the inclusion in the structure outside the small clause of the LINKER head. This is the core of the account of the distribution of the copula under Predicate Inversion outlined in Den Dikken 1995a.

4.5.1.2 The Nature of the LINKER The discussion in Den Dikken 1995a was careful to point out that it would be wrong to assume that the LINKER would *always* be spelled out as an overt copula *(be)* whenever it occurs in the structure. There are three kinds of counterexamples to the claim that *be* is audible whenever the LINKER is present: two apparent and one genuine.

Consider first of all the example in (134b), the Copular Inversion counterpart of (134a).

(134) a. Imogen considers Brian (to be) the best candidate and John (to
       be) the worst.
     b. Imogen considers the best candidate *(to be) Brian and the
       worst (to be) John.

The first conjunct of (134b) shows the expected behavior: *to be* is obligatory, just as it is in (130b). But in the second conjunct, *to be* can be omitted in both (134a) and (134b), the latter apparently contradicting our earlier conclusion that *to be* must be present in the complement of *consider* in cases of Copular Inversion. The thing to note about the second conjunct of (134), however, is that it is amenable to PF *ellipsis*— material in the second conjunct can be elided under identity with material in the first (cf. *Imogen considers Brian to have given the best performance and John, the worst*). In the version of (134b) lacking *to be* in the second conjunct, therefore, what we are arguably dealing with is a case of PF ellipsis of *to be*, as in (135), where strikeout indicates ellipsis.

(135) Imogen considers the best candidate *(to be) Brian and the worst ~~to be~~ John.

In the light of the fact that the syntax forces the presence of *to be* under *consider* in Copular Inversion constructions, as seen in (130b) and the first conjunct of (134b), the grammaticality of ellipsis of *to be* in the second conjunct of (134b) tells us that this instance of ellipsis should be thought of in terms of phonological deletion or nonrealization of material that *is* present in the syntax, not in terms of the missing material being radically absent at S-structure and being "syntactically reconstructed" at LF (see also Den Dikken, Meinunger, and Wilder 2000).

A second type of apparent counterexample to the obligatoriness of the copula in constructions in which a LINKER head is present in the structure comes from (136) (adapted from Heycock 1994).

(136) a. The best solution seems *(to be) instant retreat.
       b. The best solution remains instant retreat.
       c. The best solution becomes instant retreat.

Predicate Inversion indubitably applies in (136b, c), just as in (136a), but only in this latter case do we find a token of the verbal copula to signal the application of Predicate Inversion. To accommodate (136a) versus (136b, c), one may decompose *remain* and *become* into *continue+to be* and *come+to be*, respectively, so that there will in fact be a token of *be* present in the structure of these examples.[71] Thus, like (134b), the examples in (136b, c) are merely apparent counterexamples to a general claim that says that a form of the copula pops up whenever the LINKER is projected.

But a decompositional account of the type espoused for (136b, c) will not carry over to (132b), repeated below: we cannot decompose *make* into *cause + to be* since *make* can actually embed overt *be* itself (as in *Imogen made Brian (be) more careful*; see, e.g., Ritter and Rosen 1993, 537).

(132b) If Bill has an alibi for 6 p.m., that makes the murderer John.

To understand the absence of a copula in (132b), it is important to get a perspective on the nature of the LINKER that facilitates the inversion of the predicate around its subject.

Recall from chapter 2 that I systematically spell the RELATOR of predication relationships with small capitals to indicate that it does not represent a lexical category of its own: it represents a syntactic position that can be realized by all sorts of elements (including prepositions such as *as, by, for*, and French *à*, and things like Top or the various functional categories that Cinque (1999) introduces in his syntax of adverbial modification). Analogously to my approach to the RELATOR in chapter 2, I spell LINKER with small capitals as well, to reflect the fact that, once again, I am not proposing a new lexical element but instead make a claim about the *syntax* of the constructions at hand—the claim, in particular, that the syntax needs an additional functional projection immediately outside the small clause ("RP") when (non-"beheaded") Predicate Inversion takes place. The head of that functional projection may be lexically realized as the copula (the LINKER par excellence), as in (136a), but other elements (including inaudible ones) may also serve as the host of phase-extending head movement of the RELATOR-head.

In particular, in the example in (132b), the role of LINKER is played by the functional category Asp (short for "Aspect"). Example (132b) is a resultative construction, and arguably the internal structure of the complement of verbs taking resultative secondary predicates is larger than that of verbs like *seem* or *consider*—in particular, it contains a projection of Asp (or dependent Tense; see, e.g., Guéron 1990 on particle small clauses, Guéron and Hoekstra's (1993) T-chains, and Déchaine's (1993, 21) Predicate Visibility Principle). And with Asp sitting in between the verb and the small clause (RP), its specifier position can serve as the landing site of Predicate Inversion in (132b), and its head as the receptacle for raising of R, the functional head of the small clause.

(137) [$_{VP}$ *makes* [$_{AspP}$ [*the murderer*]$_j$ [Asp+RELATOR$_i$ [$_{RP}$ [*John*] [t_i t_j]]]]]

Asp has no overt realization in (137)—there is no aspectual particle spelling it out. Thus, the result of Predicate Inversion in (137) will not give rise to any phonetic material between the raised predicate and its subject.

As a matter of fact, when the Asp-head under matrix *make* does have a phonetic realization (in the form of a particle like *out*), it turns out to be unable to serve as a host for the raised R-head: sentences like (138b) are ungrammatical. To accommodate Predicate Inversion in contexts like these, what is needed is a copula, as in the example in (139b), the Predicate Inversion counterpart to (139a).

(138) a.   They made John out the murderer.
       b.   *They made the murderer out John.

(139) a.   They made John out to be the murderer.
       b.   They made the murderer out to be John.

Similarly for *turn out* and *end up*: as (140) and (141) show, though *be* is omissible in the canonical a-examples, it is obligatorily present in the Predicate Inversion cases in (140b) and (141b). So what we see is that aspectual particles (such as *out* and *up*) are unable to serve as hosts for raising of the RELATOR—there is a ban on incorporation into these elements, ostensibly due to their lexical properties. The null Asp-head in (137), by contrast, does manage to host the raised RELATOR-head, functioning as the LINKER that facilitates Predicate Inversion.

(140) a.   John turned out (to be) the best candidate.
       b.   The best candidate turned out *(to be) John.

(141) a.   John ended up (being) the best candidate.
       b.   The best candidate ended up *(being) John.

This discussion tells us that different elements can serve as LINKERS (copulas, null aspectual heads), hence that there is no dedicated functional category "LINKER." It also shows that the use of a copula is called on only if all else fails—that is, the copula is used as a LINKER only as a *last resort*, if nothing else can serve as the LINKER that can host the raised functional head of the small clause and whose specifier can provide a landing site for the raised small-clause predicate. These are important conclusions to bear in mind in the discussion to follow.

4.5.2 Locative Inversion and the LINKER

Moving on to Locative Inversion, let me start out by returning to the analysis of "beheaded" Locative Inversion due originally to Den Dikken and Næss (1993) and adopted in the above.[72] In this analysis, the head of the PP predicate raises to the functional head position of the locative small clause and stays there, the remnant PP being fronted across its subject via Predicate Inversion. The structure in (142a) (= (56b)), then, is part of the analysis of beheaded Locative Inversion constructions such as (52c) (repeated below as (143a)). And after (142a) has been established, the next thing that happens is inversion of the remnant PP around the subject. But notice that this does not result in *på* traveling further up the tree: as the surface word order in (143a) shows, *på* stays to the right of the small-clause subject (which is in SpecRP) through the entire derivation; it is impossible to place *på* to the left of *frimerker*, as the ungrammaticality of (143b) (on the intended reading[73]) indicates. So, apparently, (142b) does *not* arise.

(142) a.   [$_{RP}$ [*frimerker*] [RELATOR+$på_i$ [$_{PP}$ t_i *brevet*]]] (= (56b))
       b.   *[$_{FP}$ [$_{PP}$ t_i *brevet*]$_j$ [LINKER+[RELATOR+$på_i$]$_k$ [$_{RP}$ [*frimerker*] [t_k
            t_j]]]]

(143) a.   brevet   ble klistret frimerker på (= (52c))
            letter-the be pasted stamps   on
       b.   *brevet   ble klistret på frimerker
            letter-the be pasted on stamps

Despite the application of Predicate Inversion, there is apparently no need for a projection of a LINKER in "beheaded" Locative Inversion constructions, therefore. This follows from the Predicate Inversion derivation built on (74a), featuring raising of the predicate head up to the RELATOR: as I showed in section 4.3.2.2, raising the predicate head up to the phase-head both establishes equidistance for the predicate and the subject and allows the predicate to be visible to probes outside the small clause. And since there is no need for one, no LINKER will be introduced into the structure—LINKERs are merged only as a *last resort*.

This in turn means that "beheaded" Locative Inversion, while possible in ECM contexts such as (144), where a landing site is available outside the locative small clause, should be impossible in the immediate complement of the verb selecting the locative small clause: regardless of whether *på* is placed to the right of to the left of the small-clause subject (*frimerker*), the output of (145) is ungrammatical.[74]

(144) jeg så   brevet   bli klistret frimerker på (Norwegian)
       I   saw letter-the be pasted stamps   on

(145) *jeg tror   at   han har   klistret [t_i brevet]$_j$ {$på_i$} frimerker
        I   believe that he   have pasted   letter-the   on   stamps
       {$på_i$} t_j
        on

It is entirely impossible, therefore, to create space inside the complement of the verb for the application of (beheaded) Locative Inversion. This comports with our earlier conclusion that there is no LINKER projected in these constructions.

What this shows is that it would be wrong to make a blanket statement to the effect that every single instance of Predicate Inversion requires the presence of a LINKER. A subtler account is needed. The difference between Copular Inversion and "beheaded" Locative Inversion lies in the question of whether or not the head of the small-clause predicate raises to the RE-LATOR, the functional head of the small clause. When it does, as in (74a), Predicate Inversion can proceed without a projection of a LINKER being introduced outside the small clause (and hence, by economy, no LINKER may be merged, with the consequence that embedded inversion, as in (105), fails). When it does not, on the other hand, a LINKER is necessary and hence obligatory.

4.5.3   The Distribution of the LINKER: Summary

What we have seen in this section is that instances of Predicate Inversion employing the strategy in (74b)—the phase-extending head-movement scenario—feature a LINKER element in the position of the small-clause external functional head. That LINKER element is spelled out as an overt *copula* whenever a small-clause external functional head needs to be produced specifically for the purpose of accommodating phase-extending head movement to facilitate Predicate Inversion. But when phase-extending head movement can exploit a preexisting F-head outside the small clause as its landing site, no copula will surface. Such is the case in the English example in (136), analyzed as in (137), where an *aspectual* head serves as the receptacle for phase-extending head movement and has its specifier position accommodate the raised small-clause predicate. With Asp serving as the LINKER, no copula surfaces.

(74) a. $[_{RP}$ DP $[\text{RELATOR}+X_j$ $[_{XP}$ t_j ... $]]]$

b. $[_{FP}$ Spec $[\text{F}+\text{RELATOR}_i$ $[_{RP}$ DP $[t_i$ $[_{XP}$ PREDICATE$]]]]]$

Cases of Predicate Inversion featuring the derivation in (74a), by contrast, never need a LINKER element outside the small clause—and because no small-clause external functional head is needed to render the predicate visible to an outside probe (since movement of the predicate head up to the RELATOR takes care of this already), no LINKER can be employed in such instances of Predicate Inversion. This explains why the raised predicate head cannot be taken up further, via movement of the RELATOR-head to a small-clause external F-head: that is, it explains why Norwegian (143b) (analyzed as in (142b)) crashes.

The distribution of the LINKER as well as its lexicalization as a copular element are strictly governed by considerations of *economy*, therefore. A small-clause external LINKER will be called upon only if phase-extending head movement is required to make the predicate attractable by an outside probe (hence only in cases in which the predicate head does not leave the predicate); and the LINKER will be lexicalized as a copular element only if no other functional category immediately outside the small clause can take care of hosting the raised RELATOR-head.

These are key conclusions that will serve as the starting point for a discussion of Predicate Inversion and LINKERs in the nominal domain—the topic of the next chapter.

4.6   Concluding Remarks

In this chapter, I have occupied myself with the analysis of Predicate Inversion within the theory of principles and parameters—specifically, its most recent incarnation, the minimalist program (Chomsky 1995 and subsequent work). I have found occasion to make a rough cut, within the realm of Predicate Inversion constructions, between Copular Inversion and Locative Inversion, the latter in its turn factoring out into two subtypes, dubbed "true" and "beheaded" Locative Inversion.[75]

What all Predicate Inversion constructions, regardless of their specific flavor, share is the fact that their derivation involves *A-movement* of the small-clause predicate into a specifier position—either SpecTP or (in cases in which Predicate Inversion takes place in embedded contexts that are smaller than TP) a lower A-specifier position. As a result of A-movement of the predicate across its subject, the latter becomes the FOCUS of the construction, something that has important consequences in the domain of A′-extraction, as section 4.4.4 showed in detail.

The head of the raised predicate is systematically empty—either a null pro-predicate (as in the case of Copular Inversion and "true" Locative Inversion constructions) or the trace of a raised P (in "beheaded" Locative Inversion cases). It is the emptiness of the predicate head that was isolated as the *trigger* for Predicate Inversion: the need to get the null predicate head licensed is what drives predicate raising to subject.

In all instances of Predicate Inversion, the raised predicate satisfies the EPP property of the probe in its final resting place. But all Predicate Inversion constructions add something "greedy" to this altruistic scenario: the need to get the predicate's own null head licensed. If the predicate had not raised and T had attracted the small-clause subject up to satisfy its EPP property, the predicate and its null head would have been trapped inside the small clause, with no hope for salvation.

The account of the properties of Predicate Inversion constructions developed in these pages relies heavily on a theory of locality of the type developed in Chomsky's minimalist work, featuring equidistance and what I have dubbed phase-extending head movement.[76] It is the need for phase-extending head movement in Predicate Inversion constructions in which the predicate head does not raise up to the RELATOR (all Copular Inversion constructions, in particular) that gives us a window on the distribution of copular elements in such constructions. For the need for domain-extending head movement translates into a need for a small-clause external functional head, the LINKER.

(146) A LINKER is an RP-external functional head facilitating phase-extending head movement.

This LINKER-head is lexicalized as a copular element (with *copula* literally meaning "linker") whenever there is nothing else (such as aspect) to represent this functional category. This outlook on the relationship between Predicate Inversion and the LINKER gives us a well-defined and explanatory perspective on the distribution of the copula in inversion constructions.

Appendix: On the Limited Distribution of Copular Inversion

In section 4.2.1.2, I drew attention in passing to the fact that not just any small-clause predicate can undergo inversion with its subject. Thus, simple predicational copular constructions like (147a) radically resist inversion.

(147) a.　Imogen is a girl. (= (19))
　　　b.　*A girl is Imogen.

I pointed out in that subsection that the restriction operative here is not formulable in any straightforward way in terms of a definite versus indefinite dichotomy on the part of the predicate nominal—for (148a) and (149a) (which repeat (20) and (21)) do support Copular Inversion.

(148) a. Brian is an excellent doctor. (= (20))
      b. An excellent doctor is Brian.

(149) a. The Vietnam War and the Gulf War are examples of this.

                                                              (= (21))
      b. Examples of this are the Vietnam War and the Gulf War.

My conclusion in section 4.2.1.2 was that only the *specificational* and *equative* members of Higgins's (1979) typology of copular sentences are eligible for Copular Inversion (see also Campbell's (1997, 169) claim that definite and *specific*-indefinite nominal predicates, but not nonspecifics, can undergo Copular Inversion). This generalization covers both the familiar cases in which the inverted predicate is definite (such as (1b), *the best candidate is Brian*) and the examples in (148b) and (149b) (which are specificational by the criteria that Higgins isolates: in particular, they have the characteristic of specifying a value for a variable, reflected in the prosody by colon or list intonation following the copula), and correctly excludes (147b).

By this criterion, examples of the type in (150), due to Emonds 1976 and discussed in Hoekstra and Mulder 1990 (see also Birner 1994 and Ueno 2005), qualify as specificational copular sentences as well: they, too, feature the list intonation characteristic of these constructions.

(150) a. More important has been the establishment of legal services.
      b. Equally difficult would be a solution to Russell's paradox.
      c. Speaking at today's lunch will be our local congressman.
      d. Taking tickets at the door was a person I had previously
         roomed with.

But Heycock (1994, 1998b) points out that there are significant differences between inverse copular sentences such as (1b), *The best candidate is Brian*, on the one hand, and examples of the type in (150), on the other. One major—and from our perspective essential—difference between them is the fact, noted in Heycock (1994, 16), that while genuine Copular Inversion always forces the emergence of a copula (the lexicalization of the LINKER) in contexts in which in the absence of inversion no copula would be necessary (see (151)), inversion in examples of the type in (150) does not.[77]

(151) a. Brian is considered (to be) the best candidate.
      b. The best candidate is considered *(to be) Brian.

(152) a. ?Most embarrassing would have been considered losing your
         keys.
      b. ?Most incompetent were judged the students of the French
         department.

This leads me to conclude that, whatever they are,[78] sentences of the type
in (150) are *not* instances of Predicate Inversion in the sense in which I
used this label in the foregoing—that is, they do not involve raising of
the predicate to subject position. The fact that the predicate in these
examples does not appear to be empty-headed, unlike in the case of genuine Predicate Inversion constructions (see section 4.2.2), also casts doubt
on the viability of a predicate-raising to subject analysis of these sentences: there would appear to be no motivation for such movement.

The examples in (148b) and (149b) do pass the LINKER test: (153a, b)
are grammatical only with *to be* included.

(153) a. An excellent doctor is considered *(to be) Brian.
      b. Examples of this are considered *(to be) the Vietnam War and
         the Gulf War.

But Heycock (1998b) notes that even these examples differ in significant
ways from the Copular Inversion constructions discussed in this chapter.
The differences between standard Copular Inversion and the cases in
(148b) and (149b) manifest themselves on four planes: agreement, binding of variable pronouns, embedding in nonbridge contexts, and subject-
auxiliary inversion. I illustrate these differences in turn.[79]

• Agreement

While, as we have seen, Copular Inversion constructions derived via raising of the predicate to subject position have the fronted predicate trigger
agreement on the finite verb (see (154), but recall note 13 for some qualification), constructions of the type in (148b) and (149b) give rise to agreement with the postcopular noun phrase, as shown in (155).

(154) The biggest problem is/*are the factory closings.

(155) a. Delinquency is a major problem in today's society; also a big
         problem are/*is factory closings and fascist propaganda.
      b. A case in point are/*is their remarks about passive sentences.
                                                         (See note 14)

· Binding of variable pronouns

In Copular Inversion constructions, a pronoun embedded in the raised predicate cannot be bound by a quantified postcopular noun phrase (see (156b)). There are a number of explanations available for this. First, the predicate, by virtue of having undergone raising to subject position (A-movement), is not reconstructible into its base position, from which it would be c-commanded by the QP. Second, as Heycock and Kroch (1999) point out, the postcopular subject of a genuine Copular Inversion construction can never be a true quantified noun phrase (recall section 4.4.4.3); so a bound-variable interpretation is unavailable for the pronoun inside the fronted predicate for that reason as well. In any event, in constructions of the type in (148b) and (149b), it *is* possible to have a pronoun inside the precopular constituent bound by the postcopular QP, as shown in (157).

(156) a. [Every country in Western Europe]$_i$ was the enemy of its$_i$ neighbor.
      b. *The enemy of its$_i$ neighbor was [every country in Western Europe]$_i$.

(157) (In the late nineteenth century Japan became a threat to its neighbors.)
      Also a threat to its$_i$ neighbors was [every/more than one country in Western Europe]$_i$.

· Embedding in nonbridge contexts

There is no problem whatsoever with embedding garden-variety Copular Inversion constructions—both under bridge verbs such as *think* and in nonbridge contexts, the result of such embedding is fine (see (158)). Constructions of the type in (148b) and (149b), on the other hand, are embeddable under bridge verbs only: the example in (159b) is not fully acceptable.[80]

(158) a. Imogen thinks that the best candidate is Brian.
      b. Imogen wonders whether the best candidate is Brian.

(159) a. Imogen thinks that a fine candidate would be Brian.
      b. ?Imogen wonders whether a fine candidate would be Brian.

· Subject-auxiliary inversion

Inverting the order of the raised predicate and the finite auxiliary in yes/ no questions is generally grammatical in Copular Inversion constructions of the familiar sort (see (160)).[81] But in constructions of the type in (148b) and (149b), it does not work.

(160) a. Was the cause of the riot a picture of the wall?
      b. Is the biggest problem the factory closings?

(161) *Are a big problem the factory closings?

To account for the properties of constructions of the type in (148b) and (149b), Heycock (1998b) suggests a treatment that basically follows the analysis of Copular Inversion constructions advanced originally in Heggie 1988, according to which the precopular constituent is raised to SpecCP. Of course, Heggie's analysis is unsuitable for genuine Copular Inversion constructions, as has become abundantly clear. But it is indeed a reasonable candidate, a priori, for the analysis of sentences such as *A big problem is the fascist propaganda*. It will capture the four properties just mentioned without much ado: since the precopular noun phrase never makes it to SpecTP, it will be unable to control subject agreement; its raising to SpecCP, being an instance of A'-movement, is reconstructible, allowing for the binding of a variable pronoun inside the precopular noun phrase; and its occupying SpecCP makes it incompatible with embedding in nonbridge contexts,[82] and with subject-aux inversion.

But one thing does not quite fit in with the raising-to-SpecCP approach: sentences of the type in (159b) are "not bad enough" to support the analysis. While it is indeed entirely impossible to embed a full-fledged CP below *whether* (see (162)), (159b) is only marginally deviant (see also note 80).

(162) *Imogen wonders whether how good a candidate {is Brian/Brian is}.

As an alternative to the raising-to-SpecCP approach, I suggest an analysis of sentences like *A big problem is the fascist propaganda* that treats the precopular constituent as a topic base-generated in SpecTopP. And in so doing, I assimilate inverse copular sentences of this type to a subtype of specificational pseudocleft constructions identified by Den Dikken, Meinunger, and Wilder (2000): the "Type A" specificational pseudocleft.

Den Dikken, Meinunger, and Wilder (2000) present an extended argument to the effect that, within the class of specificational pseudocleft constructions (SPCs), one should distinguish two subtypes, Type A and Type B SPCs. Type B is the familiar type, arguably involving Predicate Inversion (as argued in Heggie 1988; see our discussion of Copular Inversion constructions as concealed SPCs of this type). Type A is different—not pragmatically (the *wh*-constituent is a topic in both cases, and the post-copular constituent is the focus) but syntactically. While the precopular *wh*-constituent in Type B SPCs sits in SpecTP, that of Type A SPCs is base-generated in the topic position, SpecTopP. Unlike in the case of Type B SPCs (whose *wh*-constituent is arguably a free relative), the *wh*-constituent of Type A SPCs is a full-fledged *wh*-question. The gross structure of Type A SPCs is thus that of a question-answer pair, with the *wh*-clause in SpecTopP serving as the question and the constituent in the complement of Top^0 (the comment, a full TP) functioning as the answer.

(163) [$_{TopP}$ [*wh*-clause] [Top [$_{TP}$ . . .]]]

Many specificational pseudoclefts are presumably ambiguous between Type A and Type B. But SPCs that have a polarity item in the postcopular constituent, such as (164a), are amenable only to a Type A analysis. Den Dikken, Meinunger, and Wilder (2000) show in detail that a Type B approach to (164a) cannot get the postcopular polarity item licensed. The Type A analysis, by contrast, base-generates (164a) as (164b), which, for many speakers, is grammatical as is (see Clifton 1969, 38; Ross 1972, 89; Kayne 1998, 26; Schlenker 2003; Higgins (1979, 86), however, finds things like (164b) "irremediably anacoluthic") and has the polarity item licensed perfectly straightforwardly within the TP that serves as the comment.

(164) a. What nobody bought was any wine.
     b. What nobody bought was [$_{TP}$ nobody bought any wine].

Having established that SPCs of the type in (164a) are only analyzable as Type A SPCs, we can use the properties of these pseudoclefts to check the syntactic distribution of the structure in (163). And what Den Dikken, Meinunger, and Wilder (2000) have found is that they marginally resist embedding in nonbridge contexts but are completely incompatible with subject-auxiliary inversion.[83]

(165) a. ?Imogen wonders why what nobody bought was any wine.
     b. *Was what nobody bought any wine?

In this respect, Type A SPCs closely mimic the behavior of inverse cop-ular sentences like *A big problem is the fascist propaganda*—there, too, we found that embedding in nonbridge contexts is marginal (see (159b)) and subject-aux inversion is entirely impossible (161).

Let us assume, then, that sentences such as *A big problem is the fascist propaganda* are like Type A SPCs, with the base-generated topic being the precopular noun phrase. Within the TP that serves as the comment, we will still need to take care, of course, of the fact that the subject surfaces in postcopular position, and that the precopular subject position is apparently empty. The way to ensure this is naturally the same as in the case of Germanic-style Locative Inversion constructions. There, too, I argued that the preverbal constituent is a base-generated topic, and I took the topic to be linked to a null pro-predicate that inverts with its subject by raising to SpecTP, as in (166a). Carrying this analysis over to inverse copular sentences of the type in (148b) and (149b), I now suggest (166b) (featuring the words of the running-text example *A big problem is the fascist propaganda*) as the structure of these constructions.

(166) a. [$_{\text{TopP}}$ [$_{\text{PP}}$ *on this wall*]$_i$ [Top$_\varnothing$ [$_{\text{TP}}$ [$_{\text{PP}}$ PRO-PREDICATE]$_i$ … [$_{\text{RP}}$ *a picture of Brian* [RELATOR t_i]]]]]

b. [$_{\text{TopP}}$ [$_{\text{DP}}$ *a big problem*]$_i$ [Top$_\varnothing$ [$_{\text{TP}}$ [$_{\text{PP}}$ PRO-PREDICATE]$_i$ … [$_{\text{RP}}$ *the fascist propaganda* [RELATOR t_i]]]]]

Via the Type A SPC route, then, we have ended up with an analysis of inverse copular sentences such as (148b) and (149b) that treats them on a par with Locative Inversion constructions—which is highly desirable in the light of the fact that the two have mostly parallel syntactic distributions (see the restrictions on embedding Germanic-style Locative Inversion, the impossibility of subject-aux inversion, and the fact that the finite verb agrees with the postverbal subject). Though I will not develop the analysis of these inverse copular sentences any further, I believe that there is a reasonable case to be made for the idea that they instantiate a structure of the type in (166b), with the precopular constituent occupying SpecTopP.

If, then, sentences like *A big problem is the fascist propaganda* have essentially the properties of Type A SPCs, we can conclude that, in fact, *all* inverse copular sentences are hidden specificational pseudoclefts. For in the case of garden-variety Copular Inversion constructions, I had already reached the conclusion (in section 4.2.2.1) that these feature a reduced free relative raised to SpecTP, mimicking the derivation of Type B SPCs (for which I assume, in line with Heggie 1988, that the *wh*-constituent is a free relative originating as the predicate of a small clause).[84]

One of the questions that stand out at this point is why the split between Type A and Type B structures of inverse copular sentences appears to be determined on the basis of the definiteness of the predicate nominal. Sugita 2001 is an interesting attempt to derive the definiteness requirement imposed on Type B cases from the semantics of these constructions, the key idea being that these sentences must involve set identification (of the sets denoted by the two noun phrases) in order to be grammatical.[85] But work remains to be done for the syntax. For there are copular sentences whose predicate nominals are introduced by the definite article and for which a semantics of set identification would appear to be perfectly feasible but that nonetheless are altogether ineligible for inversion: as Heycock (1998b) notes, while the canonical copular sentence in (167a) is perfect, (167b) is bad. This particular pair appears to be a member of a class of copular sentences that resist inversion as a consequence of the quantificational properties of the predicate nominal. Thus, Heycock (1998a) points out that (168b), with a universally quantified predicate nominal, is likewise ungrammatical; and to this we may add that (169b), with a negative QP serving as the predicate, fails as well.

(167) a. Brian is the one thing I want a man to be (i.e., he's honest).
       b. *The one thing I want a man to be is Brian.

(168) a. Brian was everything I needed (he was smart, considerate, resourceful).
       b. *Everything I needed was Brian.

(169) a. Brian is none of the things I would like a man to be.
       b. *None of the things I would like a man to be is Brian.

Due to the quantificational properties of their predicate nominals, the b-sentences in (167)–(169) are unanalyzable as Type A constructions, with the predicate nominal base-generated in a high topic position of the type that hanging topics originate in: QPs will not serve as hanging topics.[86] But apparently, a Type B analysis, with the QPs as part of a reduced free relative raised to SpecTP, fails as well. Notice that the variants of the b-examples with full-blown free relatives are also ungrammatical, as is shown in (170a–c), which all contrast sharply with something like *What's our biggest problem is the children*, the grammatical full free relative counterpart of *Our biggest problem is the children*.

(170) a. *What is the one thing I want a man to be is Brian.
       b. *What was everything I needed was Brian.
       c. *What is none of the things I would like a man to be is Brian.

The parallel between the ill-formedness of the b-examples in (167)–(169) and that of the sentences in (170) supports the analysis of inverse copular sentences involving fronting of the physical predicate to SpecTP that I have developed in the foregoing, according to which the fronted predicate is a reduced free relative. But it still begs the question of *why* these sentences are ungrammatical. Answering this question, which seems to be more about the restrictions on pseudoclefts than about the properties of inverse copular sentences per se, is beyond the scope of this work.

I am fully aware that the preceding paragraphs have by no means succeeded in solving all the problems surrounding the analysis of inverse copular sentences such as *A big problem is the fascist propaganda*. These paragraphs are not intended as a full-blown analysis of these constructions. Their purpose in the context of this work is basically to show that standard Copular Inversion constructions of the type in (1b), *The best candidate is Brian*, and apparently similar but in some vital respects quite different cases like *A big problem is the fascist propaganda* can both be treated as instantiations of the general schema of Predicate Inversion: in both, an underlying predicate is raised to an A-specifier position across its subject, the latter staying in its base position. What makes them differ from each other is the question of whether the precopular noun phrase is physically the raised predicate itself or instead is sitting in a topic position and is associated with a null pro-predicate that undergoes Predicate Inversion. This difference has important consequences both with respect to the clause-internal properties of the construction (agreement, in particular) and when it comes to the external syntactic distribution of the construction (embedding, subject-aux inversion). These properties fall out directly from the position of the physical predicate nominal: SpecTP or SpecTopP. But regardless of where the physical predicate nominal is placed, all inverse copular sentences are derived via Predicate Inversion.

Chapter 5

Predication and Predicate Inversion inside the Nominal Phrase

In chapter 2, where I developed my perspective on the syntactic representation of predication relationships, I argued that there are two ways, in principle, in which a predicate can be related to its subject via a RELATOR—the predicate may either be the complement or the specifier of the RELATOR, with the subject sitting in the other position inside RP.

(1) a. [$_{RP}$ [$_{XP}$ SUBJECT] [$_{R'}$ RELATOR [$_{YP}$ PREDICATE]]]

                             (Predicate-complement structure)

   b. [$_{RP}$ [$_{XP}$ PREDICATE] [$_{R'}$ RELATOR [$_{YP}$ SUBJECT]]]

                             (Predicate-specifier structure)

In chapter 4, I subsequently argued that the predicate-complement structure in (1a) may serve as input to Predicate Inversion in syntax, with the predicate raising to a higher A-position, crossing the base position of its subject along the way. In cases in which the head of the predicate does not raise out of the predicate prior to Predicate Inversion, I showed that the application of Predicate Inversion leads to the inclusion in the syntactic structure of a projection of a LINKER element, which serves multiple purposes: it provides a landing site for the raised predicate, it procures a host for the raised RELATOR (which must raise up to the LINKER in order to render the subject's base position and the predicate's landing site equidistant from the predicate's extraction position), and it is an extended phase (thanks to movement of the RELATOR to the LINKER).

(2) [$_{FP}$ [$_{XP}$ PREDICATE]$_j$ [$_{F'}$ LINKER+RELATOR$_i$ [$_{RP}$ [$_{NP}$ SUBJECT] [$_{R'}$ t_i t_j]]]]

In chapters 2–4, I made the case for the existence of both (1a) and (1b) as well as for the operation of Predicate Inversion on the basis of subject-predicate relationships in the clause—mostly copular sentences. But there is no reason, a priori, to expect (1) and (2) to be *confined* to the clausal domain. Predication relationships are not in any way the privilege or prerogative of clauses; we would expect to find them elsewhere in the syntax as well. A good place to look for nonclausal instances of (1) and (2) is the complex noun phrase. For as Abney (1987) and Szabolcsi (1983, 1994) (and others in their wake) have argued in detail, there is considerable parallelism between the syntax of the clause and the syntax of the noun phrase. Without duplicating Abney's and Szabolcsi's arguments to this effect, what I will do in this chapter is present a further piece of support for the parallel between clauses and nominal phrases by showing in detail that both predication structures in (1) as well as Predicate Inversion (2) are attested inside the noun phrase.

5.1   Qualitative Binominal Noun Phrases and the Nondirectionality of Predication

I will start the discussion of predication and Predicate Inversion inside the nominal phrase by studying in detail the most complicated case known to me—the QUALITATIVE BINOMINAL NOUN PHRASE (QBNP).[1]

(3) a. a jewel of a village
    b. an idiot of a doctor

QBNPs come in two general flavors—a point first made, to my knowledge, in Napoli 1989 and picked up in Doetjes and Rooryck 2001. I argue, in the latter's wake but on the basis of different evidence, that both involve noun-phrase internal predication but only one of them features Predicate Inversion. The noun phrase in (3a) instantiates what I will refer to as the *comparative* QBNP (on account of the fact that it draws a *comparison* between a village and a jewel). I will argue that it has an underlying predicate-complement structure that is input to Predicate Inversion, with *jewel* (the predicate nominal) inverting with its subject (*village*) in the course of the derivation. The QBNP in (3b) supports this derivation as well, but is more saliently interpreted in such a way that it ascribes a property to the referent of the noun phrase *in his or her capacity of a doctor*. On that latter interpretation, the noun phrase in (3b) exemplifies what I will call the *attributive* QBNP, drawing an explicit parallel here with attributive constructions of the type discussed in chapter 2 under the rubric of the predicate-specifier structure (e.g., *big for a butterfly* and *an idiot as a doctor*). In attributive QBNPs (in which N_1 is typically a specimen of what Milner (1978) calls the closed class of *noms de qualité* 'quality nouns' and N_2 names a professional occupation), then, the two noun phrases are base-generated in their surface order, with the predicate nominal (*idiot*) preceding its subject.

It will be good, right at the outset, to show that the distinction between attributive and comparative QBNPs is not merely an interpretive distinction. That it plays an important role in syntax is shown particularly clearly by Napoli's (1989, 203) observation (attributed to Giulio Lepschy) that, while English (3b) is ambiguous between an attributive and a comparative reading, Italian formally distinguishes between the two interpretations.

(4) a. quell' ignorante di dottore (Attributive) (Italian)
        that   ignoramus of doctor
    b. quell' ignorante del   dottore (Comparative)
        that   ignoramus of-the doctor

Thus, (4a), with a "naked" noun phrase in the position following *di* 'of', is unequivocally attributive (the referent of the complex noun phrase is an ignoramus *in his capacity as* a doctor, while he may be quite knowledgeable otherwise) whereas (4b), whose second noun is adorned with a definite article, is unambiguously comparative, with the property of being ignorant applying to an individual that happens to be a doctor by profession (and may, in fact, excel in that capacity).

While in both (3a) and (3b), the second noun phrase is marked with its own indefinite article and is separated from the predicate nominal by the element *of*, a variant of the attributive QBNP exists that has the two noun phrases juxtaposed without the intervention of any lexical material between the two nouns.

(5) a. (*)a jewel village
    b.   an idiot doctor

The construction in (5b) is a third subspecies of QBNP, a subspecies of the attributive type. Though the fact that it features two nouns in direct juxtaposition makes it look like a case of N-N root compounding, it differs radically from a root compound like *brain doctor* both in its interpretation and with respect to its prosodic contour: it has the semantics of an attributive QBNP like (3b), and it has the *second* noun carry the intonation peak (cf. *an idiot dóctor* versus *a bráin doctor*). For the comparative QBNP in (3a), there is no counterpart in which the two nouns are directly juxtaposed: though (5a) is fine as a root compound, with stress on the first noun (interpretable as something like 'a village with lots of jewels' or 'a village where jewels are made'), it does not support a reading in which it corresponds to (3a), with its characteristic intonation contour with stress on the second noun (whence the bracketed asterisk on (5a)). Since comparative QBNPs do not have an *of*-less counterpart, this means that examples of the type in (5b) are unambiguously attributive—unlike (3b), which supports two readings (teased apart in Italian by the distribution of the definite article on N_2, as seen in (4)), the noun phrase in (5b) can only ascribe to its referent the property of being an idiot in his or her capacity of being a doctor, not as an individual.[2] We can bring out this difference between (3b) and (5b) by putting these noun phrases in contexts such as those in (6) (see Hulk and Tellier 2000): while (6a), which highlights the attributive reading, is felicitous both with and without *of a*, (6b) is awkward if *of a* is left out.

(6) a. That idiot (of a) doctor prescribed me the wrong medicine.

$\qquad\qquad\qquad\qquad\qquad\qquad\qquad\qquad\qquad\qquad\qquad$ (Attributive)

$\quad$ b. That idiot #(of a) doctor just wrecked my car.   (Comparative)

From this brief introduction, it will have become clear that QBNPs present a variety of challenges, in the area of the distribution of the element *of* in between the two noun phrases and the (im)possibility of having an articleless, bare noun phrase serve as the subject of predication. I will try to meet these challenges in what follows, where, among other things, I will argue that the *of* of QBNPs should be likened to the clausal copula *be*.

(7) *Of* is a nominal copula.

Like *be*, the "nominal copula" *of* can serve as a lexicalization of the RELATOR-head of the small clause, and in Predicate Inversion constructions, it spells out the small-clause external LINKER.

At the outset of this exercise, let me point out that what unites all qualititative binominal noun phrases is that they are characterized by the fact that the first noun phrase ascribes a property to the noun phrase that follows it. On the assumption (see chapter 2, sections 2.1 and 2.2.4) that property ascription, in general, is structurally represented in the form of a predication structure, with the ascriber of the property being the predicate and the ascribee the subject, this leads us to the postulation of a syntactic structure underlying *all* QBNPs according to which there is a predicational relationship between the two noun phrases (see Napoli

1989 and Suñer 1990; also Kayne 1994, Den Dikken 1995a, Español-Echevarría 1997, 1998, and Hulk and Tellier 1999).[3] In the linear string of all QBNPs, the predicate precedes its subject, but only in what I am referring to as *comparative* QBNPs does this order result from inversion of the predicate around its subject. I will turn to the derivation of comparative QBNPs of the type in (3a) (*a jewel of a village*) in section 5.3, after having laid out the syntactically rather simpler analysis of *attributive* QBNPs such as (3b) (*an idiot of a doctor*), to which I turn right away.

5.2 Attributive QBNPs: A Predicate-Specifier Structure

In this section, I will be concerned with the syntax of QBNPs of the type in (3b) and (5b), which are characterized by their *attributive* reading: the referent of the noun phrase is said to be an idiot *in his or her capacity as* a doctor. The attributivity of these constructions leads me back to facts discussed in chapter 2.

5.2.1 Attributive Constructions: A Recapitulation

In the discussion of the fundamental nondirectionality of predication relationships in chapter 2, we looked at constructions of the type in (8a) and identified them as instances of the predicate-specifier structure in (1b).

(8) a. Imogen is beautiful as a dancer.
    b. Imogen is a beautiful dancer.

Modeling the analysis of (8a) on that of (8b), which has a reading in which it is equivalent to (8a), I analyzed both constructions in terms of a structure in which *beautiful* is a predicate of *dancer* originating in the specifier position of the RELATOR phrase. In (8b), the predicate-specifier structure constituted by *beautiful dancer* (with a silent RELATOR) is embedded under an indefinite article and the noun phrase in the complement of the RELATOR is itself a bare NP (see (9b)); in (8a), by contrast, the noun phrase in the complement of the RELATOR (which is spelled out here as *as*) includes an indefinite article, and concomitantly the RP comprising *beautiful as a dancer* is not NumP-embedded (see (9a)).[4]

(9) a. $[_{RP_2}$ *Imogen* $[_{RELATOR_2}=be$ $[_{RP_1}$ $[_{AP}$ *beautiful*$]$ $[_{RELATOR_1}=as$ $[_{NumP}$
    a $[_{NP}$ *dancer*$]]]]]]$
    b. $[_{RP_2}$ *Imogen* $[_{RELATOR_2}=be$ $[_{NumP}$ *a* $[_{RP_1}$ $[_{AP}$ *beautiful*$]$
    $[_{RELATOR_1}=\emptyset$ $[_{NP}$ *dancer*$]]]]]]$

Concretely, then, the difference between (8a) and (8b) lies primarily in the question of whether the predicate-specifier RP is NumP-embedded or not. And correlated with that seem to be two other things: the presence or absence of an article on the second noun phrase, and the presence or absence of an overt lexicalization of the RELATOR-head (*as* in (8a)). In section 2.6.4, I concluded from the facts in (8) versus (10) that when the RELATOR takes a bare nominal complement (as in (9b)), it must be silent.

(10) a. *Imogen is a beautiful as dancer.
    b. *Imogen is beautiful a dancer.

5.2.2   The Analysis of Attributive QBNPs

With this in mind, consider the facts in (11), whose b-examples were studied in Napoli 1989, 242–255.

(11) a. He is an idiot as a doctor.
       He is a fool as a policeman.
       He is a madman as a driver.
       He is a simpleton as a judge.
       He is a nincompoop as a technician.
    b. He is an idiot doctor.
       He is a fool policeman.
       He is a madman driver.
       He is a simpleton judge.
       He is a nincompoop technician.

Aarts (1998) claims that these b-examples are "contractions" of their counterparts in (11a) featuring *of a*.[5] He suggests that *of a* is "a pragmatic marker, which signals that phrases that contain it should receive an evaluative reading" (p. 150), and that "for literal [Q]BNPs, such as *fool of a policeman*, compression is unproblematic because they do not lose their evaluative feel when *of a* is deleted" (p. 151).[6] But as I will show in a protracted argument permeating this entire chapter, *of* is not a marker of any semantic or pragmatic notion whatsoever—it is a semantically empty copula, present for purely structural reasons. A moment's reflection should make it clear that there is little hope of deriving the "evaluative reading" of the constructions in (11a) (let alone those in (11b)) from *of* (or *of a*): as is of course well known and scarcely in need of illustration, *of* occurs in all sorts of noun-phrase types, most of which have no "evaluative reading" at all. At the risk of stating the obvious, let me just mention here the fact that a noun phrase like (12) has a wide range of interpretations (including at least possessive, objective, and agentive interpretations: 'a picture possessed by a woman', 'a picture depicting a woman', and, somewhat marginally, 'a picture painted by a woman') alongside the (not hugely salient but definitely available) "evaluative" (comparative) QBNP reading in which the woman in question is said to be like a picture (so beautiful).

(12) a picture of a woman

Since *of* (or *of a*) does not bring in any meaning, there is little point in deriving the b-examples in (11) from the a-cases via what Aarts calls "compression."

Instead, the approach to the alternation between the a- and b-examples in (11) that I will take here assimilates it to that seen in (7a, b). Such an assimilation is entirely straightforward. In fact, all that needs to be done is to replace the AP in the specifier position of RP_1 with a nominal constituent, as in (13) and (14). As in the case of (9a, b), we find that the RELATOR is null in the structure in which it takes a bare noun phrase as its complement, as in (14b).[7]

(13) a. Doctor Slop is an idiot as a doctor.
    b. $[_{RP_2}$ *Slop* $[$RELATOR$_2$=*be* $[_{RP_1}$ $[_{NumP}$ *an* $[_{NP}$ *idiot*$]]$ $[$RELATOR$_1$=*as* $[_{NumP}$ *a* $[_{NP}$ *doctor*$]]]]]]$

(14) a. Doctor Slop is an idiot doctor.
    b. $[_{RP_2}$ *Slop* $[$RELATOR$_2$=*be* $[_{NumP}$ *an* $[_{RP_1}$ $[_{NP}$ *idiot*$]$ $[$RELATOR$_1$=$\varnothing$ $[_{NP}$ *doctor*$]]]]]]$

The part of the structure following *be* in (14b) is a nominal phrase; in (13b), on the other hand, what follows *be* is another small clause, with two nominal subconstituents. The structures in (13b) and (14b) lead us to expect, therefore, that *an idiot doctor* should have the external syntactic distribution of a noun phrase while *an idiot as a doctor* should not. This is borne out, as seen in (15a, b).

(15) a. *Some idiot as a doctor prescribed me the wrong medicine.
    b. Some idiot doctor prescribed me the wrong medicine.
    c. Some idiot of a doctor prescribed me the wrong medicine.
    d. [Idiot {of/*as} a doctor] that you are!

To complete the paradigm, I added, in the c-example, the attributive QBNP featuring *of*. And as a moment's glance reveals, the c-example patterns like the b-example and unlike the a-sentence (see also the exclamative in (15d)). Thus, even though *an idiot of a doctor* is like *an idiot as a doctor* in featuring a prepositional element (*of*/*as*) and an indefinite article sandwiched between the first and second nouns, the two constructions exhibit entirely different external syntactic distributions: only the structure dominating *an idiot of a doctor* should bear a nominal label.

For the analysis of the attributive QBNP with *of*, what we are looking for, therefore, is a structure that shares with that of *an idiot doctor* its outward nominality, but patterns with that of *an idiot as a doctor* in its internal makeup. The structure in (16b) does just that.[8]

(16) a. Doctor Slop is an idiot of a doctor.

   b. [$_{RP_2}$ *Slop* [RELATOR$_2$=*be* [$_{DP}$ D$_\varnothing$ [$_{RP_1}$ [$_{NumP}$ *an* [$_{NP}$ *idiot*]]
        [RELATOR$_1$=*of* [$_{NumP}$ *a* [$_{NP}$ *doctor*]]]]]]]]

Since the individual nominal subconstituents of the small clause RP$_1$ are already as large as NumP (each has its own indefinite article), I labeled the top node of the predicate nominal constituted by *an idiot of a doctor* as "DP," headed by a null determiner.

The fact that, while the RELATOR of the inner small clause is lexicalized (after all, its complement is not a bare noun phrase) in both (13) and (16), the form of the RELATOR is different (*as* versus *of*) is arguably relatable to the presence of this D-head in the structure in (16b). In (13b), the RP within which the relationship between *an idiot* and *a doctor* is established is the complement of the verbal copula *be*; in (16b), this RP is the complement of D, with the RELATOR thus being embedded in a *nominal* structure. My claim in this chapter is that, in English, copular elements in the nominal domain are realized as *of* (recall (7)), and the lexicalizer of the RELATOR-head in (16b) is a copular element.[9] The fact, then, that the RELATOR in (16b) is DP-embedded causes its spell-out to be *of*, the nominal copula.

5.2.3 Some Consequences of the Analysis

With the structures of attributive QBNPs with and without *of* in place, let us address some of the consequences of the analysis.

One issue that comes up once we broaden the scope of the discussion to include languages other than English is that attributive QBNPs lacking a nominal copula between the two noun phrases are quite rare: while English has them, they are ungrammatical, for instance, in Dutch (see (17a)[10]). Nor am I familiar with "bare" attributive QBNPs from other languages.

(17) a. *hij is een idioot dokter (Dutch)
          he is an idiot   doctor
      b.   hij is een idioot van een dokter
           he is an idiot of   a   doctor

By contrast, the attributive use of an AP in constructions of the type in
(7b) (*a beautiful dancer*) is commonplace. And the crosslinguistic distribution of the attributive QBNP with *of* (*an idiot of a doctor*) is also substantially broader than that of (14a). It is rather surprising, in fact, that Dutch
and English should differ from each other the way they do here. What
characterizes (14a), as analyzed in (14b), is the fact that the predicate
nominal (as well as its subject) is a bare NP; and while Dutch is known
to allow bare NPs as predicate nominals in copular sentences (cf. (18);
see De Swart, Winter, and Zwarts 2005 for recent discussion), the English
counterparts of such sentences are almost always ungrammatical (except
in such isolated cases as *George W. Bush is president*).

(18) a. hij is dokter (van beroep) (Dutch)
          he is doctor of   profession
      b. zij   zijn dokter (van beroep)
          they are doctor of   profession

For the particular case of the Dutch/English contrast,[11] what this leads
me to suggest is that the distribution of bare NP predicate nominals is
sensitive to the size of its subject: in English, bare NP predicates are licit
only if the subject is likewise a bare NP (assimilation), while in Dutch
they are ungrammatical in that context (while they are legitimate in a
structure in which the subject is a nominal extended projection, as in
(18)—a case of dissimilation).

It is worth staying with Dutch a little bit more to consider the status of
the indefinite article preceding the second noun phrase of attributive
QBNPs. The structure in (16b) for English *an idiot of a doctor* treats this
indefinite article as a constituent of the second noun phrase. And in fact,
it has no other options: the head position immediately outside the projection of the second noun is filled by the nominal copula, *of*. In attributive
QBNPs, in other words, the indefinite article preceding N_2 *has to* form a
constituent with N_2. That means that it will have to agree in number features with N_2. Thus, we never expect to find the singular indefinite article
a preceding a plural second noun. For English, this is hardly an exciting
prediction: after all, in English, *a* never precedes a plural noun, period.[12]
But for Dutch, the prediction is of some interest. Dutch allows plural

nouns to be preceded by the singular indefinite article *een* in certain contexts, a fact recorded and discussed extensively in Bennis, Corver, and Den Dikken 1998. One of the contexts in which Bennis, Corver, and Den Dikken report this "spurious" *een* is precisely the QBNP, as seen in (19). The status of (19b) is particularly interesting in the context of the present discussion.

(19) a. die   idioten van (een) kerels (Dutch)
        those idiots of   a   guys
     b. die   idioten van (een) doktoren
        those idiots of   a   doctors

First, let me briefly return to (3b), *an idiot of a doctor*. In isolation, a QBNP such as (3b) is compatible with two interpretations, as I pointed out in section 5.1. It can receive an *attributive* QBNP reading (which says that the referent of the noun phrase is an idiot *in his capacity as* a doctor), but it also supports (albeit less saliently) a *comparative* QBNP reading (such that the referent of the entire noun phrase *an idiot of a doctor* is ascribed the property of being an idiot, not just in this person's capacity as a doctor but per se: he or she is simply an idiot who happens to be a doctor by profession, and may actually be a very good doctor).[13] This, of course, is a fact familiar from constructions of the *big butterfly* type as well: a big butterfly can be big *for a butterfly* but nonetheless a very small creature, but it can also be big in absolute terms. Now, on the *attributive* reading of (3b), (20a, b) are perfectly sensible statements. On a *comparative* reading, by contrast, (20a, b) are contradictory: schizophrenia aside, one cannot be and not be an idiot at the same time, nor can one simultaneously be a nitwit and a genius (assuming that *nitwit* and *genius* are antonyms). This is clearer, of course, for QBNPs that are unambiguously comparative in nature, such as *an idiot/a nitwit of a man* (for which an attributive paraphrase like '*x* is an idiot/a nitwit in *x*'s capacity as a man' makes no sense): the statements in (21a, b) are incoherent.

(20) a.   That idiot of a doctor is not an idiot (as a person). (Attributive)
     b.   That nitwit of a doctor is a genius—he just happens to have
          chosen the wrong profession.

(21) a.   #That idiot of a man is not an idiot. (Comparative)
     b.   #That nitwit of a man is a genius.

When we now return to the Dutch example in (19b), we find that its incarnation lacking "spurious" *een* is grammatical in the context of (20a), as seen in (22a), but the variant of (19b) containing *een* is distinctly odd in this context, as (23a) illustrates. Examples (22b) and (23b) replicate this result for (20b).

(22) a.   die   idioten van doktoren zijn (op zichzelf)   geen
           those idiots of   doctors   are (on themselves) no
           idioten (Attributive)
           idiots

      b.   die   stommelingen van doktoren zijn genieën—ze   hebben
           those nitwits   of doctors are geniuses they have
           alleen het verkeerde beroep   gekozen
           just   the wrong   profession chosen

(23) a.   #die idioten van *een* doktoren zijn (op zichzelf) geen idioten
                                                            (Comparative)

      b.   #die stommelingen van *een* doktoren zijn genieën—ze hebben
           alleen het verkeerde beroep gekozen

This confirms the prediction that the analysis of attributive QBNPs in (16b) makes. Recall that in this structure the only place to insert the indefinite article preceding N_2 is in a Num-head taking the projection of (singular) N_2 as its complement. It is impossible to place an indefinite article under the RELATOR-head, which is where Bennis, Corver, and Den Dikken (1998) generate their "spurious" indefinite article: the RELATOR in attributive QBNPs is occupied in the base by the nominal copula *van* 'of'. The fact, then, that there is no room for a "spurious" indefinite article in attributive QBNPs featuring the nominal copula supports the analysis of these constructions presented in (16b).[14]

When it comes to articles, there is one other thing worth highlighting in the context of attributive QBNPs featuring *of*, this time concerning the indefinite article preceding the *first* noun. It appears that this indefinite article resists association with a sentential negation. Thus, while *He is not a fool* and *He is no fool* can receive the same interpretation, the example in (24b) is unacceptable on a reading in which it corresponds to (24a). To be sure, *He is no fool of a president* does have a reading in which it is perfect—a instance of litotes that can be paraphrased as 'He is quite a president.'[15] But on that reading, *no fool* is *itself* the predicate nominal, and *no* has no connection with a sentential negation (i.e., on its litotic reading, (24b) is not a negative statement). What seems to be impossible is for (24b) to be equivalent to the negation of *He is a fool of a president* (i.e., (24a)). Thus, when a speaker asserts that George W. Bush is a fool of a president, it seems that a simple denial of this assertion uttered by his or her disagreeing interlocutor cannot take the form of (24b). Similarly, a sentence such as (25b), with its contrastive negation, is unacceptable;[16] to make a statement of this sort, one would need to resort to (25a), featuring *not* instead of *no*.

(24) a.   He is not a fool of a president.
     b. (*)He is no fool of a president.

(25) a.   He is not a fool of a PRESIDENT but a fool of a PROFESSOR.
     b. *He is no fool of a PRESIDENT but a fool of a PROFESSOR.

The fact that the negative indefinite article *no* on the first noun phrase of attributive QBNPs cannot convey sentential negation can be made to follow from the structure in (16b), where the indefinite article preceding the first noun comes out as a constituent of the predicate nominal, embedded inside a larger DP. Located in this position, this indefinite article will be unable to establish a connection with a sentential negation, such a relationship being blocked by the intervening D-head.

5.2.4 Summary

In sum, then, there is evidence to suggest that in the structure of attributive QBNPs featuring the nominal copula *of*, the indefinite articles preceding each of the two nouns form a constituent with the nouns that they precede, such that the structure of these constructions includes two NumPs, one of which serves as the predicate of the other, with the predicate sitting in the specifier position of the small clause. The entire predicate-specifier structure is embedded inside a DP whose (null) head is responsible for the fact that the RELATOR-head of the small clause is lexicalized as *of* (rather than, for instance, as *as*).

5.3 Comparative QBNPs: An Inverted Predicate-Complement Structure

5.3.1 Comparison and Metaphor

With these conclusions about attributive QBNPs in place, let me move on to comparative QBNPs. In these constructions, the property denoted by the first noun phrase in the *N of a N* sequence is taken to apply not just to the second noun phrase but to the referent of the entire QBNP qua individual. Thus, on the comparative reading of *He is an idiot of a doctor*, the subject is not merely an idiot in his capacity as a doctor but as a person, per se. QBNPs such as *an idiot of a man* or our initial example in (3a), *a jewel of a village*, cannot plausibly be interpreted attributively at all—as I pointed out above, 'He is an idiot in his capacity as a man' makes little sense. For such unambiguously comparative QBNPs, we find that they systematically resist the kinds of alternations we found for attributive QBNPs. Thus, while for each of the attributive QBNPs in (26), their variants given in the three columns are all essentially equivalent, those in (27) are not—though things like *horror story* or *beauty parlor* do indeed exist, they are unequivocally N-N root compounds, not "bare" QBNPs of the type instantiated by the right-hand examples in (26).

(26) a. an idiot of a doctor   ~ an idiot as a doctor
                                      ~ an idiot doctor

    b. a fool of a policeman   ~ a fool as a policeman
                                      ~ a fool policeman

    c. a simpleton of a judge   ~ a simpleton as a judge
                                      ~ a simpleton judge

    d. a nitwit of a technician   ~ a nitwit as a technician
                                      ~ a nitwit technician

(27) a. an idiot of a man   ≁ an idiot as a man
                                     ≁ an idiot man

    b. a jewel of a village   ≁ a jewel as a village
                                     ≁ a jewel village

    c. a horror of a story   ≁ a horror as a story
                                     ≁ a horror story

    d. a beauty of a parlor   ≁ a beauty as a parlor
                                     ≁ a beauty parlor

Comparative QBNPs are often metaphorical in nature, establishing a comparison between the two noun phrases in the *N of a N* sequence. In (3a), *a jewel of a village*, the village is compared to a jewel; *jewel* is used as a metaphor for the village here. Since there are myriad things that something can be compared to metaphorically, it will be clear that the set of predicative nouns that can be used felicitously in a comparative QBNP is very large. While, as I pointed out in section 5.1, attributive QBNPs have the choice of its N_1 largely confined to members of Milner's (1978) closed class of *noms de qualité* 'quality nouns', comparative QBNPs can employ any N_1 denoting something that it is deemed suitable to compare N_2 to. As a result, while attributive QBNPs are quite restricted in their range of possibilities, comparative QBNPs can be created on the spot. The comparison made is always evaluative, often negative (see Ruwet's 1982 characterization of N_1 as any noun construable as an insult). Thus, in a QBNP like (28a), *schoolmaster* stands for a set of (typically negative) properties that schoolmasters are stereotypically thought to have (such as being authoritarian, correcting people all the time, and so on), much as in its epithetic use in copular sentences like *He's a real schoolmaster*, which have the same interpretation.

(28) a. that schoolmaster of a man
     b. that barge of a woman
     c. that plonker of a plumber
     d. some rotten little fig of a human being
     e. a colorless mouse of a woman
     f. another bitchy iceberg of a woman
     g. that clumsy oaf of a newscaster
     h. some shrinking violet of a civil servant
     i. a curate's egg of a book
     j. a bummer of a summer

The examples in (28) (most of which I took from Aarts (1998), who, in turn, culled many of his examples from corpora of English texts) are a small testament to the versatility of the comparative QBNP when it comes to the choice of N_1, as well as to the fundamentally comparative nature of the construction.

It will not come as a surprise, in light of the discussion in the previous paragraph, that comparative QBNPs may alternate with constructions in which the comparison between the two noun phrases is established with the aid of a connective like *like*. For Spanish (see Español-Echevarría 1998, 75) and Dutch (Bennis, Corver, and Den Dikken 1998), this is illustrated in (29) and (30)–(31); the English renditions of these examples are grammatical as well.

(29) a. la rata de tu   hermano (Spanish)
         the rat of your brother
     b. tu   hermano es como una rata
         your brother is like a   rat

(30) a. een beer van een vent (Dutch)
         a   bear of a   bloke
     b. een vent als een beer
         a   bloke like a   bear

(31) a. kolenschoppen van (een) handen (Dutch)
         coal shovels   of   a   hands
     b. handen als (*een) kolenschoppen
        hands   like   a   coal shovels

It is alternations of the type in (30) and (31) that Bennis, Corver, and Den Dikken (1998) exploit in their quest for an analysis of comparative QBNPs. Observing that the b-examples are the canonical expression of the predicational relationship between the two noun phrases, with the noun phrase following *als* 'like' serving as the predicate nominal, they go on to derive the QBNP constructions illustrated by the a-examples via an application of Predicate Inversion—an analysis for which the observations discussed in the next subsection provide further support.

5.3.2 Comparative QBNPs and the "Spurious" Indefinite Article

Bennis, Corver, and Den Dikken (1998, 97) point out that in the QBNP in (31a), a "spurious" token of the indefinite article *een* may show up between *van* 'of' and the subject noun phrase *handen*. Recall from the discussion in section 5.2.3 that Bennis, Corver, and Den Dikken treat this "spurious" indefinite article (which clearly belongs to neither of the two constituent noun phrases of the construction) as a lexicalization of the functional head of the small clause of which the two noun phrases are a part. With *een* analyzed as a spell-out of the RELATOR, the fact that in the uninverted construction in (31b) no "spurious" indefinite article may surface then indicates that the RELATOR-head is not available for *een* to fill here. And indeed, with *als* and its English counterparts *like* and *as* analyzed as lexicalizations of the RELATOR-head (see Aarts 1992; Bowers 1993), the complementary distribution of *als* and *een* in (31b) follows immediately.

That said, the lack of complementarity between *van* 'of' and "spurious" *een* in (31a) tells us that *van* is NOT base-generated in the RELATOR-head in comparative QBNPs, unlike in attributive QBNPs. One of the pieces of evidence I brought up in section 5.2 to support the claim that the prepositional element intervening between the two constituent noun phrases in attributive QBNPs lexicalizes the RELATOR was precisely the fact, illustrated in (23) (repeated here, along with (22)), that the attributive QBNP is incompatible with the use of the "spurious" indefinite article: the sentences in (23) are incoherent, unlike those in (22) (which differ in lacking a token of *een* in front of the second noun).

(22) a. die   idioten van doktoren zijn (op zichzelf)   geen
         those idiots   of   doctors   are (on themselves) no
         idioten (Attributive)
         idiots
     b. die   stommelingen van doktoren zijn genieën—ze   hebben
         those nitwits   of   doctors   are geniuses they have
         alleen het verkeerde beroep   gekozen
         just   the wrong   profession chosen

(23) a. #die idioten van een doktoren zijn (op zichzelf) geen idioten
                                                          (Comparative)
     b. #die idioten van een doktoren zijn genieën—ze hebben alleen
          het verkeerde beroep gekozen

The infelicity of (23) follows if these are unambiguously *comparative*
QBNPs—or, put differently, if the use of the "spurious" indefinite article
in front of the second noun is an earmark of *comparative* QBNPs. On the
hypothesis (for which we had already found support in our discussion of
attributive QBNPs) that the "spurious" indefinite article is a realization
of the RELATOR-head, this reinforces the conclusion reached in Bennis,
Corver, and Den Dikken 1998 on the basis of (31) that the prepositional
element *van* intervening between the two noun phrases of the comparative QBNP *cannot* be a lexicalization of the RELATOR-head of the small
clause.

5.3.3 Comparative QBNPs and the Status of the Prepositional Element between the Two Noun Phrases

We have now arrived at a point at which we have established an initial
argument for the conclusion that comparative QBNPs are built on the basis of a predicate-complement structure that they share with their cousins
featuring a lexical RELATOR (*as*, *like*, and their ilk) between the two noun
phrases in their base order (see the b-examples in (30) and (31)), and we
have also discovered, on the basis of the lack of complementarity of the
"spurious" indefinite article and the prepositional element *van* 'of', that
the latter cannot be a lexicalization of the RELATOR in comparative
QBNPs. Instead, it must be a small-clause external head of sorts. At this
juncture, two possibilities then come to mind when it comes to the status
of the element *of*/*van*—possibilities that have far-reaching consequences
for the analysis of comparative QBNPs.

(32) a. *Of* in comparative QBNPs is a copular element serving as a
         LINKER.
     b. *Of* in comparative QBNPs is a complementizer-like element,
         sitting in D.

In light of our earlier conclusion that in *attributive* QBNPs *of* is a copular
element lexicalizing the RELATOR, (32a) would certainly be a more attractive option, a priori, than (32b), which would presumably compel us to
set up (at least) two separate lexical entries for *of,* one as a copula and
one as a complementizer-like element. I will take this to be an initial indication that (32a) is the correct approach (see Den Dikken 1995a; Bennis,
Corver, and Den Dikken 1998), identifying *of* in comparative QBNPs as
a LINKER, similar to the obligatory copula in Copular Inversion constructions of the type discussed in chapter 4 (see (33)).

(33) a. Imogen considers Brian (to be) the best candidate.
     b. Imogen considers the best candidate *(to be) Brian.

With *of* identified as a LINKER, this directly leads to an analysis of comparative QBNPs in terms of Predicate Inversion—an analysis that will of
course capture the alternation between the a- and b-examples in (29)–(31)
as well. In the following subsections, I will lay out the Predicate Inversion
derivation of comparative QBNPs (originally presented in Den Dikken
1995a), and then make a case for it, primarily by taking a close look at
the distribution of articles in the comparative QBNP—a distribution
that weighs heavily against the extant A′-movement accounts (see Kayne
1994 as well as Doetjes and Rooryck 2001; Heycock 1998b also hints at
an A′-movement account in her critique of Den Dikken 1998b). After
having made my case for a movement account of comparative QBNPs
(more specifically, one in terms of Predicate Inversion), I will address the
restrictions on quantifiers and articles in QBNPs, and subsequently I will
return to the nature and distribution of *of* and its relatives in these constructions, looking at some of the base-generation approaches to QBNPs
along the way.

5.3.4 The Predicate Inversion Analysis of Comparative QBNPs

The analysis of comparative QBNPs that I advocate can be summarized
as follows. The predicate nominal (the first noun phrase in the surface
sequence) originates as the predicate of a small clause of the predicate-
complement type, as in (1a) (repeated below). The predicate nominal can

stay in its base position in principle, in which case we get the b-examples in (30) and (31) as our output. But the predicate may also *invert* with its subject, as depicted in (2).

(1a) [$_{RP}$ [$_{XP}$ SUBJECT] [RELATOR [$_{YP}$ PREDICATE]]]

(2)   [$_{FP}$ [PREDICATE]$_j$ [$_{F'}$ LINKER+RELATOR$_i$ [$_{RP}$ [SUBJECT] [$_{R'}$ t_i t_j]]]]]

In (2), the predicate raises to the specifier position of a small-clause external functional head F that receives the RELATOR-head of the small clause. As a result of phase-extending movement of the RELATOR up to the small-clause external F-head, the predicate is allowed to cross over its subject on its way to a higher A-position thanks to the fact that the subject position of the small clause and the predicate's prospective landing site (SpecFP) have been rendered equidistant, and that the RP phase has been extended up to FP, as a result of which the predicate becomes visible to RP-external probes (including F). The small-clause external F-head is lexicalized by a LINKER—the nominal copula *of*.

This is the essence of the account. But important questions remain to be addressed. For one, we need to know what the nature of the predicate is in comparative QBNPs. The name of the construction is actually helpful in answering this question. In an example such as (3a), *a jewel of a village*, the village is *compared to* a jewel. Let us assume that this semantic aspect of comparison is structurally encoded, in the form of an abstract predicate "SIMILAR." Concretely, then, we have the following underlying representation for (3a).[17]

(34) [$_{RP}$ [*village*] [RELATOR [SIMILAR *jewel*]]]

This representation presents us not only with the semantics of comparison but also with an empty-headed predicate—and that is something we can exploit in answering another question arising in the context of the Predicate Inversion analysis of comparative QBNPs: Why does the predicate invert with its subject?[18]

In chapter 4, I argued that raising of the predicate is driven by a property of the raised predicate—specifically, the fact that it has an empty head. The representation in (34) has just delivered us such an empty head: abstract SIMILAR. On the assumption that this empty predicate head is in need of licensing, and that Predicate Inversion satisfies this need, we have an answer to the question raised at the end of the previous paragraph. But recall from the discussion of alternations of the type in (29)–(31) that inversion is apparently not *obligatory* in comparative

QBNPs: if the RELATOR-head is spelled out as *as/like*, the predicate is apparently allowed to stay in situ.

The lexicalization of the RELATOR as *as/like* in the b-examples in (29)–(31) thus raises the question of how it can keep the predicate from raising, but it raises another question as well. Recall from the discussion of the *attributive* QBNP in section 5.2 that there, the RELATOR establishing the relationship between the predicate-specifier and its subject is lexicalized as *of* rather than *as/like*, something I ascribed there to the fact that the RELATOR in attributive QBNPs is in a nominal environment. Indubitably, the RELATOR is in a nominal environment in *comparative* QBNPs as well, yet spelling it out as *as/like* is possible here (while, in fact, lexicalizing it as *of* is not; recall the discussion above).

What I would like to suggest is that, in comparative QBNPs in which the predicate does not invert, the abstract predicate head SIMILAR in (35) is licensed by the RELATOR, and that this is possible *if and only if* the RELATOR is spelled out as *as/like*. Specifically, the idea is that *as/like*, which themselves can be used to establish a comparison (*Brian is as tall as Imogen, Brian is very much like Imogen*), can content-license the empty predicate SIMILAR, with formal licensing being taken care of via incorporation of the null predicate head into the RELATOR (see Baker 1988 on incorporation and "morphological licensing").[19] If one is to keep the predicate in situ in comparative QBNPs, then, one has to choose *as/like* as the lexicalization of the RELATOR.

If, on the other hand, the RELATOR has no lexical realization or is spelled out as the "spurious" indefinite article, the empty predicate head SIMILAR in (34) cannot be licensed if the predicate stays in situ. The predicate is then forced to invert with its subject (its null head probably being licensed by the outside Num-head in (46)/(46′), below), producing the structure in (2) and the concomitant emergence of a LINKER in the small-clause external functional head F. In the absence of a licensing element under the RELATOR, therefore, Predicate Inversion is triggered just as in the cases discussed in chapter 4, by the need to license the empty predicate head.

There are, however, instances of comparative QBNPs to which an approach along the lines of (34) is not applicable. Thus, Español-Echevarría (1998, 74–75) notes the alternation in Spanish between (35a) and (35b), and adds that while (35a) can be rendered as a copular sentence featuring *como* 'like', as in (35a′), (35b) cannot be so paraphrased: (35b′) is ungrammatical with *como* included (though fine without it).[20]

(35) a. la   rata de tu   hermano (Spanish)
         the.F rat.F of your brother.M
         'your evil brother, your rat of a brother'
     a′. tu   hermano es (como) una rata
         your brother.M is   like   a.F rat.F
         'Your brother is evil, (like) a rat.'
     b. el   rata de tu   hermano
         the.M rat.F of your brother.M
         'your stingy brother'
     b′. tu   hermano es (*como) un rata
         your brother.M is   like   a.M rat.F
         'Your brother is stingy.'

For the comparative QBNP in (35a), an analysis along the lines of (34) is of course perfectly straightforward in light of the grammaticality of (35a′) with *como*. But such an analysis is unavailable for (35b). Interestingly, however, even here the need to license a null predicate head can still be held accountable for the inversion of subject and predicate. For Español-Echevarría (1997, 1998) presents an analysis of the peculiar gender mismatch between the feminine noun *rata* and its masculine determiner in (35b, b′) according to which *rata* is treated as a modifier of a null-headed noun phrase.[21] Concretely, then, what we have is a structure underlying (35b) in which the predicate nominal is headed by a null noun (whose gender features are determined under agreement with its subject, as Español-Echevarría (1998, 70–71) shows): [$_{NP}$ *rata* [N$_{\varnothing}$]]. And it is the need to get this null noun licensed that, in the particular case of (35b), drives Predicate Inversion.

Thus, the comparative QBNP in (35b) is actually closer to the cases of Copular Inversion discussed in chapter 4, where we likewise found the fact that the predicate nominal is empty-headed to be the driving force for inversion. But even though (35a) and (35b) differ with respect to what exactly is the empty head, arguably all cases of Predicate Inversion inside the complex noun phrase are triggered by the need to license that empty head. And in this respect, they both fit perfectly under the general umbrella of Predicate Inversion and its trigger as presented in chapter 4.

In the previous paragraphs, I have presented a general outlook on Predicate Inversion in comparative QBNPs, and a rationale for inversion in cases in which the RELATOR is not realized as *as/like*.[22] But the structures in (1b), (2), and (34) still look very abstract—they abstract away particularly from questions concerning the placement and distribution of articles and quantificational elements in comparative QBNPs. I have already had occasion to comment on the fact that the indefinite article preceding the second noun in Dutch comparative QBNPs can be "spurious," originating in the RELATOR-head rather than as a subconstituent of the second noun phrase. But much more remains to be said about the distribution of articles in comparative QBNPs—a distribution that, as I will show in the next subsection, is incompatible with the A'-movement approaches to comparative QBNPs available in the literature.

5.3.5 The Distribution of Articles in Comparative QBNPs: Evidence against A'-Movement Accounts

Kayne's (1994) account of QBNP constructions,[23] schematically represented as in (36a), shares with mine the idea that these constructions are built on an underlying predicate-complement structure, with the surface order of constituents being derived via overt-syntactic movement. Kayne's approach differs from mine, however, in explicitly assimilating the QBNP construction to the English "partitive-genitive" construction (*that picture of John's*), whose structure—on Kayne's (1993, 1994) assumptions—reads as in (36b), where *of* is treated as a complementizer-like element lexicalizing the D/P-head.[24]

(36) a. *that* [$_{D/PP}$ [*jewel*]$_j$ [$_{D/P}$ *of*] [$_{IP}$ *a village* I^0 t_j ...

$\qquad\qquad\qquad\qquad\qquad\qquad\qquad\qquad$ (Kayne 1994, 106)

$\quad$ b. *that* [$_{D/PP}$ [*picture*]$_j$ [$_{D/P}$ *of*] [$_{IP}$ *John* [$_I$ *'s*] t_j ...

$\qquad\qquad\qquad\qquad\qquad\qquad\qquad\qquad$ (Kayne 1993; 1994, 102)

This assimilation of QBNP and "partitive-genitive" constructions is problematic, though, for reasons that primarily have to do with restrictions on determiners. In (36b), the D/PP structure cannot be preceded by a genitive-marked possessor, nor can *that* be replaced with the definite determiner *the*, as (37) and (38) show.

(37) *your picture of John's

(38) *?the picture of John's

But in the QBNP construction, external possessors are fine (see (39), from Aarts 1998), and although the first noun in the QBNP construction is not normally preceded by a definite determiner—examples like those in (40a) (once again taken from Aarts 1998) being questionable—Austin (1980), in her detailed inventory of the properties of the QBNP construction, identifies the Det_1 position as unrestricted. And in fact, Curme (1931, 85) cites (40b) as acceptable, and QBNP constructions with a definite article that refer back to a definite DP in the preceding discourse are possible as well (see (40c), from Aarts 1998).[25]

(39) your jerk of a brother

(40) a. ?*the* nincompoop of a civil servant
      b. *the* rascal of a landlord
      c. (I went to see my bank manager, but) *the* sly fox of a man had just left.

The examples in (37) and (39) constitute a sharp minimal pair, and though the contrast between (38) and (40) is not as robust (with (40) being dialectally and contextually restricted), those (mostly British) speakers who accept (40) still resolutely reject (38). Moreover, while definite QBNPs of the type in (40) constructions can be made fully acceptable when properly contextualized, as (40c) shows, it does not seem to be the case that (38) can be similarly improved (see **I went to see my bank manager$_i$, but [the friend of mine]$_i$ had just left*).

   The parallel between QBNP constructions and "partitive genitives" is further compromised by the properties of indefinite QBNP constructions. In *a picture of John's*, the indefinite article is an integral part of the constituent raised to SpecD/P (filled by *of*) in Kayne's analysis. Indefinite articles are generated within the raised phrase. This is shown in (41a).

(41) a. [$_{D/PP}$ [*a picture*]$_j$ [$_{D/P}$ *of*] [$_{IP}$ *John* [$_I$ *'s*] t_j ...
      b. [$_{D/PP}$ [*a wretch*]$_j$ [$_{D/P}$ *of*] [$_{IP}$ *a woman* I^0 t_j ...

If QBNP constructions are truly parallel in structure and derivation to (41a), we expect that in indefinite QBNPs like *a wretch of a woman* the indefinite article preceding the first noun is an integral part of the constituent in SpecD/PP as well. This is depicted in the structure in (41b). But although section 5.2 has brought forth evidence to suggest that in *attributive* QBNPs both the first noun and the second noun do indeed form constituents with the indefinite articles that precede them, there is evidence to show that in *comparative* QBNPs, the articles do not belong to the individual nouns.

   To see this, it is particularly instructive to look at comparative QBNPs whose second noun is a proper name, such as in (42) (based on an example due to Thackeray; see Austin 1980). Comparative QBNP constructions with a proper-name subject, while apparently common in the English of Thackeray's day,[26] are highly marked in present-day English—but even speakers of present-day English detect a marked difference between (42) with *that* (which is awkward but conceivable) and the same noun phrase with *a* (which is entirely impossible).[27]

(42) %That/*a clever little wretch of a Rebecca

For Dutch the picture is sharper, as the examples in (43) (taken from Everaert 1992, 47) show.

(43) a. die/*een schat   van een Marie (Dutch)
          that/a   darling of a   Marie
      b. dat/*een serpent van een Marie
          that/a   serpent of a   Marie

The examples in (43) with the demonstrative *die/dat* are perfectly fine, while their counterparts with *een* in initial position are awful. These examples show us two things. First, it is immediately plain, of course, that the indefinite article preceding the second noun cannot form a constituent with it: proper names, in Dutch and English alike, do not normally take indefinite articles.[28] So the indefinite article preceding *Rebecca* in (42) and *Marie* in (43) must be the "spurious" indefinite article familiar from some of our earlier examples.[29] And second, the fact that the outer determiner cannot be an indefinite article when the subject of the DP-internal predication is a proper name would come as a complete surprise if the outer indefinite article in QBNP constructions belonged strictly to the predicative noun (as in Kayne's 1994 analysis; see (41b))—why should it forfeit its indefinite article precisely whenever the subject is a proper name? What these facts show beyond doubt is that we need an analysis of QBNP constructions in which the outer determiner (the one to the left of the first noun) belongs to the entire sequence that follows it, not just to the first noun's projection.

That the indefinite article preceding the first noun belongs to the entire comparative QBNP rather than to the predicate nominal is shown also by the behavior of negative QBNPs. Recall from section 5.2.3 that in *attributive* QBNPs, a *no* inserted in front of the first noun belongs unequivocally to that first noun alone, and cannot be a negative indefinite article belonging to the entire attributive QBNP. I showed this there with the aid of the examples in (24), repeated below.

(24) a.   He is not a fool of a president.
      b. (*)He is no fool of a president.

As I pointed out above, the example in (24b) is unacceptable on a reading in which it corresponds to (24a), though it does support a litotic interpretation ('He is quite a president') on which *no fool* is, in its entirety, the predicate nominal. The inability on the part of the negative indefinite article *no* on the first noun phrase of attributive QBNPs to convey sentential negation was shown, in section 5.2.3, to follow from the structure of attributive QBNPs in (16b), repeated here as (44). Here, the indefinite article preceding the first noun is a constituent of the predicate nominal.

(44) $[_{RP_2}$ *Slop* $[_{RELATOR_2}=be$ $[_{DP}$ $D_\varnothing$ $[_{RP_1}$ $[_{NumP}$ *an* $[_{NP}$ *idiot*]]
      $[_{RELATOR_1}=of$ $[_{NumP}$ *a* $[_{NP}$ *doctor*]]]]]]]]

Now, if *comparative* QBNPs were to map the indefinite articles into constituents inside the small clause, we would expect *no N of a N* in its comparative incarnation to resist a sentential-negation interpretation just like it does on its attributive reading. But this is not in fact the case. Thus, a statement such as (45a) can be denied as in (45b) or corrected with contrastive stress on the second noun as in (45c)—things we found to be impossible in attributive QBNPs (recall (24)–(25)).[30]

(45) a. This is a jewel of a village.
      b. No, I disagree—it's no jewel of a village at all; in fact, it's an utterly detestable place.
      c. No, this is no jewel of a VILLAGE, it is a jewel of a TOWN.

So what we want for *comparative* QBNPs is that the indefinite articles preceding neither of the two nouns form a constituent with those nouns. For the indefinite article preceding N_2, we can ensure this by generating it under the RELATOR-head, as a "spurious" indefinite article. For the article preceding N_1, which shows a certain sensitivity to its environment in that it depends for its distribution on the properties of the semantic *head* of the construction (N_2; see the facts in (42) and (43)), what we need to do is insert it in a Num-head outside the FP in (2). That way, it can "see" the semantic head of the construction while at the same time being able to establish a link with a sentential negation outside the QBNP.[31] So we can extend our partial structure of *comparative* QBNPs in (2) a little further, as in (46).

(46) $[_{NumP}$ Num$(=a/no)$ $[_{FP}$ [PREDICATE]$_j$ [LINKER+RELATOR$_i$ $[_{RP}$ [SUBJECT]
      $[t_i$ $t_j]]]]]

The argument against Kayne's (1994) account of QBNPs based on the distribution of articles in comparative QBNPs militates even more acutely against Doetjes and Rooryck's (2001) approach to QBNP constructions (based on French examples), according to which *any* determiner element preceding the first noun (not just indefinite articles but demonstratives as well) forms a constituent with the first noun (see (47a, b)).[32]

(47) a. ce   bijou   d' église (Comparative QBNP)
        that.M jewel.M of church.F
        [$_{CP}$ [$_{DP}$ *ce bijou*]$_i$ [$_{C'}$ *de* [$_{SC}$ [$_{NP}$ *église*] t_i]]]

   b. ton   phénomène   de fille ("Pure-degree" QBNP)
        your.M phenomenon.M of girl.F
        [$_{EvalP}$ [$_{DP}$ *ce phénomène*] [Eval [$_{DP}$ [$_{D'}$ *de* [$_{NP}$ *fille*]]]]]

Doetjes and Rooryck (2001) deserve ample credit for pioneering the structural dichotomy within the realm of QBNP constructions, as well as for the hypothesis that *only* the derivation of *comparative* QBNPs involves Predicate Inversion.[33] But though (47a) may help circumvent the problems that Kayne's (36a) has with QBNPs of the type in (39) and (40), Doetjes and Rooryck's analysis of comparative QBNPs still errs on the other end, in wrongly ruling in the ungrammatical variants of the examples in (42) and (43): if the article preceding the first noun of the comparative QBNP genuinely belongs to that noun, there is no reason these examples should be bad.

In addition, Doetjes and Rooryck's (2001) assumption that even demonstratives preceding N_1 belong strictly to the predicate nominal, while having the distinct advantage of accounting for the fact that it systematically shows gender agreement with N_1 (see (47), where "M" and "F" stand for "masculine" and "feminine," respectively), makes awkward claims about the semantics of QBNPs: in (47a) there is no comparison made between a church and *this* jewel, but instead between a church and a jewel, with the demonstrative taking the entire *N of a N* sequence as its complement. Even more clearly, in (47b) the possessive *ton* does not "belong to" *phénomène*: it is not *ton phénomène* that ascribes some property to *fille*; rather, *phénomène* by itself modifies *fille*, with *ton* forming a constituent with all of *phénomène de fille*.

I take the preceding paragraphs to have demonstrated that the analysis of (comparative) QBNPs in Kayne 1994 and accounts drawing on Kayne's movement-to-SpecDP approach (including Español-Echevarría 1997, 1998, and Doetjes and Rooryck 2001) have serious shortcomings, both concerning the landing site and nature of the movement operation that they take the predicate nominal to undergo, and (partly as a result) in the consequences of their analysis for the distribution of articles and other determiners in comparative QBNPs. The Predicate Inversion analysis in (46) has much better credentials when it comes to accommodating the article facts—though more work is still needed to fill in some of the missing pieces of the puzzle. I will turn to those pieces in the next section, devoted in its entirety to the restrictions on quantification in QBNPs.[34]

5.4   Quantification in Qualitative Binominal Noun Phrases

5.4.1   The Structures of Attributive and Comparative QBNPs Juxtaposed

In section 5.2, I argued for an analysis of attributive QBNPs according to which the predicate originates as the specifier of the RELATOR phrase, and I showed that the size of the subconstituents of the RELATOR phrase depends on where NumP is generated in the structure. In attributive QBNP constructions in which nothing intervenes between the two nouns, such as (14a) (repeated below), NumP is located outside the RELATOR phrase, as a result of which the constituent noun phrases are bare NPs (see (14b)). In attributive QBNPs featuring *of* as a lexicalization of the RELATOR, on the other hand, each of the nominal constituents of the small clause is itself a NumP, as depicted in (16b).

(14) a. Doctor Slop is an idiot doctor.

  b. [$_{RP_2}$ *Slop* [$_{RELATOR_2}$=*be* [$_{NumP}$ *an* [$_{RP_1}$ [$_{NP}$ *idiot*] [$_{RELATOR_1}$=$\varnothing$ [$_{NP}$ *doctor*]]]]]]

(16) a. Doctor Slop is an idiot of a doctor.

  b. [$_{RP_2}$ *Slop* [$_{RELATOR_2}$=*be* [$_{DP}$ D$_\varnothing$ [$_{RP_1}$ [$_{NumP}$ *an* [$_{NP}$ *idiot*]] [$_{RELATOR_1}$=*of* [$_{NumP}$ *a* [$_{NP}$ *doctor*]]]]]]]

The interim structure of comparative QBNPs that I arrived at toward the end of the previous section (see (46), repeated here) shares with (14b) the fact that there is a NumP base-generated outside the small clause.

(46) [$_{NumP}$ Num(=*a/no*) [$_{FP}$ [PREDICATE]$_j$ [LINKER+RELATOR$_i$ [$_{RP}$ [SUBJECT] [t_i t_j]]]]]

But (46) remains unspecific, in its present form, with respect to the size of the subconstituents of the small clause. By juxtaposing attributive and comparative QBNPs in an investigation of the quantificational restrictions on these constructions, I will try to reach some conclusions concerning the details of (46) that remain to be filled in. I will begin my investigation by looking at pluralization.

5.4.2 Number in QBNPs

Since the constituents of the small clause in (16b) are both NumPs, there is no particular reason to expect pluralization to be in any way restricted in *attributive* QBNPs. And indeed, Aarts (1998) cites some attributive QBNPs from English, reproduced here as (48a, b).

(48) a. those fools of doctors
     b. many idiots of football hooligans

But Napoli (1989, 237) gives *those scoundrels of lawyers* a star. It seems that plural attributive QBNPs are generally rejected by present-day American English speakers (though (49a) is an example produced by a native of Portland, Oregon, and (49b), whose provenance is harder to establish, seems to stem from an American English speaker as well). They may be a relic of times past (note the fact that (49c) is from a text produced in the nineteenth century).

(49) a. So long as fools of doctors don't take such things as weakness
         and play on the sufferer's ego or ignor [*sic*] it, the sufferer may
         accept and laugh away the condition.
         www.aiprojects.net/library/hypertext/fournobletruths.html
     b. When those vermin who killed your mother left you out in the
         forest to die, when those fools of doctors left you to burn to
         death in the sun ...
         www.shininghalf.com/cv/alucard2.html
     c. Those idiots of doctors had been treating me for extravagance.
         From *Australian Tales*, by Marcus Clarke (1846–1881)

Though the precise root of the problem with pluralization in English attributive QBNPs remains to be investigated further, it seems to me that there is a connection between the paucity of QBNPs of the type in (48) and (49) and the fact that the plural b-examples in (50)–(51), which correspond to the perfectly well-formed and abundantly attested singular a-cases, are not at all common and strike the native speaker as awkward.[35]

(50) a. We have a fool for a doctor.   He is a fool for a doctor.
     b. We have fools for doctors.   They are fools for doctors.

(51) a. He has a fool as a father.   He is a fool as a father.
     b. They have fools as fathers.   They are fools as fathers.

The parallel between (48)–(49) and the b-examples in (50) and (51), if real (as it appears to be), is interesting because the constructions in (50) and (51) were diagnosed in chapter 2 as reverse-predication constructions—that is, instantiations of the predicate-specifier structure. In section 5.2, I argued that attributive QBNPs are likewise instances of the predicate-specifier structure.

There appears to be a generalization, therefore, that pluralization of predicate-specifier constructions is highly restricted in the English-speaking world. I have no clear insights or even speculations to offer on the subject of why this should be the case. It seems that the problem is specifically one connected to the *second* noun phrase in the sequence. For in British English (where nouns like *committee* and *government*, while formally singular, can outwardly behave like plural noun phrase, as in *the government are a bunch of idiots*; see Elbourne 1999 and Den Dikken 2002 for discussion), attributive QBNPs such as (52) are grammatical (see Bennis, Corver, and Den Dikken 1998, and Matushansky 2002),[36] and so are the examples in (53).

(52) a. those fools of a police force
     b. those nincompoops of a government
     c. those (three) idiots of a committee

(53) a. We have fools for a police force.
     b. We have a bunch of nincompoops as our government.
     c. We have (three) idiots as our committee.

In these examples, the predicate nominal is a morphological plural and even accepts a numeral quantifier (as Matushansky 2002 notes; see also note 36), while the postcopular subject is morphologically singular. It seems to be the latter's formal singularity that makes (52) (in the relevant dialects) more readily acceptable than things like (48). This generalization is not straightforwardly translatable into more formal terms on the basis of the structure in (14b): one would expect pluralization to be unproblematic in predicate-specifier structures of this type. The restrictions on pluralization in English attributive QBNPs thus stand out as a bit of a mystery. Much more "well-behaved," from my perspective, is the behavior of Dutch, where there is no problem with pluralization of predicate-specifier constructions—(19b), which supports an attributive reading when *een* is absent, is perfectly grammatical (see section 5.2.3).

(19b) die   idioten van (een) doktoren (Dutch)
      those idiots of   a   doctors

With *een* included, (19b) unequivocally instantiates a *comparative* QBNP, which can thus be seen to allow pluralization as well. For English comparative QBNPs, there are no examples on record in the linguistic literature that feature two plural noun phrases. A web search turned up a couple of plural variants of our original comparative QBNP in (3a), *a jewel of a village*—a very *British* English set:

(54) a. Sparkling little jewels of villages like, Killin, Kenmore and
        Fortingall are spread along the length of Breadalbane.
        www.trossachs.fsworld.co.uk

   b. But the foothills of the Apenines south of Forli and Faenza hold
      a variety of small jewels of towns in a lovely setting.
      balick.home.sprynet.com/italy.html

   c. We will explore and photograph several gems of villages such as
      Peacham, East Corinth and Strafford, which are quintessential
      New England.
      www.lightandland.co.uk/holidays/vermont.html

   d. The land is crossed by rivers along the banks of which stand
      many gems of villages.
      www.wwnorton.com/thamesandhudson/new/spring02/551072
      .htm

   e. The area was full of lakes and little gems of villages and small
      towns.
      www.citroen-2cv.org.uk/Events/20020500frenchNational.htm

But even in British English, it seems that the plural comparative QBNP is hardly productive (while inverse copular sentences such as *the biggest gems are these villages* are of course perfectly general in the English-speaking world and beyond). In Dutch, by contrast, it is perfectly normal (see (19b) with *een* included). It is interesting to note in this connection that a web search conducted for the sequence *darlings of children* produced precisely one specimen of the QBNP type (alongside such irrelevant non-QBNP cases as *playgrounds are the darlings of children*), given in (55a)—clearly a translation from Dutch (55b): the site on which it occurs is the English version of the private website of a proud Dutch father of two children.

(55) a. I'm very proud and feel very rich with my darlings of children.
        www.ook-kinderen-hebben-rechten.com/08-03-03-engels.html

   b. mijn schatten   van (een) kinderen (Dutch)
      my   treasures/darlings of   a   children

That the postcopular noun phrase of comparative QBNPs may be as large as NumP in Dutch is suggested also, and in fact more strongly so, by the fact that the counterparts of the English examples in (56a) are grammatical in Dutch (albeit marginal for some speakers; see Den Dikken 1995a for the original observation, and see also Bennis, Corver, and Den Dikken 1998).

(56) a.   *that disaster of (a) number agreement facts
           *that scandal of (a) managers' salaries
     b. (?)die ramp   van een getalscongruentiefeiten (Dutch)
           that disaster of a   number-agreement-facts
        (?)dat schandaal van een directeurssalarissen
           that scandal   of a   managers-salaries

(57) a.   Those number-agreement facts are a disaster.
           The biggest disaster is those number-agreement facts.
     b.   die   getalscongruentiefeiten zijn een ramp (Dutch)
           those number-agreement-facts are a   disaster
           de grootste ramp   zijn die   getalscongruentiefeiten
           the biggest disaster are those number-agreement-facts

The contrast in (56a, b) is striking in view of the fact that, in copular sentences (both "straight" and inverted), Dutch and English behave essentially alike when it comes to number disagreement between the subject and the predicate nominal, as seen in (57).[37] If in English, for reasons that remain largely obscure, the postcopular noun phrase of no QBNP is ever allowed to be plural-marked (though it might still become plural via subject-predicate *agreement* if the predicate is plural-marked, as in (54)), (56a) is essentially uninteresting. But (56b) shows that, in Dutch comparative QBNPs, the subject can be pluralized independently of the predicate nominal. This number disagreement between subject and predicate follows if the postcopular subject of a comparative QBNP is allowed to have a NumP of its own, independently of the predicate nominal.

It is worth noting in this connection that the fact that the postcopular subject has its *own* NumP in Dutch (56b) should make it impossible for the small-clause external Num-head in the structure in (46) to establish a relationship with the postcopular subject; this Num-head will only be able to check features against the raised predicate nominal, which is singular. This has two interesting consequences. First, we expect it to be impossible to insert a >1 numeral quantifier in front of the binominal sequence in

(56b)—a prediction borne out by the facts in (58a, b): *twee* 'two' in (58b) is grammatical only if the predicate nominal is plural.[38]

(58) a. één grote ramp   van een feiten (Dutch)
        one big   disaster of a   facts
     b. die   twee ramp*(en) van een feiten
        those two disaster(s) of a   facts
     c. die ramp   van een feiten ?komt/*komen zeer ongelegen
        that disaster of a   facts comes/come   very inconvenient
     d. dat schandaal van een salarissen is/*zijn ongehoord
        that scandal   of a   salaries   is/ are unheard-of

And second, we expect the fact that the postcopular noun phrase in (56b) has a NumP of its own to disqualify it from triggering agreement on the finite verb—the small-clause external Num-head in (46) is obviously the closer candidate for establishing an Agree relationship with T, and since this Num agrees with the predicate nominal, we expect singular agreement. And indeed, Broekhuis, Keizer, and Den Dikken (2003, 571) point out that in comparative QBNPs of the type in (56b), we get singular agreement on the verb, as is illustrated in (58c, d).[39]

   While the grammaticality of plural postcopular subjects in comparative QBNPs may so far look like a quirk of Dutch, it is important to note that there are other languages that allow it, too. Thus, note Spanish (59) (due to Suñer 1990), where, as in the Dutch examples in (56b), the predicate nominal is singular and its postcopular subject is plural and where, like the outer demonstratives in Dutch (56b), the outer indefinite article agrees with N_1.

(59) un   asco   de croquetas (Spanish)
     a.MSG disgust.MSG of croquettes.FPL
     'some disgusting croquettes'

And Den Dikken and Lipták (1997) show in detail that Hungarian has a counterpart of the Indo-European comparative QBNP (see (60a)), featuring the nouns *csoda* 'wonder, miracle', *fene* 'hell', and *kutya* 'dog' in initial position, separated from their subject by *egy*, a token of the indefinite article that, like its Dutch counterpart, has "spurious" uses in comparative QBNPs whose second noun is a plural (as in (60b)).[40]

(60) a. csoda/fene/kutya egy nap (Hungarian)
         wonder/hell/dog a   day
         'a wonder/hell/dog of a day'

b. csoda/fene/kutya egy napok
    wonder   a   days
    (Lit.) 'a wonder/hell/dog of days'
b'. *csodák/fenék/kutyák egy napok
    wonders/hells/dogs   a   days

The Hungarian facts closely resemble those of Dutch—in both languages, there is a "spurious" indefinite article, and in both languages, the postcopular subject is allowed to be a plural (even when its predicate is singular).[41] I conclude, therefore, that Hungarian, like Dutch and Spanish, accepts NumP in the position of the postcopular subject in (46).

It is interesting to stay with Hungarian QBNPs a little longer. As Den Dikken and Lipták (1997) note, while the postcopular subject in (60b) is plural, its predicate is singular—and in fact, it *must* be singular: (60b') is ungrammatical. In this regard, there appears at first sight to be a striking difference between noun-phrase internal predication and clause-internal predication in Hungarian. For as (61a) shows, number agreement is obligatory in a garden-variety copular sentence with *napok* as its subject and *csoda* as the predicate.

(61) a. a   napok {csodák/*csoda} voltak (Hungarian)
         the days   wonders/wonder were
         'The days were wonders.'
     b. *napok csodák   voltak
         days   wonders were

But note that (61b), with an articleless plural subject, is ungrammatical (see É. Kiss 1994). Den Dikken and Lipták (1997, 71) relate the ungrammaticality of (60b') to that of (61b) by drawing attention to the independent fact that "the subject in a nominal-internal predication construction must be smaller than DP" (see (62)), which is also true for Germanic nominal-internal predication constructions (see English *a wonder of a/ *the day*, Dutch *een wonder van een/*de dag*).[42]

(62) *csoda/fene/kutya egy a   nap(ok) (Hungarian)
     wonder/hell/dog a   the day(s)

If the subject of a plural predication must be a full DP in Hungarian but if, independently, the subject of a nominal-internal predication cannot be a full DP, the ungrammaticality of (60b') follows.

The Hungarian data thus confirm in an interesting way the fact that there are languages in which the postcopular subject of a comparative

QBNP can be a NumP. And they also suggest that the postcopular subject cannot be as large as DP (see also section 5.4.4). That still leaves us some territory in between D and Num to investigate. What about quantifiers in QBNPs? I will turn to this next.

5.4.3   Quantifiers in QBNPs

While Dutch allows its postcopular subjects in comparative QBNPs to be NumPs, it still resists the inclusion of most quantifiers in the second noun phrase. Thus, (63b, c), with the universals *alle* 'all' (which, like its English counterpart, takes a plural) and *ieder* 'every', are ungrammatical—in the case of (63b), regardless of whether the predicate nominal is singular or plural. For (63a), on the other hand, I accept the variant with a singular predicate nominal.[43]

(63) a.   ?die ramp(*en) van een twee feiten (Dutch)
             that disaster(s) of a   two facts
       a′. *een ramp   van een twee feiten
             a. disaster of a   two facts
       a″. *die twee ramp   van een feiten
             that two disaster of a   facts
       b.   *die ramp(en) van (een) alle feiten
             that disaster(s) of   a   all facts
       c.   *die ramp   van (een) ieder feit
             that disaster of   a   every fact

Two things are worth drawing attention to in connection with (63a). First, it should be noted that (63a) becomes ungrammatical if the outer demonstrative is replaced with an indefinite article (see (63a′)).[44] This suggests that the indefinite article preceding N_1 does not form a constituent (exclusively) with N_1—for if it did, (63a′) ought to pattern with *twee feiten zijn een ramp* 'two facts are a disaster', which, however, is grammatical. In other words, (63a′) suggests that the predicate nominal is quite limited in size in comparative QBNPs. But the postcopular subject cannot be too small in size: there is a world of difference between the grammatical variant of (63a) (?*die ramp van een twee feiten*), which while not brilliant is acceptable, and the entirely impossible example in (63a″), with *twee* 'two' placed to the left of the singular predicate nominal (cf. (58b), which also shows that a plural predicate nominal is grammatical here). The ungrammaticality of (63a″) follows if the NumP belonging to the postcopular subject cannot be erected outside the small-clause subject in comparative QBNPs; if the subject's NumP could be projected in the complement of the outer D-head, on top of the LINKER phrase, then *twee* 'two' ought to be able to precede the raised predicate, *quod non*.

The Dutch examples in (63) show that there is a basic split, within the realm of quantification, between numeral quantifiers on the one hand, and other quantifiers on the other. This split is further confirmed by the behavior of Hungarian comparative QBNPs. We saw in the previous section that Hungarian, like Dutch, allows its postcopular subject in comparative QBNPs to be a NumP and to take on plural morphology independently of the predicate. And in Hungarian, as in Dutch, there are speakers who allow the subject to harbor a numeral quantifier.

(64) a. %csoda   egy két könyv (Hungarian)
        wonder a   two book
    b. *csoda   egy kevés könyv
        wonder a   few   book
    c. bárcsak János ne   olvasott   volna (*csoda   egy) akár egy
       if-only János NEG read-PAST would   wonder a   any one
       könyvet   se
       book-ACC NEG
       'If only János had read (*a wonder of) any book.'

But even for those speakers who accept (64a), pure quantifiers like *kevés* 'few' are entirely impossible in that position (see (64b)), and so are negative-polarity items featuring *akár egy* 'any one' (see (64c), taken from Den Dikken 1998b, 189).

In English, too, constructions of the type in (64b, c) are impossible.[45] And for Dutch, we had already seen that pure quantification fails in comparative QBNPs; the same is true when it comes to embedding a negative-polarity item inside the postcopular noun phrase (i.e., the counterpart of Hungarian (64c) is ungrammatical in Dutch as well). Taking NPIs to belong in the set of pure quantifiers, we may conclude that for all three languages investigated, pure quantification of the postcopular subject is impossible in comparative QBNPs.

At this juncture one might in principle pursue two lines of thought when it comes to explaining the ban on pure quantifiers and NPIs in the postcopular subject of comparative QBNPs. One would be to blame it on restrictions on the size of the postcopular noun phrase; the alternative would be to find the cause in a ban on extraction (including QR) and of and from the postcopular noun phrase.

I pursued the latter line of attack in my earlier work (see especially Den Dikken 1998b), seeking a parallel between Copular Inversion constructions, where, as we know from Moro's (1997) work discussed in chapter 4, extraction of and from the postcopular noun phrase is likewise strictly impossible. Under the same rubric of a ban on extraction, I went on to capture the ungrammaticality of *wh*-extraction examples of the type in (65b, c) as well.

(65) a. Brian thinks that this is a wonder of a sentence.
  b. *{What/which sentence} does Brian think this is a wonder of (a) *t*?
  c. *This is the sentence {that/which} Brian thinks this is a wonder of (a).
  d. Brian thinks that this is a wonder of *(a) WHAT?
  e. *Who thinks that this is a wonder of what?

But as Heycock (1998b) is right to note, this account of the *wh*-extraction facts in (65b, c) founders in a number of respects. First, it should be noted that (65b) is ungrammatical even with *what*, a non-D-linked *wh*-element. This is surprising, from the point of view of an analysis that seeks to blame the ill-formedness of (65b) on a ban on *wh*-extraction of the postcopular subject of Predicate Inversion constructions, because in Copular Inversion constructions, *wh*-extraction of plain *what* is not actually ungrammatical (see {*What/*which picture*} *do you think that the cause of the riot was?*). Moreover, Heycock (1998b) points out that even echo-*wh*'s are impossible in comparative QBNPs: example (65d) is impossible without *a*, which shows that *what* simply cannot replace the postcopular noun phrase.[46] That multiple *wh*-questions with an in situ *wh*-element inside the QBNP are impossible as well (see (65e)) fits in with that conclusion.

What we find, then, is that the postcopular noun phrase in a comparative QBNP cannot be a *wh*-phrase at all. And this in all likelihood has everything to do with the size restrictions on the postcopular noun phrase of a comparative QBNP.[47] These size restrictions will also give us an account for the fact that this noun phrase is cannot be a true QP, on the assumption that QPs are larger than NumP (i.e., the functional head Q introducing true quantifiers is higher than Num). É. Kiss (2002, 153) explicitly makes a case to this effect for the structure of the Hungarian noun phrase, proposing that numeral quantifiers (like *két* 'two' in (64a)) occupy SpecNumP while other quantifiers (specifically, for her, those ending in -*ik*, including *melyik* 'which', *mindegyik* 'each', and *bármelyik* 'any') are sitting in the specifier position of a QP dominating NumP.

(66) a.   [$_{QP}$ *melyik* [Q [$_{NumP}$ *két* [Num [$_{NP}$ *kérdés*]]]]] (Hungarian)
              which   two   question
          'which two questions'
     b.   ?[$_{DemP}$ *ezen* [Dem [$_{QP}$ *bármelyik* [Q [$_{NumP}$ [Num [$_{NP}$ *kérdés*]]]]]]]
              this   any   question
          'any of these questions'

On the assumption that quantifiers like *kevés* 'few' and the NPI *akár egy* 'any' belong to the latter class, we then have a basic understanding of the facts in (64), with the subject of a QBNP extending maximally to NumP.

That the size approach is right is further suggested by the fact that the ban on pure quantifiers and *wh*-elements observed above for comparative QBNPs carries over in its entirety to *attributive* QBNPs, which, as I argued in section 5.2 (see also Doetjes and Rooryck 2001), are not derived via Predicate Inversion.

(67) a.   an idiot of {a/*every} doctor
     b.   If only there had been an idiot of {a/*any} doctor around.
     c.   Brian thinks that Slop is an idiot of *(a) WHAT?
     d.   *Who thinks that Slop is an idiot of what?

For attributive QBNPs, I had established in section 5.2 that the post-*of* noun phrase is a NumP. So on the plausible assumption that *wh*-phrases and true QPs are necessarily larger than NumP, the ungrammaticality of the relevant variants of (67a–d) follows straightforwardly. By the same token, that of the relevant variants of (63)–(65) falls out as well—given that the postcopular noun phrase of a comparative QBNP, like that of an attributive QBNP, is a NumP, no smaller than a NumP (recall Dutch (63a) versus (63a″)) and no larger than that.[48]

5.4.4   The Size of the Subconstituents of Comparative QBNPs

Let us take stock at this point. We have just reached the conclusion that the postcopular noun phrase of comparative QBNPs is a NumP—no smaller, no larger. For the precopular noun phrase, our discussion in section 5.3 had already led to the conclusion that demonstratives and indefinite articles that linearly precede it do not form a constituent with it. For demonstratives, I argued this on the basis of the fact that postulating *that N* as the predicate nominal does not deliver a sensible semantics for comparative QBNPs.[49] With regard to the indefinite article, I presented the contrast between (24) and (45), repeated below, to show that attributive and comparative QBNPs differ minimally when it comes to the location of the outer indefinite article: in the former, it forms a constituent with N_1 (as a result of which *a* N_1 can be converted into *no* N_1 within the small clause, but there is no chance of interpreting *no* as an associate of sentential negation), but in the latter it takes the entire *N of a N* sequence as its complement, allowing a sentential negation reading for *no N of a N*, as in (45b, c).

(24) a.   He is not a fool of a president.
     b. (*)He is no fool of a president.

(45) a.   This is a jewel of a village.
     b.   No, I disagree—it's no jewel of a village at all; in fact, it's quite an ugly place.
     c.   No, this is no jewel of a VILLAGE, it is a jewel of a TOWN.

While (45) suggests is that it is possible for the outer indefinite article to take the entire *N of a N* sequence as its complement, it does not tell us whether the precopular noun phrase is a bare NP or larger than that. An indication that the predicate nominal can be as large as NumP was provided by the Dutch example in (58a), where N_1 is preceded by a numeral and an attributive modifier that form a constituent with N_1 (given that (58a) is the nominal-internal counterpart of the copular sentence *Die feiten zijn één grote ramp* 'Those facts are one big disaster', where *één grote ramp* as a unit serves as the predicate nominal; see note 38).

(58a) één grote ramp   van een feiten (Dutch)
      one big   disaster of   a   facts

For English, the question of whether the predicate nominal is a bare NP or a NumP is perhaps harder to answer on empirical grounds with specific reference to the comparative QBNP. But from the discussion in 5.2.3 of the distribution of bare NP predicate nominals in Dutch and English, the reader may recall that in English, bare NP predicates are licit only if the subject is likewise a bare NP (as in *of*-less attributive QBNPs such as *an idiot doctor*). That conclusion, in conjunction with our finding that the postcopular subject of comparative QBNPs is a NumP, leads us to an analysis of the precopular noun phrase in English QBNPs as a NumP as well.

Pulling these findings together, we can update the representation of comparative QBNPs in (46) by filling in the category labels for the constituent noun phrases of this structure: both the precopular noun phrase and the postcopular subject are NumPs, just as in attributive QBNPs.

(46′) [$_{NumP}$ Num [$_{FP}$ [SIMILAR [$_{NumP}$ Num NP$_{Pred}$]]]$_j$ [LINKER+RELATOR$_i$ [$_{RP}$ [$_{NumP}$ Num NP$_{Subj}$] [t_i t_j]]]]]

Outside the outer NumP in (46′), other nominal material (including demonstratives and, with certain restrictions,[50] definite articles as well) can be added, but (46′) is the core structure of comparative QBNPs. The key difference between comparative and attributive QBNPs, then, lies not in the size of their nominal subconstituents but in the question of whether the predicate originates as the specifier of the RELATOR or instead as its complement, with Predicate Inversion obtaining in the latter case due to the empty-headedness of the predicate.[51]

One last question. We have now reached the general conclusion that in QBNPs of all types (attributive QBNPs featuring *of*, *of*-less attributive QBNPs, and comparative QBNPs) the nominal constituents of the DP-internal small clause are systematically no larger than NumP. A question that arises at this point is why they cannot be any larger—why, in particular, can the nominal constituents of the small clause not be DemPs or DPs? Let me start with the question of why DP is unsuitable. Here I follow Kayne (1994, 86) in assuming that D cannot take a DP complement, which Kayne takes as given. And for demonstratives (which originate lower in the tree than determiners; see Bernstein 1997 and Giusti 1997), I assume that they are systematically dependent on a strictly local D-head (note that demonstratives in the Germanic languages are typically amalgams of the definite determiner and some deictic marker: English *th+at/is*, Dutch *d+at/it/ie/eze*; see also the discussion of Spanish demonstratives in section 5.5.1), which prevents them from being structurally severed from the D-head. The biggest the nominal constituents of QBNPs can ever get, therefore, is NumP.

5.5   Real and "Spurious" Articles in Qualitative Binominal Noun Phrases

5.5.1   "Your Feet's Too Big"—or Are They? "Spurious" Definite Articles in Romance QBNPs

The claim that the constituent noun phrases of QBNPs are no larger than NumP seems to be flatly contradicted by the Italian example in (68a), from Napoli (1989, 203) (recall (4), from section 5.1), and their Spanish counterparts in (69a, a′, a″) featuring a definite article (the *-l* of *del*) in front of N_2 (Español-Echevarría 1997, 1998, and personal communication; also Longenecker 2002).[52,53]

(68) a.   quell' ignorante del   dottore (Comparative QBNP)
          that ignoramus of-the doctor   (Italian)
     b.   quell' ignorante di (*un[54]) dottore (Attributive QBNP)
          that   ignoramus of a   doctor

(69) a.   %ese ignorante del   doctor (Comparative QBNP) (Spanish)
          that ignoramus of-the doctor
     a′. el   imbécil de(%l) doctor ese
          the idiot   of(the) doctor that
     a″. el   imbécil ese de(%l) doctor
          the idiot   that of(the) doctor
     b.   ese ignorante de (*un) doctor (Attributive QBNP)
          that ignoramus of a   doctor

Let us start the discussion from the vantage point of Spanish (69a″). It would appear at first sight that we are dealing here with a demonstrative noun phrase *imbécil ese* that serves as the predicate nominal. But I already pointed out in the discussion of Doetjes and Rooryck (2001) in section 5.3.5 that taking the demonstrative to form a constituent with the first noun phrase makes for a very implausible semantics (a predication relationship between 'that idiot' and 'doctor'). Moreover, our crosslinguistic investigations in the foregoing have led to the conclusion that the precopular noun phrase is never larger than NumP. More likely, therefore, *ese*, in all of (69a, a′, a″), forms a constituent with the entire *N de(l) N* sequence. That is, underlyingly, we are dealing with a structure in which the demonstrative *ese* occupies the head position of a DemP generated outside the constituent harboring the *N de(l) N* sequence, as in (70a).[55] The surface outputs in (69a′, a″) then result from raising to Spec-DemP of either the entire *imbécil de(l) doctor* sequence (producing (69a′)) or just the predicate nominal *imbécil* (resulting in (69a″)). These derivations are depicted in (70b, c), where the outer D-head is spelled out as *el*. Alternatively, the outer D may be null, in which case the demonstrative *ese* raises up to it, producing the word order in (69a), where *ese* precedes the rest of the noun phrase thanks to having raised up to D.[56]

(70) a. [DP D [DemP _____ [*ese* [[*imbécil*] [*de (el) doctor*]]]]]
    b. [DP *el* [DemP [[*imbécil*] [*de (el) doctor*]]ᵢ [*ese* t_i]]]
    c. [DP *el* [DemP [*imbécil*]ⱼ [*ese* [t_j [*de (el) doctor*]]]]]]

This analysis has the advantage of keeping the predicate nominal small and generating the demonstrative where it belongs: on this construal, the predicate nominal in (69a″) does not in fact contain a demonstrative; the demonstrative instead belongs to the entire QBNP, as desired.

That this approach to (69a″) is superior to one in which the demonstrative forms a constituent with the predicate nominal is suggested as well by some observations presented in Casillas Martínez 2001, 54–55.

(71) a.   ese   libro   redondo (Spanish)
         that.M book.M round.M (e.g., a children's book)
    b.   esa   mierda de libro   redondo
         that.F shit.F of book.M round.M
         'that shit of a round book'
    c. ??esa   mierda redonda de libro
         that.F shit.F round.F of book.M
    d.   esa   mierda redonda de libro   no cabe en la caja
         that.F shit.F   round.F of book.M NEG fit   in the box
         cuadrada
         square
         'That round shit of a book won't fit in the square box.'

Casillas Martínez notes that the modifier *round* would normally go onto *book*, as in (71b), paraphrased in English as *that shit of a round book*, where *round* clearly forms a constituent with the second noun phrase. But (71d) is grammatical in the context given (though out of context it is distinctly odd, as (71c) shows). It would appear at first blush that *redonda* in (71d) forms a constituent with the predicate nominal. But of course "round shit" is nonsense, no matter what the context. Spanish (71d) is paraphrased in English as *that round shit of a book*, which is readily compatible with a construal of *round* as a modifier of the entire *N of a N* sequence. For Spanish, surface word order seems to resist such a construal: *redonda*, after all, surfaces to the immediate right of *mierda*, not to the right of *mierda de libro*. But we can nonetheless structurally represent it as a modifier of all of *mierda de libro* if we insert it to the left of the entire *N de N* sequence and raise the predicate nominal around it, into a higher specifier position—specifically, the specifier position of DemP. With the demonstrative *esa* raising up further to the D-head (base-generated empty in this case, as in (69a)), the desired surface word order then results.

(72) a. [$_{DP}$ D [$_{DemP}$ _____ [*esa* [*redonda* [[*mierda*] [*de libro*]]]]]]

     b. [$_{DP}$ D+*esa*$_j$ [$_{DemP}$ [*mierda*]$_i$ [t_j [*redonda* [t_i [*de libro*]]]]]]

The thing to note is that the derivation of (71d) exploits exactly the same operation (raising to SpecDemP) that is also employed in the proposed derivation of (69a″), depicted in (70c). I take it, then, that the facts in (69a″) and (71d) mutually reinforce each other and confirm the conclusion that, despite surface appearances, the predicate nominal of the Spanish QBNP is never as large as a DemP.

So far, this discussion of Spanish (69) has yielded two beneficial results—we have managed to keep the predicate nominal smaller than it appears to be in (69a″), and we have gained an understanding of the syntax of demonstratives in Spanish QBNPs: these are heads base-generated outside the small clause, and they raise up to D whenever D is not base-filled with a definite determiner. With this in mind, I would like to address the question of what to do with the definite article preceding N$_2$ in the Italian and Spanish examples in (68a) and (69a, a′, a″).

The discussion by Español-Echevarría (1997, 1998) of what he calls "definiteness-agreement" effects in Spanish QBNPs is particularly germane to this question. As Español-Echevarría points out, while Spanish QBNPs with an outer demonstrative for many speakers allow the alternation illustrated in (69a, b), QBNPs with an outside definite or indefinite article have only one grammatical output: one in which the two noun phrases agree in definiteness, as seen in (73) and (74).[57]

(73) a. el imbécil del doctor   (74) a. *un imbécil del doctor
        the idiot of-the doctor   an idiot of-the doctor

     b. *el imbécil de doctor   b. un imbécil de doctor
        the idiot of doctor   an idiot of doctor

This "definiteness-agreement" effect is quite puzzling. It is not found in demonstrative QBNPs, as we have already seen (see (69a–a″)): there, we find an alternation between *de* and *del*, and we get this alternation even in cases in which the demonstrative (*ese*) occurs to the right of N$_1$ or all the way at the end of the sequence, as illustrated in (69a′) and (69a″). The significance of these examples, in relation to (73), is that here we find the outer D-head spelled out as *el*, as in (73), but unlike in (73) we still have a choice when it comes to the lexicalization of a definite article in front of N_2. Moreover, the "definiteness-agreement" effect seen in (73) is not found in other complex noun phrases featuring *de* in Spanish (see, e.g., (75a)), nor is it a property of Spanish nominal predication constructions that the predicate nominal and its subject must agree in definiteness (see (75b)).

(75) a. la/una casa del   doctor (Spanish)
        the/a house of-the doctor
     b. el   doctor es un imbécil
        the doctor is an idiot

From (75b) we learn that it would be wrong to treat the "agreement effect" as a case of subject-predicate or Spec-Head agreement, nor would we want it to be some sort of Agree relationship between the outer D-head and the D-head of a DP embedded within the complex noun phrase—or else (75a) would be tough to accommodate. We do arguably want it to be an Agree relationship emanating from D, but as in the case of Agree relationships in general, we want the target to be the closest available match. So let us take this as our starting point: the outer D-head has a specification for definiteness and seeks to establish an Agree relationship with the closest available bearer of a definiteness feature.

For all cases in which there is a demonstrative base-generated right below D, this Agree relationship can straightforwardly be established between D and Dem: on the natural assumption that demonstratives share their specification for definiteness with the definite article (but see the text below (78) for a qualification in the light of Español-Echevarría 1997, 1998), any Agree relationship emanating from D qua probe will target the Dem-head. This is sufficient, for now, to ensure that, whenever a demonstrative is present in Spanish QBNPs (as in (69)), no definiteness requirements are placed on the marker preceding N_2: it can be either *el* or null.

Now consider what happens when there is no demonstrative right below D. In that case, D will have to establish an Agree relationship with something lower down in the structure—to be precise, with something inside RP in the case of attributive QBNPs, and something inside the LINKER's projection (FP) in comparative QBNPs.

(76) a. [$_{DP}$ D [$_{RP}$ [$_{NumP}$ Num NP$_1$] [RELATOR [$_{NumP}$ Num NP$_2$]]]]
     b. [$_{DP}$ D [$_{FP}$ [SIMILAR NP$_1$]$_j$ [LINKER+RELATOR$_i$ [$_{RP}$ [$_{NumP}$ Num NP$_2$] [t_i t_j]]]]]

Recall from the discussion in chapter 4 that the small clause (RP) in (76a) is a phase, and that in (76b) movement of the RELATOR up to the LINKER extends the RP-phase up to FP. So in (76a) D will be unable to establish an Agree relationship with anything inside the RELATOR's complement, and in (76b) it cannot Agree with anything inside RP. The constituents in the specifier positions of RP in (76a) and FP in (76b) *are* possible targets for D qua probe, but so is the *head* of D's complement. That head would, if specifiable for a matching definiteness feature, be *closer* to D than the head of the specifier of RP/FP. That is, in an abstract structure of the type in (77), where δ is the head of the specifier of α's complement and ε is the head of α's complement, α (which has a formal feature matched by both δ and ε) should prefer to establish an Agree relationship with ε rather than with δ: α and ε are separated by fewer maximal projections than are α and δ.[58]

(77) $[\alpha_{FF}\ [\beta\ [\gamma\ \delta_{FF}]\ [\varepsilon_{FF} \ldots]]]$

Now suppose that the RELATOR-head of Spanish QBNPs is specifiable for definiteness, by being spelled out as the definite article. Then specifying it for the feature [+DEF] should be optimal in a QBNP whose outside D-head is likewise specified as [+DEF]: by having the RELATOR specified for a matching definiteness feature, D can get its own definiteness feature checked in the most economical of ways. In (76a), the structure of an attributive QBNP, the RELATOR is spelled out as the nominal copula, *de* in Spanish, so generating a definite article there is out of the question. But in (76b), it would certainly be possible to have the RELATOR spelled out as the definite article. Given a choice between generating *el*, which is inherently [+DEF], under the RELATOR (as in (73a)) or having the precopular noun phrase specified as [+DEF] (as in (73b)), the former should be chosen because it produces a more economical way of checking the outer D-head's [+DEF] feature.[59] And since, with *el* being a spell-out of the RELATOR, (73a) can only be derived via (76b), this predicts that the QBNP in (73a) should be unambiguously *comparative* (i.e., the referent of the noun phrase is an idiot as an *individual*). This prediction is borne out: Manuel Español-Echevarría and Ana Longenecker (personal communication) confirm that (73a) supports no attributive reading ('an idiot as a doctor').[60]

In (74), *el* under the RELATOR has no chance of survival since there is nothing to match its [+DEF] specification. So (74a) is ruled out via that route on account of a violation of Full Interpretation. And note that the fact that (74a) is ungrammatical also shows that it would be a mistake to contemplate the possibility of generating the definite article as a constituent of the postcopular noun phrase. If *el* could be mapped into a constituent with N_2, there would be no obvious reason why (74a) should be bad—after all, *El doctor es un imbécil* 'The doctor is an idiot', with a definite subject to an indefinite predicate nominal, is perfectly well formed. We must conclude that the definite article preceding the second noun in a Spanish QBNP absolutely cannot form a constituent with that noun.

If this analysis of the "definiteness-agreement" effect in (73) and (74) holds water, it strongly suggests that the token of the definite article intervening between *de* and N_2 in examples such as (73a) originates under the RELATOR-head, and is thus a "spurious" definite article—in effect, the definite counterpart of the "spurious" indefinite article found in Dutch QBNPs (see Bennis, Corver, and Den Dikken 1998 and the discussion above). This has the significant advantage that it keeps the size of the postcopular noun phrase in Spanish QBNPs of the type in (73a) smaller than it would appear to be at face value. After all, all we need in postcopular position in (73a) is a NumP. Thus, treating the definite article following *de* in (73a) as a "spurious" definite article allows us to reconcile the Spanish facts with the conclusion, drawn on the basis of our investigation of the quantificational properties of the second noun phrase in QBNPs, that the postcopular noun phrase of QBNPs is never larger than NumP.

Treating the definite article following *de* as a "spurious" definite article occupying the RELATOR-head will also give us a perspective on the alternations in (68) in Italian and (69) in Spanish, and the interpretive contrast that they exhibit. For ease of reference, let me repeat the key examples here.

(68) a.   quell' ignorante del   dottore (Comparative QBNP) (Italian)
           that   ignoramus of-the doctor
     b.   quell' ignorante di (*un) dottore (Attributive QBNP)
           that   ignoramus of   a   doctor

(69) a.   %ese ignorante del   doctor (Comparative QBNP) (Spanish)
           that ignoramus of-the doctor
     b.   ese ignorante de (*un) doctor (Attributive QBNP)
           that ignoramus of   a   doctor

In the introductory discussion in section 5.1, I noted that Napoli (1989, 203) points out, insightfully, that in Italian (68b) the referent of the complex noun phrase is an ignoramus *in his capacity of being a doctor*, while in (68a) being a doctor by profession is incidental to the fact that he is an idiot: the referent of *quell'ignorante del dottore* is an ignorant *individual* (and may actually be an excellent doctor). So (68b), with bare *di*, is unambiguously an *attributive* QBNP, whose derivation is based on the predicate-specifier structure in (14b), whereas (68a) is what I have called a *comparative* QBNP. The Spanish facts in (69) show a similar interpretive distinction between the a- and b-examples.[61]

Interestingly, then, we find that in the *comparative* QBNP in (68a), whose derivation involves Predicate Inversion and raising of the RELATOR head up to the LINKER (*di/de*), a definite article in front of the second noun is obligatory. In the *attributive* QBNP, on the other hand, the postcopular noun phrase must be completely articleless: even adding the indefinite article *un* between *di/de* and N_2 is impossible. What I said in the discussion of (73) (with (73a) unambiguously comparative) allows us to make sense of this pattern.

The fact that (68a) and (69a) are unambiguously comparative while (68b) and (69b) are attributive means that (68a) and (69a) are derived via Predicate Inversion and the word order in (68b) and (69b) is base-generated in a predicate-specifier structure. The structures in (78) illustrate this for the Spanish examples. The structure in (78b) is perfectly well formed with a token of *de* sitting under the RELATOR-head, and with D checking its [+DEF] feature against the matching feature of the demonstrative in Dem^0. No "spurious" indefinite article is called upon—in fact, there is no space for one in (78b): the RELATOR-head is already being realized by *de*, and as in the discussion of Dutch "spurious" articles (see section 5.2.3), the nominal copula and the "spurious" article are in complementary distribution as lexicalizations of the RELATOR (recall (73a)). So (78b) yields an output in which there is no definite article between *de* (the RELATOR) and *doctor*—as desired: (69b) is attributive. In (78a), on the other hand, *de* lexicalizes the LINKER. Hence, the RELATOR-head is available in principle for *el* to spell out. With *el* lexicalizing the RELATOR and *de* spelling out the LINKER, we obtain the example in (69a), an unambiguously *comparative* QBNP that can only result from (78a).

(78) a. [DP D [DemP *ese* [FP [SIMILAR NP_1]ⱼ [LINKER+RELATORᵢ [RP [NumP Num NP_2] [t_i t_j]]]]]]

     b. [DP D [DemP *ese* [RP [NumP Num NP_1] [RELATOR [NumP Num NP_2]]]]]

Viewed this way, then, the facts in (68) and (69) confirm a conclusion we had reached in section 5.2.3 on the basis of an investigation of the facts of Dutch: that "spurious" articles can only be used in *comparative* QBNPs. While this is an interesting result that addresses our most pressing concerns about (69) (and Italian (68) as well), two questions remain that I will briefly address in closing this subsection. One is the question of why the RELATOR should be spelled out as *el* at all (given that a null RELATOR would also seem to have done the job: D's definiteness has already been checked against the demonstrative). Another is why there should be variation among Spanish speakers when it comes to the acceptability of (69a). To this latter question, Español-Echevarría (1997, 1998) suggests an answer that capitalizes on the feature content of demonstratives in Spanish: demonstratives possess the feature specification [+DEF] only in a subset of dialects of Spanish; in others they have no specification for [DEF] at all. The latter dialects will never enable the demonstrative to satisfy D's [+DEF] feature; a "spurious" definite article under the RELATOR-head is then called for in all demonstrative QBNPs, on a par with (73a). On the other hand, in dialects in which demonstratives *are* specified [+DEF], there is no reason for the RELATOR-head of comparative QBNPs to be spelled out as the "spurious" definite article—and by general considerations of economy, one will then forgo the lexicalization of the RELATOR as a "spurious" article.[62] For those speakers, then, there is no formal contrast between comparative and attributive QBNPs (as in French; see Hulk and Tellier 1999, 2000, and note 53, above).[63]

5.5.2   On the Distribution of "Spurious" Articles

This leaves us with one last thing to take care of in the discussion of the Romance facts: the bareness of the noun phrase following the nominal copula in examples such as (68b), (69b), and (74b). From English and Dutch, we are not familiar with such bare noun phrases in postcopular position—in fact, in these languages, bare noun phrases are systematically impossible there. The case of Dutch is perhaps particularly striking. For while Dutch would normally have mass nouns such as *spinazie* 'spinach' occur without an indefinite article, as in (79a) (where, as a matter of fact, *spinazie* linearly follows *van* 'of', as in (79b)), it demands an indefinite article in front of *spinazie* in the comparative QBNP in (80b) (see Bennis, Corver, and Den Dikken 1998).

(79) a. Brian houdt niet van (*een) spinazie (Dutch)
     Brian holds not of   a   spinach
  b. die pracht van *(een) spinazie
     that beauty of   a   spinach

Bennis, Corver, and Den Dikken (1998) treat the indefinite article preceding *spinazie* as an instance of the "spurious" indefinite article, and present
an analysis of the distribution of the "spurious" indefinite article that
ensures that *een* must be lexicalized in (79b). I refer the reader to the
aforementioned article for the details of this analysis, which are irrelevant
here. What matters for our purposes here is that, even in contexts in
which Dutch would otherwise want the noun phrase to be bare, it forces
an indefinite article in front of N_2 in its QBNPs. Romance is the exact
opposite of Dutch in this respect. For in Romance, indefinite articles
that are otherwise obligatory (see Italian **(Un) dottore è un ignorante*
'A doctor is an ignoramus') suddenly disappear in QBNPs (as in attributive *quell' ignorante di (*un) dottore* 'that ignoramus of a doctor', (68b)).

German holds an interesting middle ground between Dutch (and English) and Romance in this respect. German (80) is a near-minimal pair
(from Van Caspel 1970, 286, via Aarts 1998, 151) of which the a-example
is not particularly exciting from a Germanic perspective. But (80b) (which
is from Heinrich Heine's work) is interesting, in two respects: it lacks an
indefinite article on N_2, and, apparently concomitantly, it shows nominative rather than dative case on the second noun phrase.

(80) a. ein Schurke von einem Bedienten (German)
     an villain   of a-DAT servant-DAT
  b. ein alter Schelm von Lohnbediener
     an old   villain of waged servant-NOM

While examples of the type in (80b) for many present-day German
speakers have a distinctly archaic flavor, there are varieties of German in
which alternations of the type in (80) are still entirely natural. Thus,
Abraham (1998) mentions the example in (81) without commenting on
any particular awkwardness of its variant lacking *einem*.[64]

(81) ein Biest von (einem) Direktor (German)
    a   beast of a-DAT manager

It is important to note, however, that alternations of this type are not possible across the board in German QBNPs. Thus, (82), while perfect with
einem included, is deviant with a bare noun phrase following *von*.[65]

(82) ein Schatz von *(einem) Kind (German)
     a   treasure of   a-DAT   child

The contrast between (81) and (82) suggests that omission of the indefinite article in front of N_2 is grammatical in German in *attributive*
QBNPs only: (81) is of course perfectly compatible with an attributive interpretation ('an animal in his capacity as a manager'), but (82) does not
support such a reading. That the attributive/comparative dichotomy does
indeed underlie the omissibility of the indefinite article preceding N_2 is
further confirmed by the fact that of the examples in (83) (modeled on
Napoli's (1989) Italian examples in (68)), (83b) is unambiguously attributive (as Werner Abraham, personal communication, tells me). The example in (83a), on the other hand, is compatible with both readings of
English *that nitwit of a doctor*—the doctor can either be a nitwit as a doctor or as an individual.

(83) a. was für ein Armleuchter von einem Arzt! (German)
        what for a   nitwit   of a-DAT doctor
     b. was für ein Armleuchter von Arzt!
        what for a   nitwit   of doctor
        Both: 'What a nitwit of a doctor!'

Thus, omission of the indefinite article in front of N_2 disambiguates German QBNPs toward their attributive interpretations. This is an interesting result since, as we saw in the discussion of (68) and (69), omission of
the definite article in front of N_2 in Romance QBNPs disambiguates them
toward their attributive readings as well.

The German and Romance facts are not entirely parallel, however:
while the a-examples in (68) and (69) are unambiguously comparative
('The doctor is a nitwit as an individual'), German (83a) is ambiguous.
This is readily understandable from the point of view of the account of
QBNPs developed in the foregoing. Recall that the nominal constituents
of the small clauses in both comparative and attributive QBNPs are maximally NumPs. That means that the definite article preceding N_2 in Italian (68a) and Spanish (69a) *cannot* be mapped into the second noun
phrase; in other words, it *must* be a "spurious" definite article. And with
"spurious" articles occupying the RELATOR-head and therefore competing
with the nominal copula in attributive QBNPs (after all, in attributive
QBNPs the nominal copula occupies the RELATOR position), it then follows that (68a) and (69a) cannot support an attributive interpretation.

Things are different for German (83a). There, there is nothing to force *einem* to be construed as a "spurious" indefinite article: since *einem* is an indefinite article, it can be mapped perfectly well into the postcopular singular noun phrase of an attributive QBNP. So German (83a) is correctly predicted to be perfectly compatible with two interpretations (like its English counterpart).

What, then, makes (83b) and the Romance examples in (68b) and (69b) incompatible with the comparative interpretation? The answer must take cognizance of the fact that, in the absence of an article between the nominal copula (*di, de, von*) and the second noun phrase, the RELATOR-head of comparative QBNPs is radically *empty*. Apparently, this is illegitimate.

(84) The RELATOR-head of comparative QBNPs must have feature
content.[66]

What are the roots of this generalization? My answer to this question capitalizes on the fact, established in chapter 4, that in Predicate Inversion constructions in which the head of the predicate does not move up to the RELATOR, the RELATOR must raise up to a small-clause external functional head (the LINKER) to make inversion of the predicate around its subject legitimate. Comparative QBNPs are instances of this scenario: their derivation involves nonbeheaded Predicate Inversion, and hence the RELATOR must raise. Now, on the minimalist assumption that movement is driven by the need to check a feature of the probe, this means, for the specific case of movement of the RELATOR up to the LINKER, that the RELATOR must possess (a) certain feature(s) that it can check against the LINKER once it gets there. The nature of the feature(s) in question is not particularly relevant—I have no proposal to make with regard to this. But *that* there must be some feature that the LINKER checks against the RELATOR that it attracts in overt syntax is a given, on the assumptions laid out in Chomsky's (1995) work.

Now, if the RELATOR head were to be radically empty (i.e., lack features altogether), that would make movement of the RELATOR up to the LINKER illegitimate, on minimalist assumptions. But we know that Predicate Inversion succeeds perfectly well in the derivation of comparative QBNPs, which means, in turn, that raising of the RELATOR to the LINKER must be successful as well. And in order for the RELATOR to be eligible for movement, it must have features. That then means that the RELATOR cannot be radically empty in comparative QBNPs—*QED*.

Thus we derive the conclusion that in comparative QBNPs, the RELA-TOR head must have feature content (84). And with this conclusion in place, we can return to the question that I raised at the beginning of the previous paragraph: why (68b), (69b), and (83b) are incompatible with a comparative interpretation. The answer is now straightforward: to procure a comparative interpretation, a Predicate Inversion derivation built on a predicate-complement structure must be executed. But in order for such a derivation to converge, a "spurious" article is needed under the RELATOR-head, to provide the RELATOR with the requisite features and thereby make raising of the RELATOR up to the LINKER possible. Since the examples in (68b), (69b), and (83b) all distinguish themselves precisely in *lacking* a "spurious" article, that is what makes them ungrammatical qua comparative QBNPs.

This then takes us back, in closing, to the grammaticality of these examples on their attributive readings, and to the question of why the indefinite article that seems to belong to N_2 is absent in these QBNPs. One possible answer would be: because the postcopular subject is a bare NP in these examples. That answer would cause some friction with the conclusion, reached in section 5.2, that the postcopular noun phrase of attributive QBNPs is a NumP. That conclusion could have been arrived at prematurely, of course. It seems unlikely, however, that the postcopular noun phrases in Romance and German attributive QBNPs are indeed bare NPs. To see this, consider first constructions of the type in (18), repeated below. These are good candidates for featuring a truly bare NP as their predicate nominals.

(18) a. hij is dokter (van beroep) (Dutch)
      he is doctor of   profession
    b. zij   zijn dokter (van beroep)
      they are doctor of   profession

The fact that the predicate nominal in (18b) does not have any plural-marking (even though its subject is plural) suggests that its structure radically lacks a NumP (hence plural-marking, which is to be checked against Num, is not licensed). Moreover, adjectival modification of the bare predicate nominal is usually impossible (see (85)).[67]

(85) a. hij is een uitstekende/beroemd(e) dokter (Dutch)
       he is an excellent/famous(AGR) doctor
    b. *hij is uitstekend/beroemd dokter
       he is excellent/famous   doctor

The ungrammaticality of (85b) follows if the predicate nominal in constructions of the type in (18) is a truly bare NP, and if attributive adjectival modification is dependent on the presence, outside the bare NP, of a functional projection harboring the modifier (see Cinque 1999; also see the discussion in chapter 2, above: the Cinquean functional head will serve as a RELATOR of the attributive modifier (a predicate-specifier) and the bare noun phrase).

The relevance of these observations in connection with the question of whether the apparently bare noun phrase following the nominal copula in the QBNPs in (68b), (69b), and (83b) is truly a bare NP will become clear when we go back to the Spanish examples in (59) and (71b), repeated here.

(59) un   asco   de croquetas (Spanish)
  a.MSG disgust.MSG of croquettes.FPL
  'some disgusting croquettes'

(71b) esa   mierda de libro   redondo (Spanish)
   that.F shit.F   of book.M round.M
   'that shit of a round book'

Note first that, as (59) shows, the bare second noun phrase of Spanish QBNPs can be pluralized (independently of the predicate nominal), while truly bare noun phrases such as the predicate nominal in Dutch (18b) cannot. The fact, then, that plural marking is possible on N_2 in (59) indicates that its extended projection must include NumP. Consonant with this is the fact that the second noun can be independently modified even when bare, as seen in (71b): here, *redondo* is a modifier strictly of the second noun (with which it agrees in gender).[68] In light of the fact that truly bare NPs are unmodifiable (see (85b)), the fact that this QBNP is grammatical and features an articleless noun phrase in postcopular position confirms the conclusion that the postcopular noun phrase in QBNPs of the type in (68b), (69b), and (83b) is not in fact a bare NP.

This conclusion is sufficient for my purposes here—for with this conclusion in place, we have eliminated the threat that (68b), (69b), and (83b) apparently pose to the generalization reached in section 5.2 that the postcopular noun phrase of attributive QBNPs is a NumP. These examples do not actually threaten this conclusion: the postcopular noun phrases in these attributive QBNPs *are* in fact NumPs, but the head of these singular NumPs is not lexically realized. This naturally gives rise to broader questions concerning the licensing of the null Num-head of singular NumPs—questions whose urgency is stressed by the fact that in Dutch, which is closely related to German, articleless singular noun phrases following *van* 'of' are strictly impossible. For lack of clear insight into these questions, I will leave them aside here. But whatever the answers to these questions (which are well beyond my present reach), the conclusion drawn from the grammaticality of modification (see (71b)) will stand: the postcopular noun phrase of attributive QBNPs is *never* a bare NP, not even when it looks like one at first glance.

5.5.3   Concluding Remarks

In this section, I discussed the distribution of articles, real and "spurious," in the two types of QBNP. The conclusion reached at the end of section 5.4 that the pre- and postcopular noun phrases of both attributive and comparative QBNPs are NumPs was shown to stand up to scrutiny in the face of apparently serious threats posed by QBNPs in Romance and German. I argued that demonstratives intervening between N_1 and the nominal copula in Spanish do not form a constituent with N_1 but instead take the entire *N of a N* sequence as their complement. I also showed that apparently bare postcopular noun phrases are not truly bare NPs, and that there are solid grounds for believing that the definite article preceding N_2 in comparative QBNPs in Italian and Spanish is a lexicalization of the RELATOR-head—a "spurious" definite article, in other words.

The isolation of a "spurious" definite article in the syntax of Romance comparative QBNPs led me to an investigation of the distribution of "spurious" articles in qualitative binominal noun phrases. Arguing that the need for phase-extending movement of the RELATOR up to the small-clause external LINKER requires the RELATOR to have feature-content, I concluded that the obligatory presence of an overt RELATOR (in the form of a "spurious" article) can largely be explained on account of the fact that in comparative QBNPs the RELATOR is not allowed to be radically empty.[69]

5.6   The Nominal Copula

What all QBNPs discussed in this chapter so far (except for English-specific "bare" attributive QBNPs such as *an idiot doctor*) share is the presence, in between the two constituent noun phrases, of a meaningless prepositional element, *of* in English. I have analyzed this element as the nominal counterpart of the copula *be*—a purely grammatical marker.

(7) *Of* is a nominal copula.

In this section, I will undertake to further support this approach to *of*, by first of all confronting it with other approaches to *of* in QBNPs in the extant literature, and subsequently by presenting some interesting cross-linguistic evidence underpinning the account.

5.6.1 *Of* in Previous Analyses

The question of what to do with *of* in QBNPs is not an easy one. While some options are readily discarded, settling on a satisfactory analysis has proved tougher. When it comes to eliminating analyses, we can make short shrift of the approach to QBNPs taken in Abney 1987, Napoli 1989, and Everaert 1992, which takes *of* to be a preposition heading a PP-complement to the first noun.

(86) [$_{NP}$ *a/that* [$_{N'}$ *jewel* [$_{PP}$ *of* [$_{NP}$ *a village*]]]]

This analysis is refuted on a number of counts. First, the fact that—productively in British English, but on a much more limited scale in American English (see Napoli 1989; Aarts 1998)—the first noun can take a complement of its own (as in (87)) pleads strongly against an approach to the *of* + N$_2$ sequence of the QBNP as a complement of N$_1$. Second, the fact that extraposing and preposing the *of* + N$_2$, as well as quantification of and extraction of and from the second noun phrase, are all barred in QBNPs (see (88)) would be entirely unexpected on a complementation approach à la (86): such an analysis assigns *a picture of a girl* the exact same parse on its QBNP reading ('a very beautiful girl') as on its more familiar interpretations ('a picture belonging to a girl, taken by a girl, depicting a girl').[70]

(87) a.   that son of a bitch of a boss
     b.   %that manipulator of people of a mayor
     c.   %that destroyer of education of a minister

(88) a.   He saw a picture of a girl yesterday.   √QBNP ('a very
                                                    beautiful girl')
     a′.   He saw a beauty of a girl yesterday.
     b.   He saw a picture yesterday of a girl.   *QBNP
     b′. *He saw a beauty yesterday of a girl.
     c.   Of a girl, he saw a picture yesterday.   *QBNP
     c′. *Of a girl, he saw a beauty yesterday.
     d.   The girl that he saw a picture of yesterday. *QBNP

d'.   *The girl that he saw a beauty of yesterday.
e.   He saw a picture of every girl yesterday.   *QBNP
e'.   *He saw a beauty of every girl yesterday.

More microscopically, with specific reference to *of*, we may point out as evidence against (86) that the *of* of QBNPs crosslinguistically does not give rise to the same kind of behavior that purely prepositional incarnations of *of* give rise to. Thus, in German, the *von* of QBNPs does not *have to* mark the noun phrase that follows it as dative—recall the pair in (80), repeated below.

(80) a. ein Schurke von einem Bedienten (German)
         an villain   of   a-DAT servant-DAT
     b. ein alter Schelm von Lohnbedienter
         an old   villain of   waged servant-NOM

While (80b), from Heinrich Heine's work, is archaic (not least because of its use of the obsolete noun *Lohnbedienter*), we have seen that examples of this type are by no means rare in present-day German. And systematically, we find that, in cases in which morphological case is marked on the lexical noun, the second noun in these articleless cases bears (default, morphologically unmarked) nominative case.[71]

(89) a. ein Biest von einem Präsident-*(en) (German)
         a   beast of   a-DAT president-CASE
     b. ein Biest von Präsident-(*en)
         a   beast of   president-CASE

Kayne (1994), who assimilates the structure of QBNPs to that of possessed noun phrases (recall the discussion in section 5.3.5), would not expect this behavior on the part of *von* in (80) and (89) either. Thus, (80) and (89) count as evidence against both (86) and Kayne's (36a), repeated here.

(36a) *that* [D/PP [*jewel*]ⱼ [D/P *of*] [IP *a village* I⁰ tⱼ ... (Kayne 1994, 106)

What also argues against an assimilation of QBNPs and possessed noun phrases is the fact, stressed in Abraham 1998, that *von* + DAT, in German QBNPs, cannot be replaced with the genitive case: while (89a') is grammatical on a reading in which the beast is the president's possession (a reading that is also available for (89a)), it is entirely impossible on its QBNP reading.[72]

(89a′) *ein Biest eines Präsidenten (German)
        a   beast a-GEN president-CASE

In this regard, QBNPs behave robustly differently from possessed noun
phrases, which show the alternation between dative and genitive familiar
from the literature.

A fourth reason for rejecting (86), which once again carries over to
Kayne's (36a), concerns the postulation of the string $a\ N_2$ as a constituent, with the indefinite article being the determiner of the second
noun phrase. Recall from the previous discussion that (as Den Dikken
1995a and Bennis, Corver, and Den Dikken 1998 show) tokens of the
"spurious" indefinite article can be found sandwiched between *of* and N_2
in constructions in which the properties of both N_1 and N_2 are such that
een clearly cannot team up with either one of them.[73]

(90) a.   die pracht van een Westertoren (Dutch)
           that beauty of a   Westertoren
     b. (?)die ramp   van een getalscongruentiefeiten
           that disaster of a   number agreement facts
     c. (?)dat tuig   van een voetbalsupporters
           that scum of a   soccer supporters
     d.   die pracht van een spinazie
           that beauty of a   spinach
     e. (?)die   idioten van een regering
           those idiots of a   government
     f.   die   schatten van een kinderen
           those darlings of a   children

The analysis of QBNPs proposed in Aarts 1998, reproduced in (91),
does not face the problems that the Dutch examples in (90) pose for the
structures put forth in Abney 1987, Napoli 1989, Everaert 1992, and
Kayne 1994. Since he analyzes *of a* as an essentially unanalyzed string of
words (a syncategorematic chunk tagged on to the first noun's projection), there is no dependency of *a* on either of the two nouns.

(91) [NP *a/that* [N′ [MP *jewel of a*] [N′ *village*]]][74]

But while Aarts's (1998) structure does indeed steer clear of a collision
with the facts in (90) as far as the *possibility* of a "spurious" indefinite article in front of N_2 is concerned, it remains empty-handed when it comes
to accounting for the fact that a token of the "spurious" indefinite article
is in fact *obligatory* in (90a–e) while not in (90f). Thus, ultimately,

Aarts's analysis also fails to shed light on the distribution of the "spurious" indefinite article—and it does not enlighten us either when it comes to the nature and function of the marker *of* following the first noun.

5.6.2   *Of* as the Nominal Copula, and the Distribution of Copular Elements

The discussion in the previous pages of this chapter has shown that, by contrast, an analysis that treats the marker *of* as a nominal copula in QBNPs accurately captures the nature and distribution of this element in both attributive and comparative QBNPs.[75] In the former, *of* is the lexicalization of the RELATOR, which is overt here because its complement is larger than a bare NP (see *of*-less attributive QBNPs of the *idiot doctor* type) and realized as *of* rather than, say, *as* or *like* because it is embedded in a nominal rather than verbal structural environment (see section 5.2 for discussion). In comparative QBNPs, on the other hand, *of* is the lexicalization of the small-clause external LINKER, whose presence is forced as a consequence of the fact that the predicate nominal inverts with its subject in the course of the derivation of comparative QBNPs (recall section 5.3). Just as there are heterogeneous forces that cause copulas to show up in the clause (providing support for Tense, lexicalizing the LINKER), so also is there more than one route along which a nominal copula may show up in the structure.

Thus, we have an analysis according to which *of* as the nominal copula is one of a variety of possible lexicalizations of the RELATOR (see (92) for English), in addition to being the spell-out of the LINKER inside nominal phrases (see (93)).

(92) a. The RELATOR is realized as *of* in the complement of D.
    b. The RELATOR is realized as *be* in the complement of T or Asp.
    c. The RELATOR is realized as *as, for, like* in the complement of the RELATOR or specific Vs.

(93) a. The LINKER is realized as *of* in DP.
    b. The LINKER is realized as *be* in TP.
    c. The LINKER is null in AspP.

The statements in (92) and (93) together give us a comprehensive picture of the landscape of English copular elements as we know it to date. We have now built to completion a protracted argument to the effect that copular elements exist both in clauses and inside nominal phrases.

5.6.3 Language Variation in the Distribution of the Nominal Copula

It is well known that not all languages employ copular elements in all contexts in which languages like English employ them. So with the conclusion in mind that copulas are not confined to the clause but exist in noun phrases as well, let us take a look at some of the variation in the use of copular elements in the nominal domain. I will present two brief case studies here, of Hebrew and Hungarian.[76] Since in the foregoing we have already come across the Hungarian QBNP, let me start with the Hungarian facts.

5.6.3.1 Hungarian In section 5.4.2, we encountered some Hungarian examples of comparative QBNPs, a representative of which is (94).

(94) csoda egy könyv (Hungarian)
     wonder a   book
     'a wonder of a book'

An interesting feature of this comparative QBNP is that it lacks an element corresponding to English *of*: the only thing separating the two nouns is a token of what I identified as being a "spurious" indefinite article. The lack of a counterpart to *of* in Hungarian (94) turns out to tie in with the lack of a copular element in Hungarian (present-tense) sentences with predicate nominal and a third-person subject. Thus, consider (95).

(95) a. ⟨*van⟩ János ⟨*van⟩ a   legjobb diák   ⟨*van⟩ (Hungarian)
        is   János is   the best   student is
        'János is the best student.'
     b. ⟨*van⟩ a   legjobb diák   ⟨*van⟩ János ⟨*van⟩
        is   the best   student is   János is
        'The best student is János.'

Regardless of the relative order of subject and predicate in (95), the third-person singular present-tense form of *lenni* 'be'—that is, *van*—may not surface, no matter where it is placed.[77]

I went out of my way to rule out placement of *van* in all the various positions surrounding the two noun phrases because Hungarian is a free word-order language. To be more precise, Hungarian is a discourse-configurational language (see É. Kiss 1995)—a language in which the information-structural properties of constituents are the prime determinants of word order. And precisely because of its discourse configurationality, it is not very easy to be sure whether (95b) does or does not involve

Predicate Inversion in the sense of this study. In all likelihood, *a legjobb diák* 'the best student' does not sit in SpecTP at Spell-Out: it will likely occupy a TP-external Topic position. It would, however, be difficult to *rule out* a derivation of Hungarian (95b) involving Predicate Inversion: Predicate Inversion (i.e., movement of the predicate to SpecTP) is an operation made available in UG, and Hungarian is known to have A-movement to SpecTP; there is no reason to expect Hungarian *not* to have Predicate Inversion, therefore. Thus, though it arguably is not its *only* possible derivation, (95b) does presumably have a grammatical derivation involving Predicate Inversion, with movement of the predicate around its subject into the specifier position of a LINKER head *cum* raising of the RELATOR head up to the LINKER.

This said, it is interesting to see that Predicate Inversion apparently does not give rise to an overt copular element in sentences of the type in (95b). What this suggests is that Hungarian lacks an overt realization of the LINKER at the clausal level—while English *be* does double duty as a supporter of tense, aspect, and agreement and as a LINKER, Hungarian *lenni* 'be' performs only the former task; the LINKER is not lexicalized. With this in mind, the fact that the Hungarian comparative QBNP in (94) also lacks an overt LINKER can now be seen to be part and parcel of a broader generalization: Hungarian lacks overt LINKERs. The absence of a LINKER element in both (94) and (95b), apart from further enhancing the parallelism between clauses and nominal phrases (see Szabolcsi 1994), thus lends support to the analysis of comparative QBNPs in terms of Predicate Inversion.

5.6.3.2 Hebrew   Hebrew copular sentences have received a good deal of attention in the literature (see especially Doron 1983 and Rapoport 1987). It will not be necessary for me, therefore, to present a detailed catalog of their properties here. Suffice it to make a couple of remarks about the distribution of copular elements in Hebrew clauses.

In Hebrew predicative copular sentences with a nominal predicate, the element *hu* (which is identical with the third-person nominative *h*-pronoun *hu* 'he') or the appropriate gender variant thereof (depending on the gender features of the subject) surfaces optionally in between the subject and the predicative noun phrase. Doron (1983) and Rapoport (1987) analyze this element *hu* (to be glossed as "H") as a lexicalization of Infl; in line with the preceding discussion, I will assume instead that it is a realization of the RELATOR-head inside the nominal small clause.

(96) a. dani more (Hebrew)
        Dani teacher
     b. dani *hu* more
        Dani H teacher
        Both: 'Dani is a teacher.'

In specificational copular sentences, the facts are more complicated, the occurrence of *hu* depending on a number of factors, one of which is linear order. Consider first the canonical specificational copular sentence in (97a).

(97) a. dani %(*hu*) ha-more   a'. ani (*hu*) ha-more (Hebrew)
        Dani H   the-teacher   I   H   the-teacher
        'Dani is the teacher.'   'I am the teacher.'
     b. ha-more   *(*hu*) dani   b'. ha-more   *(*hu*) ani
        the-teacher H   Dani   the-teacher H   I
        'The teacher is Dani.'   'The teacher is me.'

According to Rapoport (1987), the question of whether the variant of this sentence lacking *hu* is acceptable gives rise to some speaker variation: though most speakers would want *hu* to be present in (97a), some allow *hu* to be omitted. It seems that omitting *hu* is particularly easy in canonical specificational constructions with a pronominal subject: (97a') without *hu* is acceptable to all speakers. In *inverse* specificational sentences, on the other hand, the picture is straight and simple: *hu* is systematically obligatory, for all speakers, regardless of the nature of the subject. This is shown in (97b, b'). We need not concern ourselves here with the difficult question of what is responsible for the optionality of *hu* in a subset of canonical copular sentences. For our purposes, the point of interest is that in *inverse* copular sentences, *hu* is obligatorily present (see (97b, b')).

With this in mind, let us take a look at the Hebrew counterparts of comparative QBNPs like *a jewel of a village*, discussed in Shaked 2001.[78] The examples in (98) give an initial impression. What we find in these examples is a token of *šel* between the two nouns.

(98) a. zot [buba *šel* yalda] (Hebrew)
        this doll of girl
        'This is a doll of a girl.'
     b. ze [xara *šel* kelev]
        this shit of dog
        'This is a shit of a dog.'

Readers familiar with the syntax of possessed noun phrases in Hebrew will recognize this element as the "genitival marker" of Hebrew. That there are indeed close ties between genitival noun phrases and QBNPs in Hebrew is suggested in a particularly telling way by the pair in (99).

(99) a. ha-pitsuts   *šel* mesiba ha-ze (Hebrew)
        the-explosion.M of party.F the-this.M
        'this explosion of a party' (genitival reading)
     b. ha-pitsuts   *šel* mesiba ha-zot
        the-explosion.M of party.F the-this.F
        'this explosion of a party' (QBNP reading)

While English does not distinguish morphologically between the two readings of *this explosion of a party*, in Hebrew there is a key difference between the two interpretations when it comes to which noun determines the choice of demonstrative: the first noun on the genitival interpretation, the second on the QBNP reading.[79]

With these morphological and semantic distinctions correspond differences in relativizability.

(100) a. mesiba še-ze   ha-pitsuts   šel-a (Hebrew)
         party that-this.M the-explosion of-RES.F
         'a party that this is the explosion of'
      b. *mesiba še-zot   pitsuts   šel-a
         party that-this.F explosion of-RES.F

This of course recalls what I had observed earlier in the discussion about A′-extraction in QBNPs. The Hebrew binominal construction is thus completely well behaved.

Despite their differences, what the genitival and QBNP cases share is their word order *and* the presence of the element *šel* between the two noun phrases. The element *šel* is typically likened, in the literature on Hebrew noun phrases, to English *of*. For English *of*, I argued in the foregoing that, in comparative QBNPs, it is the lexicalization of a LINKER-head. For *šel* in Hebrew comparative QBNPs, we can now make precisely the same assumption. The presence of *šel* in (98) and (99b) can be seen to be directly on a par with the presence of *hu* in inverse specificational copular sentences in Hebrew (see (97b, b′)). The generalization is that whenever Predicate Inversion applies in predicate nominal constructions, whether in a clause or within a nominal phrase, this gives rise, in Hebrew as in English, to the emergence of a copular element.

The Hebrew results are in a way more spectacular than the ones we found for English, for two reasons. One is that, in Hebrew simple sentences with a predicate nominal, a copular element is strictly obligatory only in *inverse* copular sentences (while in English simple predicate nominal constructions, a copula is *always* present, for reasons having to do with the checking of tense and agreement features). The other reason Hebrew is such a striking piece of support for the approach to QBNPs taken in this work is that there is in fact a variant of the Hebrew *N šel N* construction that differs from (98) and (99b) in *two* respects: it has the opposite (i.e., underlying) order of the two nouns, and it lacks the element *šel*. The examples in (101) illustrate these points.

(101) a. ha-pitsuts   *šel* mesiba ha-zot (=(99b)) (Hebrew)
           the-explosion.M of party.F the-this.F
      b. ha-mesiba pitsuts   ha-zot
           the-party   explosion.M this.F
           Both: 'this explosion of a party'

The beauty of this alternation is that it implicates *šel* directly in the process of Predicate Inversion: *šel* shows up precisely when the predicate (*pitsuts*) inverts with its subject.[80] This goes along just perfectly, of course, with an account of the *šel* in Hebrew comparative QBNPs as a lexicalization of the LINKER head: there is a LINKER generated only in the context of Predicate Inversion.

Those familiar with Hebrew syntax will be struck by the partial parallel between (101) and the alternation between the so-called free state and construct state of possessed noun phrases.

(102) a. ha-bayit *šel* ha-mora ("Free state") (Hebrew)
           the-house of the-teacher
      b. beit   ha-mora ("Construct state")
           house the-teacher

What is shared between (101) and (102) is the *šel*/no-*šel* alternation. This suggests some sort of parallel between QBNPs and possessed noun phrases. And a quick look back at Hungarian further enhances such a parallel. For just as the Hungarian QBNP lacks a token of the nominal copula, so also do Hungarian possessed noun phrases with a nominative possessor have no copular element between the two nouns.

(103) a. csoda   egy könvy (=(94)) (Hungarian)
         wonder a   book
         'a wonder of a book'
      b. János könyv-e
         János book-AGR
         'János's book'

But while there are indeed conspicuous parallels between QBNPs and possessed noun phrases, there are immediately eye-catching differences as well. Thus, (101) and (102) differ in that, in the latter pair but crucially not in the former, the two members have identical word orders: in both *house* precedes *teacher*. Another significant difference between (101b) and (102b) is that each of the two nouns of (101b) can be marked definite (with the aid of *ha-*; see note 80), while in the "construct state" the first noun can never be preceded by *ha-* (cf. **ha-beit/ha-bayit ha-mora*). A third difference is that, in the "construct," the first noun is typically a phonologically reduced variant of the possessum of the "free state" (cf. *beit* versus *bayit*), while in the *šel*-less QBNP there are no phonological reductions. The Hungarian possessed noun phrase also differs from its QBNP, in featuring agreement (with the possessor) on the second noun. These notes suggest that, on the one hand, there is reason to find some sort of common ground between QBNPs and possessed noun phrases, but on the other, there are significant differences between the two that need to be captured.

In this study, I will not present a full-fledged treatise on the structure of possessive constructions—a topic that lies well outside the bounds of this book. But in the next section, where I will examine a number of other cases of predication and Predicate Inversion inside the nominal phrase, the possessed noun phrase will come up as one of the candidates.

5.7 Other Cases of Predication and Predicate Inversion inside the Nominal Phrase

With the analysis of QBNPs of the type in (3a) (*a jewel of a village*) and (3b) (*an idiot of a doctor*) now firmly in place, I will broaden the scope of the discussion by analyzing, in this final section, a number of other instances of predication and Predicate Inversion inside nominal phrases, including *wh*-interrogative and *wh*-exclamative constructions, instances of adjectival predication and inversion, possessed noun phrases, and relative-clause constructions. The discussion throughout draws on my earlier work on predication inside the complex noun phrase (see, in particular, Den Dikken 1995a, 1995c, 1998b, 1999; Den Dikken and Lipták 1997; Bennis, Corver, and Den Dikken 1998; Den Dikken and Singhapreecha 2004).[81]

5.7.1 *Wh*-Interrogative and *wh*-Exclamative Noun Phrases

The *wh*-element *wat* in Dutch serves a variety of purposes (see Postma 1994, 1995a, 1995b, Bennis 1995; also see Moro 2000, section 3.2.2). In one of its uses, it is a counterpart to indefinite *iets* 'something' (see (104a)); on this construal, *wat* remains inside the verb phrase. Alongside its indefinite use, *wat* also has two ex-situ construals, one as an interrogative pronoun (see (104b)), and one as a marker of exclamatives (see (104c)).[82]

(104) a. Brian heeft *wat* gegeten (Indefinite) (Dutch)
     Brian has   what eaten
     'Brian ate something.'

   b. *wat*   heeft Brian gegeten? (Interrogative)
     what has   Brian eaten
     'What did Brian eat?'

   c. *wat*   heeft Brian gegeten (zeg)! (Exclamative)
     what has   Brian eaten   DPRT
     'Boy, did Brian eat!'

All three interpretations of *wat* resurface inside complex noun phrases, as shown in (105), as well as in complex adjective phrases, as in (106)—though the latter paradigm is incomplete, *wat* not being able to serve as a *wh*-interrogative marker in adjectival contexts (*hoe* 'how' being used instead).

(105) a. Brian heeft [*wat* bessen] gegeten (Indefinite) (Dutch)
     Brian has   what berries eaten
     'Brian ate some berries.'

   b. [*wat* voor bessen] heeft Brian gegeten? (Interrogative)
     what for   berries has   Brian eaten
     'What kind of berries did Brian eat?'

   c. [*wat* een bessen] heeft Brian gegeten (zeg)! (Exclamative)
     what a   berries has   Brian eaten   DPRT
     'Boy, did Brian eat a lot of berries!'

(106) a. die   bessen zijn [*wat* zoet] (Indefinite)
         those berries are what sweet
         'Those berries are somewhat/kind of sweet.'[83]
      b. [**wat*/*hoe*   zoet] zijn die   bessen? (Interrogative)
          what/how sweet are those berries
          'How sweet are those berries?'
      c. [*wat* zoet] zijn die   bessen (zeg)! (Exclamative)
         what sweet are those berries DPRT
         'Boy, how sweet those berries are!'

Letting ourselves be informed by the observation that the *wh*-element
wat can serve as a predicate in predicate-complement structures, as in
(107a–c), we are led to the hypothesis that in constructions of the type in
(105)–(106), *wat* serves as a predicate inside the confines of the bracketed
phrases.

(107) a. *wat*$_i$ is [$_{RP}$ dat [RELATOR t_i]]? (Dutch)
         what is that
         'What's that?'
      b. die   feiten zijn [een probleem als *wat*]
         those facts are a   problem as what
         'Those facts are quite a problem, a serious problem.'
      c. die   bessen zijn [(zo) zoet   als *wat*]
         those berries are   so sweet as what
         'Those berries are extremely sweet.'

This line of thought brings forth an analysis of constructions of the
type in (105) and (106) that postulates a small clause of the predicate-
complement type, with *wat* serving as the predicate and the nominal or
adjectival phrase to its left as its subject, as the core of the structure underlying them. I will confine my discussion here, for the sake of brevity,
to the complex noun phrases in (105), which are all underlain by the partial structure in (108).

(108) [$_{RP}$ [$_{Subject}$ *bessen*] [RELATOR [$_{Predicate}$ *wat*]]]

From this base structure, one gets to the *wat*-indefinite and *wat*-
exclamative constructions in (105a) and (105c) by performing a simple
A′-movement operation on the small-clause predicate, *wat*. In the indefinite noun phrase in (105a), *wat* arguably lands in the specifier position of
a QP generated outside the small clause (see (109a)),[84] while for (105b),

the exclamative case, Bennis, Corver, and Den Dikken (1998) argue that *wat* is A′-moved into SpecDP (as depicted in (109b)).

(109) a. [$_{DP}$ D$_\varnothing$ [$_{QP}$ [$_{Predicate}$ *wat*]$_i$ [Q$_\varnothing$ [$_{RP}$ [$_{Subject}$ *bessen*] [RELATOR t_i]]]]]
     b. [$_{DP}$ [$_{Predicate}$ *wat*]$_i$ [D=*een*$_j$ (...) [$_{RP}$ [$_{Subject}$ *bessen*] [t_j t_i]]]]

An obvious difference between (105a) and (105b) is the fact that *wat* in the latter is obligatorily separated from its subject by the indefinite article *een*—something which holds for *all* Dutch *wat*-exclamative constructions, entirely regardless of the number features of the subject (see *wat *(een) idioten!* 'what an idiots'). The fact that *een* is oblivious to the number properties of the subject makes it clear that this *een* does not form a constituent with the subject noun phrase—it is an instantiation, in other words, of the "spurious" indefinite article, originating under the RELATOR-head. The very appearance of the "spurious" indefinite article in *wat*-exclamatives thus provides support, in the light of the analysis of "spurious" articles presented earlier in this chapter, for the underlying structure in (108) for *wat*-exclamatives: without the presence in the structure of the RELATOR, one would be at a loss accommodating the "spurious" indefinite article in these constructions.[85]

The fact that "spurious" *een* is obligatory in *wat*-exclamatives (while in comparative QBNPs it can be left out in contexts in which both constituent noun phrases are plural: *die schatten van (een) kinderen* 'those treasures of (a) children') suggests that there is a structural reason why the RELATOR cannot be null in these constructions. Bennis, Corver, and Den Dikken (1998) suggest that this structural reason is a requirement on the part of the D-head to be lexically realized whenever something raises to its specifier—something akin to the Verb Second requirement in root-CPs. This requirement forces the RELATOR, realized as "spurious" *een*, up to the D-head, resulting in the desired surface word order in which the "spurious" indefinite article shows up between the *wh*-element in SpecDP and the subject in the specifier position of the small clause. On the assumption that no requirement of the type imposed by D holds for the Q-head in the structure in (109a),[86] there is no obligation to lexicalize the RELATOR-head here; considerations of economy then presumably dictate that no overt lexicalization of the RELATOR should be used (note that *wat een bessen* 'what a berries' is ungrammatical on an indefinite construal).

With (105a) and (105c) thus taken care of, this leaves us with the *wat voor*-construction in (105b).[87] Bennis, Corver, and Den Dikken (1998) argue, on the basis of the distribution of the "spurious" indefinite article in these constructions, that *wat voor*–interrogatives are structurally ambiguous, in many cases, between two derivations, one involving direct A′-movement to SpecDP and one featuring Predicate Inversion followed by A′-movement to SpecDP. Since the latter derivation is the more interesting one from my perspective in this chapter, let me focus on that one here (referring the reader to Bennis, Corver, and Den Dikken 1998 for detailed discussion of the direct A′-movement derivation). It is depicted in (110).

(110) [DP [Predicate *wat*]$_i$ [D=*voor* [FP t_i [LINKER+*een*$_j$ [RP [Subject *bessen*]
      [t_j t_i]]]]]]

In this structure, *voor* originates under D (as it does in the straight A′-movement derivation of *wat voor*–interrogatives), as a lexicalization of the [+WH] D-head. Apparently the fact that *voor* is present under D renders it unnecessary (in fact, impossible) to spell out the LINKER in (110) as *van* (cf. the ungrammaticality of **wat voor van een bessen* 'what for of a berries')—in striking contrast to what we have found to be the case in other noun-phrase internal instances of Predicate Inversion in Dutch, where *van* shows up systematically. The suggestion that presents itself is that the presence of an overt meaningless functional element (*voor*) under D causes the emptiness of the LINKER in a context in which it would otherwise be obligatorily overt. This can be thought of as a kind of "nonproliferation treaty"—a desire to keep the amount of meaningless material to a minimum. While D would normally force a LINKER in its complement to be overt, a D-head filled by the meaningless marker *voor*, whose presence is forced independently by the requirement that the [+WH] D-head be spelled out overtly, causes the LINKER to be silent.[88] Precisely because the LINKER is not independently spelled out in *wat voor*–interrogatives, the application of Predicate Inversion is somewhat harder to diagnose than it is in other instances of noun-phrase internal Predicate Inversion—but as Bennis, Corver, and Den Dikken (1998) show in detail, the distribution of the "spurious" indefinite article *een* still gives the language user a positive clue to the effect that Predicate Inversion *can* indeed occur in the derivation of *wat voor*–interrogatives.

The paradigm in (105) does not have a match in English. But French comes close to having a perfect counterpart to the triplet in (105), featuring the *wh*-element *quel* (and its gender- and number-inflected forms).

(111) a. Brian nous a   donné [*quel*ques   leçons] (Indefinite) (French)
          Brian us   has given   WH-QUE-PL lessons
          'Brian gave us some lessons.'
      b. [*quelle* leçon] Brian nous a   donnée? (Interrogative)
          WH-F lesson Brian us   has given-F
          'What lesson did Brian give us?'
      c. [*quelle* leçon] Brian nous a   donnée là! (Exclamative)
          WH-F lesson Brian us   has given-F there
          'Boy, what a lesson Brian gave us!'

The match with Dutch (105) is not perfect because in the indefinite member of the triplet, (111a), the form of the *wh*-element is slightly different from the form that it takes in the interrogative and exclamative cases. But it nonetheless remains significant, it seems to me, that the indefinite quantifier *quelque(s)* 'some' is morphologically a *wh*-element composed of (uninflected) *quel* 'what/which' and an element *-que* (which Kayne (2003, 11) identifies with the complementizer *que*).

If indeed there is merit in assimilating the analysis of French (111) to that of Dutch (105), it will be interesting to draw attention to an observation made in Obenauer (1994, 365): the fact that subject clitic inversion in exclamatives with *quel* is sensitive to the interpretation of the *wh*-expression in the left periphery.

(112) a.   quelle leçon il nous a   donnée là! (French)
           what lesson he us   has given   there
      a'. quelle leçon nous a-t- il donnée là!
           what lesson us   has he given   there
      b.   quelle chance il a   eue!
           what luck   he has had
      b'. *quelle chance a-t- il eue!
           what luck   has he had

Obenauer points out that in (112a/a') we are dealing with a 'type of' interpretation, while in (112b/b') the *wh*-constituent is interpreted as an expression of 'high degree'. On the assumption (motivated by the parallel with Dutch (105)) that the *wh*-word (*quelle* in (112)) is a predicate of the noun phrase it is construed with, this brings forth an interesting link between (112) and the QBNPs in (113) (see Hulk and Tellier 1999, 2000; Doetjes and Rooryck 2001; and note 39, above). Doetjes and Rooryck (2001) argue that the difference in behavior with respect to external agreement between (113a) and (113b) is a consequence of a difference in syntactic structure between the two examples, and that this difference in syntactic structure, in turn, is reflected in a difference in interpretation. They claim that of the two examples in (113), only (113a) involves a *comparison*: while (113a) is paraphrasable as 'the quality of the church is such that it resembles a jewel', a similar paraphrase for (113b) (i.e., #'the quality of your daughter is such that she resembles a phenomenon') would be absurd. In (113b), they say that we are dealing with "pure degree" qualification: the only thing *phénomène* does is contribute "a strongly positive or negative evaluation of *fille* 'daughter', and as such [it] expresses high/ low degree of quality."

(113) a. ce   bijou   d' église   a   été   reconstruit(*e) (French)
         that.M jewel.M of church.F has been rebuilt-M/*F
      b. ton   phénomène   de fille   est bien
         your.M phenomenon.M of daughter.F is   quite
         distrait*(e)
         absentminded-F/*M

The interpretive parallel between the example pairs in (112) and (113) should be transparent: in both cases, the a-example involves a comparison (with Obenauer's "type of" reading subsumed under comparison) while the b-cases involve degree. And it turns out that, systematically, it is only in the a-cases that we find that the properties of the predicate (*bijou* in (113a), *quelle* in (112a/a′)) assert themselves externally to the complex noun phrase, triggering agreement in (113a) and bringing about inversion of the clitic subject and the finite auxiliary in (112a′).[89] In the b-cases, the predicate plays no role outside the complex noun phrase— something that seems to be related to the fact that it is a mere expression of high degree.

Figuring out the precise way of ensuring that the predicate asserts itself outside the complex noun phrase of which it is a part is a major challenge which I am not prepared to face at this time (see Hulk and Tellier 1999, 2000, Doetjes and Rooryck 2001, and Casillas Martínez 2001 for discussion; it is likely that "semantic agreement" or what Casillas Martínez calls "index agreement" (as distinct from concord or morphosyntactic agreement) plays a role in this context). But the relevance of the parallel between (112) and (113) in the context of the discussion in this chapter should be clear, regardless of how the analysis of the details will come out in the end. For the QBNPs in (113), I established on the basis of a detailed investigation in the opening sections of this chapter that their syntax involves predication inside the complex noun phrase. The fact, then, that there is a certain degree of syntactic parallelism in the behavior of these QBNPs and in that of exclamatives with *quel* of the type in (112) provides us with an additional piece of support for the claim (defended at length in Bennis, Corver, and Den Dikken 1998; see also the references cited there, and Moro 2000) that *wh*-exclamative constructions are built on a noun-phrase internal predication structure of the type in (108)/ (109b).

5.7.2 Adjectival Predication and Predicate Inversion inside the Complex Noun Phrase

Staying with French a little longer, let us proceed to cases of adjectival predication inside the complex noun phrase.[90] In particular, consider the pair in (114) (whose b-member has been discussed in ample detail in Milner 1978; Huot 1981; Azoulay-Vicente 1985; Hulk and Verheugd 1994; Kupferman 1981, 1994a, 1994b; Lagae 1994; Hulk 1996, among other works).

(114) a. une pizza chaude (French)
            a-F pizza hot-F
      b. une pizza de chaude
            a-F pizza DE hot-F
            Both: 'a hot pizza'

The example in (114a) is a garden-variety case of attributive modification in French, with the modifier surfacing to the right of the head noun— something usually taken to be the result of movement of the head noun or (more likely) its projection to a position higher up in the structure of the noun phrase. But (114b) is interesting in that it features the element *de* 'of' between the head noun and the adjective.

Alternations of this sort are not peculiar to French. Thus, the Thai pair in (115) is parallel in all relevant respects to the French pair in (114)—a parallelism that, as Den Dikken and Singhapreecha (2004) show in detail, extends to the nitty-gritty details of syntax (quantificational restrictions, in particular) and interpretation.

(115) a. khon   kèng (Thai)
            person smart

    b. khon   thîi kèng
       person THÎI smart
       Both: 'the/a smart person'

I will focus here on the interpretive properties of the alternations in (114) and (115).

The use or nonuse of *de* in examples of the type in (114) is not meaningless. The presence of *de* has a clear interpretive effect: (114b) has the following interpretive hallmarks, which set it apart from its *de*-less variant in (114a).[91]

• Example (114b) receives a CONTRASTIVE interpretation: a contrast between hot pizzas and pizzas that are not hot; see Milner 1978.

• Example (114b) has AP represent OLD INFORMATION (whereas in the *de*-less counterparts, AP represents new information); see Lagae 1994.

That AP represents old information in the "NP–*de*–AP" construction is perhaps particularly clear from the fact that it cannot be focally stressed (see Hulk and Verheugd 1994, 43, note 16):

(116) *il y a deux places de LIBRES et deux places d'OCCUPÉES (French)
      There are two places of free and two places of occupied.

Lagae (1994) refers to the information structure of "NP–*de*–AP" constructions, which has the unusual property of featuring the AP as old information, as an "inverted" information structure. Taking this point literally, I will translate it into a syntactic derivation of the "NP–*de*–AP" construction involving inversion of the predicate around its subject, with *de* serving as a LINKER, as it does in other instances of noun-phrase internal Predicate Inversion in French. The Predicate Inversion approach to (114b) makes immediate sense of the "inverted" information structure of the construction, assimilating it straightforwardly to that of inverse copular sentences (see (117b)). The default information-structure representation of a canonical copular sentence is one in which the subject represents old information and the predicate supplies new information about it. In the inverse copular sentence in (117b), by contrast, the focus or new information is *John*, and *my best friend* is old information (see section 4.1, above)—and this information-structure representation for inverse copular sentences is basically fixed: when you invert a predicate around its subject, the result is an information-structure representation in which the postcopular noun phrase is invariably the focus (see Declerck 1988 and references cited there for detailed discussion; also recall sections 4.1.1 and 4.2.1.1).[92]

(117) a. Brian is my best friend. (Canonical copular sentence)
     OLD   NEW

    b. My best friend is Brian. (Inverse copular sentence)
     OLD   NEW

In the earlier sections of this chapter, I showed that Copular Inversion is attested inside the nominal phrase as well. French has constructions of that type, as we have seen—(118) is an example. In fact, French is quite a bit richer than English when it comes to Predicate Inversion inside the nominal phrase. For alongside (118), we also find (119), a case of inversion of an *adjectival* predicate around its subject inside a complex DP (see Den Dikken 1995a as well as Hulk and Tellier 2000; see also Den Dikken and Lipták 1997 for cases of adjectival Predicate Inversion inside DP in Hungarian, some of which are reproduced in (129), below). In both examples, we find that in French the LINKER element signaling Predicate Inversion inside the complex nominal phrase is realized as *de*.

(118) a. un imbécile de garçon (French)
       a idiot   of boy

    b. ... [FP *imbécile*ᵢ [LINKER=*de* [RP [*garçon*] [RELATOR *t*ᵢ]]]]

(119) a. un drôle de type (French)
       a funny of guy

    b. ... [FP *drôle*ᵢ [LINKER=*de* [RP [*type*] [RELATOR *t*ᵢ]]]]

With the analysis of (119a) given in (119b) in place, we are well on our way toward an account of the construction in (114b), repeated here as (120a).

(120) a. une pizza de chaude (French)
       a   pizza of hot-AGR

    b. ... [FP *chaude*ᵢ [LINKER=*de* [RP [*pizza*] [RELATOR *t*ᵢ]]]]

The combination of the fact that the linker element *de* occurs in (120a) *and* that (120a) shares its peculiar information-structural profile with Predicate Inversion constructions tells us securely that the derivation of (120a) involves Predicate Inversion: the adjectival predicate *chaude* inverts with its subject *pizza* in the course of the derivation of (120a), as shown in (120b). Support for an analysis that treats the AP as an underlying predicate-complement (rather than as an attributive predicate-specifier) comes from Milner's (1978) observation (reproduced in Azoulay-Vicente 1985, 26–27) that there is a contrast between (121a) and (121b), a contrast that is mirrored by the one seen in the copular sentences in (122). Apparently, the fact that the adjective *policier* cannot be used predicatively in a copular sentence is responsible for its ungrammaticality in (121b).

(121) a.   j' en   ai   vu   un de bon
           I of-them have seen one of good
      b. *j' en   ai   vu   un de policier (French)
           I of-them have seen one of police$_A$

(122) a.   ce film   est bon
           this movie is   good
      Cf. un bon   film
           a   good movie
      b. *ce film   est policier
           this movie is   police$_A$
      Cf. un film   policier
           a   movie police$_A$

The part of the derivation depicted in (120b) is parallel in all respects to what happens in (119b). But while in (119) the derivation stops there, an additional step must be taken in the derivation of (120a) that will reinstate the underlying order of subject and predicate. Den Dikken and Singhapreecha (2004) discuss this additional step with specific reference to the parallel Thai facts (see (115)), which are particularly helpful because of the fact that Thai heavily exploits classifiers, elements which make specifier positions available for phrasal movement in syntax.

The pair of examples to consider is the one given in (123).

(123) a. rôm   (khan) jàj săam khan nán (Thai)
          umbrella CLF   big three CLF DEM
          'those three big umbrellas'
      b. rôm   thîi jàj săam khan nán
          umbrella THII big three CLF DEM
          'those three big (as opposed to small or medium-size)
          umbrellas'

The *thîi*-less example in (123a) serves to set things up for the analysis of (123b), which is the example we are particularly interested in. As (123a) shows, the syntax of the complex noun phrase in Thai is robustly head-final. What this means, on the assumption that syntactic structure is antisymmetric (Kayne 1994), is that the syntax of Thai noun phrases involves massive leftward pied-piping movement. To get the demonstrative *nán* to surface in final position, we need to raise the entire complement of Dem into SpecDemP. Continuing on from right to left, the next-to-last item in the complex DP is the classifier *khan*, arguably another head (see Singhapreecha 2001). Interestingly, this classifier can occur *twice* in the complex noun phrase in (123a): once between the head-noun and the adjective, and once in penultimate position. And even more interestingly, the occurrence of the classifier *khan* between the head-noun and the adjective turns out to be in *complementary distribution* with the linker element *thîi*, as a comparison of (123a) and (123b) shows. This tells us that the head position of the Classifier Phrase realized by the leftmost token of *khan* in (123a) serves as the landing site of movement of the LINKER *thîi* in (123b). Since this Classifier Phrase also makes a specifier position available, we can then proceed to exploit this specifier position as the landing site for movement of the remnant small clause in the partial structure in (120b), which, for the Thai example at hand, reads as in (124). The resulting derivation of the complex noun phrase in (123b) is depicted in (125).[93]

(124) ... [$_{FP}$ *jàj*$_i$ [LINKER=*thîi* [$_{RP}$ [*rôm*] [RELATOR *t*$_i$]]]]]

(125) a. [$_{RP}$ NP [R AP]]
$\rightarrow$ merging F; AP–to–SpecFP (Predicate Inversion), with spell-out of F as LINKER *thîi* $\rightarrow$

b. [$_{FP}$ AP$_a$ [*thîi* [$_{RP}$ NP *t*$_a$]]]]
$\rightarrow$ merging Clf1 (null); remnant-RP-to-SpecClf1P + *thîi*–to–Clf1 $\rightarrow$

c. [$_{Clf1P}$ [$_{RP}$ NP *t*$_a$]$_i$ [*thîi*$_x$ [$_{FP}$ AP$_a$ [*t*$_x$ *t*$_i$]]]]
$\rightarrow$ merging Q (=*sǎam*); Clf1P–to–SpecQP $\rightarrow$

d. [$_{QP}$ [$_{Clf1P}$ [$_{RP}$ NP *t*$_a$]$_i$ [*thîi*$_x$ [$_{FP}$ AP$_a$ [*t*$_x$ *t*$_i$]]]]$_j$ [*sǎam* *t*$_j$]]
$\rightarrow$ merging Clf2 (=*khan*^{2}); QP–to–SpecClf2P $\rightarrow$

e. [$_{Clf2P}$ [$_{QP}$ [$_{Clf1P}$ [$_{RP}$ NP *t*$_a$]$_i$ [*thîi*$_x$ [$_{FP}$ AP$_a$ [*t*$_x$ *t*$_i$]]]]$_j$ [*sǎam* *t*$_j$]]$_k$ [*khan*^{2} *t*$_k$]]
$\rightarrow$ merging Dem (=*nán*); Clf2P–to–SpecDP $\rightarrow$

f. [$_{DP}$ D [$_{DemP}$ [$_{Clf2P}$ [$_{QP}$ [$_{Clf1P}$ [$_{RP}$ NP *t*$_a$]$_i$ [*thîi*$_x$ [$_{FP}$ AP$_a$ [*t*$_x$ *t*$_i$]]]]$_j$ [*sǎam* *t*$_j$]]$_k$ [*khan*^{2} *t*$_k$]]$_m$ [*nán* *t*$_m$]]]

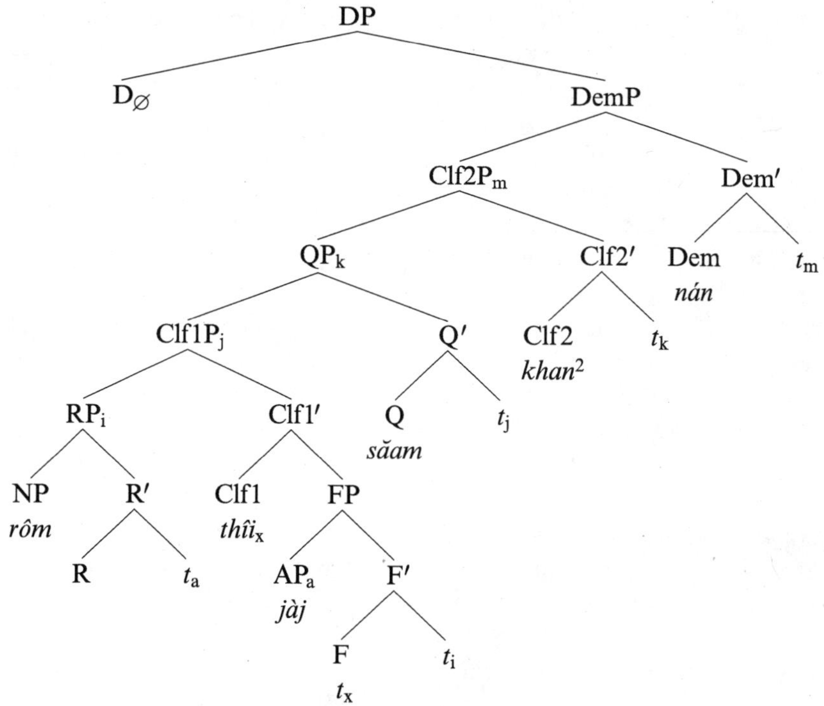

This account of Thai (123b) will carry over to French on the assumption that French noun phrases feature a projection of Clf1 as well, whose specifier serves as a landing site for remnant-RP movement and for the raised LINKER.[94]

One advantage of this analysis of constructions of the type in (114b) and (115b) is the fact that it has no trouble accommodating cases of *recursion* such as French (126a) or Thai (126b).

(126) a. quelque chose *d'* autre *de* grave (French)
           something   DE other DE serious
           'something else serious'
       b. rot *thîi* jàj *thîi* phææng khan níi (Thai)
           car THII big THII expensive CLF   DEM
           'that big expensive car'

An analysis that treats *de* or *thîi* as a LINKER readily assimilates these facts to the recursivity of English QBNPs such as *an idiot of a doctor*, illustrated in (127a).[95] By contrast, an account that would place *de/thîi* all the way up in D would run up against the problem of how DP recursion is apparently legitimate in (126) but not in other contexts—a particularly clear indication that embedding a DP inside a DP is not normally grammatical (see Kayne 1994, 86) coming from the ill-formedness of examples such as (127b).

(127) a.   that asshole *of* an idiot *of* a doctor
      b. *that idiot *of* the/that/my doctor

There is converging evidence, therefore, for the point of view that constructions of the type in (114b) and (115b) involve Predicate Inversion, the concomitant emergence of a LINKER element (*de, thîi*), and "restoration" of the base word order via an operation that takes place *below* the DP level.

French and Thai are not the only languages exhibiting inversion of adjectival predicates around their subjects. Close to French, we find plenty of examples in Spanish that are structurally similar to the example in (119a), *un drôle de type* 'a funny of guy'. Español-Echevarría (1997) presents some examples of this type, reproduced in (128a, b); Aarts (1998) mentions (128c), and also points out that the *A de(l) N* construction is attested in Portuguese as well, as witness (128d).[96]

(128) a. el listo del   doctor (Spanish)
         the smart of-the doctor
      b. el hábil del   doctor
         the skillful of-the doctor
      c. la tonta de Juana
         the silly of Juana
      d. a   stupida da Flora (Portuguese)
         the stupid of Flora

And Den Dikken and Lipták (1997) present cases from Hungarian that are parallel in all relevant respects to the cases of predicate-nominal inversion inside DP brought up in section 5.4.2. Thus, compare our earlier examples in (60) (repeated below) and the adjectival cases in (129). Den Dikken and Lipták (1997, 70) note that what supports a Predicate Inversion analysis of (129) is the fact that adjectives that can only be used attributively cannot figure in this construction (recall French (121)): of the two adjectives meaning 'little', *kicsi* and *kis*, only the latter can be used predicatively in sentences, and concomitantly, only the latter occurs in (129b).

(60) a. csoda/fene/kutya egy nap (Hungarian)
        wonder/hell/dog a   day
        'a wonder/hell/dog of a day'

    b. csoda/fene/kutya egy napok
       wonder   a   days
       (Lit.) 'a wonder/hell/dog of days'

(129) a. véres   egy nap(ok) (Hungarian)
          bloody a   day(s)
          '(a) bloody day(s)'
      b. {kicsi/*kis} egy kocsi
          little   a   car
      Cf. a   kocsi {kicsi/*kis}
          the car   little
          'The car is small.'

In fact, even in English we find inverse adjectival predications—though
these are dialectally restricted. Thus, Bolinger (1972a, 136) mentions
(130), which may be an instance of AP-inversion inside the complex
noun phrase (though the absence of an outer determiner makes this hard
to ascertain with certainty). And rather more productively, standard English (131a) alternates in many dialects (especially of American English;
see Abney 1987) with the construction in (131b), featuring *of* between
the *wh*-AP and its subject.[97]

(130) considerable of a fool

(131) a. How big a problem do you think this is?
      b. How big of a problem do you think this is?

The alternation in (131) reminds one of the claim made in Bennis, Corver,
and Den Dikken 1998 that Dutch *wat voor*–interrogatives are structurally
ambiguous, in principle, between a derivation involving A′-movement of
the predicate (*wat*) to SpecDP and one in which the predicate first inverts
with its subject via Predicate Inversion and subsequently raises on to
SpecDP. Thinking along these lines, we can analyze (131a) in terms of direct A′-movement and (131b) as a case of Predicate Inversion (triggering
of) followed by movement to SpecDP.

5.7.3 Possessed Noun Phrases and PP-Predicate Inversion inside the Complex Noun Phrase

In the previous section, we discovered that in French there are two surface outputs for cases of DP-internal adjectival Predicate Inversion: in
one, the AP actually surfaces to the left of its subject, separated from it
by the LINKER *de* (see (119a), repeated below as (132a)); in the other (see

(114b), repeated here as (132b)), word order does not lead us to suspect that inversion has taken place at all.

(132) a. un drôle de type (French)
         a   funny of guy
      b. une pizza de chaude
         a   pizza of hot

But there are nonetheless solid indications that inversion *has* in fact taken place in (132b): the LINKER *de* shows up, there are syntactic restrictions on the construction that are hard to accommodate if it was derived in the same way as garden-variety cases of attributive quantification, and it has a special interpretation (or information-structural profile) that reveals that it is a product of Predicate Inversion.

While English does not have anything like the alternation in (132), it has something entirely similar to it in the realm of possessed noun phrases. Thus, consider pairs such as the following.

(133) a. Brian is [a man of means].
      b. the means of that man

(134) a. Brian is [a man of many talents].
      b. the many talents of that man

(135) a. Pooh is [a bear of very little brain].
      b. the small amount of brain of Pooh bear

(136) a. This is [an analysis of great significance/potential].
      b. the great significance/potential of this analysis

(137) a. This is [a gemstone of enormous value].
      b. the enormous value of this gemstone

As in the French cases in (132), both members of each pair contains the nominal copula *of*. The possibility presents itself, therefore, that the examples in (133)–(137) all involve Predicate Inversion as an ingredient of their syntactic derivation, and that one of the two members of each pair is derived from the other via an operation that reinstates the underlying order of constituents, much in the way that French (132b) is derived from a structure of the type reflected by (132a) via remnant movement of the small clause to a position above the landing site of the inverted predicate (see section 5.7.2; especially (125)).

If (133)–(137) are to be derived via Predicate Inversion, what is their underlying structure such that it can be input to a Predicate Inversion derivation? In much of my previous work (see Den Dikken 1995a, 1998b, 1999), I answered this question by drawing a parallel between possessed noun phrases and double-object constructions. In Den Dikken 1991, 1995c, chap. 3, I argued that the double-object construction in (138b) is syntactically derived from the prepositional dative construction in (138a) via an instance of Predicate Inversion targeting the dative PP—which, on the evidence of the fact that it can trigger Locative Inversion (see (139)), is analyzed as a small-clause predicate.[98]

(138) a. Imogen gave the book to Brian.
       b. Imogen gave Brian the book.

(139) a. To Brian was given the book.
       b. To Imogen was sent a postcard.
       c. To Amnesty International was donated the bulk of his estate.

The key ingredients of this approach (slightly updated in light of the discussion in chapter 4) are summarized in (140).

(140) a. The dative preposition has a null allomorph, $P_\varnothing$.
       b. $P_\varnothing$ incorporates into the RELATOR head, making its PP the closest goal for an outside probe.
       c. The outside probe attracts the beheaded PP overtly yielding inversion of subject and predicate.

With the double-object construction derived from a structure more directly reflected by the prepositional dative construction via A-movement of the dative PP predicate (i.e., via Predicate Inversion), we are led to the conclusion that both members of the pair in (138) are underlain by a structure in which the possessor is the complement of a dative preposition whose projection serves as a predicate that takes the possessum as its subject, as in (141).

(141) [RP [SUBJECT POSSESSUM] [R′ RELATOR [PREDICATE=PP P_{dative} POSSESSOR]]]

This underlying structure is not realized in English possessed noun phrases (*the book to Brian). But we do not need to look far to find it attested on the surface: French has it, for instance, as (142a) illustrates.

(142) a. une voiture à Jean (French)
           a   car   to Jean
       b. une voiture de Jean
           a   car   of Jean

French (142a) alternates with (142b), which has exactly the same linear order of its major constituents but differs from (142a) in that it features the nominal copula *de* in between the possessum and the possessor. But the linear order of constituents does not *have to* be like this in French possessed noun phrases featuring *de*: French also has things like (143).

(143) une femme de moeurs légères/faciles (French)
      a   woman of mores   light/easy
      'a woman of easy virtue'

It seems to me that the alternation between (142b) and (143) is parallel to that seen in (132)—or, for that matter, to the one found in the English pairs in (133)–(137). Given an underlying core structure for possessed noun phrases as in (141), the a-examples of all these pairs (as well as French (143)) reflect the output of Predicate Inversion on the surface: the possessor, which underlyingly follows the possessum and is introduced by a dative preposition (see (142a)), shows up to the left of the possessum, and is separated from it by the nominal copula, *of*/*de*. These "pure" Predicate Inversion cases are convertible into surface orders in which the possessor comes to show up to the right of the possessum (just as in the base representation) via fronting of the remnant small clause around the inverted possessor, much as in the derivation of French (132b).

The details of the derivations of the a- and b-members of the pairs in (133)–(137) are not particularly relevant in the present context.[99] Whole bookshelves can be filled with studies of possessed noun phrases and possessive constructions more generally. The purpose of the foregoing remarks has been simply to show that an analysis of possessed noun phrases of the type in (133)–(137) is readily available within the confines of the approach to predication, Predicate Inversion and the distribution of the copula laid out in this work—an analysis that rests crucially on an underlying representation of these constructions of the type in (139), a small-clause structure whose predicate is a dative PP. This analysis, originally developed on the basis of the English dative alternation, allows a natural extension to the alternation between *be* + DATIVE and *have* constructions as well (see Benveniste 1966; Kayne 1993; Den Dikken 1995a, 1995c). I thus conclude that there is good evidence for the existence of constructions whose underlying structure involves a dative-PP predicate and whose surface syntax is derived via inversion of the dative PP with its subject—constructions that are attested both in clauses and within the nominal phrase. This confirms that, alongside the cases of nominal and adjectival inversion canvassed in the foregoing, noun-phrase internal *prepositional* Predicate Inversion exists as well.

5.7.4 Potpourri: Predicate Inversion and the LINKER in Mandarin Chinese Nominal Phrases

By way of a microscopic case study at the end of this long journey through the realm of noun-phrase internal predication and Predicate Inversion constructions, I will present, in closing, the interesting case of Mandarin Chinese—one of the most impressive arrays of nominal-internal Predicate Inversion constructions known to me, a paradigm case of the exploitation, to the full, of a syntactic mechanism made available by Universal Grammar. The Mandarin Chinese functional element *de* is used in a variety of ways, discussed in detail in work by Cheng (1986, 1997a, 1997b), Simpson (2001, 2002), and Tang (1983, 1993), among others. The examples in (144) (from Simpson 2001, 2002) give a representative sample.

(144) a. hao de shu (Mandarin)
         good DE book
         'good books'
      b. wo de shu
         I   DE book
         'my book'
      c. zai Beijing de ren
         in Beijing DE people
         'people in Beijing'
      d. wo mai de shu
         I   buy DE book
         'the book that I bought'
      e. Deng Xiao-ping shishi de xiaoxi
         Deng-Xiao-ping die   DE news
         'the news that Deng Xiao-ping had died'

Of the examples in (144), the first shows a clear resemblance to the Thai and French examples discussed in section 5.7.2 (recall (114b) and (115b), repeated below): it involves a noun and an adjective predicated of that noun, the two being separated by a meaningless element (*de*) linking them.

(114b) une pizza de chạude (French)
a-F pizza DE hot-F
'a hot pizza'

(115b) khon thîi kèng (Thai)
person THÎI smart
'the/a smart person'

The obvious difference between the Thai and French cases on the one hand, and Mandarin (144a) on the other, is the relative order of the adjective and the noun: while in (114b) and (115b) the order is "NP–LINKER–AP," in (142a) we find "AP–*de*–NP." What this means is that the remnant small-clause movement step that figures in the derivation of the French and Thai examples (and that reinstates the underlying relative order of noun and adjective) is not taken in Mandarin (144a). The adjectival predicate in (144a) simply inverts with its subject, and that is the end of it.

(145) [$_{DP}$ D (...) [$_{FP}$ [$_{AP}$ *hao*]$_i$ [LINKER=*de* [$_{RP}$ [*shu*] [RELATOR t_i]]]]]

In light of what was said in section 5.7.3, an entirely parallel account can be given for the possessive noun phrase in (144b), as in (146). An extension of this PP-inversion analysis is of course immediately applicable to (144c) as well, so we need not tarry on the analysis of (144c): we can model it directly on that of (144b), and represent it as in (147).

(146) [$_{DP}$ D (...) [$_{FP}$ [$_{PP}$ P$_\varnothing$ *wo*]$_i$ [LINKER=*de* [$_{RP}$ [*shu*] [RELATOR t_i]]]]]

(147) [$_{DP}$ D (...) [$_{FP}$ [$_{PP}$ *zai Beijing*]$_i$ [LINKER=*de* [$_{RP}$ [*ren*] [RELATOR t_i]]]]]

For relative-clause constructions such as (144d) and noun-complement clauses like (144e), an extension of the Predicate Inversion *cum* LINKER approach is available as well. What we need to make this happen, in the case of relative clauses, is an analysis that treats them as predicates of the noun phrases they are combined with, in line with standard wisdom: relative clauses have long been recognized as predicates of the head-noun phrases. The traditional right-adjunction approach to relative clauses captures their predicativity by assimilating them to other adjoined modifiers, such as adverbials.[100] On the present assumptions, adverbial modification involves a predication structure featuring a RELATOR phrase—in section 2.6.7, I argued that the predicate-complement structure in (148a) and the predicate-specifier structure in (148b) are both available for adverbial modification (the two making different predictions in the domain of scope in multiple-adverb constructions).

(148) a. [$_{RP}$ [$_{vP}$ DP [$_{v}$ VP]] [RELATOR AdvP]]
     b. [$_{RP}$ AdvP [RELATOR [$_{vP}$ DP [$_{v}$ VP]]]]

Continuing on the assumption that, as the traditional right-adjunction approach to relative clauses would have it, there is a structural parallel between relative-clause constructions and adverbial-modification constructions, we would then expect relative clauses to be connected to the "head" of the relativized noun phrase via a RELATOR and eligible in principle for predicate-complement as well as predicate-specifier status.

(149) a. [$_{RP}$ ["head"] [RELATOR [$_{CP}$ RelCl]]]
     b. [$_{RP}$ [$_{CP}$ RelCl] [RELATOR ["head"]]]

Both options may indeed be made available by Universal Grammar, though my present understanding of relative-clause constructions is not such that I will be able to make firm claims at this point.[101] Rather than pursuing the broader questions of whether (149a) and (149b) are available side by side and, if so, what determines their distribution, I will confine myself here to showing that, for Mandarin, translating the predicativity of relative clauses into an analysis according to which the relative clause serves as the predicate of a canonical small clause, as the complement of a RELATOR (see (149a)), readily produces an analysis of the example in (144d) that makes it entirely parallel to the examples in (144a–c).

(150) [$_{DP}$ D (...) [$_{FP}$ [$_{RC}$ *wo mai*]$_i$ [LINKER=*de* [$_{RP}$ [*shu*] [RELATOR t_i]]]]]

Throughout, we start out from a structure in which the predicate of the head noun originates to the right of the head noun and inverts with its subject via Predicate Inversion, with the LINKER *de* showing up as a reflex of the application of Predicate Inversion. For the specific case of (144d), the predicate that inverts with its subject is a full-fledged relative clause, but otherwise, (144d) is no different from (144a–c). A comparison of the structures in (145)–(147) and the one in (150), for the relative-clause case in (144d), makes this clear.

In the light of our discussion of quantificational restrictions on nominal-internal predication constructions in section 5.4.3, above, there is one thing that deserves some discussion in connection with the properties of relative-clause constructions in Mandarin. In section 5.4.3 we found that the postcopular noun phrase of QBNPs, while accepting numeral quantifiers to some extent (although this is already subject to crosslinguistic and idiolectal variation), is not allowed to contain a pure quantifier like *every*. Interestingly, however, the examples in (151) (adapted from Simpson 2001) show that it is possible to have the relative clause predicated of both numerically and universally quantified noun phrases.[102]

(151) a. [wo zuotian   mai] de liang-ben shu (Mandarin)
          I   yesterday buy DE two-CLF   book
          'two books I bought yesterday'
       b. [wo zuotian   mai] de mei-ben   shu
          I   yesterday buy DE every-CLF book
          'every book I bought yesterday'

This difference between relative-clause constructions and the noun-phrase internal AP/NP predication cases discussed earlier in this chapter turns on the maximum size that the small-clause subject is allowed to have. For QBNPs, I argued at some length that the postcopular subject may not be larger than NumP, and hence does not tolerate any quantifiers other than numerals. Apparently, the subject of a relative clause is allowed to be larger than NumP. I believe this difference between relative clauses and other noun-phrase internal predication constructions is a re-flex of the fact that relative clauses involve internal operator movement, with the "head" of the relative clause connected to the operator. Opera-tors must minimally be as large as QP. Hence, on the assumption that the operator and its binder must be phrase-structurally identical, the "head" of the relative clause *must* in fact be larger than NumP—minimally a QP.[103] Thus, far from compromising the Predicate Inversion analysis of Mandarin (144d), the facts in (151) actually lend support to the conclu-sion reached in section 5.4.3, that the quantificational restrictions on the postcopular noun phrase in QBNPs are a consequence of the size restric-tions imposed on this noun phrase.

Finally, let us take a closer look at the noun-complement clause case in (144e). The traditional analysis of noun-complement clauses literally takes these to be the complement of the noun, so that in *the claim that John was asleep* we are dealing with a clause base-generated in the com-plement of the noun *claim*. But as is well known, this analysis (especially when embedded in the *Barriers* framework of Chomsky 1986) has severe trouble capturing the familiar CNPC effect in sentences such as ?**Who did Imogen discuss the claim that Brian had kissed?** There is an alternative analysis, however, which does not take the so-called noun-complement clause to be a complement of the noun—an analysis due to Stowell (1981) (see also Napoli 1989, 250). On that analysis, the projection of the noun *claim* and the *that*-clause are taken to entertain a predication relationship, with the former serving as the predicate of the latter, as in (152a).

(152) a. $[_{DP}$ D $(\ldots)$ $[_{RP}$ CP $[_{RELATOR}$ $[_{NP}$ *claim*$]]]]$

     b. $[_{DP}$ D $(\ldots)$ $[_{FP}$ $[_{NP}$ *claim*$]_i$ $[_{LINKER+RELATOR_j}$ $[_{RP}$ CP $[t_j$ $t_i]]]]]$

In the course of the syntactic derivation, the predicate nominal inverts with its CP subject via Predicate Inversion, as depicted in (152b). In English, apparently, this does not give rise to the emergence of an overt realization of the LINKER (unlike in cases in which the head noun is *question* and its subject is a *wh*-CP: *the question of whether John was asleep*). English is somewhat unexpected that way, especially in view of the fact that at the clausal level, it does produce the key evidence for Predicate Inversion: in (153a), the copula *to be* is inomissible (on the intended reading), as in the by now familiar case of Copular Inversion (see (153b)).

(153) a. I consider the claim *(to be) that Imogen kissed Brian.

     b. I consider the best candidate *(to be) Brian.

The Mandarin facts are better behaved in this respect: in (144e) we do indeed find the expected surface reflex of the Predicate Inversion operation, the linker *de*. In other words, the *de* in between the "noun-complement clause" and the head noun in (144e) can readily be assimilated to the instances of the LINKER *de* discussed earlier in this section.[104]

Thus, the syntax of all of the Mandarin examples in (144) has been found to involve nominal-internal Predicate Inversion, with *de* serving as the LINKER. By treating all these examples this way, the analysis captures Simpson's (2001) observation that "the function which might seem to be constant and always associated with *de* is to introduce some kind of predication on a nominal." As a consequence of the fundamental connection between *de* and predication, it is impossible to use *de* in a DP in which nothing is predicated of the head noun, as in (154).[105]

(154) a. *de* shu

     DE book

    b. *shu *de*

     book DE

From the analysis of the Mandarin facts outlined in the previous paragraphs, this follows without further ado: *de* is a LINKER popping up as a reflex of a fully general Predicate Inversion operation, an operation that, as its name suggests, can only apply in contexts in which there is a predicate inside the complex noun phrase.

5.8   Concluding Remarks

While the preceding chapters documented and analysed the vicissitudes of predication and Predicate Inversion in the clause, this chapter put the spotlight on predication relationships within the complex noun phrase and on cases of inversion of the noun-phrase internal predicate around its subject. The existence of both straight (predicate-complement) and reverse (predicate-specifier) structures was demonstrated primarily on the basis of an in-depth investigation of the syntax of qualitative binominal noun phrases (QBNPs), which were shown to come in two types: the comparative QBNP (see (3a)) and the attributive QBNP (see (3b), on its most salient reading: 'an idiot in his or her capacity of being a doctor').

The syntax of the latter is relatively straightforward, instantiating the predicate-specifier structure and thus base-generating the major constituents of the complex noun phrase in their surface order. The meaningless element (English *of*) appearing in between the predicate and its subject is a copular element lexicalizing the functional head of the small clause, the RELATOR, on a par with elements such as *as, for, like* in the attributive constructions discussed in chapter 2 (e.g., *big for a butterfly*).

Since comparative QBNPs start life as predicate-complement structures, their syntax is considerably more involved. The discussion in section 5.3 has shown in detail that the way the predicate ends up to the left of its subject is via an application of Predicate Inversion (in the technical sense of the term discussed in chapter 4). The copular element *of* appearing between the predicate and the subject in this case is a spell-out of the small-clause external LINKER, its presence forced as an integral part of the Predicate Inversion process.

Qualitative binominal noun phrases exhibit a variety of severe restrictions on their nominal subconstituents in the realms of determination and quantification. These restrictions can be attributed to the fact that neither the subject nor the predicate of a QBNP is allowed to be any larger than NumP. Romance QBNPs in which one or even both of the major constituents of the small clause do appear to be larger were shown to conform to the generalization, with the definite article preceding the second noun in a subset of Romance comparative QBNPs being analyzed as a lexicalization of the RELATOR-head of the small clause—a "spurious" definite article akin to the "spurious" indefinite articles that are ubiquitous in comparative QBNPs in Dutch. "Spurious" articles, being spellouts of the RELATOR, are restricted to occur in comparative QBNPs only, a conclusion that was shown to be robustly confirmed by the empirical facts.

The distribution of noun-phrase internal predication, Predicate Inversion, and the nominal copula (*of* in English) is by no means confined to qualitative binominal noun phrases. In section 5.7, I documented a variety of other DP-internal predication constructions, whose syntactic properties strongly vindicate the conclusions reached on the basis of the detailed investigation of QBNPs in sections 5.1–5.6. Thus, it is clear that predication inside the nominal phrase exists, and so does Predicate Inversion; concomitantly, copular elements are abundantly represented inside the complex nominal phrase, both as spell-outs of the RELATOR and as lexicalizations of the LINKER. These conclusions at once enhance the parallelism between clauses and nominal phrases (pioneered by Szabolcsi 1983, 1994 and Abney 1987) and further the program laid out in the preceding chapters.

Chapter 6

Predication, RELATORS, and LINKERS

The general objective of this work has been to present a syntax of predication and the inversion of the predicate around its subject, putting its emphasis on meaningless elements (meaningless in the sense of having no semantic load) that play an essential role in the establishment and syntactic manipulation of predication relationships: RELATORS and LINKERS.

Chapters 2 and 3 of this study developed the hypothesis that all subject-predicate relationships are syntactically mediated by a RELATOR, and argued that subject-predicate relationships are both configurational and fundamentally nondirectional. While Napoli's (1989) approach to predication is both nondirectional and nonconfigurational, and Rothstein's (1983) configurational approach to (primary) predication explicitly includes a directionality clause stipulating that the predicate must follow the subject, this study has presented an extended argument for the view that predication relationships are systematically established in a RELATOR phrase, with the predicate originating either as the complement of the RELATOR (with the subject in the RELATOR's specifier), as in the familiar small-clause structure, or as the specifier of the RELATOR (with the subject occupying the RELATOR's complement position). Against this background, chapter 2 looked not only at core cases of predication (both primary and secondary) but also at the syntactic representation of topicalization, focalization, and adverbial and adjectival modification. In chapter 3 I explicitly refuted claims to the effect that "bare" small clauses or "bare" copular sentences exist, insisting on an asymmetrical and underlyingly predicational approach to all copular sentences (including what have variously been referred to as equative or identifying/identificational copular sentences) and reducing the typology of copular sentences of Higgins 1979 (or the expanded version of Declerck 1988) to just two types (see also Verheugd 1990): Moro's (1997) canonical and inverse copular sentences, the latter derived in syntax via Predicate Inversion.

With Predicate Inversion thus introduced, chapter 4 put the focus on the restrictions on inversion of the predicate around its subject and the distribution of LINKER elements surfacing between the inverted predicate and the subject. It presented an in-depth analysis of the syntax of Predicate Inversion (including Copular Inversion, Locative Inversion, "beheaded" Locative Inversion, and Dative Shift constructions), showing that Predicate Inversion constructions in general involve A-movement of a null-headed small-clause predicate around the subject, with the licensing requirement imposed on the null head of the predicate giving us the trigger for Predicate Inversion. It was shown that the grammar solves the locality problem facing A-movement of the predicate around its subject in either of two ways (raising of the predicate head to the RELATOR, or raising of the RELATOR to the small-clause external LINKER), giving rise to two different types of Predicate Inversion constructions with predictably distinct syntactic behaviors.

The discussion in chapter 5 of predication and Predicate Inversion in the nominal domain, the most extensive case study featured in the book, addressed, among other things, the syntax of *wh*-interrogative and *wh*-exclamative DPs, cases of DP-internal adjectival predication, possessed noun phrases, and relative-clause constructions, but its main focus was on the syntax of qualitative binominal noun phrases such as *a jewel of a village* and *an idiot of a doctor*. I argued at length that while all qualitative binominal noun phrases share the fact that the first noun phrase serves as the predicate of the second, one type of qualitative binominal noun phrase (the attributive type) base-generates the surface order of predicate and subject in a predicate-specifier structure and the other type (the comparative one) is derived from a predicate-complement structure via Predicate Inversion. Both types of qualitative binominal noun phrase give rise to a "nominal copula" (English *of*) between the predicate and the subject: in the predicate-specifier type, this copula is the lexicalization of the RELATOR, while in the predicate-complement type, whose derivation involves Predicate Inversion, the nominal copula is a spell-out of the small-clause external LINKER. The case study of qualitative binominal noun phrases thus lent support to the nondirectionality of predication, highlighted the pervasiveness of predication and Predicate Inversion in the grammar, and by identifying a copular element inside the nominal phrase and analyzing its distribution, it both furthered the parallelism between clauses and nominal phrases and vindicated the view that copular elements are meaningless spell-outs of functional heads inside or immediately outside small clauses (RELATORs and LINKERs).

The opening paragraph of this study emphasized that these were neither the first nor the last words written on predication. It is my hope, however, that the previous pages have made a contribution to the ongoing discussion of predication relationships and their syntax by seeking to establish a number of important points, which I will present here as bullet statements summarizing the exposition in the preceding paragraphs:

• Predication relationships are asymmetrical but nondirectional, projected in syntax in either of two ways—the predicate-complement or predicate-specifier structures.
• All predication relationships are mediated in syntax by a RELATOR; consequently, all predication relationships are asymmetrical.
• Predicate-complement structures may serve as input to the syntactic process of Predicate Inversion, a movement operation raising the predicate to an A-specifier position above the base position of its subject.
• Inversion of predicate and subject is subject to locality conditions that can be met in either of two ways—via raising of the predicate head to the RELATOR, or via phase-extending movement of the RELATOR to a small-clause external functional head, the LINKER.
• Predication and Predicate Inversion exist both in clauses and in nominal phrases; their workings are identical in the two structural domains.
• Copular elements manifest themselves as spell-outs of RELATOR and LINKER heads; since such heads are found both in clauses and in nominal phrases, copular elements exist in both structural domains.

Whether or not a RELATOR is spelled out depends on an interplay of factors in which the structural environment of the RELATOR plays a key role. The LINKER is generally forced to be spelled out whenever the language has an element to lexicalize it, to signal the application of phase-extending head movement, on which successful application of Predicate Inversion depends.

RELATORS and LINKERS are the vital syntactic cement of predication relationships and the inversion thereof. Studying the behavior of these elements has proved beneficial in bringing forth new perspectives on time-honored questions about predication and the distribution of copular elements, and in opening up new empirical domains of investigation. Pursuing these perspectives will doubtless further our understanding of the many questions surrounding the syntax of equation, (pseudo)clefting, relativization, and possession as well.

Notes

Chapter 1

1. I should note here that my use of the term LINKER is rather different from that in Collins's (2003) recent work on African languages. Collins's "linker" is a *v*P-internal functional category whose specifier position may serve as a landing site for movement—not of a predicate but typically of a subject. Unlike my LINKER, therefore, Collins's "linker" does not serve as the connection between a moved predicate and the small clause from which the predicate was extracted. From the perspective of the theory of predication laid out in this work, the Collins-type "linker" showing up in sentences such as (i) (where the numbers in the gloss represent noun-class markers, AFF stands for the affirmation prefix, and EXT is the extended aspect marker; see Baker and Collins 2003) seems in fact to be a good candidate for RELATOR status: the noun phrase to the left of (and, on Collins's analysis, in the specifier position of) k'- is the subject of the PP to its right. I will not address the analysis of Collins-type "linker" constructions in any detail in this work, bringing (i) up merely to forestall terminological confusion with regard to the term *linker*/LINKER.

(i) mo-n-a-hir-ire okugulu k'- omo-kihuna (Kinande)
 AFF-1SG.SU-T-put-EXT leg.15 LK.15 LOC.18-hole.7
 'I put the leg in the hole.'

Chapter 2

1. Some parts of this section were informed by the discussions of predication scattered throughout Seuren 1998.

2. The small-caps notation *RELATOR* is meant to bring out the idea that the term is a cover for anything that may be used to connect a predicate to its subject (see sections 2.2.3 and 2.5 for further discussion). It is explicitly not proposed to represent a syntactic category (as opposed to the otherwise similar approach in Bowers 1993, where *Pr*—which functions much like my RELATOR—*is* introduced as a new functional category (see also Moro 1988 and Adger and Ramchand 2003)). The tree in (1) is a shorthand notation, therefore. It is important to keep this in mind throughout.

3. The notion "minimal domain" used in (2) is defined as in Chomsky 1995; for our purposes here, the minimal domain of a head can basically be thought of as the set of nodes comprising the complement position and the specifier of that head.

4. I have chosen the term *reverse predication* to refer to predicate-specifier structures, rather than *inverse predication*, in order to avoid confusion with Predicate Inversion constructions, which share with predicate-specifier structures the fact that the predicate occupies a specifier position but differ crucially in that the predicate is not *base-generated* as a specifier but becomes a specifier as a result of the application of Predicate Inversion, an overt-syntactic movement operation. Predicate Inversion will be discussed in detail in chapters 4 and 5.

5. I call elements such as *as, for*, and also *like* prepositions in light of the fact that all of them are strandable under A'-extraction (cf. *What do you regard him as?*, *What do you take me for?* and *What is it like?*). The Russian element *v* 'into' in (i), which like English *as, for*, and *like* serves as a lexicalization of the RELATOR (see Bailyn 2004, who identifies it as a spell-out of Bowers's Pr^0), is presumably to be classified as preposition as well—with the nominative marking on the predicate nominal being an "inanimate accusative," according to Franks and Pereltsvaig (2004).

(i) a. Putin soglasen ballotirovat'sja v   prezidenty (Russian)
       Putin agrees   to-run   into presidents(NOM)
       'Putin agrees to run for president.'
    b. gruppa graždan vydvinula Putina   v   prezidenty
       group citizens nominated Putin-ACC into presidents(NOM)
       'A group of citizens nominated Putin for president.'

6. Though perhaps confusing, I will continue to use the abbreviation "RP" in the syntactic representations of subject-predicate relationships; but throughout, I will indicate, with the aid of an "=" sign following the RELATOR-head, what the RELATOR actually corresponds to in the specific example at hand (see, e.g., (8a)). "RELATOR" will be spelled with small caps to indicate its abstract nature.

7. Chomsky (1986) assumes, plausibly, that Infl's VP-complement in (8b) is not an *argument* of Infl: the legitimacy of intermediate adjunction to VP is crucial in *Barriers*; such would be forbidden, however, if VP were an argument of Infl (since Chomsky (1986, 6) explicitly rules out adjunction to arguments). Yet at the same time, Chomsky (1986, 20) argues that Infl must *θ-govern* the VP-predicate in its complement, on the basis of the fact that VP-movement out of a *wh*-island (as in *?Fix the car, I wonder whether he will*) gives rise to a mere subjacency effect, not the ECP effect that would be expected if the moved VP left a non-θ-governed trace. The conclusion that Infl's VP-complement is θ-governed by Infl but not an argument of Infl is basically incoherent. The grammaticality of VP-extraction from *wh*-islands is unlikely to support the alleged θ-government relationship between Infl and VP: in *Barriers* the role of θ-government in the licensing of traces is essentially reduced to zero. I will not take the VP-topicalization facts to support a thematic relationship between Infl and VP, therefore (see also the discussion in

section 2.4, and Rothstein's (1983) argument that predicates cannot be assigned a θ-role). In general, I take the RELATOR in (1) to be thematically inactive—a point to which I return in section 2.5.1.

8. On the standard assumption that "coordination of likes" is the only type of co-ordination allowed, no problems arise when it comes to the syntactic category of the conjunction on this approach. Things become tricky, however, when one considers examples of the type in (i), where, apparently, the two conjuncts belong to different syntactic categories. Unless one adopts a more abstract analysis (e.g., one in terms of coordination of small clauses, with "small clause" being a category in its own right—see below for more discussion of the structure and category membership of small clauses), such examples pose an insurmountable conundrum for approaches to conjunction of the type in (9).

(i) I consider John [[an idiot] and [out of his mind]].

9. I will not explore this semantic hypothesis any further in this work, which confines itself to the *syntax* of predication. Execution of the hypothesis that the semantics of predication uniformly involves set intersection ($\cap$) is not entirely straightforward. Thus, predications such as *Few linguists are good teachers* or *Nobody likes this* are not directly interpretable in terms of set intersections (there is no set denoted by *few linguists* that would be intersectible with *good teachers*). This does not necessarily defeat a uniform set-intersection approach to all predication, however: one could represent such sentences in terms of a structure in which the quantified subject occupies a nonargument position, being linked to a variable (a null name) in subject position, the latter denoting a set that may then intersect with the set denoted by the predicate. Thanks to Anna Szabolcsi for discussion of this point.

10. The hypothesis is usually known as the *VP–Internal Subject Hypothesis*, but though the debate about its validity has focused primarily on verbal predications, the hypothesis is obviously wider in scope. The text formulation applies it to all *lexical* projections (with $L \in \{A, N, P, V\}$).

11. In this representation, the SpecVP position is available as an escape hatch for extraction out of the VP, hence is always a θ'-position.

12. To see this, consider the structure in (i)—an ungrammatical structure corresponding to a grammatical sentence. Here, the intermediate trace t_i' of the adjunct-*wh* in the embedded SpecCP (which cannot be deleted since it serves to license the original trace of the adjunct at LF) cannot be properly governed by its immediate antecedent (the intermediate t_i'' adjoined to the matrix VP) due to the intervention between the two of V', the immediate X-bar projection of the governor of t_i'. Chomsky (1986) notes this problem and seeks to solve it by assuming (Chomsky 1986, 4) that the X' node is projected only when it makes a difference. With V' not projected, VP would become the minimality barrier, but since VP does not exclude the antecedent t_i'', no ECP violation ensues. Notice now that nonprojection of V' will be a possibility *only* if the subject of the VP is not projected inside the VP, in SpecVP—in the structure in (i), V' cannot be omitted on pain of the creation of a ternary-branching structure. In order for Chomsky's

(1986) way around the minimality problem with long-distance adjunct extraction to succeed, therefore, the external argument of VP must not be base-generated in SpecVP (see (8b)).

(i) *$[_{CP}$ *how*$_i$ do you$_j$ $[_{VP}$ t_i'' $[_{VP}$ t_j $[_{V'}$ think $[_{CP}$ t_i' that Mary did it $t_i]]]]]$

Chomsky's "patch" for unwanted minimality violations under long-distance adjunct extraction (i.e., the nongeneration of X$'$) should lead to the *general* conclusion that "specifier positions" never serve as subject positions—positions that the subject is born in, moves to, or transits through. Consider, for instance, the example in (ii), featuring long-distance adjunct extraction across the overt subject of an adjectival small clause. Thus, though Chomsky (1986) explicitly embraces an analysis of small clauses à la Stowell (1981), with the external argument of all small-clause predicates being base-generated inside their maximal projection, as a specifier, the minimality problem that such an analysis would present in cases like (ii) suggests that treating predicate-internal subjects as *specifiers* is fundamentally at odds with the technicalities of the *Barriers* framework. That does not mean, however, that *Barriers* is incompatible with predicate-internal base generation of external arguments per se: the particular variant of the LP–Internal Subject Hypothesis depicted in (11b), with its *adjunction* approach to the external argument, would fit *Barriers* just fine. It is just the predicate-internal base generation of the subject as a *specifier* (11a) that wreaks havoc for (i) and (ii).

(ii) How do you consider Mary likely to have done it?

13. It is worth stressing that, common misconceptions of Hale and Keyser's use of Larsonian "VP-shells" notwithstanding, the outer "VP-shell" in the structures in (15) does *not* correspond to Chomsky's (1995) *v*P (see (13))—the outer VP does not have a specifier at all (and could not have one, crucially, because the outer V-head's complement is not a predicate, or unsaturated constituent). So the *v*-head introducing the external argument would be projected *outside* the outer "VP-shell" in (15).

14. I will return in chapter 3 to the question of how to define a small clause from the perspective of the approach to predication taken in this work.

15. I thus give an affirmative answer to the question of whether small clauses are projections of functional heads or not, but I am not assuming here (contrary to what I did in some of my earlier work; see Den Dikken 1987, 1995a) that that functional head is Agr (among other works, see also Hornstein and Lightfoot 1987; Cardinaletti and Guasti 1992; Hoekstra and Mulder 1990; Chomsky 1995, chap. 3). Moro (1997) rightly objects to an Agr-based approach on the basis of the fact that the subject and the nominal predicate of a small clause can differ in number properties (as in *The children are a problem*). More generally, it is fundamentally wrong to take "Agr" to exist as a functional category—agreement is a *relationship*, perhaps one mediated by a functional category, but certainly not *identified as* that functional category. See also Chomsky (1995, chap. 4) for a rejection of Agr-heads within minimalism.

16. Where "specifier," as before, is a shorthand for "A-specifier"; if readers wish to believe in escape-hatching movement through A$'$-specifier positions of lexical

projections (see note 11), they may equip lexical projections with as many A'-specifiers as they see fit. But since the discussion in this work does not bear on this point, I will not address the issue.

17. In current minimalist terms, one would say that the light verb *v* can have an "EPP property" (Chomsky's 2001 "OCC").

18. We can continue to call the RELATOR of the predication relationship between a VP and its subject a light verb *v*, as long as it is clearly understood that this light *v* is just an instantiation of a general-purpose functional head that helps establish predication. Recall from the discussion in section 2.2.3 that "RELATOR" is not to be taken to stand for a lexical primitive—there is no such thing as a lexical category "RELATOR"; the term "RELATOR" is a shorthand intended as a cover for all the various functional categories that can mediate a predication relationship.

19. The predication relationship between the VP and the surface subject is established only after movement of the subject to SpecTP has taken place. That is, predication cannot be a "D-structure" affair here. In general, with the abolition of D-structure in minimalism, there can be no sense in which predication is confined to D-structure, or the "premovement" part of the derivation. Predication may happen at any point—and we know that it can apply postmovement: the *tough*-movement construction (see (i)) is a case in point. Ever since Browning 1987, it has been entirely standard to assume that in *tough*-movement constructions of the type in (i), the predicate is created as a result of movement of a null operator within the infinitival clause (see also Mulder and Den Dikken 1992; Chomsky 1995). Neither from a theoretical point of view nor from an empirical one is there anything suspicious, therefore, about treating unaccusative constructions in terms of a predication relationship established after movement between the VP and the surface subject.

(i) Imogen is tough to please.

20. For sentences like *I saw Imogen fall*, the question of what serves as the RELATOR depends on one's assumptions concerning the complement structure of perception verbs taking bare infinitival complements. If these lack T, then T cannot be the RELATOR. That still does not mean that we need a light verb *v* to establish the relationship, though. If the complement of *saw* in *I saw Imogen fall* is a small clause (lacking T), then the nature of the RELATOR head will be identical with that of RELATOR heads in other small-clause complementation constructions, including *I consider Imogen smart/a pretty girl/out of this world*.

I should add that the text discussion does not rule out the possibility that a light verb *v* is present in the structure of unaccusative constructions for reasons independent of the predication relationship established by the VP and the (raised) subject. Thus, if one subscribes to the view (championed in Marantz 1997 and subsequent work in Distributed Morphology) that roots are category-neutral and that a light verb *v* is needed to "make" a verb out of the lexical root, then a *v* will need to be included in all verbal structures, irrespective of the predication relationships established in them.

21. In languages, such as Japanese, that allow multiple nominative constructions, (20a) does potentially converge, with T checking its nominative Case feature twice, against both the subject and the object. If this is a sensible approach to nominative object constructions such as (ia) (contrasting with ungrammatical (ib), featuring an accusative object), then reining in the distribution of nominative objects will be a matter of determining the distribution of (20a) and (20b), a task I cannot undertake here.

(i) a.   John-ga   orandago-*ga* dekiru (Japanese)
         John-NOM Dutch-NOM   can-do
         'John can speak Dutch.'
    b. *John-ga   orandago-*o* dekiru
         John-NOM Dutch-ACC can-do

22. For more detailed discussion of Rotuman *ne*, see Den Dikken (2003b). In that work (which does not adopt the distinction between "RELATOR" and "LINKER" elements introduced in this book), I call *ne* a linker; with the term *LINKER* confined to grammatical markers in *inverse* predications (see chapters 4 and 5, below), it will presumably be better to rechristen *ne* as a RELATOR (given that it is not obvious that there has been inversion of the subject and the predicate in examples of the type in (23a, b)). In Chinese and Burmese, the element serving as a linker of (systematically *inverse*) subject-predicate relationships inside the noun phrase doubles as a topic marker as well. See Den Dikken and Singhapreecha 2004 and the references cited there.

23. The use of *ec* rather than *t* in these structures reveals that I am not prepared to commit myself to a movement analysis of topicalization. In chapter 4, I will in fact adopt a base-generation approach to certain PP-topicalization constructions, but for others a movement analysis is likely to be correct. My use of the term *topicalization* glosses over these potential differences (see Grohmann 2003 for careful discussion). Arguably, it also extends to dislocation constructions and "hanging-topic" constructions. I will not discuss these in any detail here (but the fact that hanging *as for* topics in English seem to combine two lexicalizers of the RELATOR head—*as* and *for*—is an interesting potential avenue toward an analysis of this construction).

24. Of course we should be free to continue to use the label "TopP" and express *syntactic* generalizations (such as ordering and selectional restrictions) in terms of that label (see Rizzi's 1997 et passim work on the left periphery).

25. On adverbs as predicates, see also Davidson 1975; Rothstein 1983.

26. Alternatively, *-ly* can be treated as an inflectional suffix base-generated directly on the adjectival predicate, with the RELATOR entering into an Agree relationship with the feature bundle represented by *-ly*. The choice between these options is immaterial for my purposes here. For concreteness, I will take *-ly* to be a syntactically autonomous element lexicalizing the RELATOR.

27. I refer the reader to Aarts 1992 and Bowers 1993 for arguments to the effect that elements such as *like* are lexicalizations of the functional head of small

clauses—that is, of subject-predicate structures. I will return to *like* and the like in section 2.6.4 and also in chapter 3.

28. Szabó 2001 contains valuable discussion of the relative merits of the predicate and predicate-modifier approaches to adjectival modifiers, reaching the conclusion—to which I subscribe—that the predicative use is more basic. While there are of course attributive adjectives to which the predicative analysis seems difficult to apply (*utter, chief, former*; but see Larson 1998 on *former*), he sets these aside, noting—correctly, in my view—that it would be bad methodology to generalize to the worst case.

29. For simplicity, I take *a* to be a D-head; see chapter 5 for in-depth discussion of the nominal phrase. I also suppress here the fact that the subject of the AP predicate-specifier—that is, the NP *dancer*—is itself a predicate (with AP serving as a function from predicates (properties) to predicates (properties); see Kamp 1975 and Siegel 1976). The answer to the question of what a DP-contained NP-predicate is predicated of is not straightforward. On present assumptions, we would have to make [RP [AP *beautiful*] [RELATOR [NP *dancer*]]] the predicate-complement of another RELATOR (exactly as in (33)); its subject will either be PRO or, perhaps more likely, a null operator (see Campbell 1997 for the latter approach, which he confines to specific noun phrases: he identifies the null operator as a *specificity* operator), controlled or bound by the matrix subject, *Imogen*.

30. Strictly speaking, the predication relationship between *dancer* and *Imogen* is not direct but mediated by a null category, as discussed briefly in note 29. The only thing that the structure below (32) does not end up expressing directly is the predication relationship that (31) postulates between *Imogen* and *beautiful*(R). But this seems to me to be a good result. For while I find Szabó's (2001) treatment of the semantics of *Imogen is a beautiful dancer* generally satisfactory and insightful, I believe it is a mistake to have *beautiful*(R) predicated of *Imogen* in this particular sentence. In (32), there is no *direct* relationship between *beautiful*(R) and *Imogen*—instead, the RP representing *beautiful*(R) is contained in a DP that serves as a predicate nominal, and it is this DP that is predicated of *Imogen*.

31. In more formal registers, the *as a* in (33) can be replaced with *qua*. I will take it that *qua* is another candidate for the lexicalization of the RELATOR, but I have nothing to say about the more restrictive distribution of *qua* or about the fact that *qua* must be followed by a bare noun phrase.

32. Syntactically, though, (37a) and (37b) are robustly different when it comes to the possible presence of complements to the adjective. As I pointed out in my critique of Higginbotham's (1985) account of *big for a butterfly*, it is perfectly possible for the adjective to take an internal argument in this construction: *good at math for a three-year-old*. But as is well known, attributive adjectives within the noun phrase cannot take a complement (to their right) when they occur in prenominal position: **a good at math girl*. This restriction, known as the Head-Final Filter, has stubbornly resisted a principled account in the syntax literature. I have no enlightenment to offer, and must leave the matter open.

33. Recall note 5 on reasons for believing that these elements are prepositional.

34. It should be clear that the b-examples in (45) and (46) do not involve compounding: they have exactly the opposite prosodic contour of English root compounds (cf. *bráin doctor* versus *idiot dóctor*). Peculiarly, while Napoli (1989, 235) base-generates these examples as [$_{N'}$ N NP], she restructures them at S-structure into complex nominals, [$_N$ N N], indistinguishable from compounds.

35. Pesetsky (1989) shows unequivocally that a derivation in terms of extraposition around the adverbial modifier is untenable: it makes the wrong predictions with respect to extraction (*What did Imogen thank Brian profusely for?*) and relative scope (the fact that (ia) features the scopal relation between *intentionally* and *twice* that is also found in (ib), and not that of (ic): in the former two sentences, *intentionally* scopes over *twice*, while in the latter *twice* takes scope over *intentionally*; see Andrews 1983 for original discussion, as well as Cinque 1999, 25–28, and Takano 2003, the last-mentioned author arguing for right-peripheral base generation of adverbs on the basis of an interesting argument that I do not have the space to reproduce or critique here).

(i) a. Brian knocked intentionally twice on the door.
    b. Brian intentionally twice knocked on the door.
    c. Brian knocked on the door intentionally twice.

36. I am representing the subject of the adverbial as *v*P in recognition of the outcome of the discussion in section 2.6.1 (see (29)) as well as to facilitate a remnant movement analysis for examples of the type in (51); generating *v* outside RP and having the adverbial predicated directly of the VP would lead *v* to be separated from its associate VP in ways that are disallowed both in Chomsky 1995, chap. 4, and in the theory laid out in this book. (The label "AdvP" in (52) serves expository purposes only; I do not recognize a lexical category "Adv.")

37. I would like to thank Erika Troseth for her help with the examples in (53) and (54).

38. Cinque (1999, 179, note 72) takes (53b) to reflect the base order, with (53a) derived from it via leftward movement of the PP *on the door* ("for informational reasons"). But how (53a) is base-generated remains unclear, as does the fact that extraction from the allegedly leftward-moved PP in (53a) is perfectly grammatical (*Which door did Imogen knock on twice?*). In any event, Cinque's approach to (53a, b) makes exactly the same predictions with respect to scope as does the main-text proposal; the fact that (53b) perhaps tends a little more strongly toward a single-event reading than does (53a) thus remains unaccounted for on both approaches.

39. The discussion in what follows was directly inspired by Hoekstra (1996) (see also Benveniste 1966 with respect to the analysis of periphrastic perfects). Hoekstra takes my (55b) to be the *only* underlier of verbal predication relationships, and derives active (55a) from passive (55b).

40. A case in point here are Baker, Johnson, and Roberts's (1989, 223) remarks about the *by*-phrase. Taking *-en*, the passive morpheme, to be the "absorber" of

the external θ-role, they assimilate it to a clitic, and go on to assume that "long passives" (i.e., passives including a *by*-phrase) are clitic-doubling constructions. But clitic-doubling constructions of the familiar type are subject to restrictions (involving definiteness, specificity, and pronominality) that are not mimicked by "long passives"; moreover, Baker, Johnson, and Roberts do not make it explicit what the clitic-doubling hypothesis entails for the syntactic status and position of the *by*-phrase. This is not to say that the clitic-doubling hypothesis cannot be on the right track—it is merely to illustrate the text claim that the position of the *by*-phrase and the way it is linked to the external θ-role have remained largely unclear in the extant literature on the active/passive diathesis alternation.

41. Active constructions are not necessarily built on (55a): those in which there is no [tense] feature to be checked by V against T can be built on either (55a) or (55b); see below for reverse predication in perfective *have*-sentences, and section 2.7.2 for discussion of predication alternation in Romance causatives.

42. In all likelihood, the structure of participial constructions involves more than just a bare VP, and may not even be verbal in nature (note the fact that passive participles double as adjectives: *the unspoken truth*), but to keep the representations in (55) simple, I have chosen to abstract away from this. I will return to the matter in section 2.8.2, where an aspectual projection (AspP) will be inserted between T and RP in the structure in (55c).

Note that substitution of the (homophonous) past-tense form *kissed*, providing a bearer of a matching [tense] feature, results in a tensed active like *Imogen kissed Brian* on Hoekstra's (1996) assumptions (see also Den Dikken 1996). In this connection, note Guéron (2003) for the idea that English past-tense and past-participial forms are essentially the same things, differing with respect to whether or not they check a [tense] feature in T, and for interesting discussion of Arabic and Latin as languages in which participial forms can raise to T. (To be sure, the past-tense and past-participial forms of English verbs are not systematically identical, but for the *regular* verbs, they always are.)

If, on the other hand, simple actives like *Imogen kissed Brian* are not derived from passive sentences but generated via (55a), one must assume (and derive) that (55b) cannot converge if V bears a [tense] feature. To this end, one may follow Hale and Keyser (1993) in assuming that heads of specifiers cannot be moved. In the *Barriers* framework, this was straightforwardly derivable from the fact that the constituent in specifier position was a blocking category for lack of L-marking, hence being an inherent barrier itself and propagating barrierhood via inheritance to the constituent dominating the specifier. A massive ECP violation hence results from raising the head of a specifier to an external head position. In current minimalism, guaranteeing T's failure to establish an Agree or Attract relationship with the verbal head in (55b) is not entirely straightforward. What must be ensured is that (i) there is a *phase* boundary between T and V and (ii) the V-head is not on the edge of that phase. RP is arguably a phase (see section 4.3.2.1 for discussion; RP is "propositional" and hence qualifies, by Chomsky's (2000, 2001) general rationale, for phasehood). VP in (55b) is on the phase edge, and V is the head of this VP. But apparently, being the head of the constituent on the edge of the RP-phase does not make V itself sit on the phase edge. I will not develop a theory that ensures this but will assume that, in general, the head of a constituent sitting on the edge of a phase is not itself on the edge of a phase.

43. Passives of course do not *have* to feature an overt *by*-phrase. While for analyses of passives à la Baker, Johnson, and Roberts (1989), the emergence of an overt *by*-phrase is somewhat troublesome (given that *-en*, passive morphology, absorbs the external θ-role), for the present proposal it is the *non*occurrence of a *by*-phrase that gives rise to some further discussion. It is commonly assumed in the literature that in "short passives" like *Brian was kissed*, there is in fact an external argument represented in the syntax—note the familiar argument (from Manzini 1980 and Roeper 1983) based on rationale clauses in sentences like *The ship was sunk to collect the insurance*, where the PRO subject of the rationale clause needs a syntactic controller. Williams (1987) countered this argument by pointing to sentences such as *Grass is green to promote photosynthesis*, where there can be no implicit agent controlling the PRO subject of the rationale clause (see also Whelpton 1995, chap. 5, for discussion). It seems obvious to me, however, that the two types of sentences are in different ballparks: while an "event-control" approach to the latter is reasonable (the sentence states, right or wrong, that the grass's being green is what promotes photosynthesis), such an analysis is obviously absurd for the former type of example (the ship's being sunk is not the collector of the insurance). See Roberts (1987, 113–114) for a compendium of arguments against an event-control approach (the most significant of these being the anaphor binding facts in pairs like *The President was impeached publicly (by the Republicans) PRO to secure themselves extra votes* versus **The President was impeached publicly PRO to reveal/expose itself to the electorate*, and the fact that **The house was struck by lightning PRO to start a fire* is ungrammatical even though there is in fact an event ("the house being struck by lightning") that should be able to control PRO). An implicit yet syntactically represented external argument does indeed seem necessary, therefore, for passives. I will represent it as a *pro* in the complement of the RELATOR in the structure in (55b)—with the RELATOR being null in this case. Thus, a potentially interesting correlation emerges between the overtness of the agent in the RELATOR's complement and the overtness of the RELATOR: when the former is overt, the latter is as well (being realized, in English, as *by*; in case-marking languages, it is represented by some lexical case, e.g. instrumental).

44. The existence, in Italian, of *averci* 'have-there' (see Moro 1997, 236ff.—*I professori (c') hanno molti libri* 'The professors there-have many books') does not compromise the Benvenistian adage: *ci* is not a preposition. See Ferrazzano 2002 for discussion of the syntax of *averci* constructions.

45. As in the case of the passive construction in (55b), the VP in the specifier of the RELATOR phrase in (61b) is arguably dominated by functional structure of its own (e.g., Kayne's 1989 "InfP"). But as before, I have chosen to keep the structures simple, for expository convenience.

46. The Case-checking preposition that lexicalizes the RELATOR can also be the counterpart of the *by* of English passive *by*-phrases (as in the *faire-par* construction). In light of the brief discussion of the active/passive diathesis alternation in the previous subsection, it is likely that the structure of *faire-par* constructions is very similar to that of *faire*-infinitive constructions. In particular, the relationship between the causee and the causativized VP will be established in the same configurational way, via a prepositional RELATOR in a predicate-specifier structure of the type in (3b). This still leaves room for differences between *faire*-infinitive and *faire-par* causatives, however. It is in fact highly likely that in *faire-par* constructions there is more functional structure between the causative verb and the RP constituting the lower predication. Since the text discussion serves merely to sketch the outlines of an analysis of Romance-type causative constructions from the perspective of the approach to subject-predicate relations taken in this study, I will not go into the details of these constructions here, referring the reader to Den Dikken and Longenecker 2004 for further discussion.

47. See Den Dikken and Longenecker 2004, section 5.1, for further details, including a discussion of clitic-case alternations in unergative-based causatives. The structure of *ergative/unaccusative*-based *faire*-infinitive constructions is of course different from that of transitive and unergative-based causatives: these constructions have no "external argument" in the complement of the causative verb; the causee is introduced, not with the aid of a RELATOR instead but as the complement of the infinitival verb and checks accusative Case against the matrix "light verb" v under Agree (see (ib)).

(i) a. Imogen laisse/fait tomber le livre (French)
       Imogen lets/makes fall   the book
       'Imogen lets/makes the book fall.'
   b. [$_{vP}$ [$_{DP}$ CAUSER [$_{v'}$ v [$_{VP2}$ V$_{CAUS}$ [$_{VP1}$ V1$_{Inf}$ [$_{DP}$ CAUSEE]]]]]]

48. There is variation, in (66a), with respect to the size of the nominal subconstituents of the small clause. In the discussion here, this variation is inconsequential; I will return to it at more length in chapter 5. In section 2.8.1, I will conflate the reverse nominal predication cases with the reverse adjectival cases because, as we have seen, there are no fundamental differences between the two types. I will not address prepositional predication (see (42c)) in much detail. (Recall from note 36 that the label "AdvP" in (66c) serves expository purposes only; I do not recognize a lexical category "Adv.")

49. This is not to say that predicates cannot bear *morphological* case—they most certainly can. There are two ways predicates can end up with morphological case: (i) via "case agreement" (agreement in case with the subject), or (ii) as a result of the presence of a case particle or preposition under the RELATOR-head. (In chapter 3, we will encounter some examples of the latter type from Russian and Hungarian; see section 3.2.1.2.) The fact that the infinitival complementizer *for* cannot be omitted in Copular Inversion constructions such as **(For) the culprit to be Brian would be surprising* cannot be ascribed to *the culprit*'s Case needs (since it has none)—instead, it could be attributed to *Brian*'s need to get its Case feature checked, via the link between it and the raised predicate.

50. Recall from note 29 that (66b) is a somewhat simplified structure; the full-fledged representation would arguably include a double-RP structure à la (66a) with a null category in the specifier position of the outer RP.

51. By "attributive" I mean precisely what Higginbotham (1985) means when he says that the *for*-phrase serves as an "attribute." It restricts the meaning of the adjectival (or nominal) predicate in the RELATOR's specifier position (see also section 2.6.3).

52. The structure of (68c) includes an aspectual projection (AspP) between the causative verb and RP; see Den Dikken and Longenecker 2004, section 4.2, for detailed discussion of Romance *faire-par* causatives that leads to the conclusion that an AspP is needed outside RP. The Asp-head can plausibly be held responsible for the realization of the RELATOR as *da* 'by' rather than *a* 'to' (which we see in the causative in (68b), where there is no AspP projected on top of the RELATOR phrase).

53. The fact that the verbal material preceding the subject may be more complex than a single inflected verb (as in the complex tense in (70.A2)) makes it clear that a simpleminded verb-raising approach to postverbal subject placement in unergative "free-inversion" constructions will not do.

54. See Pinto 1997 for detailed discussion. I should add that (70.A2) is not ungrammatical per se—it works just fine in a narrow-focus context, as the answer to the question *Chi ha mangiato le mele?* 'Who has eaten the apples?', with focus on the subject. I assume that the syntax of subject-focus constructions is different, involving A′-movement of the subject.

Pinto (1997) notes that there are a few apparently transitive constructions allowing for clause-final subject placement in a wide-focus context, (i) being a case in point, but she points out that the verb and the object form an idiomatic unit in such cases, counting essentially as an intransitive VP.

(i) in questo ufficio hanno dato le   dimissioni   molti ministri (Italian)
    in this   office have   given the resignations many ministers
    'Many ministers resigned in this office.'

55. The fact that sentences like (70.A2) become grammatical, in the wide-focus context at hand, when the direct object is cliticized (Pinto 1997) is compatible with the text analysis on the assumption that object clitics (like incorporated nouns) are not Case-feature checkers, hence do not depend on the presence in the structure of the "light verb" *v*.

56. The passive seems rare in ergative languages—though perhaps this generalization should be stated in the other direction: as Nichols (1992, 158) points out, languages that have an antipassive but no passive are systematically ergative (there certainly are (morphologically) ergative languages that have a passive, Eskimo being a case in point; see Dixon 1994, section 6.1, for discussion and exemplification). This may follow if, as seems plausible as a first stab, syntactically ergative languages assign transitive sentences a structure in which (63b) merges with T and T establishes an Agree relationship with V's object, as a result of

which V's object checks absolute Case (the counterpart in ergative/absolute languages to nominative Case in nominative/accusative languages). The subject, in the RELATOR's complement position, is then left to check Case against the RELATOR, which is morphologically reflected in the form of ergative case (it is perhaps significant here that ergative case is called *"relative* case" in the literature on Eskimo languages). Viewed this way, transitive constructions in ergative languages are in fact structurally *identical* with the passives of nominative/accusative languages—which may explain why lack of passive and ergativity typically go together.

57. Postverbal subjects of unaccusative/ergative verbs do not arise via (69) but instead have a familiar genesis, with VP serving as the complement of T and V's complement staying in situ, checking Case against T under Agree, the EPP being checked via verb movement. This difference between postverbal subjects of unergative and unaccusative/ergative verbs should be responsible for the difference in behavior with respect to extraction (*ne*-cliticization in Italian, for instance) and past-participle agreement.

(i) a. ne   sono venuti   molti (Italian)
        of.them are   come-M.PL many-M.PL
        'Many of them came.'
    b. *ne   hanno telefonato   molti
        of.them have   telephoned-M.SG many-M.PL

58. This approach to (73) generates some nontrivial questions. One thing that comes up is why T, in constructions in which SpecTP is occupied by an adverbial, cannot be filled by a modal (which would then end up preceding the subject). Another question is why the distribution of adverbials that can sit in SpecTP is restricted in ways that are not in any obvious way linkable to tense. These questions are brought sharply into the focus by the analysis suggested in the main text—but in all fairness, I should add that Culicover's (1993) approach to (73b) does not provide immediate(ly insightful) answers to these questions either. These are open questions that future research should address.

59. I say "by and large" because (67), as it stands, does not follow from the theory, but (67) aside, the distribution of (63) reduces in its entirety to independent properties of the system.

Chapter 3

1. Recall from chapter 2 (note 4) that the adjectives *reverse* and *inverse* are used systematically to refer to two profoundly different things in this study: reverse predications are base-generated with the predicate higher than the subject, in the form of a predicate-specifier structure; inverse predications have the predicate higher than the subject thanks to movement of the former on the basis of an underlying predicate-complement structure.

2. I will not review these mechanisms here; see Den Dikken 1995c for relevant discussion.

3. See the discussion in section 2.8.2 for an answer to the question of why *da*, not *a*, must be chosen as the lexicalization of the RELATOR-head in passive (6c), whereas there is a choice of RELATOR in causative constructions (i.e., (4b) alternates with a *faire-par* causative).

4. I reiterate that the fact that there are reverse predications that cannot serve as primary predications does not undermine the text approach. Failure of turning a reverse RP into a primary predication generally has independent causes—such as the one hinted at in the previous paragraph in the discussion of the ill-formedness of (6b); or the apparently general (albeit still poorly understood) fact that adjectival and nominal reverse predications can only be attributive (see section 2.8.1), which is responsible for the fact that the lower RP in (i) cannot form a primary predication (cf. **skinny is (for) an American*).

(i) Imogen finds Brian skinny for an American.

[$_{VP}$ *finds* [$_{RP}$ *Brian* [RELATOR=$\varnothing$ [$_{RP}$ [$_{AP}$ *skinny*] [RELATOR=*for* [$_{DP}$ *an American*]]]]]]

Notice, by the way, that, on the text approach, the sentence in (i) has *two* small clauses embedded under *find*: the outer RP is a straight predication with *Brian* as its subject, and the inner RP is a reverse predication featuring the predicate *skinny* in the specifier position of RP. (Recall from the discussion in chapter 2 that the AP of *skinny* is a function from predicates (properties) to predicates (properties), with the complement of the RELATOR being simultaneously the subject of the AP and the predicate nominal of the containing embedded RP.)

5. It goes without saying that, given (8), the results of Moro's (2000) creative use of the notion of a "bare" small clause within his "dynamic antisymmetry" framework will be lost. But as I will show in detail in the chapters to follow, we do not need "dynamic antisymmetry" to account for the facts of Predicate Inversion, one of Moro's case studies. I will have nothing to say here about his other applications of "dynamic antisymmetry"—to the extent that these do not involve predication relationships, they are unaffected by what is argued here.

6. Two constructions discussed in my earlier work that present particularly strong evidence against symmetrical, "bare" small clauses will be brought up briefly in this note. For resultative constructions, the Norwegian Locative Inversion construction with P-stranding illustrated in (i) provides key support for a functional head inside the small clause that serves as a landing site for movement of the prepositional head of the moved PP-predicate. This construction is discussed in great detail in Den Dikken and Næss 1993, to which I refer the interested reader. See also the discussion in chapter 4, below.

(i) jeg tror   at [$_{PP}$ t_i brevet]$_j$ ble klistret [$_{RP}$ frimerker [RELATOR+*på*$_i$ t_j]]
   I   believe that   letter-the was pasted   stamps   on
   'I believe that there were stamps pasted on the letter.' (Norwegian)

And in the domain of predicate nominal constructions, the distribution of the indefinite article *een* in Dutch noun-phrase internal Predicate Inversion constructions of the type in (ii) serves as an argument for the existence of a functional head inside the small clause as well (see Bennis, Corver, and Den Dikken 1998).

(ii) die   schatten van (*een*) kinderen (Dutch)
  those darlings of a   children
  'those adorable children'

Since *een*, the Dutch counterpart of English *a*, cannot form a constituent with either of the two noun phrases inside the complex DP, it cannot be base-generated as such. Instead, Bennis, Corver, and Den Dikken argue, *een* originates in the functional head position of the DP-internal small clause, to the right of *kinderen* 'children', which is the subject of that small clause (*schatten* 'darlings' being the predicate).

(iii) [DP D . . . [RP kinderen [RELATOR=*een* [schatten]]]]

The surface word order of (ii) is derived via Predicate Inversion *cum* raising of R to a higher functional head "F," realized as the LINKER *van* 'of'. The details of Predicate Inversion will be discussed in chapter 4. I will return to Dutch (ii) in chapter 5.

7. See also Kondrashova 1996. The question arises at this point why the lexicon of English should feature two different "dummies" performing the task of tense support, *be* and *do*. Why doesn't English use just one of them for all cases in which tense support is needed? What needs to be assumed is that the "dummy" *do* is not entirely devoid of features—*do* is used as a tense supporter only in combination with *verbs*, while *be* is used in the complement case. A suggestion that comes to mind is that the "dummy" *do* possesses an event role (E-role), and that this prevents *do* from being used with predicates that have no E-role. Two questions spring up in connection with that hypothesis, though: (i) *do* is used in imperatives with *be* (though these may involve eventive *be*, possessing an E-role); (ii) some take all stage-level predicates (whether they be verbal or nonverbal) to possess an E-role (see, e.g., Kratzer 1988, 1995), which would lead one to expect *do* to be used with stage-level APs, *quod non* (cf. *Brian is/*does sick*).

8. Kondrashova (1996, 57–58) presents interesting "*be*-doubling" data from Church Slavonic and Northwestern dialect varieties of Russian (see (i)), which suggest that, in these varieties, the functions of providing tense support and serving as a RELATOR of the subject-predicate relationship are strictly separated, such that no single *be*-element could perform both functions at the same time. As a result, two forms of *be* are needed to do what needs to be done in (i) (with *byla/byli* providing tense support and *esti/est'* being the RELATOR).

(i) a. zhara   taka byla   esti (Northwestern Russian dialects)
     heat-3SG.F such was-SG.F is
     'There was such a heat.'
  b. jarmanki byli   est' chastye
     fair-PL   were-PL is   frequent
     'There were frequent fairs.'

For English and most other languages, however, a single token of *be* does manage to take care of both connecting the predicate and its subject and providing tense support. Hence, in such languages, economy will prevent the inclusion of more than one RELATOR or copula in the structure.

9. This is only straightforwardly the case for instances of (14) in which both DP-dependents of the larger DP do indeed have exactly identical sets of features. We can safely abstract away from phonological and purely semantic features, since these should play no role in syntactic computation. But as far as ϕ-features are concerned, it seems that Pereltsvaig will need to make a distinction between *He is the culprit* on the one hand, and *I am/you are the culprit* or even *He is the problem* on the other: in the latter two cases, α and β are not featurally identical (assuming that [+animate] or [+human] is a morphological feature, not a purely semantic one). Thanks to Andrea Moro for pointing this out to me.

10. In this context it is also worth mentioning the obligatory use of the dative case on predicates in Hungarian (ib, c) (see É. Kiss 2002, 68, 217n.). Unlike in Russian, no minimal pairs of the type in (15) can be constructed for Hungarian: in (ia) the use of the dative case on the predicate is impossible regardless. The distribution of the dative case on the adjectival/nominal predicate in Hungarian partially tracks that of English spell-outs of the RELATOR such as *as*, *for*, and *like* (see (12)): cf. *Brian is (*as) pushy* versus *Imogen regards Brian *(as) pushy*. This suggests that the dative case in (ib, c) lexicalizes the RELATOR. The details of the distribution of the RELATOR-dative in Hungarian remain somewhat elusive, though.

(i) a. János rámenős-(*nek) volt (Hungarian)
     János pushy-DAT   was
     'János was pushy.'
  b. Mari Jánost   rámenős-*(nek) tartja
     Mari János-ACC pushy-DAT   consider-3SG
     'Mari considers János pushy.'
  c. Mari engedte   János   rámenős-*(nek) lenni
     Mari let-PST-3SG János-ACC pushy-DAT   be-INF
     'Mari let János be pushy.'

11. In this study I will not occupy myself any further with the question of how the interpretive peculiarity of sentences of this type is to be derived. I refer the interested reader to the references listed in Pereltsvaig 2001, 196—in particular, Wierzbicka 1980, Bailyn and Rubin 1991, Smith 1999, and Geist 1999. It is interesting, in light of the discussion of Celtic to follow immediately below, that Doherty (1996) and Adger and Ramchand (2003) make highly similar observations about the interpretation of copular sentences featuring the "defective copula" *is/bu*—sentences that seem to correspond by and large to Russian NOM-NOM copular constructions. I will show in the next subsection that Celtic specificational copular sentences with *is/bu* should not be analyzed in terms of a structure of the type in (14). If this is right, then it further confirms the conclusion that Pereltsvaig's attempt to derive the special interpretive properties of Russian NOM-NOM copular constructions from the structure in (14) is a failed one.

12. The Scottish Gaelic examples in this section are taken from Adger and Ramchand 2003, the Irish examples from Doherty 1996.

13. Adger and Ramchand present interesting evidence for their account from the domain of intonation, pointing out that while normally focal stress is final in Scot-

tish Gaelic, in (16b) it must fall on the noun phrase following *e*, which in this sentence is the rightmost element in an A-position.

14. My remarks in this section on the structure of English copular sentences such as *Brian is the culprit* pertain to cases that (like (13)) have the *canonical* word order, with the predicate following the copula. On *inverse* specificational copular sentences, see chapter 4 for detailed analysis.

15. Though Aristotle took the copula to be a meaningless provider of a tense specification, modern Western philosophy (see, e.g., Mill 1856, 86; Russell 1903, 64) has generally subscribed to the idea that *be* is a polysemous lexical item with a variety of different meanings (corresponding to the different types of copular sentence enumerated in standard typologies of copular sentences, such as Higgins 1979 and Declerck 1988; see section 3.2.3, below, for discussion). In the linguistic literature, Huddleston (1971), Akmajian (1979), Seuren (1985), Rapoport (1987), Higginbotham (1987), Safir (1985), and Zaring (1996), among many others, subscribe to this point of view, recognizing two different *be*'s. Montague (1973) gives *be*-sentences two treatments as well ($x = y$ and $f(x) = y$). Halliday (1967, 66) and Bolinger (1972b, 98) go even further and distinguish between three different types of *be*—for Bolinger, an equational *be*, a locational *be*, and a nonequational *be*. All these approaches assign some sort of meaning to *be*. For a recent principles-and-parameters study of copular constructions (with special reference to Hebrew) and the meaning of the verb *be*, see Rothstein 2000. At the other side of the spectrum, many scholars (not just within the generative tradition but outside it as well; see Dik 1983 for a Functional Grammar approach) hold the view that the copula is a meaningless connective, hence does not come in a variety of flavors. Jespersen (1961) explicitly refutes the idea that the copula can be used as an expression of identity. Stowell (1981) likewise denies the copula a meaning of its own, as do, among others, Rapoport (1987), Heggie (1988), Scholten (1988), and Moro (1997). Partee (2000) points out that "in the Slavic literature, it has long been noted that insofar as differences in the semantics of different copular sentences can be predicted from differences in the semantics of the 'arguments' of the copula, it should not be necessary to posit ambiguities in the copula itself"; she refers to Chvany 1975 and Padučeva and Uspenskij 1979 in this context. While Kondrashova (1996, 43) explicitly takes issue with an approach that derives the semantic (or, more specifically, the thematic) differences between the arguments, she does subscribe to a "one-*be*" approach, calling it an expletive. I, too, consider there to be only one *be*, a semantically meaningless syntactic connective.

16. See also Adger and Ramchand 2003 for important differences with transitive sentences in Scottish Gaelic.

17. See chapter 4 for detailed discussion of the syntax of inverse copular sentences. We will see there that there is indeed a direct syntactic match between equative and inverse copular sentences: both involve a reduced free relative predicate.

18. They do offer an interesting footnote (note 9 on p. 378) in which they point out that coordination constructions exhibit some of the same restrictions as equative copular sentences in the domain of A′-extraction—particularly intriguing here

is their observation that, like coordinate structures, equatives allow "across-the-board" extraction: *Which city is your opinion of t my opinion of t?*

19. Heycock and Kroch explicitly state that they reject an analysis in terms of an equative copula, noting correctly that "equative semantics is independent of the presence of the copula" (1999, 381). As Heycock (1994) notes, in examples such as those in (i), no copula is necessary at all.

(i) a. If Bill has an alibi for 6 p.m., that makes John the murderer.
     b. If Bill has an alibi for 6 p.m., that makes the murderer John.

20. The full free relative is presented here only for the sake of comparison. There is no claim that the reduced free relative in (28) is the spitting image of the full free relative *what Cicero is*—clearly, **What Cicero is is Tully* is not a well-formed sentence. Heycock and Kroch's (1999, 376) observation that tautologies like *Honest is honest* cannot be paraphrased as **What honest is is what honest is* ("such sentences are always ungrammatical and uninterpretable") similarly shows that we should not want to draw too close a connection between *overt* free relatives in pseudoclefts and the *reduced* free relative in (28). Though the analysis in (29) runs parallel, in its essentials, to Heggie's (1988) account of *wh*-initial specificational pseudoclefts, I am not claiming that equative copular sentences are *identical* to pseudoclefts (though they do share some essential properties). It may be possible to localize the difference between pseudoclefts and equatives in the emptiness of (the head and) the operator of the free relative in the latter, in conjunction with the assumption that the null operator is of a different semantic type than *what* (a type that remains to be identified).

21. The extraction facts will be addressed more fully in chapter 4. Notice that the analysis straightforwardly accommodates (23) since both overt noun phrases in the structure of equative constructions are arguments (specifically, subjects), hence both can be modified by nonrestrictive relative clauses. The fact that in Italian the uninflected pro-predicate clitic *lo* can be used to pronominalize one of the two constituents of equative copular sentences is accommodated by having *lo* replace the *entire* reduced free relative that originates as the predicate of the small clause. (Thanks to Andrea Moro, personal communication, for raising this point; see Moro 1997, 71ff., for discussion of the pro-predicate clitic *lo* in Italian copular sentences.)

22. For the sake of completeness (and avoidance of possible confusion), it should be noted that, while semantically entirely neutral in equatives, inversion in pseudoclefts is not entirely innocuous as far as their interpretation is concerned. It is certainly true that (ia) and (ib) can have an identical interpretation—the so-called *specificational* reading that I am after in the main text (whence the label "specificational pseudocleft"): 'Brian doesn't eat the following: food for the dog.' (On the term "specificational," see also note 29.) But both sentences in (i) in addition support nonspecificational (or predicational) readings in which what follows the copula is a predicate nominal. On a predicational reading, (ia) is paraphrasable as 'the stuff that is left over on Brian's plate is fed to the dog, serves as dog food,' with *food for the dog* as a predicate nominal; and (ib) has a predicational

reading featuring *what Brian doesn't eat* as a predicate nominal such that to the referent of *food for the dog* is ascribed the property of being that which Brian does not eat.

(i)   a. What Brian doesn't eat is food for the dog.
      b. Food for the dog is what Brian doesn't eat.

These readings are entirely irrelevant in the context of the text discussion. In the main text, I chose examples in which the kinds of ambiguity just discussed are unlikely (or at least, less likely) to arise. A completely disambiguated case is (ii) versus (iii) (from Higgins 1979), where the sentences in (ii) are exclusively specificational (because of the use of *himself*) and concomitantly allow for inversion, whereas the example in (iiia), featuring *him*, is unambiguously predicational and as a result is not invertible.

(ii)   a. What John is is important to himself. (Specificational only)
       b. Important to himself is what John is.

(iii) a.   What John is is important to him. (Predicational only)
       b. *Important to him is what John is.

23. There is talk of an equative copular construction in Irish in Carnie 1995—but by this term, Carnie refers to constructions of the type in (17b), which are not equative but specificational copular sentences, a distinct type (Higgins 1979; Declerck 1988).

24. In Slavic and Hebrew, true equatives like *the Morning Star is the Evening Star* use what seems to be the counterpart of the Scottish Gaelic pronominal augment—a (demonstrative) pronoun. Consider the following example from Russian (taken from Kondrashova 1996, 38, note 8, who points out that in equatives "it is always possible (and is often preferable, in some cases even obligatory) to use a structure with a pronominal element"; the use of *be* is disallowed in these constructions, as in many others).

(i) utrennjaja zvezda eto vechernjaja zvezda (Russian)
     morning star   this evening star

Slavic and Hebrew also use the pronoun as a connective in specificational copular sentences. There an assimilation to Celtic along the lines of Adger and Ramchand's approach is feasible, with the (demonstrative) pronoun serving as a small-clause predicate. But for equatives such an approach is unavailable (otherwise Scottish Gaelic (32a) ought to be grammatical). I tentatively follow Adger and Ramchand's (2003) suggestion for Hebrew that grammaticalization may lead to a reanalysis of the pronominal predicate as a spell-out of the functional head of the small clause (my RELATOR, their "Pred"). See also chapter 5 on articles (definite and indefinite) as spell-outs of the RELATOR-head.

25. Welsh (33) is arguably the closest counterpart of an Irish/Scottish Gaelic specificational copular sentence with a pronominal augment: (i) it features a defective copular element (cf. the *yw* of Welsh (33) with the *is*/*'s* of my Irish and Scottish Gaelic examples), and (ii) the focus in (33) is on the subject rather than the clause-final constituent, as Rouveret points out.

26. The English translation does not bring out clearly that (34) is indeed a *speci-ficational*, not a predicational pseudocleft. That is, it is semantically equivalent to 'John is a nuisance.'

27. Though Zaring (1996) talks of "identity-*be*," the constructions she discusses (such as (34)) are consistently specificational.

28. This section will not address copular sentences from a *language*-typological point of view, nor will the remainder of this study; comparative investigations will be limited to specific contexts in which they serve a direct purpose. For a crosslinguistic study of copular sentences (examining over 150 languages), see Pustet 2003. The present section addresses the inventory of copular sentence types.

29. Declerck (1988) presents an even more elaborate system. I will not talk about identificational copular sentences in the discussion to follow; I will assume without discussion that their syntax can be wholly assimilated to that of specificational copular sentences. Specificational copular sentences are sentences whose predicate is what Higgins (1979) calls "superscriptional," providing the heading of a (possibly quite short) list, and whose underlying subject identifies one or more members of that list, thereby specifying a value for the variable predicate. They typically have the surface form [Predicate-*be*-Subject] (cf. *My best friends are Tom, Dick, and Harry*), but they can also surface in the other order (which, for Higgins, is the "inverted" order; terminology is confusing here since, on my assumptions, specificational copular sentences of the form [Subject-*be*-Predicate] are of course *un*inverted constructions): thus, Higgins (1979, 233–234) himself notes the word-order alternation in (i), where both members of the pair are specificational copular sentences; and Declerck (1988) points out, outside the realm of pseudoclefts, that (iia) and (iib) are both felicitous as specificational copular sentences serving as answers to a question such as *Who is the culprit?*

(i) a. This is what I think we should do.
    b. What I think we should do is this.

(ii) a. Brian is the culprit.
     b. The culprit is Brian.

Notice that in both orders, the noun phrase that specifies the value (*this*/*Brian*) attracts focal stress—and this, in fact, is a quintessential property of specificational copular sentences: the fact that the subject, regardless of whether it follows or precedes its predicate in the surface string, is interpreted and prosodically treated as the focus of the sentence (see also the discussion in section 4.1.1). Such a construal is definitely easier, in general, for postcopular noun phrases: focus gravitates to the right; hence specificational copular sentences typically feature a [Predicate-*be*-Subject] order. But as (i) and (ii) show, English specificational copular sentences are not strictly required to undergo Predicate Inversion in the syntax.

When they do have the predicate in precopular position, specificational copular sentences show a strong tendency for "copula doubling" in present-day spoken English: *The reason is is that S*, or *What I said was was/is that S*. Conceivably, the syntax of these "copula-doubling" constructions involves a Topic-Comment structure with Predicate Inversion (of a null pro-predicate linked to the noun phrase in topic position) inside the Comment, with the two copulas lexicalizing the Topic-head (see Den Dikken, Meinunger, and Wilder's 2000 analysis of "Type A" specificational pseudoclefts, discussed at more length in the appendix to chapter 4, below) and a Comment-internal LINKER (see chapter 4). But "copula doubling" cannot be taken to be a diagnostic for (inverted) specificational copular sentences since, as Patrick McConvell (who was one of the first to study "double *be*" constructions; see McConvell 1988) pointed out in a posting on *LinguistList* (see posting 15.427 for his summary), it has started to rear its head in indubitably predicational copular sentences as well: *The headline is is kinda cute*, or *Crime policy is is a very political and emotional issue.*

30. Though this sentence corresponds to *the Morning Star is the Evening Star*, for someone who utters (39d)—someone who holds the (mistaken) belief that the Morning Star and the Evening Star are different entities—it is not entirely clear that it represents an equative. The same is true for the variant of (38d) that has *misidentified* instead of *identified*. But the person's interlocutor may continue the conversation as in (ia, b), where the complement of *mistake/misidentify* arguably is equative, just as in copular (ic).

(i) a. Look, you idiot, nobody could mistake the Morning Star for the Evening Star because they are the same thing!

   b. Look, you idiot, nobody could misidentify the Morning Star as the Evening Star because they are the same thing!

   c. Look, you idiot, nobody can rightly claim that the Morning Star is *not* the Evening Star: they are the same thing!

31. For readers who are not familiar with Dutch, it may be useful to know that there is a fair amount of discussion of Blom and Daalder's (1977) analysis of copular sentences throughout Den Dikken 2005.

32. Declerck (1988, 93) claims that the Blom and Daalder–type approach to specificational sentences (which treats them as predicational underlyingly) is incompatible with Givón's (1973, 119) universal that "a predicate may never be less general than its subject"—but this is mistaken: for advocates of the inversion approach to specificational copular sentences, the precopular NP (the hyperonym) is indeed the predicate underlyingly, with the postcopular NP (the hyponym) being its subject. Declerck dismisses the Blom and Daalder approach, stressing that "specificational sentences do not express a hyponymy relation" (1988, 93). In defense of his position, Declerck draws on Higgins 1979 and Halliday 1967, 1968: Higgins points out that the essence of the specificational relationship is that the contents of the concept expressed by the superscriptional NP (see note 29) are specified, which "naturally means that the NP denoting the concept and the NP specifying its contents cannot differ in generality or specificity" (Declerck 1988, 92–93); and Halliday argues that the two NPs of specificational sentences have "the same degree of specificity, and that this is precisely the reason why such sentences are reversible" (Declerck 1988, 93, note 98). This point is significant—but it does not, in and of itself, jeopardize an analysis of specificational copular sentences that assigns them a predicational small-clause structure underlyingly. Such

an approach leaves room, as we saw in the discussion in section 3.2.2.2, for the possibility that neither of the two noun phrases is itself a predicate, predicatehood being borne instead by a reduced free relative of which one of the two noun phrases is a subconstituent.

Chapter 4

1. Copular Inversion constructions of the type in (1b) have attracted a good deal of attention in the literature, being discussed in great detail in the work of Andrea Moro (especially Moro 1988, 1990, 1991, 1993, 1997, 2000) and also in Heggie 1988, Heycock 1994, and Heycock and Kroch 1999. Locative Inversion constructions such as (2b) figure prominently in Joan Bresnan's work (see, e.g., Bresnan 1977, 1990, 1994), and have also been discussed in Rochemont and Culicover 1990, Culicover and Levine 2001, and Hoekstra and Mulder 1990. Hoekstra and Mulder, following Emonds 1976, bring up AP Inversion constructions of the type in (ib) (called "marginal" by Bresnan (1994, 76, note 4), who gives them "??") as well, though they do not analyze these in any detail. Heycock (1994, 1998b) is careful to set them aside from Copular Inversion constructions like (1b). I will return to these cases in the appendix.

(i) a.   Losing your keys would have been considered most embarrassing.
   b.   ?Most embarrassing would have been considered losing your keys.

2. Culicover and Levine (2001) contrast (ia) with (ib) and proceed to regard only the former type of sentence, with a fronted locative and a nonheavy and not necessarily clause-final postverbal subject, as a genuine case of Locative Inversion. They never discuss the intonational and information-structural properties of constructions of the type in (ia). It seems to me that (ia) is not at all a quintessential Locative Inversion construction—unless *slowly* is read with comma intonation (which is not what Culicover and Levine had in mind), it seems impossible to assign focus intonation to the postverbal subject (*Robin*) in (ia), whereas the clause-final subject in (ib) is of course a natural recipient of focus intonation. While it is presumably correct to say that (ia) should be treated differently from (ib), I would certainly classify the latter as a possible case of Locative Inversion, with the small-clause subject staying in situ rather than raising across the VP-adjoined manner adverb. For Bresnan (1994, 105) (who, unlike me and unlike Mikkelsen (2002a) for Danish Locative Inversion, assumes a rightward VP-adjunction for the postverbal subject in English Locative Inversion), the postverbal subject of a Locative Inversion construction will also necessarily follow VP-adjoined adverbials.

(i) a. Into the room walked Robin slowly.
   b. Into the room walked slowly a very large caterpillar.

The above is not to suggest that the small-clause subject *cannot* undergo Heavy NP Shift; it merely seeks to cast doubt on the idea that (ib) is *necessarily* derived thereby. See Whitman 2004 for interesting discussion of Heavy NP Shift turning otherwise ungrammatical instances of English "transitive expletive constructions" into well-formed sentences (*There have eaten lunch in this hash house some of the strangest men ever to visit our godforsaken outpost*); the same is true for Locative

Inversion (*In this hash house have eaten lunch some of the strangest men ever to visit our godforsaken outpost*), not surprisingly if *there*-sentences and Locative Inversion constructions both involve Predicate Inversion in syntax, à la Moro 1997 and Hoekstra and Mulder 1990. On the analysis of Heavy NP Shift and its compatibility with Predicate Inversion, see section 4.4.4.1.

3. It is hard to think of felicitous questions corresponding to examples of the type in (7b–d), which is why I resorted to topicalization in (9b–d). These sentences are rather strained; some people actually find them unacceptable, but (9b–d) and similar sentences are not generally rejected by my informants. It does seem much easier to extract the complement of *for*=RELATOR in predicate-complement structures: thus, *I take you for a fool* supports A′-extraction of *for*'s complement without difficulty (cf. *What do you take me for?*); similarly for *as*=RELATOR in *What do you regard him as?* The fact that in predicate-specifier constructions of the type in (7b–d) the noun phrase in the complement of the RELATOR is itself a predicate, while in (7a) it is not, may be responsible for the relatively poor status of the examples in (9b–d), featuring extraction of a predicate nominal across a predicate-specifier that is itself predicated of the extractee.

4. Culicover and Levine (2001, 287–288), while accepting Bresnan's conclusion that the fronted locative is a subject, reject Bresnan's argument from raising, pointing out that in sentences in which there is a manner adverb following the postverbal subject, such as (ia), raising delivers an ungrammatical result. They contrast (ia) with grammatical (ib), in which the manner adverb precedes the heavy subject of the fronted locative and raising is fine. Culicover and Levine take (ia) to instantiate Locative Inversion proper. But recall from the discussion in note 2 that (ia) does not have the intonational profile of a typical Locative Inversion construction, and that (ib) is more likely to be a genuine instance of Locative Inversion. I therefore set aside Culicover and Levine's objection, based on the ungrammaticality of raising in (ia), to Bresnan's raising argument for the A-movement analysis of Locative Inversion.

(i) a. Into the room (*appeared to have) walked Robin slowly.
     b. Into the room (appeared to have) walked slowly a very large caterpillar.

5. Bresnan (1977, 180) also presents *that*-trace effects in Locative Inversion constructions as evidence for A-movement (cf. (i)). Culicover and Levine (2001, 301) object to this argument, however, saying that extraction of the fronted locative succeeds only if the postverbal noun phrase is sufficiently heavy: *Into the room I claim/believe walked {*Robin/√ROBIN}*. They claim the *that*-trace effect in (i) is a reflex of Heavy NP Shift performed on the subject. But note that when the locative is not extracted into the matrix, *that* is preferably realized overtly (*She thinks ??(that) on the wall hung a picture of a Politician, She believes ??(that) into the room walked ROBIN*): apparently, the *that*-trace effect otherwise triggered by HNPS is lifted by preposing the locative (à la Culicover 1993, perhaps). But then, why couldn't the *that*-trace effect be lifted in the same way in examples like (i), via locative preposing internal to the embedded CP? It seems, then, that Culicover and Levine's (2001) HNPS alternative is incomplete (as they themselves note on pp. 307–308). But the fact remains that Bresnan's original *that*-trace

argument for A-movement should presumably be handled with some care. Note also that it does not carry over to Copular Inversion constructions in any event; see (ii).

(i)   *On which wall* do you think (*that) *t* hung a picture of Imogen?

(ii) **How good a candidate* do you think (that) *t* is Brian?

6. Szendrői (2003, 71) claims, contra Horvath, that Hungarian postverbal "foci" are not foci; but on page 73 of her paper, she does nonetheless countenance the existence of postverbal foci, interpreted nonexhaustively, in line with the text discussion.

7. Example (20b) was inspired by Guéron (1992, 1994), (21b) by Declerck (1988). The appendix to this chapter returns to these examples. Birner (1994, 252) notes that Predicate Inversion cases with an indefinite preposed constituent make up only 10 percent of all relevant Predicate Inversion examples in her 1,458-token corpus.

8. I will continue to ignore Higgins's "identificational" copular sentences (such as *Brian is that man over there*), which in note 29 of chapter 3 I tentatively assimilated to specificational copular sentences.

9. The root of these restrictions will be discussed in detail in section 4.4; for now, they serve the purpose of identifying equative copular sentences as systematically inverted copular sentences.

10. One would expect (27) to be universal, not subject to parametric variation. I will assume so.

11. The example in (29c) is mildly deviant due to a violation of the Specificity Condition, barring extraction from a specific noun phrase. But it is still much better than the c-examples in (25), (26), and (30).

12. I use *embedded* sentences to illustrate Dutch inverse copular constructions to circumvent the distracting Verb Second effect.

13. Of note in this connection is also Declerck's (1988, 79) example in (i), which can only be assigned a specificational reading (due to the presence of the negative polarity item *any* in the postcopular constituent)—concomitantly, only singular verb agreement is possible.

(i) What the book does not offer is/*are any solutions to the problems that are noted.

As Declerck (1988, 79–80) (see also Berg 1998 and Den Dikken 2005, section 4.2) points out, however, the link between finite verb agreement and specificational interpretation is less than strict. Though there certainly are strong tendencies of the type just illustrated, it is often possible for either noun phrase to control finite verb agreement, as shown by Declerck's examples below.

(ii) a. The aim of our policy {is/*are} improved relations with the Soviet Union.
     b. Improved relations with the Soviet Union {is/?are} the aim of our policy.

(iii) a. More books {is/?are} what I need.
      b. What I need {is/??are} more books.

(iv) a. Theft and robbery {is/are} what I despise most.

   b. What we can't have here {is/?are} theft and robbery.

14. The parallel between specificational pseudoclefts and sentences of the type in (1b) in the domain of agreement effects may go further. Thus, while (33b) is ungrammatical with plural agreement, the inverse specificational copular sentence in (ib) does feature plural *are*, obligatorily so; and concomitantly, the somewhat clumsy pseudocleft paraphrase of (ib) shows plural agreement as well.

(i) a. The following examples are/*is a case in point.

   b. A case in point are/*is the following examples.

(ii) What is a case in point are/*is the following examples.

   Of course, by assimilating (33)/(34) and (35)/(36) we have not thereby *explained* the agreement behavior of specificational copular sentences and pseudoclefts in English and Dutch. This is a topic that I have to leave aside here.

15. Guéron (1992) makes a distinction between what she calls the *récit* and the *commentaire*; inverse specificational copular sentences, for her, belong to the *commentaire*.

16. Unless the postverbal subject is heavy (and presumably not in its base position), as Culicover and Levine (2001, 300) point out. Cases like (i) should be carefully kept distinct from the main-text examples of "pure" Locative Inversion.

(i) We heard from this pulpit preach [HNP a close associate of Cotton Mather].

17. I will return to the A′-extraction facts of Predicate Inversion constructions at more length in section 4.4. See also Den Dikken and Næss 1993 for discussion of Norwegian Locative Inversion constructions in this connection.

18. The variants of (49a) given in (i), involving what Culicover and Levine call "heavy inversion" (in which the postverbal subject forms its own intonational phrase and is typically a heavy noun phrase), are grammatical. See note 5, above, for relevant discussion.

(i) a. Into the room I claim/believe *ec* walked/will walk … BRIAN!

   b. Into the room I claim/believe *ec* walked/will walk a ravenous horde of angry Tolstoy scholars.

19. I deliberately chose a relative clause construction (see (49b)) to illustrate this point rather than a *wh*-question: the *wh*-constituent in a *wh*-question is always a focus, hence *wh*-question formation involving the fronted locative as the *wh*-phrase is out of the question quite independently of any syntactic restrictions for the simple reason that the fronted locative in a Locative Inversion construction is a *topic* and therefore inherently ineligible for focalization. Surprisingly from this perspective, Culicover and Levine (2001, 304) give as perfectly grammatical instances of *wh*-questions involving full PPs rather than the pro-PP *where* (see *To which place went Robin?*, which they contrast with **Where went Robin?*). But these constructions do not have the information-structural profile of Locative Inversion constructions and arguably should not be analyzed as such.

20. Information-structural properties of sentence constituents are determined precisely once in a complex sentence—that is, a topic is the topic of a particular

clause and of that clause only; it is impossible for a constituent to be the topic of multiple clauses at the same time. The same, mutatis mutandis, is true for foci (see also section 4.4.3). Successive-cyclic topic or focus movement (i.e., movement from a SpecTopP or SpecFocP position to a higher position of the same type) is not allowed, something that follows straightforwardly if SpecTopP and SpecFocP positions are never potential extraction sites.

21. In Copular Inversion constructions, the pro-predicate is content-licensed by the reduced relative clause attached to it; hence in Copular Inversion constructions there is no need for a topic (in fact, there cannot be one: it would be redundant). Formal licensing is taken care of by T in Copular Inversion and Locative Inversion constructions alike, hence fronting the pro-predicate to SpecTP is obligatory in both cases, by (37).

22. Cinque's (1990) claim that the ill-formedness of (48b) (repeated below as (ib)) is due to the general unavailability of a null pro-PP should be reevaluated in light of this. It seems unlikely that (48b)/(ib) can be blamed on the putative nonexistence of prepositional pro-forms: *(in) there* can in fact serve as a resumptive for long-distance locative A′-dependencies, as in (ia). The fact that a *null* locative *cannot* be used in this kind of context is arguably due to the fact that a locative pro-predicate is unlicensable in the position that it occupies in (48b)/(ib). Conversely, in Locative Inversion constructions, the pro-PP *must* be null, precisely because of the fact that the pro-predicate here occupies a position in which it is fully licensed to be null.

(i) a.   In that room, I wonder whether anyone would be able to work (in) there
          for more than a day.
   b.   ?*In that room, I wonder whether anyone would be able to work for more
          than a day.

23. A quick search on the Internet using a generic search engine (Google) delivered about 150 examples of "been paid little/much attention to"—though I should note that many of the specimens were from websites that presumably were not composed by native speakers of English (with remarkably many hits from Japan and China, and also—not particularly surprisingly given the well-formedness of "beheaded" Locative Inversion constructions in these languages—from Scandinavia). Two attested examples from unequivocally native-English-speaking sources are worth mentioning here. The sentence in (i) was uttered by Steve Forbes, a former Republican presidential candidate in the United States, while talking to Wolf Blitzer (CNN); (ii) is attributed to Lauren J. Sugarman, in a transcript of the Advisory Committee on Construction Safety and Health of the Occupational Safety and Health Administration of the U.S. Department of Labor.

(i) And two other things, Wolf, that haven't been paid much attention to.
    www.cnn.com/TRANSCRIPTS/0108/05/le.00.html

(ii) It really set the tone for a lot of the safety and health regulations that
     previously had been paid little attention to and was an impetus for a lot of
     the regulations we take for granted now.
     www.osha.gov/doc/accsh/transcripts/accsh_031497.html

24. It does not seem possible to blame the fact that the postverbal subject in (51c) is not extractable on the idiomatic character of the collocation *pay attention to X*—after all, *wh*-extraction succeeds perfectly well in (51a). The idiom *pay attention to X* is not nearly as "frozen" as, for instance, *kick the bucket*—as witness the fact that passivization is grammatical here as well, as in (50a).

25. Den Dikken and Næss (1993) call (52c) the "transitive pseudopassive," because of the fact that it seems to resemble a pseudopassive like *This bed was slept in by Napoleon*. But their analysis of this construction is in terms Locative Inversion. In what follows, I will refer to this construction as the "beheaded Locative Inversion" construction.

26. The step from (56b) to (56c) is a rough first stab. The details of this derivation will be addressed in section 4.3.2. Note also that I am treating Norwegian here as though it was English as far as the structure of subject-initial root clauses is concerned, with the subject in SpecTP and the finite auxiliary raised to T. This simplification is innocuous in the context of the discussion here.

27. Luhya (57c) shows that the noun phrase in the complement of the P-trace entertains an agreement relationship with the finite verb. English (i) shows that in its "beheaded" Locative Inversion constructions, the same thing happens. For Norwegian this cannot be demonstrated, for the simple reason that Norwegian lacks subject agreement altogether. But the fact that, when the NP in the complement of P is pronominalized, it comes out as nominative (see (ii)) is a reliable indication that in Norwegian "beheaded" Locative Inversion constructions as well, the NP inside the beheaded PP in SpecTP manages to establish a feature-checking relationship with T.

(i) These issues have/*has been paid little attention to in the literature.

(ii) hun   ble klistret en tøybit   på (Norwegian)
     she.NOM be pasted a   patch of fabric onto

Den Dikken and Næss (1993) argue that in the structure in (56c) the complement of the P-trace is in the checking domain of T. I will assume so without further argument, and adopt Den Dikken and Næss's (1993) analysis of "beheaded" Locative Inversion wholesale.

28. While Baker's (1988) approach to applicatives is compromised by the virtually systematic lack of morphophonological similarity between prepositions and applicative morphemes in Bantu (see Den Dikken 1995c, chap. 5, for discussion), a P-incorporation approach to the Luhya locative suffix in (57b, c) is entirely natural: *ho* is transparently related to *ha*, the locative marker.

29. Kayne's (1994, 96) constraint on the spell-out of copies (reproduced in (i), below) straightforwardly allows for this optionality: since at Spell-Out neither copy of P c-commands the other, both may be lexicalized without incurring a violation of the LCA, but of course it is by no means obligatory to lexicalize both copies. When the P-copy inside PP is spelled out, its presence blocks a feature-checking relation between T and P's complement; instead, T establishes an agreement relationship with the PP, resulting in locative agreement (57b).

(i) A given chain link c_k can license PF deletion of another link c_l of the same chain only if c_l does not c-command c_k.

30. Example (64b) becomes grammatical once the particle is dropped. For discussion, see Den Dikken 1995a, 1995c, chap. 4.

31. Word orders of the type in (65c) are grammatical in varieties of Germanic in which there is morphological dative case (such as German and Icelandic; see Den Dikken 1995c for discussion). In those languages, PP is never actually decapitated: although P itself is null, it is "alternatively realized" (in Emonds's 1985 terminology) by the dative morphology on P's complement.

32. The exact details of this structure will be worked out in section 4.3.2, once we have a better picture of the locality restrictions on Predicate Inversion. For now, (67) will suffice.

33. In the case of Norwegian "beheaded" Locative Inversion (52c), the preposition raises no further than the RELATOR-head in overt syntax. It would seem, therefore, that (52c) will never constitute a locality of licensing problem for the P-trace. I will assume (without being able to provide concrete evidence for this) that the preposition does ultimately make its way up to V in the covert component: the RELATOR-head is not the end station of P-movement, even in Norwegian. With this assumption made, (52c) reduces to the cases of "beheaded" Locative Inversion discussed in the main text under the rubric of (66) and (67).

34. Apparent garden-variety Locative Inversion in Luhya is arguably a case of "beheaded" Locative Inversion as well, as I pointed out in the discussion of (57b), above. For Chicheŵa Locative Inversion (see (58b)) I tentatively suggest that it, too, involves P-incorporation—except that there is no reflex of P on the verbal complex. That is, (58b) is like (57b) except for the absence of an overt locative suffix on V. If Chicheŵa Locative Inversion involved fronting of a full-fledged PP to SpecTP, it would be difficult to isolate a syntactic trigger for its application. Even Germanic-style Locative Inversion may involve incorporation of the head of the pro-predicate in (46b) into the verb, if the agreement facts in (84) are an indication that (83) is employed here.

35. Collins says (note 15) that he knows of no language in which Locative Inversion is accompanied by some affix. There are such languages, though—Luhya Locative Inversion constructions systematically feature a locative suffix on the verb; see (57b, c).

36. I assume here, in line with Chomsky (1995, chap. 4) but contra Chomsky's more recent work (where v is assumed to be omnipresent), that v is only present in the extended projection of transitive and unergative verbs—verbs that are associated with an external argument and that are (potential) accusative Case checkers. See section 2.5.2 on unaccusatives and T as a RELATOR.

37. Moro's (1997, 87) observation that in sentences such as (i), *himself* can be legitimately bound by *Brian* does not militate against RP's status as a CFC—it straightforwardly does not if the local domain for binding is not defined as the least CFC within which the relevant binding-theoretic principle can be satisfied

(contra Chomsky 1985 but in line with, for instance, Reinhart and Reuland 1993, to which I appealed in section 2.3). Anaphors in *picture*-noun contexts do not reflexivize the predicate, and behave in many ways more liberally than anaphors that are a predicate's direct dependents.

(i) Brian$_i$ considers [$_{RP}$ this [$_{R'}$ RELATOR [the best picture of himself$_i$]]]

I should add that, even if small clauses should turn out not to be CFCs, their status as phases is not in and of itself jeopardized thereby. The conceptual grounds on which to identify phases remain rather unclear in current theory; Boeckx and Grohmann (2004) are right to conclude that the arguments for phases must be empirical. What I hope the following discussion will show is that there is a solid empirical basis for believing that small clauses are indeed phases.

38. In our specific example, α is the base position of the predicate, β the small-clause subject, and τ the landing site of Predicate Inversion.

39. Definition (76b) is a restatement of Chomsky's (1995, 178) equivalent but substantially more cumbersome definition in (i).

(i) For any set S of categories, let us take Min(S) (minimal S) to be the smallest subset K of S such that for any $\gamma \in S$, some $\beta \in K$ reflexively dominates γ.

40. Here, $\delta/\delta_{MIN}(\alpha)$ and $\delta/\delta_{MIN}(\beta)$ are computed via (76a, b); it is immaterial whether $\delta/\delta_{MIN}(\alpha)$ are computed from α's base position or from its landing site. Empirically, this modification of the definition of the minimal domain of a head-movement chain does not have any repercussions beyond the fact (to which (77) was specifically tailored) that it includes the complement of the head of the chain in the domain of the chain; (77) continues to guarantee, as desired (see section 4.3.2.3), that the specifier of the head of the chain, the specifier of the foot of the chain, and the complement of the foot of the chain are included in the chain's minimal domain. Theoretically, (77) requires treating the host of the moved head as a separate entity for which a minimal domain is computed independently of the raised head. Since the host head must in any event be merged prior to head movement, and hence exists autonomously prior to head movement, this does not seem to be an adverse consequence of the redefinition of the minimal domain of a head-movement chain.

41. In line with the general hypothesis that all movement is feature-driven, one would assume that the head F has some feature to check against R, and that this feature has the EPP property of needing to be checked in overt syntax. The nature of this feature is an open question. I will not address the question, not thereby meaning to trivialize it.

42. This result is obtained both on Chomsky's (1995) own definition of the minimal domain of a head-movement chain (see (76b)) and on my revision thereof, given in (77). By (76b), the minimal domain of the chain CH=(RELATOR, t) is the set of nodes {SpecLP, SpecRP, Pred}. By (77), the minimal domain of the chain CH=(RELATOR, t) resulting from raising of the RELATOR up to the LINKER-head is the union of the minimal domain of the LINKER (i.e., {SpecLP, RP}) and the minimal domain of the RELATOR (i.e., {SpecRP, Pred}, or, if we compute

δ/δ_{MIN}(RELATOR) for the upper copy, {SpecLP, SpecRP, Pred}; see note 40)—in other words, δ_{MIN}(CH) is the set of nodes {SpecLP, RP, SpecRP, Pred}. On both approaches, δ_{MIN}(CH) includes the landing site of the raised predicate (SpecLP) and the position it skips on its way there (SpecRP, the base position of the subject).

43. For Locative Inversion, see Rochemont 1986, 114; Bresnan 1994, 86. The default accusative of the postcopular subject can either be assumed not to be a reflex of structural Case-feature checking or instead, à la Reuland (1983) (who discusses the accusative form of the subject in subject gerunds: *Him being a confirmed bachelor surprised us*), to be the morphological realization of an indirect Case-checking relationship—*i.c.*, a situation in which the postcopular subject has its Case feature checked "by proxy," by the raised predicate, with which it agrees. (The latter approach may be more readily compatible with the observation that the infinitival complementizer *for* is obligatory in Copular Inversion contexts: *(For) the culprit to be Brian would be surprising*; see the last part of note 49 of chapter 2 for brief discussion.)

Recall from the discussion in section 4.2.2.1 that the agreement facts in inverse copular sentences with a singular predicate and a plural full-DP subject are different in Dutch: the plural DP-subject controls agreement in (34b) and (36a). But when the subject of the inverted predicate nominal is a personal pronoun, we find that Copular Inversion is severely restricted: while the root clauses in (ia) are perfect (doubtless because their Verb Second syntax obscures their TP-internal derivation: (ia) could simply result from A′-fronting of the predicate nominal to SpecCP without Copular Inversion taking place), the embedded clauses in (ib) are ungrammatical—ostensibly because of a failure of feature checking against the subject of the inverted predicate. The breakdown of a feature-checking relationship between the subject and T in (ib) is as expected from the point of view of the text discussion; the general fact that the inverted predicate nominal fails to check features against T in Dutch Copular Inversion constructions and the success of a feature-checking relationship between T and the DP-subject in (34a) and (36b) remain open questions, however.

(i) a.   het grootste probleem {ben ik/ ben jij/ is hij} (Dutch)
          the biggest problem   am I   are you is he
   b. ?*dat het grootste probleem {ik ben/ jij   bent/ hij is}
          that the biggest problem   I am   you are   he is

The fact that Italian behaves differently from English, both with respect to agreement and as regards Case (cf. *Il colpevole sono io* 'the culprit am I'), is discussed in detail in Moro 1997.

44. T can indeed establish a feature-checking relationship with the NP contained inside the fronted beheaded PP for all of its features: the P-trace is not a Case checker (hence P's object still has its Case feature available for checking against T), and it does not prevent the establishment of a ϕ-feature agreement relationship between T and its object either—the P-trace does not count as an intervener for any relationship.

45. As Postal (2004, 240–243) discusses and illustrates in detail, however, the ban on *The book was given the boy* is by no means categorical outside British English. It may well be a simplification (or even an error) to represent the variation in the English-speaking world as dialectal, but for our very limited purposes here, such a representation will suffice.

46. Ideally, the question of whether PrtP counts as a phase or not would be relatable to other properties of verb-particle constructions in the languages in question. We know that, when it comes to the placement of particles, there is variation within the Mainland Scandinavian languages (see Svenonius 1996 for overview and discussion), Norwegian once again being the most liberal variant, allowing both "inner-particle" and "outer-particle" constructions. Swedish is often described as allowing only verb-adjacent particle placement (though the issue is actually much subtler than this: see Vinka 1999 and Stenshoel 2004 for discussion), while Danish systematically places the particle to the right of the noun phrase. Taking this into account, we might generalize that languages in which particles are in a fixed position vis-à-vis the noun phrase assign phasehood to their PrtPs while languages in which particles allow variable placement do not. But besides the fact that this kind of generalization can hardly be called insightful, it should be clear that it will not carry over to the variation we find in English: all varieties of English show a particle placement alternation similar to the one found in Norwegian. It remains unclear, therefore, what other consequences (88) might have, and what it ultimately follows from. This question will need to be addressed in future research.

47. As Moro (1997, 268, note 45) points out, (i) is grammatical, potentially contradicting the text claim that *wh*-extraction of the postcopular subject across its inverted predicate is impossible. But he observes that extraction of *who* fails in the nonrestrictive relative clause in (ii). This indicates that *who* cannot be interpreted as a *referential* constituent in these examples, which in turn suggests that (i) is not in fact an inverse copular sentence but instead a *canonical* one featuring *wh*-extraction of the predicate (*who*), with *the culprit* serving as the subject. The fact that *who* is used to question the predicate nominal (rather than *what*) then raises a question, however. Heycock (1994, passim) takes the correct generalization to be that D-linked *wh*'s cannot extract in inverse copular sentences (while non-D-linked *wh*'s such as plain *who* or *what*) can. I will systematically use D-linked *wh*-phrases here.

(i) Who do you consider the culprit to be?

(ii) *I met Brian, who I consider the culprit to be.

48. Recall from note 30 that (94b) becomes grammatical when the particle (*out*) is dropped. In general, double-object constructions lacking a particle are more liberal (see also the discussion at the end of the previous subsection). In Den Dikken 1995c, chap. 4, a possible explanation for the behavior of particleless double-object constructions is given. Here, as in that work, I will take the properties of double-object constructions *with* a particle to be the quintessential properties of double-object constructions proper.

49. The fact that A′-extraction across a phase boundary is possible is explained in Chomsky's (2000, 2001) recent work along the same lines as A′-extraction across a barrier used to be explained in the *Barriers* framework—with an appeal to *intermediate adjunction* to the phase (or barrier). Thus, in a sentence such as (ib), derived from (ia) (where the object of the preposition is deeply buried inside the *v*P phase and does not check any features against either *v* or anything outside *v*P), *wh*-extraction of *which shelf* is perfectly grammatical thanks to intermediate adjunction to *v*P, driven by some EPP property of the head of the phase.

(i) a. Brian put the book down on that shelf.

   b. Which shelf did Brian put the book down on?

Note that, as in *Barriers*, Chomsky (2000, 2001) assumes that intermediate adjunction is impossible in the case of A-dependencies. Sauerland (2003) has constructed a subtle argument to the effect that even A-movement proceeds via intermediate adjunction to *v*P. His argument, however, rests crucially on the assumption (not argued for there or elsewhere) that raising verbs like *seem* are associated with a *v*P of their own (see Chomsky's generalized light verb *v*). If raising verbs do not have a *v* in their extended projection (see section 2.5.2), Sauerland's argument for A-movement via intermediate *v*P-adjunction loses its force. Here I will assume, in line with the tradition, that A-movement is different from A′-movement in not being able to proceed via intermediate adjunction. This, then, leaves the text discussion of L-related dependencies in the preceding subsections unaffected.

50. Notice, however, that (100) does not seem to help us out in the case of (ib) if, as I will argue in section 4.5.1.2, the role of LINKER in instances of Copular Inversion of the type in (ia) is performed by Asp: AspP is certainly not a meaningless category; hence one would expect intermediate adjunction to be legitimate here, *quod non*. (Note that (ib) is trivially grammatical on a reading in which the bracketed noun phrase is the predicate nominal, but on the intended reading, according to which *the murderer* is the predicate nominal and we are dealing with an inverse predication, this sentence is impossible.) It may be, therefore, that the ban on adjunction to the projection of the LINKER has a different root than the one suggested in the main text. I will leave this open.

(i) a. If John is a friend of Brian, and John committed the murder, that makes the murderer a friend of Brian.

   b. *Who does that make the murderer [a friend of *t*]?

51. In this connection, recall also my critique of Pereltsvaig's (2001) coindexation approach to "equative" copular sentences in section 3.2.1.1.

52. This approach was inspired by Heggie (1988) and Guéron (1992, 1994); see also Bresnan and Kanerva 1989 on Locative Inversion.

53. Unlike Heggie (1988) and Guéron (1992, 1994), however, I am not denying foci the right to have something extracted from them—such is in fact perfectly possible in principle, as we saw in (98b) and (99b). That it is impossible in Copular Inversion and "true" Locative Inversion constructions has an independent cause: (100) in the former, subjacency (the topic-island effect) in the latter.

54. The formulation in (105b) should be thought of as a convenient shorthand. It is not meant to make syntax "prescient" of the pragmatic interpretation of its output, or to have pragmatics be input to syntax; recall the discussion in section 4.2.1.1. The syntactic structure does not "know" yet what the pragmatic interpretation of its constituents will end up being. Rather, as the text discussion below (102) is careful to express, a syntactic chain including multiple positions to which a pragmatic function is assigned is rejected in the pragmatic component.

55. Culicover and Levine (2001) argue that apparent Locative Inversion constructions featuring Heavy NP Shift have a different derivation entirely from true Locative Inversion constructions. I have already had occasion to cast doubt on some of Culicover and Levine's arguments to this effect (see notes 2, 4, 5, above). I will assume that genuine Locative Inversion constructions support Heavy NP Shift.

56. As Takano points out, extraposed heavy noun phrases differ in this respect from negative adverbials in right-peripheral position, which do license polarity items to their left (see (i), due to Branigan 1992).

(i) a. Brian paints pictures at all well only rarely.
    b. Imogen tells jokes with any gusto only occasionally.

57. See Koster 2000 and also De Vries 2002 for detailed discussion of an asyndetic coordination approach to a variety of extraposition phenomena, with the extraposed constituent being base-generated as the complement of a colon head "∶" that takes the clause preceding the extraposed phrase as its specifier. For Heavy NP Shift, this gives rise to a paraphrase of a sentence such as (ia) along the lines of (ib).

(i) a. [:P [TP Imogen met *ec* yesterday] [: [DP her favorite uncle from Cleveland]]]
    b. Imogen met someone yesterday: (namely,) her favorite uncle from
       Cleveland.

58. Notice that this is a restructuring construction; even though the pronoun originates as the object of the embedded infinitive, it will be able to undergo A-movement into the matrix clause such that it will end up c-commanding the anaphor contained in the matrix adverbial. See Lasnik and Saito 1991 and Lasnik 2001 for discussion of similar cases not involving Heavy NP Shift.

59. I took (112) from Heycock and Kroch (1999, 386). Moro's (1997, 26) original Italian examples are reproduced in (i).

(i) a. ogni libro fu l'aquisto   di molti studenti (Italian)
       every book was the-purchase of many students
    b. l'acquisto   di molti studenti fu   ogni libro
       the-purchase of many students was every book

60. Thanks to Tor Åfarli, Arild Hestvik, Helge Lødrup, and Tarald Taraldsen for their help with these examples; Taraldsen provided the example in (115), which is pragmatically plausible on both scope readings. For some speakers, *hver* "every" demands wide scope systematically; those speakers may substitute *alle brevene* for *hvert brev* to check their scope judgments for (115).

61. See Kayne 1998 for another variant of the overt movement approach, one by which the higher copy of the moved QP is pronounced; the lack of surface displacement results from remnant movement around the moved QP.

62. I am not sure why the postverbal subject is apparently unable to gain scope over negation in Norwegian "true" and "beheaded" Locative Inversion (see (i)).

(i) a. mange frimerker ble ikke klistret på brevet *many>/<not*
       many stamps   be not pasted on letter-the
    b. på brevet   ble ikke klistret mange frimerker *many??>/<not*
       on letter-the be not pasted many stamps
    c. brevet   ble ikke klistret mange frimerker på *many?*>/<not*
       letter-the be not pasted many stamps   on

This is something that does not seem to follow from the account. Relevant here may be Aissen's (1975, 9) observation that in English, Locative Inversion constructions do not tolerate sentential negation (*On this wall never hung a picture of U.S. Grant*), though they do allow contrastive constituent negation (*On this wall hangs not a picture of U.S. Grant but one of Jefferson Davis*). (Bresnan (1994, 88) points out that "negation appears much more freely in Chicheŵa locative inversions.") Note also that (ii), which is of the same structural type as (ic), supports wide scope for *mange* relatively happily. The relativity of some of the judgments may be due to interference of expletive *det* constructions (*det* is always insertable after *be*; see also Mikkelsen 2002a). Thanks to Helge Lødrup and his colleagues at the University of Oslo for help with the examples in (i) and (ii).

(ii) innvandrere blir ikke gitt   mange borgerlige rettigheter *many?(?)>/<not*
     immigrants be not given many civil   rights

63. Note, then, that the scopal rigidity of double-object constructions is *not* a consequence of the fact that their derivation involves Predicate Inversion (contrary to what I have claimed in some of my earlier work (particularly Den Dikken 1999), where I was unaware of the facts in (114c) and (116b)).

64. To illustrate this for (120b), consider what would happen if we reconstructed the matrix VP into the VP-gap without taking the direct object out of the matrix VP prior to reconstruction: that would result in *Imogen* [VP *gave someone everything that Brian* [VP *gave someone everything that Brian* [VP *gave someone everything that . . .*]]], etc., ad infinitum.

65. Hornstein's (1994, 1995) own analysis of (119b) is in terms of an A-movement analysis of the operation that resolves infinite regress in ACD constructions (A-movement to SpecAgrOP, to be precise; but see Kennedy 1997 for a convincing case against the A-movement approach to ACD and quantifier scope interaction championed by Hornstein). He does not, in the end, manage to present an account of the scopal rigidity of (119a) vis-à-vis the ambiguity of (119a′), however (see Hornstein 1995, 247–248, note 75).

66. I would like to thank Robert Fiengo and Erika Troseth for their help with the examples presented and discussed in what follows.

67. In what follows, I will illustrate only the Heavy NP Shift option, not the relative-clause extraposition option. Heavy NP Shift is typically more natural in the contexts at hand than relative-clause extraposition, presumably due at least in part to the fact that the relative clause, in ACD constructions, is rather light (after all, its VP is elliptical).

68. Though pragmatically, canonical and inverse copular sentences are not equivalent (see the discussion of focus in section 4.1), the two are truth-conditionally identical.

69. Recall from note 65 that Hornstein's (1994, 1995) A-movement analysis of infinite regress avoidance in ACD constructions has been shown, convincingly in my view, to be problematic (see Kennedy 1997); I do not consider it a viable alternative to the QP-raising and "extraposition" approaches, and will not discuss it here.

70. Heycock (1998a) rightly draws attention to the fact that Moro argues on independent grounds (having to do with the distribution of adverbial modifiers and floating quantifiers within small-clause complements to *consider*-type verbs) that "the complement of a *believe*-type verb would be better analysed as an 'enriched' small clause, which includes some spec-positions of a higher inflectional head" (Moro 1997, 55–56). With that additional FP available, there does not seem to be a lack of space, therefore.

71. This line of attack was originally suggested to me by Dominique Sportiche (personal communication). Alternatively, one may extend to (135b, c) the AspP approach taken in the main text immediately below for the example in (136), as does Heycock (1994).

72. This section will focus exclusively on cases of "beheaded" Locative Inversion. For "true" Locative Inversion constructions, details depend on whether or not P-incorporation can be argued to be involved in their derivation (see the discussion of Luhya "true" Locative Inversion in 4.2.2.3 (the examples in (57), in particular), and note 34 for the suggestion that Chicheŵa "true" Locative Inversion might involve silent P-incorporation). I will not address these details here.

73. Of course, (143b) is trivially grammatical on a bizarre reading according to which the letter is pasted onto the stamps; on that construal, we are not dealing with "beheaded" Locative Inversion at all but instead with a plain and simple passive counterpart to 'They pasted the letter onto stamps.'

74. English (ia), the transitive version of (50c), is likewise ungrammatical. This could be attributed to lack of space as well—but the issue is substantially more complex here than it is for the Norwegian case discussed in the text. English *pay* in principle allows Dative Shift (*Imogen paid Brian a lot of money*), which on my assumptions involves "beheaded" Locative Inversion (recall section 4.2.2.3). The variant of (ia) featuring Dative Shift (i.e., the version of (ia) that has a null dative preposition, given in (ib)) is tenuous: a Google search turned up just one attested token of this construction (see www.yaledailynews.com/article.asp?AID=20641), along with some 300 instances of *paid it little attention*, and a mere 38 for *paid me little attention*, which should be compared with the tens of thousands of hits

for *paid little attention <u>to</u>*. The relative paucity of double-object tokens for *pay attention* seems due not to the complement of *pay* never making the requisite space available for "beheaded" Locative Inversion but to lexical restrictions on Dative Shift, most of which remain poorly understood (see Bresnan and Nikitina 2003 for discussion). Because of these complications, lack of space does not seem solely responsible for the ill-formedness of (ia).

(i) a.   *They have paid [t_i this issue]$_j$ {to$_i$} little attention {to$_i$} t_j.
 b.   ??They have paid [t_i this issue]$_j$ {P$_{\varnothing\text{-}i}$} little attention {P$_{\varnothing\text{-}i}$} t_j.

75. I have not addressed cases of AP or VP Predicate Inversion; see the appendix for brief discussion of English cases of these types. Massam (2001) presents an interesting analysis of VSO order in Niuean involving raising of the lexical VP to SpecTP, stranding *v*, and the object-shifted object—technically, a pure case of VP Predicate Inversion. I refer the interested reader to Massam's paper for facts and discussion.

76. Note that if this account holds water, it argues strongly for the existence of head movement in syntax, contra Chomsky's (1995, chap. 4, passim) suggestion that head movement might be a PF affair. The role that head movement plays in the extension of domains and phases, which are computed in core syntax, entails that head movement is itself an ingredient of core syntax.

77. The examples in (152) are from Emonds (1976) as well as Hoekstra and Mulder (1990); see also note 1, above. In that note, I pointed out that Bresnan (1994) judges them to be marginal, assigning them two question marks. But Heycock seconds Emonds's judgment. I have decided to give the examples in (152) one question mark to reflect the fact that they are not universally deemed impeccable.

78. I do not have a clear perspective on the analysis of these examples, nor does anybody else, to my knowledge.

79. The AP-inversion cases in (150) pattern with the examples in (148b) and (149b) in these respects; I will not illustrate this.

80. Heycock's (1998b, 10) examples here involve *also* attached at the left edge of the precopular noun phrase. And indeed, sentences such as (159b) become fully unacceptable with *also* added. But without *also*, the result seems to be only marginally degraded. I have no account for the apparent fact that adding *also* makes embedding in nonbridge verb contexts entirely impossible.

81. Jacqueline Guéron (personal communication) has pointed out to me that (i) is not as good as (160) (not all speakers share this judgment, though). She suggests that the difference between these cases may have to do with the animacy of the noun phrase in SpecTP, but it remains obscure why subject-auxiliary inversion should be sensitive to this.

(i) ?Is your best friend John?

82. For the complement of bridge verbs, it is usually assumed (see, e.g., Iatridou and Kroch 1992) that it allows CP recursion.

83. The marginal acceptability of (165a) patterns, as Den Dikken, Meinunger, and Wilder (2000) point out, with the marginality of performing topicalization inside an embedded *wh*-question (cf. *?I wonder what to Mary, I should give*; see Emonds 1976, Baltin 1985, Pesetsky 1989, and references cited there).

84. The fact that full-fledged Type B SPCs resist subject-auxiliary inversion (see (ia), adapted from Heggie 1988, 312) is not immediately straightforward: there is no particular reason, syntactically speaking, why the fronted free relative, which after all occupies SpecTP on my analysis, should be uncomfortable with having the finite auxiliary raise past it to C. For Heggie (1988), the ungrammaticality of (ia) follows straightforwardly: she has the free relative raise to SpecCP. But that analysis (which she extends to inverse copular sentences in general) faces the insurmountable problem that embedding a Type B SPC under ECM-verbs like *consider* is grammatical—provided that a token of the copula *be* is provided (see (ii); Ross 1999). I will continue to assume a raising-to-SpecTP analysis for Type B SPCs, therefore; I have no insights to offer with respect to (ia), and must leave this important question open.

(i) a. *Is what Brian is important to himself? (Specificational)
     b. Is what Brian is important to him? (Predicational)

(ii) I consider what he is *(to be) important to himself.

85. Sugita's (2001) paper is noteworthy also because of its comparison of nominal Predicate Inversion in clauses and nominal phrases (see chapter 5 on the latter). She argues that DP-internal Predicate Inversion requires strict set intersection, not identification.

86. Thus, while (ia) is grammatical, (ib) is not (regardless of whether *as for* is included or not).

(i) a. Everything I needed, I got from my grandparents.
     b. *(As for) everything I needed, I got it from my grandparents.

Chapter 5

1. In my earlier work, I called this the *N of a N* construction. The more contentful designation "qualitative binominal noun phrase" blends terminology introduced in Aarts 1998 ("binominal noun phrase") and Hulk and Tellier 1999, 2000 ("qualititative construction"). The expression "qualititative binominal noun phrase" should be sufficiently explicit to avoid confusion with Safir and Stowell's (1988) use of the term *binominal*, for constructions like *two books each*. For (early) discussion of QBNPs, see De Groot 1949, Royen 1947–1954, Paardekooper 1956, Van den Toorn 1966, Van Caspel 1970, and Klein 1977 (all on Dutch); Eskenázi 1967, Tutescu 1969, Thomas 1970, Regula 1972, Jean-Claude Milner 1973, Jacques Milner 1978, Ruwet 1982, and Gaatone 1988 (on standard French); Gérard 1978, Noailly–Le Bihan 1984, Larrivée 1994, and Léard 1997 (on (standard and) Québécois French); and Lapesa 1962 (on Spanish). In the generative literature, discussion of QBNPs is found in Abney 1987; Napoli 1989; Suñer 1990, 1999; Everaert 1992; Kayne 1994; Den Dikken 1995a, 1998b; Den Dikken and Lipták

1997; Bennis, Corver, and Den Dikken 1998; Aarts 1998; Español-Echevarría 1997, 1998; De Wit 1997; Abraham 1998; Hulk and Tellier 1999, 2000; Doetjes and Rooryck 2001; Casillas Martínez 2001; Matushansky 2002; Malchukov 2004; and references cited there. Casillas Martínez 2001 is particularly noteworthy for its coverage of the literature on these constructions; that paper also contains a wealth of detailed information about the agreement facts in QBNPs (which I will largely leave aside in the discussion to follow). Though I have seen many of the references listed in the above, there are a number of sources that I have not had access to while writing this chapter; I occasionally draw on these sources via some intermediary (often the Casillas Martínez paper). For inadvertent misrepresentations of some of these texts, I take full responsibility.

2. The grammaticality of cases like *that madman George* (Napoli 1989) is surprising from this perspective. These might be appositives (cf. *my friend George*). Confirming the text discussion, in Dutch (ia) one does indeed get an attributive interpretation 'Jan Wolkers in his capacity as a writer (as opposed to his capacity as a sculptor)', as noted in Broekhuis, Keizer, and Den Dikken 2003, 567, where it is suggested that (ia) may not instantiate a QBNP but instead "the restrictive counterpart of the construction in [(ib)], where we are clearly dealing with a noun phrase with an appositive function."

(i) a. Jan Wolkers de schrijver is erg geliefd in Nederland (Dutch)
       Jan Wolkers the writer   is very loved in the.Netherlands
    b. Jan Wolkers, de (beroemde) schrijver, houdt hier vanavond een lezing
       Jan Wolkers the famous   writer   holds here tonight   a   lecture
       'Jan Wolkers, the (famous) writer, will give a lecture here tonight.'

3. See Napoli 1989, 186–201, 223–229, for a variety of arguments, based on Italian and English data, supporting the predication relationship between the two constituent noun phrases of QBNPs, with the first noun phrase serving as the predicate of the second.

4. In chapter 2, I treated *a dancer* as a DP, for the sake of simplicity. Now that we have moved over into the realm of complex noun phrases, it will be important to be more specific about the internal structure of nominal constructs. Throughout the discussion to follow, I will treat English indefinite articles (*a* and its null counterpart in the plural) as lexicalizations of the functional head "Num" (short for "Number"), and the definite article as a spell-out of the D-head. Whenever there are no compelling reasons to assume that the structure of the noun phrase extends beyond NumP, I will not erect any abstract structure on top of NumP (though I will leave open the possibility that, in some or even all of the cases in question, the extended projection of the noun continues all the way up to DP, with D null).

5. He refers to Quirk et al. 1985, 1285, in this connection.

6. The idea that, in attributive QBNPs, *of a* brings in some sort of lexical meaning is echoed in Español-Echevarría 1997, 164, where, with specific reference to Napoli's (1989, 203) Italian example reproduced in (4a), above (*quell'ignorante di dottore* 'that ignoramus of (a) doctor'), it is claimed that 'the preposition *di* 'of'

… acquires a certain degree of lexical meaning, close to *as*/*for*'. While Español-Echevarría is right to draw a connection between the attributive reading of *an idiot of a doctor* and the examples in (11a), it would be wrong to take their semantics to derive from the markers *of*/*as*/*for* used in these constructions—as discussed in the main text immediately below, these markers are meaningless elements; the semantics derives from the particular way the predicational relationship between the two noun phrases is established in the structure (see chapter 2).

7. A nontrivial problem is raised by British English *that fool the doctor* (Napoli 1989, 232), which cannot be accommodated by (14b). I suspect that British English has an additional structure at its disposal alongside (14b), but cannot speculate as to its nature.

8. By drawing a structural parallel between (9b) and attributive QBNPs, (16b) is to some degree reminiscent of McCawley's (1988) characterization of N_1 in the *N of a N* construction as an "adjectival noun." For a well-taken rebuttal, see Aarts 1998, note 11.

   Doetjes and Rooryck (2001, 7) draw attention, in connection with their claim that the noun phrase preceding *de* is a modifier in constructions featuring the structure in (16b), to Hulk and Tellier's (1999) observation that this first noun phrase can be one which fails to serve as a predicate in copular sentences—such as *sapristi* 'heavens' in *cette sapristi de roue* 'this heavens of wheel', or *nom de dieu* 'god's name' in *une nom de dieu de bonne femme* 'a god's name of woman' (see also Gérard 1978 and Léard 1997 on "*sacre* constructions" in Québécois: *ce tabernak de fou* 'that tabernacle of fool'). Hulk and Tellier do not actually end up accommodating their own observation. It does follow from (16b), however.

9. Abraham (1998, 342), while congenial to the text approach, gets the relationship between *of* and a nominal environment backward when he says that *of* is "ein Relationselement mit ausschließlich nominaler Selektion" ("a relational element with exclusively nominal selection"): it is not the fact that *of selects* a nominal (cf. the appearance of *of* in Romance *A of N* constructions and in possessive contexts, discussed in section 5.7—there the predicate is not nominal) but the fact that it is *selected by* D that is the key.

10. Example (17a) is redeemable on a construal in which *idioot* is an uninflected *adjective* (cf. English *idiotic*); inflection (in the form of a schwa, resulting in *een idiote dokter* 'an idiotic doctor') would be much more natural here, though. (See also De Swart, Winter, and Zwarts 2005.) Clearly, with *idioot* construed as an uninflected adjective, (17a) does not instantiate a binominal construction. This interpretation of (17a) is irrelevant, therefore.

11. At this point I have no insights to offer beyond this contrast, when it comes to the distribution of bare predicate nominals. The text discussion of the Dutch/English contrast is tentative and should be looked at in more detail in future research.

12. Besides, English QBNPs with *of* are generally quite difficult to get in the plural (see (ib)), in contradistinction to *of*-less attributive QBNPs, which pluralize perfectly well (see (ia)). (It is interesting to note that in (ia) only the second noun

is plural-marked—*idiots doctors* is entirely impossible (though I did find one example of *madmen drivers* on the web, embedded, perhaps significantly, in a text whose Canadian author emphasizes at the outset that he has "made NO effort to correct any gramatical [*sic*] or spelling mistakes contained in the document").) In British English, plural QBNPs are apparently possible to some degree (whence the "%" on (ib))—thus, Aarts (1998, 118, 143) mentions *those fools of doctors* and *many idiots of football hooligans* as grammatical instances of the construction. I will return to pluralization in QBNPs in section 5.4.2.

(i) a. They are idiot doctors.
    b. %They are idiots of doctors.

13. Peculiarly, Español-Echevarría (1997, 164) claims that English *an idiot of a doctor* lacks the attributive reading. This is false.

14. The reader may wonder at this point about the distribution of the "spurious" indefinite article in the Dutch counterparts of the examples in (6) (repeated in a simplified form as (i), below). In section 5.1, I pointed out (following Hulk and Tellier 2000) that (ia) is attributive and (ib) comparative, so one might expect (ia) in Dutch to be impossible with "spurious" *een*. This, however, is not borne out: (iia) is perfect both with and without *een*, like (iib). This does not compromise the text conclusion, however. For notice that of the examples in (i), only (ib) is categorical in accepting only one of the readings (the comparative one, in particular): while the salient reading of (ia) is certainly the attributive one, prescribing the wrong medicine is of course also something that could be done by someone who is an idiot as an *individual*, not just in his or her capacity as a doctor. As a result, the context in (ia) will not bring out any contrast in the distribution of "spurious" *een* in Dutch: (iia) with *een* involves a comparative QBNP, which is fine in the context.

(i) a. That idiot of a doctor prescribed me the wrong medicine.
    b. That idiot of a doctor just wrecked my car.

(ii) a. die   idioten van (een) doktoren hebben me het verkeerde geneesmiddel
      those idiots of   a   doctors have   me the wrong   medicine
      voorgeschreven (Dutch)
      prescribed
    b. die   idioten van (een) doktoren hebben m'n auto gesloopt
      those idiots of   a   doctors have   my car   wrecked

15. This construction appears to have been more common in nineteenth-century English. I have found several examples of *no fool of a N* on this litotic ("quite a N") reading on the web, especially in the collocation *no fool of a job*, in documents that either were written in the nineteenth century or try to mimic nineteenth-century English—especially the English of the lower classes. In African American Vernacular English, *no fool of a N* seems to be fairly common as well (e.g., *Ain't no fool of a human bean* [*sic*] *got the power to hold back the flood*, and *Master didn't raise no fool of a slave*). While *no fool of a N* appears to be dialectal, there is a variant of this litotic QBNP that has a much broader distribution: *no joke of a N*. Some examples illustrating this construction are given in (i). (Note

also the following example, spotted by Asya Pereltsvaig, personal communication, on FoodNetwork (November 4, 2004): *This is no poodle of a dessert!*)

(i) a. This is no joke of a chain letter.
      www.itd.umich.edu/virusbusters/hoaxes/disney.html, and elsewhere
   b. It has been no joke of a hard time.
      www.samoa.co.uk/books/vailima-letters/chapter8.html
   c. Bawah is no joke of a supermiddleweight.
      www.newmexicoboxing.com/cozzone/bojadolacy.html
   d. This was no joke of a wart.
      www.bmezine.com/scar/Q20810/scrcoldb.html
   e. 38 mb is no joke of a download for a modem user.
      www.ocaddiction.com/articles/misc/3dmark2001
   f. This is no joke of a concert/town/score/triathlon/name/module/task/trip/
      lie/piece/ ...

16. There is a litotic reading in which the string of words in (25b) comes out fine, equivalent to (i) (see the previous note), but for that reading, the prosodic contour indicated in (25b) with the aid of small capitalization would be inappropriate.

(i) He is quite a president but a fool of a professor.

17. The question of how large the constituent noun phrases are (bare NPs or NumPs or even larger) is addressed in section 5.4.

18. Suñer (1990) and Español-Echevarría (1998, note 5) take focus to be the trigger, but recall section 4.2 for discussion of the failure of this type of approach.

19. Though I will not pursue this here, one could argue that *as* (Dutch *als* = *al* + *s*) is a composite of a spell-out of the RELATOR and a spell-out of the adjective SIMILAR (*so*, reduced to *-s*)—compare Old English *alswa* = *al* + *swa* 'all + so'—created through incorporation of the adjective into the RELATOR. For *like*, a similar line of thought suggests itself: see Dutch *gelijk* 'like, identical', a composite of the cognate of English *like* (which by itself is sporadically usable adjectivally, as in *like minds, a like sum*) and the prefix *ge-*, which in English comes out as *a-* in the adjective *alike*. If these suggestions are on the right track, the RELATORS in *as* and *like* are presumably quantificational elements: *all* and Dutch *ge-* (which seems to be a quantificational element of sorts in *broeder~gebroeders* 'brother~brethren'; on *ge-*, see Postma 1996, suggesting that it is similar to Latin *-que*, itself presumably quantificational).

20. Casillas Martínez (2001, 45) points out that the example in (35b) has a different interpretation in Puerto Rican Spanish, paraphrasable as 'your brother the traitor'; Puerto Rican Spanish apparently does not have (35a) at all. The implications of this contrast between Iberian and Puerto Rican Spanish remain to be investigated. Milner (1978) observes facts similar to (35a, b) for French, though in French, apparently, the counterpart of Spanish (35b) allows for a choice of outer determiner (see (ib)). Note that French allows the use of "naked" N_1 as the predicate of a copular sentence corresponding in meaning to (ib) (see (iib')). In Spanish, this is impossible: unless *rata* is given a special intonation contour with two

high tones on *rata* (see Español-Echevarría 1997, note 8), **tu hermano es rata* is ungrammatical.

(i) a. ma   vache de frère (French)
         my.F cow.F of brother.M
         'my meanie of a brother'
     b. mon/ma vache de frère
         my.M/F cow.F of brother.M
         'my severe brother'
     b'. mon frère   est vache
         my.M brother.M is cow.F
         'My brother is severe.'

21. In all fairness, I should note that this is my translation of Español-Echevarría's proposal; he himself takes *rata* to be the left-hand member of a "compound headed by *pro*" (1998, 76), referring to Sleeman 1996 in this connection. Since, however, compounds are never headed by overt pronouns (even though they can sometimes serve as nonheads, as in *she-goat, she-male*), I will not take over the specifics of Español-Echevarría's proposal. The text approach takes the head of the noun phrase of which *rata* is a part to be a null noun; see Panagiotidis (2003) for discussion of null nouns versus *pro*. Note that this analysis is readily compatible with the observation (made in Español-Echevarría 1997, 154, and replicated in full detail in Casillas Martínez 2001) that *rata* in this context is adjectival in nature, accepting degree modifiers (cf. *tu hermano es muy/bastante rata* 'Your brother is very/quite stingy', which is unambiguously of the (35b') type): with *rata* construed as a modifier of a (null-headed) NP, it behaves essentially like an adjective.

22. Notice that this discussion provides an answer to the question of why there are no "straight" predicate-complement structures in the nominal domain that have no lexicalization of the RELATOR—that is, why there are no counterparts to the bracketed part of (i) in the nominal domain. The answer is that the null predicate head SIMILAR would not be licensable in the absence of either a RELATOR lexicalized as *as/like* or Predicate Inversion. But this raises the question of how (i) can be grammatical, or, put differently, how null SIMILAR is licensed here. The key here seems to be that the small clause in (34) is embedded under a licenser in (i)—I assume that, even in the absence of a lexical RELATOR, the null predicate head can still be licensed if, after raising to the RELATOR, it can incorporate into the verb (see Baker 1988 on incorporation into the verb as a mechanism to accomplish "morphological licensing"; the copula is included in the set of licensers: see the Benvenistian analysis of the *be/have* alternation in terms of P-incorporation into *be*, as discussed in Freeze 1992, Kayne 1993, and Den Dikken 1995a).

(i) a. I consider [this village a jewel].
     b. This village is [*t* a jewel].

23. Throughout the discussion to follow, it should be borne in mind that, with the exception of Doetjes and Rooryck (2001), none of the accounts discussed structurally distinguish between different types of QBNPs.

24. In Kayne's more recent work (see especially Kayne 2002a, b), radically different analyses of constructions featuring *of* and its ilk in other languages are proposed—analyses in which *of* is generated outside the complex noun phrase, in the functional domain of the clause, so that the string *jewel of a village* is not a constituent. The present chapter unfolds an extended argument to the effect that QBNPs and possessed noun phrases should receive an analysis that derives their syntax via operations within the confines of the complex noun phrase.

25. While the use of *the* as the outer determiner of QBNPs is perhaps somewhat more common in British English (see (i) for some attested examples from the work of British authors Kate Kingsbury and Gladys Mitchell, brought to my attention by Asya Pereltsvaig, personal communication), it occasionally surfaces in American English as well (see (ii), which I spotted in a column by Joseph Rappaport published in the October 30, 2003, edition of *amNewYork*, a free daily newspaper distributed in New York City).

(i) a. That girl gives him the devil of a time. (Kingsbury, *Berried Alive*, 59)
   b. I'm having the devil of a job. (Kingsbury, *Dig Deep for Murder*, 154)
   c. I found myself in hospital with the devil of a headache.
                                      (Mitchell, *Cold, Lone and Still*, 197)
   d. Only because the idiot of a caretaker or whatever he calls himself
      misdirected me. (Mitchell, *Cold, Lone and Still*, 151)

(ii) How could the Metropolitan Transportation Authority be running out of
     money, just five months after the whopper of a [fare] hike last May?

In his corpus-based study of the Dutch QBNP construction, Pekelder (1994) notes that *de* and *het*, the definite determiners of Dutch, can occasionally be found in this construction: 5 percent of his ninety-eight definite instances of the construction involve *het*, 7 percent feature *de*. Clearly, *de/het*-marked QBNP constructions are extremely rare in Dutch, as in English. Spanish, Catalan, and Portuguese are freer than Germanic and the rest of Romance in this regard, as Español-Echevarría (1997) points out: in Spanish, Catalan, and Portuguese, definite articles are freely allowed to head QBNPs (and to this we may add that outer definite articles seem to be allowed to some degree in Québécois as well: cf. *l'imbécile à Jean*; Noailly–Le Bihan 1984). The contrast in (iii), between Spanish and Italian, is minimal.

(iii) a.   el loco   del   doctor (Spanish)
        the madman of-the doctor
    b. *il matto   del   dottore (Italian)
        the madman of-the doctor

26. Or J. R. R. Tolkien's, for that matter: in his *Lord of the Rings* trilogy (specifically, in *Moria's Revenge*) from the 1930s, we find the dialogue in (i), featuring a comparative QBNP in Gandalf's statement that has a proper name (*Took*) as the second noun (Peregrin Took, also known as Pippin Took, is one of the hobbits).

(i) Pippin: Are you sure you don't want Gimli to read that?
   Gandalf: No, fool of a Took!

(In the history of French, things apparently developed in the opposite direction, judging from Lapesa (1962), who claims that in Old French, in contradistinction to other Old Romance varieties, N_2 in the QBNP could not be a proper name; in Modern French it certainly can, as in the other modern Romance languages.)

27. English shows the contrast between demonstratives and indefinite articles as outer determiners of QBNPs more clearly in *of*-less QBNPs featuring a proper name as N_2, as the example in (i) (from Napoli 1989) indicates. (Napoli (1989, 242–255) analyzes these constructions in some detail; recall also note 2, above, and the discussion of *of*-less attributive QBNPs in section 5.2.)

(i) that/*a madman George

28. When they do, as in (i), the interpretation one gets is a type reading—we have someone on our team who has the (stereo)typical characteristics of David Beckham (a British soccer player excelling, among other things, in bending a ball like only he can). This reading (discussed, e.g., in Longobardi 1994, 636, 693) is not the one we get for *Rebecca* or *Marie* in (42) and (43).

(i) We have a David Beckham on our team.

29. In English, the use of the "spurious" indefinite article is quite restricted—only with proper names, it seems (and even then, only in older varieties); certainly not with plurals. See Bennis, Corver, and Den Dikken 1998 for relevant discussion.

30. Dutch *geen* 'no' (which on the surface looks like a morphological derivative of the indefinite article *een*; but see Broekhuis, Keizer, and Den Dikken 2003, 665ff., for evidence that synchronically it is not analyzable this way) works like English *no* in comparative QBNPs: the example in (ib) is perfect (typing in *geen dijk van een* into Google will find the interested reader a list attested examples), with a sentential-negation interpretation.

(i) a. dit is een dijk van een tapijt (Dutch)
         this is a   dyke of   a   carpet
         'This is an excellent carpet' (a carpet that is like a dyke, having the solidity and durability of a dyke).
     b. dit is geen dijk van een tapijt
         this is no   dyke of   a   carpet

31. Questions remain as to how exactly the indefinite article in Num teams up with N_2. These questions are part and parcel of a larger set of questions concerning the selection of gender and number forms of outer determiners of comparative QBNPs, as well as the selection of outside agreement. I will not make a systematic effort here to unravel these elusive data, but see notes 33 and 39.

32. Doetjes and Rooryck (2001, 4–5) base their analysis on Milner's (1978) observations about coordination in French QBNPs.

(i) a. elle avait acheté quelques merveilles de robes et de souliers rouges qui lui allaient à ravir
         *'She had bought some marvels of dresses and of red shoes that fit her like a glove.'

    b. *elle avait acheté quelques merveilles de robes et splendeurs de soulier
        rouges qui lui allaient à ravir
        'She had bought some marvels of dresses and splendors of red shoes that
        fit her like a glove.'

(ii) a.   nous avons visité plusieurs bijoux d'abbayes médiévales et d'églises
          romanes
        *'We have visited several jewels of medieval abbeys and of Roman
        churches.'
    b. *nous avons visité plusieurs bijoux d'abbayes médiévales et chefs-d'oeuvre
        d'églises romanes
        'We have visited several jewels of medieval abbeys and masterpieces of
        roman churches.'

Apparently, it is impossible in French to coordinate what follows the quantifier introducing the *N of a N* construction with another *N of a N* sequence: the b-examples are impossible in French, while those in (ia)/(iia) are well formed. Doetjes and Rooryck (2001) take the ungrammaticality of the b-examples to indicate that any determiner or quantifier that precedes N_1 must form a constituent with N_1. It is difficult to appreciate the strength of this argument, however. As my grammaticality markings on the English paraphrases of the French sentences indicate (see also Aarts 1998), the French facts are the exact opposite of what we find in English. One would not want to argue that syntactic constituency in French QBNPs is drastically different from that in their English counterparts. Since there is strong evidence from indefinite articles (which carries over to French: *ce/*un bijou de Marie* 'this/*a jewel of Marie') that tells us that the determiner element preceding N_1 does *not* form a constituent with N_1 in QBNPs, we must conclude that (i)/(ii), while interesting, do not show what Doetjes and Rooryck take them to show. I leave the analysis of (i)/(ii) open here.

33. Though note that their particular dichotomy is not entirely identical to mine. Doetjes and Rooryck (2001) distinguish between comparative and "pure-degree" constructions, taking (47b) to instantiate the latter. Representation (47b) is not in any obvious sense a specimen of what I have called the *attributive* QBNP (i.e., (47b) is not saying that the referent of the noun phrase is a phenomenon in her capacity of being a sister). I would in fact classify it as a *comparative* QBNP. Since Doetjes and Rooryck show that there are some interesting syntactic differences between (47a) and (47b) (especially as regards outward gender agreement), there may be occasion to further subdivide the class of comparative QBNPs into two subtypes. But I will not undertake such a bifurcation here. Whatever its fate, it will leave the text dichotomy (attributive versus comparative QBNPs) entirely unaffected, there being ample evidence for it in the facts presented in the foregoing. (I refer the interested reader to Napoli 1989, Hulk and Tellier 1999, 2000, Doetjes and Rooryck 2001, Casillas Martínez 2001, Longenecker 2002, and Szekely 2002 for discussion of the French, Italian, and Spanish agreement facts, some of which are extremely subtle; see note 39 for some illustration for French. An important role appears to be played, especially in the French data, by semantic agreement, or what Casillas Martínez (2001) calls "index agreement.")

34. Readers not interested in the details of the quantificational and determiner restrictions on QBNPs may want to skip the discussion of the rather intricate facts presented in sections 5.4 and 5.5, and proceed directly to section 5.6, about the nominal copula.

35. I have not supplied the b-examples in (50)–(52) with any diacritics marking their degree of awkwardness, as in the case of (48) and (49). The status of these examples remains to be researched further. But what is clear is that, while the a-examples in (50)–(52) are entirely natural and are readily produced, the b-cases are awkward and entirely unattested in my Google searches.

36. Bennis, Corver, and Den Dikken (1998, 98) note that (52) is also marginally possible in Dutch (?*die idioten van een regering* 'those idiots of a government'), with Broekhuis, Keizer, and Den Dikken (2003, 570) adding that Dutch is unlike British English in never allowing plural agreement with nouns like *regering* 'government'. Similarly, in Italian one finds *i cretini della Mafia* 'the cretins of-the Mafia' (Napoli 1989, 198), which accepts a QBNP reading ('the Mafiosi, all of whom are cretins'), but *la Mafia* never triggers plural agreement. In this context, one might also bring up the following quote from Woody Allen's 1971 movie *Bananas*: "This trial is a travesty. It's a travesty of a mockery of a sham of a mockery of a travesty of two mockeries of a sham." The last portion of this chain of QBNPs is of particular interest: in *two mockeries of a sham*, the inverted predicate is plural, and even numerically quantified. (Thanks to Rachel Szekely, personal communication, for drawing my attention to this quote.) For more on such number disagreement cases, see the main-text discussion below (57)/(58).

37. To be sure, there is one remarkable difference between English (57a) and Dutch (57b): the fact that, in the inverse cases, the finite verb agrees with the precopular noun phrase in English but with the postcopular subject in Dutch (recall the discussion in section 4.2.2.1). But it remains obscure how this difference could be held responsible for the contrast between (56a) and (56b), or for the more general fact that the second noun phrase of English QBNPs (whether attributive or comparative) cannot be a morphological plural. I will not pursue a potential parallel between the verb agreement facts in (57) and the distribution of number in QBNPs.

38. Example (58a) is grammatical only with the modifier *grote* included; *één* forms a constituent with the predicate nominal here (cf. *die feiten zijn één *(grote) ramp* 'Those facts are one big disaster')—perhaps also in English *one hell of a N* (see Matushansky 2002, and note 40, below), though that is less easy to prove. Note that (58a) triggers singular agreement (*dat is/*zijn één grote ramp van een feiten*), in stark contrast with things like *dat zijn/*is leuke feiten* 'That are/is nice facts', where plural *zijn* is obligatory.

39. Example (58c) is from Broekhuis, Keizer, and Den Dikken 2003, 571; (59d) is my own, based on the second example in (56b). In fairness, I should note that before I saw this passage in Broekhuis, Keizer, and Den Dikken 2003, my own impression of outward agreement triggered by (56b) was that it distinguished between cases in which the outer demonstrative is *die* (compatible with both sin-

gular and plural nouns) and those featuring *dat* (neuter singular), with only the latter showing a clear bias against plural agreement. It seems to me that (58c) with plural agreement becomes acceptable (in fact, preferred) once a predicate is chosen that demands *feiten* 'facts', not *ramp* 'disaster' as its subject (cf. (i); with *schandaal* 'scandal', (i) seems unacceptable either way). I also have the impression that in a sentence like (ii), the choice of *is* and *zijn* is more or less free, even with neuter *schandaal* 'scandal' heading the QBNP. The fact that *zijn* is acceptable in (ii) seems to be influenced by the presence, between the matrix copula and the QBNP, of the ethical dative *me* and the discourse particles *daar* and *toch*: dropping the sequence *me daar toch* from (ii) makes the *zijn*-variant deteriorate, particularly sharply in the case of neuter *schandaal*. This is doubtless related to the fact that (ii) with *me daar toch* included is an exclamative; "spurious" *een* is common in exclamatives.

(i) die ramp   van een feiten ??staat/?staan in iedere grammatica (Dutch)
    that disaster of a   facts stands/stand in every grammar

(ii) dat is/zijn me daar toch een ramp/schandaal van een feiten!
     that is/are me there DPRT a   disaster/scandal of a   facts

As the cocktail of Dutch facts in (58c, d) and (i)–(ii) already suggests, the behavior of QBNPs with respect to outward agreement is extremely complicated. For a discussion of French gender-agreement facts, see Hulk and Tellier 1999, 2000, and Doetjes and Rooryck 2001. According to Doetjes and Rooryck (2001), the generalization is that in French QBNPs, while the gender form of the demonstrative of the complex noun phrase seems to be systematically determined by the first noun in the string, external agreement is controlled either by the first noun or by the second, depending on whether we are dealing with a comparative or a "pure degree" QBNP: (iiia) is clearly comparative and features outward masculine agreement triggered by *bijou*, N_1; for (iiib) comparative construal would, according to Doetjes and Rooryck, be absurd (#'Your daughter is such that she resembles a phenomenon'), and here we find that the predicative adjective agrees with the second noun of the QBNP. I will not dwell on the analysis of these gender-agreement facts here, since it seems to me that they do not constitute a clear argument in favor of any of the extant accounts: all analyses have to resort to some degree of wizardry to accommodate these data, and belaboring this wizardry seems scarcely productive in the context of this chapter. (The interested reader is referred to the above-mentioned papers for discussion of the French facts, as well as to Longenecker 2002 for Spanish, and Napoli 1989 and Szekely 2002 for Italian. See especially Casillas Martínez 2001, who presents an analysis of inward and outward agreement facts in Romance QBNP constructions couched in terms of a distinction between concord (morphosyntactic agreement) and what he calls "index agreement," an HPSG notion.)

(iii) a. ce   bijou   d' église   a   été   reconstruit(*e) (French)
         that.M jewel.M of church.F has been rebuilt-M/*F

      b. ton   phénomène   de fille   est bien distrait*(e)
         your.M phenomenon.M of daughter.F is   quite absentminded-F/*M

40. The three N_1's partaking in the Hungarian QBNPs in (60), *csoda* 'wonder', *fene* 'hell', and *kutya* 'dog', all show somewhat special behavior in English. Thus, as Matushansky (2002) points out, English *hell of a N* readily allows the numeral *one* to introduce it; though she does not note this, the same is true for *dog* and *wonder* (cf. *This is one dog of a game* and *That is one wonder of a beaver*, both culled from the web). Matushansky's claim that with other N_1's, QBNPs typically do not allow *one* seems overstated: QBNPs corresponding to copular sentences in which the predicate is modified by *real* often allow for *one* to be placed to the left of the inverted predicate nominal; thus, one occasionally finds such QBNPs *He is one disaster of a president* (cf. *This president is a real disaster*), or *That is one idiot of a boy* (cf. *That boy is a real idiot*).

41. The one eye-catching difference between the Hungarian and Dutch examples of QBNPs is the absence in the former of anything corresponding to Dutch *van* (or English *of*). I turn to this in section 5.6.3.1.

42. Though apparently not universally—in Italian and Spanish, the second noun phrase of a QBNP can be introduced by the definite article. See section 5.5.1 for discussion.

43. In that variant (*?die ramp van een twee feiten*, where "spurious" *een* MUST be included; see Bennis, Corver, and Den Dikken 1998 for discussion of the obligatoriness of "spurious" *een* in all cases of number disagreement between subject and predicate nominal), (63a) corresponds to the grammatical copular sentence *die twee feiten zijn een ramp* 'Those two facts are a disaster'.

44. In this respect, comparative QBNPs behave like adjectival modification: *die rampzalige twee feiten* 'those disastrous two facts' is grammatical while **een rampzalige twee feiten* is bad (even in exclamative contexts, where "spurious" *een* would be allowed).

45. In Den Dikken 1998b, I attempted to demonstrate that NPIs are also unembeddable on a left branch within the postcopular noun phrase, by presenting examples of "modifier-NPIs" of the type in (i). Unfortunately, however, the robustness of the contrast in (ib) (between unstressed *particularly*, which distributes like an NPI, and heavily stressed *PARTICULARLY*, which is not an NPI) is undermined substantially by the fact, noted in Heycock 1998b, note 7, that putting an adverbial modifier on an attributive adjective preceding N_2 produces a very awkward result (while adverbial modification of an adjective preceding N_1 is perfectly fine); see (ii).

(i) a. I don't think that this is a beauty of an (*at all) expensive picture.
   b. I don't think that this is a beauty of a (*particularly/??PARTICULARLY) expensive picture.

(ii) a. a remarkably tall beauty of a woman
    b. a beauty of a (??remarkably) tall woman

46. The grammaticality of (65d) *with* the indefinite article (not noted by Heycock) is irrelevant in the context at hand: it is on a par with things like *John bought a big red WHAT about baseball?*, where the echo-*wh* is an N^0, not a nominal phrase. The German example in (i) (which according to Abraham 1998, 340 is grammatical)

can be treated as a case of an N^0 echo-*wh* as well. German affords us the possibility of having an N^0 echo-*wh* preceded by no article precisely because it also allows the second noun phrase of comparative QBNPs to be a bare singular. Thus, Abraham (1998, 339) notes that (ii) is grammatical both with and without *einem*, in stark contrast to what we find in Dutch or English, where a singular N_2 must always be preceded by an indefinite article. I will return to these cases in section 5.5.2.

(i) ein Traum von WAS? (German)
    a   dream of   what

(ii) ein Biest von (einem) Direktor
     a   beast of   a-DAT manager

47. The fact that I am now blaming the *wh*-restrictions on QBNPs on a size restriction applying to the second noun phrase does not mean, of course, that the claim made in my earlier work (see Den Dikken 1998b, in particular) that the second noun phrase of (comparative) QBNPs is unextractable has thereby been proven wrong. On the contrary, the parallel between comparative QBNPs and Copular Inversion constructions continues to lead one to expect there to be a ban on extraction of the postcopular constituent; but demonstrating the effect of this ban is extremely difficult given that this constituent is probably too small to ever be eligible for extraction.

48. The conclusion that the postcopular noun phrase in comparative QBNPs, as in attributive QBNPs (see section 5.2), is a NumP makes it possible to accommodate the fact that both QBNP types allow the postcopular noun phrase to undergo *one*-replacement in English. Bennis, Corver, and Den Dikken (1998, 99, note 16) give an example of *one*-replacement in what is clearly an *attributive* QBNP (see (i), provided to them by an anonymous reviewer). *One*-replacement also works in unambiguously *comparative* QBNPs such as those in (ii), culled from the Internet with the aid of the generic search engine Google.

(i) To keep the team consistently victorious, it takes a real genius of a coach,
    and to lose so consistently, it takes a real dunce of one.

(ii) a. I don't get colds very often, though Lynnie had given me a beauty of one
        when we first met.
        www.enchantments.net/swept13.htm
     b. I don't like mysteries, they give me a bellyache and I have a beauty of
        one right now.
        usf.for.net/archive/USS_Stealth_Lounge_3.html
     c. This may be the first reefer madness story out there—and a horror of one
        it is.
        site130.webhost4life.com/floridaaamc/reefermadness/comicbooks.htm
     d. (Anyway, today hasn't been to bad headache wise) i had a bitch of one
        last night though.
        necessaryevils.blogspot.com
     e. The AI in Heroes IV seems exclusively fighter and a bitch of one upon
        that.
        radiskull.pitas.com/17_01_2003.html

Napoli (1989, 236) notes that in British English (though definitely not in American English), it is even possible to perform *one*-replacement on the second noun phrase of a *bare* attributive QBNP (as in *if he's a doctor, he must be a bit of a madman <u>one</u>*, attributed to Andrew Radford). Napoli is presumably right to note that there is a connection here with the grammaticality of full-fledged DPs in second position in British English *of*-less attributive QBNPs (see *that fool <u>the</u> doctor*, mentioned in note 7).

49. In the next section, I will present an argument from Spanish comparative QBNPs showing that there are syntactic reasons as well to take the demonstrative not to form a constituent with N_1 (contra Doetjes and Rooryck 2001).

50. Recall the discussion of (40), above, as well as note 25.

51. Example (46′) adopts the null predicate SIMILAR that I argued for in section 5.3.4. Recall that in that section I also brought up the fact that certain Spanish comparative QBNPs feature an empty-headed nominal predicate; see Español-Echevarría 1997, 1998.

52. Manuel Español-Echevarría (personal communication) notes that only the variants of (69a′) and (69a″) that feature *del* (i.e., *el imbécil del doctor ese* and *el imbécil ese del doctor*) are *comparative* QBNPs (like (69a)). The ones lacking the definite article preceding N_2 (i.e., *el imbécil de doctor ese* and *el imbécil ese de doctor*, which for some speakers are hard to get; Ana Longenecker, personal communication) have an *attributive* reading—like (69b) and Italian (68b). (The latter examples seem to show that the postcopular noun phrase can be a bare NP; I will turn to this issue in section 5.5.2.) From the point of view of the text analysis of the pre-N_2 definite article as a "spurious" article, Español-Echevarría's observation reminds one of the fact (see section 5.2.3, (23)) that in Dutch, QBNPs featuring a "spurious" indefinite article are unambiguously *comparative* as well.

53. The status of (69a, a′, a″) varies depending on the speaker. Español-Echevarría (1997, note 3) suggests that this dialectal split may be related to the split in the English-speaking community between those accepting (ia) (see 7) and those who do not (the status of (ib), like that of (69b), being entirely constant): Napoli (1989, 232) points out that (ia) is acceptable in British English but not in American English. Español-Echevarría goes on to suggest that the variation regarding the judgment on (ia) may also be related to the fact on QBNPs like (40), above (*the rascal of a landlord*, and so on), get a mixed reception from native speakers, with British speakers once again being more favorably disposed (though recall the opening lines of note 25). The link between (ia) and (40), if empirically real, is analytically quite elusive, however (note that all speakers uniformly reject **that idiot of the doctor*). I will not pursue it here, though I would like to see it taken up in future work.

(i) a. %that fool the doctor
     b.   that idiot doctor

For speakers who reject (69a) with *del*, the formal distinction between the attributive and comparative readings of QBNPs with outer demonstratives evaporates. For those speakers, Spanish (69a) thus behaves like French, where, as

Hulk and Tellier (1999) point out, the interpretive difference noted by Napoli (1989, 203) between the two readings of *that ignoramus of a doctor* (see section 5.1) is never formally marked in any way within the QBNP: N_2 can only project a bare NP (see (ii)).

(ii) cet imbécile {de/*du} médecin (French)
     that idiot   of/of-the doctor

54. Napoli (1989, 203) points out that there are contexts in which an indefinite article *can* be used on N_2 in Italian QBNPs—in particular, "If that NP is used not in the genus sense, but, instead, to pick out a particular person who has the property signified by the N of the NP following *di*," or in cases in which the second noun phrase is modified by a restrictive relative clause. In the former case, Napoli's characterization suggests that we are in fact dealing with a *comparative* QBNP; in the latter context, articles generally exhibit out-of-the-ordinary behavior (cf. *the Paris *(that I knew as a child)*; see Kayne 1994 and references cited there). It seems, therefore, that the diacritic on *un* in (68b) is appropriate: genuinely *attributive* QBNPs do indeed resist any determiner on N_2.

55. I am abstracting away in this structure from the question of whether *imbécil de(l) doctor* is an attributive or a comparative QBNP—this is irrelevant here: on either analysis, *imbécil* is eligible for movement to SpecDemP.

56. Raising to SpecDemP presumably happens systematically in Spanish demonstrative-marked noun phrases: the fact that, when the demonstrative precedes the rest of the noun phrase (as in *(*el) ese imbécil de(l) doctor*), it is impossible to insert a definite article in front of it, while in (69a′, a″) the D-head is obligatorily spelled out as a definite article, suggests that when the D-head is empty, the demonstrative raises up to it, thereby ending up to the left of what is in SpecDemP.

57. Español-Echevarría (1997, 1998) points out that there is a way of making (73b) grammatical, by adding a relative clause at the right edge of the QBNP. This is illustrated in (i). Español-Echevarría presents an interesting argument to the effect that the relative clause in (i) is attached at a different level in the two variants of the example. When there is no article preceding N_2, the relative clause is attached to the entire QBNP, with the subject of the relative clause being *imbécil de doctor*, which is well formed qua INDEF-INDEF case (see (74b)). Attaching the relative clause high in the variant of (i) that has N_2 preceded by a definite article, on the other hand, would make *imbécil del doctor* the subject of the relative clause—an illegitimate INDEF–DEF case of the QBNP (see (74a)). So in (i) with *del*, the relative clause must be attached low, to the second noun.

(i) el imbécil de(l)   doctor [que tienes   en casa] (Spanish)
    the idiot   of(the) doctor that have-2SG at home

58. There is no reason to believe that δ is structurally invisible to α (if there is no phase boundary phase in between them)—and in fact, the two do indeed seem to be able to establish an Agree relationship for *gender*: in Romance it appears that it is always N_1 that agrees with the outside determiner/demonstrative in QBNPs (see Hulk and Tellier 1999, 2000; Doetjes and Rooryck 2001).

59. Note that this account of (73) compares two candidates that have different numerations, hence should not compete on standard assumptions. I take the semantic vacuity of *el* to make such a comparison legitimate.

60. Also recall note 52, and recall section 5.2.3 on "spurious" indefinite articles in Dutch comparative but not attributive QBNPs.

61. Manuel Español-Echevarría (personal communication) tells me that he agrees with Napoli (1989) that (69a) has the referent of the complex noun phrase interpreted as an ignorant *individual*, but he notes that the Spanish example in (69b) is itself ambiguous between the reading paraphrased by Napoli ('an ignoramus in his capacity as a doctor') and one according to which the referent of the complex noun phrase is, as in (69a), an ignoramus as an individual—but in the way that *all* doctors are ignorant. That is, on this particular interpretation of (69b), there is a presupposition that all doctors are ignorant people. (This presupposition is lacking for (69a).) This reading is paraphrasable as 'He is an ignoramus like any doctor (is)', which carries the same presupposition. It seems to me that this English example has the structure of attributive constructions of the *big for a butterfly* type. Thus, the second reading of Spanish (69b) that Español-Echevarría reports fits in with a characterization of the b-example as an attributive QBNP.

62. Note that, in the text account, the speakers who do *not* use the definite article following *de* in demonstrative QBNPs are the ones for whom the demonstrative *does* have a [+DEF] specification; for Español-Echevarría, by contrast, "In the dialects disallowing definite DP's as second constituents, demonstratives do not have [a definiteness] feature" (1998, 77).

63. One last note is in order before we proceed. Español-Echevarría (1997, 1998) points out that possessed noun phrases are grammatical in second position in Spanish QBNPs (see (ia)); he also tells me (personal communication) that demonstratives can intervene between *de* and the second noun, as in (iib). Español-Echevarría (1997, 1998) presents an interesting argument (based on facts mentioned in note 57) to the effect that *mi hermano* in (ia) is a constituent. He shows that the example in (iia) is ill-formed: the relative clause here can neither be attached high (for that would deliver the illicit INDEF–DEF *imbécil de mi doctor* as the subject of the relative clause; see note 57) nor low (for possessed noun phrases cannot host relative clauses; see (iib)).

(i) a. el imbécil de mi hermano (Spanish)
        the idiot   of my brother
    b. el imbécil de ese doctor
        the idiot   of that doctor

(ii) a. *el   imbécil de mi hermano [que tienes   en casa]
          the idiot   of my brother   that have-2SG at home
     b. *mi hermano [que tienes   en casa]
          my brother   that have-2SG at home

There is no denying, therefore, that *mi hermano* in (ia) is a constituent. But this does not conflict with our conclusion that the postcopular noun phrase of QBNPs is no larger than NumP: though possessed noun phrases distribute like definite

DPs, the possessor itself arguably occupies a position lower than SpecDP (see especially the facts of Hungarian: in *az én könyvem* 'the I book-1SG, i.e., my book', it is plain that the possessor is somewhere in D's complement). Assuming that in Spanish, as in Italian (where things like (ia) are grammatical as well: *quella carogna del tuo dottore* 'that scoundrel of-the your-AGR doctor'; Napoli 1989), the possessor is indeed lower than D (cf. the fact that Italian prenominal possessors inflect like adjectives), the grammaticality of (ia) can be accommodated. The fact that (ib) is likewise well formed is much harder to account for, however. The analysis of Romance QBNPs laid out in the above fails to make sense of (ib). I will not speculate here on how (ib) might be rendered compatible with the text assumptions; it will be useful to first gain a better understanding of the status of Spanish (ib) within the broader context of Romance QBNPs.

64. Thomas Leu (personal communication) tells me that in his variety of Swiss German, such alternations are common as well. What follows are some attested examples from standard German featuring *Schurke* and *Biest* as N_1 and a bare N_2, culled from the Internet. Note, by the way, that the examples in (ii) show very clearly that it is N_2 that determines the gender form of the outer determiner/ demonstrative: *Biest* is neuter, and systematically, even when N_2 is nonneuter, the gender form of the demonstrative in the examples in (ii) is neuter (*dieses*).

(i) a. ein Schurke von Mann (German)
    a   villain   of   man
    www.telekom.at/Content.Node2/de/copy/14/copy14_2.2.pdf

  b. ein Schurke von Fabrikbesitzer
    a   villain   of   factory-owner
    www.itglwf.org/displaydocument.asp?DocType=Press&Index=536&
    Language=DE

  c. ein Schurke von Adler
    a   villain   of   eagle
    www.sagen.at/texte/maerchen/maerchen_irland/elfenmaerchen/
    irrfahrten.html

  d. ein Schurke von Beruf
    a   villain   of   profession
    www.dg-gilde.de/topic,266,125,ae0d21adbb2f35b85983c0dd198bb7de.html

(ii) a. dieses Biest von Schlange (German)
    this   beast of snake
    www.blinde-kuh.de/geschichten/rotschopf.html

  b. dieses Biest von Rechner
    this   beast of computer
    www.andexlinger-berlin.de/aufruesten.htm

  c. dieses Biest von Sekretärin
    this   beast of secretary
    www.latexgeschichten.de/intro.htm

  d. dieses Biest von Song
    this   beast of song
    www.amazon.de/exec/obidos/ASIN/B00006643L/ref=pd_sim_dp_3/

    e. dieses Biest von Frau
       this   beast of   woman
       www.singles.co.at/orgien/9.html

65. Werner Abraham (personal communication); in his 1998 paper, Abraham presents (82) as allowing the same kind of alternation as (81), but he now tells me that, while in (81) omitting *einem* is indeed perfectly free, it is poor in (82).

66. This does not necessarily mean that it must be phonetically overt—see Bennis, Corver, and Den Dikken 1998 for conditions under which the null allomorph of the "spurious" indefinite article is licensed, conditions that are more lenient in English than they are in Dutch (where the "spurious" indefinite article is only ever null when the two constituent noun phrases of the small clause are both plural). The discussion there includes an account of the facts of Swedish, which is interesting in having a specialized morphological incarnation for the plural form of the "spurious" indefinite article: *ena* (distinct from both *en* and *et*, the two gender forms of the garden-variety indefinite article). See Delsing 1993 for further details. He points out that the use of the "spurious" indefinite article in Swedish is characteristic of what he calls "descriptive" (as opposed to "classifying") noun phrases—noun phrases where "the description is the view of the speaker, and hence it has a modal function" (p. 36). This evaluative effect of the use of the "spurious" indefinite article matches the use of this element in QBNPs. Particularly interesting in this context is the fact, to which Bennis, Corver, and Den Dikken 1998, 100, draw special attention, that in a Swedish example like (i), the presence of *ena* expresses that the referents of the subject "*behave like,* or *give the impression of being,* real doctors; they need not be genuine doctors at all" (original italics). The use of *ena* in (i) thus results in a *comparative* predication, with *ena* doing basically the same work that English *like* would do. This is readily compatible with the assumption that *ena* is a "spurious" indefinite article—a realization of the RELATOR head of the small clause of *comparative* QBNPs. (Also see Bennis, Corver, and Den Dikken 1998 and Leu 2003, 2004, for different accounts of the function and distribution of "spurious" indefinite articles in the so-called *was für* and *was*-exclamative constructions in Germanic.)

(i) Lisa och Kalle är ena riktiga doktorer (Swedish)
    Lisa and Kalle are a-PL real   doctors

67. This generalization is not fully airtight: examples of the type in (i) are grammatical. Here, though, the specific collocation of noun and attributive adjective seems almost to function as a compound. Such cases aside, the text generalization holds. See De Swart, Winter, and Zwarts 2005, section 2.3, for discussion of examples such as (i).

(i) hij wil   gehuwd priester worden (Dutch)
    he wants married priest   become
    'He wants to become a married priest.'

68. Aarts (1998, 133) shows that modification of N_2 is possible (albeit generally somewhat dispreferred; recall also note 45) in English QBNPs as well (cf. *a jewel*

of a crescent-shaped island, which alternates with *a crescent-shaped jewel of an island*).

69. I added the qualification "largely" here because, as shown in Bennis, Corver, and Den Dikken 1998, zero allomorphs of the "spurious" article may exist in individual languages (recall note 66). It seems that in French the "spurious" article is systematically null: French never features a definite article between the nominal copula *de* and N$_2$ in its QBNPs (see note 53: *cet imbécile de/*du/*d'un médecin* 'that idiot of (*the/*a) doctor'). What the text discussion does not shed light on is why the "spurious" article in Romance (to the extent that it is physically represented) is a token of the *definite* article while in Germanic it is the *indefinite* article.

70. Bennis, Corver, and Den Dikken (1998, 89) note similar facts from Dutch, reproduced here as (i).

(i) a.   een huis   waar hij een verdieping *t* van heeft gekocht (Dutch)
        a   house where he a   floor   of has bought
    b.   *een huis waar hij een kast   *t* van heeft gekocht
        a   huis where he a   giant (lit., closet) of has bought
   Cf.   hij heeft een kast van een huis   gekocht
        he has a   giant of a   house bought

71. Thanks to Werner Abraham (personal communication) for providing (89). He also notes that, though the use of the dative *-e* on masculine/neuter nouns is archaic, speakers still have intuitions when it comes to its distribution in (i): *-e* is usable in (ia) but certainly not in (ib).

(i) a. ein Schatz von einem Mann(e) (German)
      a   treasure of   a-DAT man(DAT)
   b. ein Schatz   von Mann(*e)
      a   treasure of   man(*DAT)

72. See Corver 2003 for interesting discussion of counterparts of English *you idiot!* in several Germanic varieties featuring possessive/genitive marking on the pronoun (cf. Danish *dit fæ!* 'your fool', noted in Jespersen 1924, 98–99). Casillas Martínez (2001), referring to Suñer 1999, points out that in Latin, QBNPs featuring genitive case instead of dative were apparently found. I have not seen any actual examples of this type, and will refrain from further discussion for lack of details. Worth noting in the context of case is the fact that in Québécois the role of nominal copula can be played by *à*, the dative preposition (cf. *l'imbécile à Jean,* from Noailly–Le Bihan 1984, cited in Casillas Martínez 2001, 4); the more familiar *de* can also be used in Québécois QBNPs, however (see *un imbécile de gendarme* 'an idiot of policeman', cited in Casillas Martínez 2001, 5).

73. In Den Dikken 1995a, I identified the *een* in constructions like (90b) as a constituent of the first noun phrase (severed from it in the course of the syntactic derivation of the construction); the grammaticality of examples like (90c, e, f) (discovered in Bennis, Corver, and Den Dikken 1998), where *een* cannot form a constituent with either of the two nouns, indicates clearly that this approach was mistaken.

74. In (91), "MP" is Aarts's (1998) label, standing for "Modifier Phrase" (an obvious anomaly); its internal constitution is never discussed in his paper, but Aarts does assume explicitly that it patterns like attributive modifiers and, concurrently, finds itself in a position adjoined to the projection of the head noun. As I have shown in the earlier sections of this chapter, there are two types of QBNPs, only one of them being of the attributive type. Aarts's analysis, apart from postulating an out-of-the-ordinary modifier constituent (*jewel of a* in (91)), will thus be ill-equipped to accommodate the differences between the two types of QBNP.

75. See also Milner 1978 as well as Abraham 1998 on *de* as a copula-like element. Azoulay-Vicente (1985, 32) rejects this hypothesis—wrongly, in view of the discussion in this chapter.

76. The Slavic languages would have made for an interesting case study as well, given that the distribution of the copula in clauses is quite intricate. However, Slavic does not seem to have a counterpart to the QBNP. Serbo-Croatian (ia) (an attested example spotted by Charles Braver) its Russian counterpart in (ib) (provided to me by Ora Matushansky) seem to carry the load of (comparative) QBNPs of the English type, but they are structurally quite different—what is the second noun in the English QBNP is an adjective in the Slavic examples (prenominal in Serbo-Croatian, postnominal in Russian). I will not attempt to analyze these cases here. I also have no answer at this time to the question of why Slavic has no QBNPs.

(i) a. onaj ciganski   brabonjak (Serbo-Croatian)
        that gypsy-ADJ.SFX piece.of.shit
    b. eto der'mo tsyganskoe (Russian)
        that shit   gypsy-ADJ.SFX

77. That Hungarian has a third-person singular present-tense form of *lenni* 'be' at all is because in nonverbal predications in which the predicate is a PP, *van* 'is' does show up (cf. *a könyv az asztalon van* 'the book the table-on is', *a hölgynek nagyon szép szeme van* 'the woman-DAT very beautiful eye is—that is, the woman has very beautiful eyes').

78. The discussion to follow draws directly on Shaked 2001—to my knowledge, the first generative study of QBNPs in Hebrew (see also Halevy 2000 and Pereltsvaig 2004). The examples in Shaked's paper are all of the comparative type.

79. The generalization that ensues is that the semantic head of the construction controls agreement. In this regard, Hebrew differs from French. According to Doetjes and Rooryck (2001), in French QBNPs, the gender form of the demonstrative of the complex noun phrase seems to be systematically determined by the first noun in the string (the Dutch facts are less categorical here: see Den Dikken 1995a and Broekhuis, Keizer, and Den Dikken 2003, 572–573, for discussion and exemplification), while external agreement is controlled either by the first noun or by the second, depending on whether we are dealing with a comparative or an attributive QBNP; see note 39.

80. Shaked (2001, 12–13) shows that (101b) does not involve a nominal compound. A particularly clear indication that no compounding is involved comes

from the fact that the second noun in this construction can be independently marked definite, as in *ha-mesiba <u>ha</u>-pitsuts ha-zot*. This also suggests that trying to assimilate (101b) to English *an idiot doctor* (which alternates with *an idiot of a doctor*, though only on its *attributive* interpretation) would be ill-advised.

81. Though not strictly speaking an instance of Predicate Inversion, Hoekstra's (1999) inversion analysis of nominalizations (whereby *the destruction of the city* is derived via leftward movement (to SpecCP on Hoekstra's assumptions) of *destruction*'s maximal projection around *the city*, with concomitant introduction of *of*) is very similar in spirit to the analyses laid out in this chapter. I refer the interested reader to Hoekstra's paper, not making an attempt here to extend the Predicate Inversion analysis to nominalizations.

82. The examples in (104) are based on those in Bennis, Corver, and Den Dikken 1998, 104, which the discussion to follow draws on directly; see also Den Dikken 2003a for relevant discussion. DPRT in (104c), (105c), and (106c) stands for "discourse particle."

83. Note English *kind of sweet*, featuring *of*—arguably, *kind* here serves as an underlying predicate as well, inverting with its adjectival subject. In this context, note as well that *hell* may also team up with adjectives, in things like *hella cool* (where *of* contracts onto *hell*; cf. *kind/sort of > kinda/sorta*). (The *hella A* construction apparently originated in the San Francisco Bay Area in the early 1990s.) What is interesting is that *hella cool* alternates with *cool as hell*, a canonical predication in which *hell* is separated from its subject (the AP of *cool*) by a lexical RELATOR, *as*.

84. Bennis, Corver, and Den Dikken (1998) do not discuss the analysis of indefinite *wat*+NP constructions; I present an account here to complete our coverage of the paradigm in (105).

85. Unless one were willing to base-generate this token of "spurious" *een* in D—but that would make it difficult to understand its obliviousness to the number properties of the complex noun phrase, which I take to disqualify such an approach to "spurious" *een* in *wat*-exclamatives.

86. Compare this to English topicalization versus *wh*-fronting: the latter triggers subject-aux inversion while the former, which arguably targets a structurally lower position (SpecTopP), does not.

87. For interesting recent discussion of the *wat voor*–construction, I refer the reader to Leu 2003, 2004, an approach that shares with the one proposed in Bennis, Corver, and Den Dikken 1998 the idea that *wat* is underlyingly a small-clause predicate. In Leu 2004, the "spurious" indefinite article in *wat voor*-constructions is argued to be a *real*, well-behaved [−PLURAL] indefinite article belonging to an abstract singular noun corresponding to something like *sort* or *kind* (see Dutch *wat voor een soort bessen* 'what for a sort berries'). He presents some suggestive evidence in favor of an approach of this sort (which, if correct, would suggest that the indefinite article in *wat voor*–constructions is different from the "spurious" *een* found in QBNPs, to which Leu's approach does not seem applicable). Leu (2003) focuses primarily on cases of *wat voor* split, where

wat 'runs away from home' (to use Szabolcsi's 1983 winged expression). I will not address *wat voor* split here at all, since it does not bear in any direct way on the issues under discussion in this book.

88. An alternative way of thinking about this would be to take *voor* to be the suppletive spell-out of the combination of the [+WH] D-head *and* the LINKER *van*; such an approach would presumably commit one to the assumption that the LINKER raises overtly up to D in the course of the derivation of *wat voor*–constructions.

89. The idea, with respect to (112), is that subject clitic inversion is triggered only by *wh*-constituents; only in (112a/a′) can the *wh*-ness of the operator manifest itself on the outside of the complex noun phrase and trigger inversion. Apparently, the *wh*-word does not *have to* trigger inversion: (112a) is grammatical alongside (112a′).

90. The discussion in this section is based on Den Dikken and Singhapreecha 2004.

91. See Den Dikken and Singhapreecha 2004 for evidence showing that the same interpretive effects manifest themselves in Thai (115).

92. Any information structure representation for (117b) that is different from the one circumscribed in the main text involves a different analysis of the construction, one in which we are *not* in fact dealing with an inverse copular sentence but with a construction in which *my best friend* is taken to be an underlying *subject*; such a reading is hard to get for the particular example in (117b), but much more readily available for *My best friend is the president of the United States*, which is genuinely ambiguous.

93. Throughout, raising of the RELATOR up to F (the LINKER head) is suppressed in the structures, in an attempt to keep them manageable. Note that the numeral *săam* 'three' is introduced outside the small clause; the subject of RP is a bare NP. This may generally be the case in classifier languages.

94. Note that Den Dikken and Singhapreecha's (2004) somewhat simplified representations employ raising of the small-clause subject NP to SpecClf1P rather than remnant-RP movement. The latter approach is more consonant with the assumptions laid out in the foregoing (especially with the conclusion, reached in chapter 4, that the subject of an inverted predicate is ineligible for movement).

95. Peculiarly, Matushansky (2002) faults the small-clause approach to QBNPs for failing to account for recursion. But of course recursion poses no problems whatsoever: the constituent formed on the first cycle (*idiot of a doctor* in (127a)) can function as the subject of another predication (here with *asshole* as the predicate), just as in *That idiot of a doctor is an asshole*.

96. Español-Echevarría (1997), Casillas Martínez (2001), and especially Longenecker (2002) point out that there are significant and systematic differences between the *N de(l) N* and *A de(l) N* constructions in Spanish. An immediately eye-catching one is that, while the former allows indefinite articles and demonstratives at its left edge, the *A de(l) N* construction does not (see (i)). I will not

address the roots of these differences here, referring the reader to the works just mentioned for discussion.

(i) a. un imbécil/*listo de doctor (Spanish)
         an idiot/smart   of doctor
     b. ese imbécil/*listo de doctor
         that idiot/smart   of doctor

97. I refer the reader to Borroff 2000 and Troseth 2004 for discussion of the alternation in (131); both note that this kind of inversion is licensed outside *wh*-contexts as well (see *he is not very good (of) a student*), and analyze the distribution of these constructions in detail. It is worth noting that (131) cannot be pluralized: **how big (of) problems* is ungrammatical, with or without *of*. That (131b) does not pluralize presumably has precisely the same root as the absence of a plural counterpart to QBNPs. Ultimately for the same reason, but via a slightly different route, **how big problems* can be excluded as well—see Kayne 2002b for discussion, based directly on Bennis, Corver, and Den Dikken 1998. That exclamative *What (?)?(big) problems!* is good is possibly due to the fact that *what* may raise to the head position that would otherwise have to be filled by the article (see Kayne 2002b, note 15, for this suggestion).

98. See also Rothstein 1983, 50, on dative PPs as predicates. Coopmans (1989, 739) presents examples similar to (139), which he notes are perhaps not brilliant but in any event no worse than the corresponding cases of PP-topicalization. Baker (1996, section 9.1.1) analyzes P as a *monadic* category, denying that P assigns a θ-role to its subject. This conclusion may stand if predication is divorced from external θ-role assignment. PPs should definitely be allowed to serve as predicates.

99. I refer the interested reader to Den Dikken 1999 for detailed discussion, primarily based on Hungarian facts. There I also draw the English "Saxon genitive" construction (*Brian's book*) into the picture, arguing that *'s* is an instantiation of the nominal copula (see Den Dikken 1995a for the original idea). Bernstein and Tortora (2005) have confronted this approach to "Saxon genitives" with some nontrivial questions that should lead one to rethink parts of the orginal analysis. I will leave the specifics of the analysis of the myriad surface manifestations of possessive constructions for a future occasion.

100. The alternative head-raising analysis (see Vergnaud 1974, revived by Kayne 1994) structurally reflects the predicativity of relative clauses only if A′-movement of the "head" of the relativized noun phrase into SpecCP is to result in predication. Kayne adopts the raising analysis to bring relativized noun phrases in line with the antisymmetric approach to syntactic structure. The analysis of relative-clause constructions to be proposed in what follows (see Den Dikken and Singhapreecha 2004, which is the origin of this account) is fully compatible with antisymmetry as well, and has the additional advantage of assimilating relativized noun phrases to other cases of DP-internal predication.

101. The well-known fact that English-type relative clauses cannot be used in clausal predications (cf. **Chocolates is that Imogen loves*) might potentially

suggest that the predicate-specifier structure, which represents *attributive* modification, is right for such relative clauses. However, the fact that replacing the null operator with an overt *wh*-operator procures a grammatical output (*Chocolates is what Imogen loves*—a (Type B) pseudocleft construction) may indicate that the predicate-complement structure *is* available for English-type relative clauses, and that the relative clause's syntactic environment influences the (null/overt) realization of the operator. This requires further study.

102. Simpson observes that quantifiers may also *precede* relative clauses, so (ia, b) are grammatical alongside (149a, b). Representation (i) is presumably derived from (151a, b) via fronting of the numeral/quantifier plus classifier complex to a position above the relative clause.

(i) a. liang-ben [wo zuotian   mai] de shu (Mandarin)
     two-CLF   I   yesterday buy DE book
   b. mei-ben   [wo zuotian   mai] de shu
     every-CLF I   yesterday buy DE book

103. See Den Dikken 2003b, sections 4.3 and 4.5, for relevant discussion supporting this conclusion, based on the facts of Rotuman noun-phrase internal predication, which shows an array of possibilities quite similar to that seen in Mandarin (144).

104. If, as (152) depicts, the head noun is the underlying *predicate* in so-called noun-complement clause constructions, then Mandarin (144e) is the only member of the paradigm in (142) in which Predicate Inversion (giving rise to the LINKER *de*) is followed by remnant movement of the small clause to reinstate the underlying word order. An alternative approach would take the CP to be the predicate of the small clause, with the head noun's projection as its subject. This would assimilate so-called noun-complement clause constructions directly to relative-clause constructions. But such an assimilation is less than straightforward: it is not at all obvious how so-called noun-complement clauses would qualify as predicates. Moreover, switching the major constituents of the small clause in (152a) around would lose an account of the obligatoriness of *to be* in (153a). I will therefore continue to assume (152a) (agreeing on this point with Napoli 1989, 250, who, incidentally, applies this analysis only to *the fact that S*, not to *the idea/proof that S*, for reasons that remain unarticulated (see p. 249)), while noting that it complicates the derivation of Mandarin (144e).

105. Simpson's own analysis, which takes *de* to be a D-head, only manages to capture the link between *de* and predication via a detour, by saying that all constructions involving *de* are basically relative-clause constructions, with *de* in D and the IP of the relative clause raised to SpecDP, as depicted in (i).

(i) a. [$_{\text{IP}}$ *wo mai shu*] (Mandarin)
     → introducing C (null); raising of *shu* to SpecCP →
   b. [$_{\text{CP}}$ *shu*$_i$ [C [$_{\text{IP}}$ *wo mai t$_i$*]]]
     → introducing D (=*de*); raising of IP to SpecDP →
   c. [$_{\text{DP}}$ [$_{\text{IP}}$ *wo mai t$_i$*]$_j$ [*de* [$_{\text{CP}}$ *shu*$_i$ [C *t$_j$*]]]]

References

Aarts, Bas. 1992. *Small Clauses in English: The Nonverbal Types*. Berlin: Mouton de Gruyter.

Aarts, Bas. 1998. Binominal noun phrases in English. *Transactions of the Philological Society* 96, 117–158.

Abney, Stephen. 1987. *The English Noun Phrase in its Sentential Aspect*. Unpublished doctoral dissertation, MIT.

Abraham, Werner. 1998. *ein Schatz von einem Kind*: zur Prädikatsyntax binominaler Nominalkonstituenten. *Deutsche Sprache: Zeitschrift für Theorie, Praxis, Dokumentation* 26, 337–347.

Ackrill, John Lloyd, ed. and trans. 1963. *Aristotle: Categories and De Interpretatione*. Oxford: Clarendon Press.

Adger, David, and Gillian Ramchand. 2003. Predication and equation. *Linguistic Inquiry* 34, 325–359.

Aissen, Judith. 1975. Presentational-*there* insertion: A cyclic root transformation. In R. E. Grossman, L. J. San, and T. J. Vance, eds., *Papers from the Eleventh Regional Meeting of the Chicago Linguistic Society*, 1–14. Chicago: Chicago Linguistic Society.

Akmajian, Adrian. 1979. *Aspects of the Grammar of Focus in English*. New York: Garland.

Alexiadou, Artemis, and Elena Anagnostopoulou. 1998. Parametrizing AGR: Word order, V-movement and EPP-checking. *Natural Language and Linguistic Theory* 18, 491–539.

Andrews, Avery. 1983. A note on the constituent structure of modifiers. *Linguistic Inquiry* 14, 695–697.

Aoun, Youssef, and Yen-Hui Audrey Li. 1989. Scope and constituency. *Linguistic Inquiry* 20, 141–172.

Aristotle. 1963. *Categories and De Interpretatione*. Ed. and trans. John Lloyd Ackrill. Oxford: Clarendon Press.

Arnauld, Antoine, and Claude Lancelot. 1660. *Grammaire générale et raisonnée*. Port Royal.

Austin, F. 1980. "A crescent-shaped jewel of an island": Appositive nouns in phrases separated by *of*. *English Studies* 61, 357–366.

Azoulay-Vicente, Avigail. 1985. *Les tours comportant l'expression* de + *adjectif*. Geneva: Librairie Droz.

Bailyn, John. 2004. Overt predicators. *Journal of Slavic Linguistics* 9, 1–2.

Bailyn, John, and Ed Rubin. 1991. The unification of instrumental case assignment in Russian. In Almeida Jacqueline Toribio and Wayne Harbert, eds., *Cornell Working Papers in Linguistics* 9, 99–126. Ithaca, NY: Cornell University.

Baker, Mark. 1988. *Incorporation*. Chicago: University of Chicago Press.

Baker, Mark. 1996. *The Polysynthesis Parameter*. Oxford: Oxford University Press.

Baker, Mark, and Chris Collins. 2003. Linkers and verb phrase structure. Unpublished manuscript, Rutgers University and Cornell University.

Baker, Mark, Kyle Johnson, and Ian Roberts. 1989. Passive arguments raised. *Linguistic Inquiry* 20, 219–251.

Baltin, Mark. 1985. *Toward a theory of movement rules*. New York: Garland.

Baltin, Mark. 1987. Do antecedent-contained deletions exist? *Linguistic Inquiry* 18, 579–595.

Barbiers, Sjef. 1995. *The Syntax of Interpretation*. Unpublished doctoral dissertation, University of Leiden/HIL.

Belletti, Adriana. 1988. The Case of unaccusatives. *Linguistic Inquiry* 19, 1–34.

Bennis, Hans. 1995. The meaning of structure: The *wat voor* construction revisited. In Marcel den Dikken and Kees Hengeveld, eds., *Linguistics in the Netherlands 1995*. Amsterdam: John Benjamins.

Bennis, Hans, Norbert Corver, and Marcel den Dikken. 1998. Predication in nominal phrases. *Journal of Comparative Germanic Linguistics* 1, 85–117.

Benveniste, Émile. 1966. *Problèmes de linguistique générale*. Paris: Gallimard.

Berg, Thomas. 1998. The resolution of number conflicts in English and German agreement patterns. *Linguistics* 36, 41–70.

Bernstein, J. 1997. Demonstratives and reinforcers in Romance and Germanic languages. *Lingua* 102, 87–113.

Bernstein, Judy, and Christina Tortora. 2005. Two types of possessive forms in English. *Lingua* 115, 1221–1242.

Birner, Betty. 1994. Information status and word order: An analysis of English inversion. *Language* 70, 223–259.

Blom, Alied, and Saskia Daalder. 1977. *Syntaktische theorie en taalbeschrijving*. Muiderberg: Coutinho.

Bobaljik, Jonathan. 1995. *Morphosyntax: The Syntax of Verbal Inflection*. Unpublished doctoral dissertation, MIT.

Boeckx, Cedric, and Kleanthes Grohmann. 2004. Barriers and phases: Forward to the past? Paper presented at Tools in Linguistic Theory (TiLT), Budapest,

May 16–18, 2004; unpublished manuscript, Harvard University and University of Cyprus.

Bolinger, Dwight. 1972a. *Degree Words*. The Hague: Mouton.

Bolinger, Dwight. 1972b. A look at equations and cleft sentences. In Evelyn Scherabon Firchow, Kaaren Grimstad, Nils Hasselmo, and Wayne O'Neill, eds., *Studies for Einar Haugen*, 96–114. The Hague: Mouton.

Bonet, Eulalia. 1989. Postverbal subjects in Catalan. Paper presented at the annual meeting of the Canadian Linguistic Association, Université de Laval, Québec City.

Borer, Hagit. 1984. *Parametric syntax*. Dordrecht: Foris.

Borroff, Marianne Law. 2000. Degree phrase inversion in the scope of negation. Unpublished manuscript, SUNY Stony Brook.

Bowers, John. 1991. The syntax and semantics of nominals. In *Cornell Working Papers in Linguistics* 10, 1–30. Ithaca, NY: Cornell University.

Bowers, John. 1993. The syntax of predication. *Linguistic Inquiry* 24, 591–656.

Branigan, Philip. 1992. *Subjects and Complementizers*. Unpublished doctoral dissertation, MIT.

Bresnan, Joan. 1977. Variables in the theory of transformations. In Peter Culicover, Thomas Wasow, and Adrian Akmajian, eds., *Formal Syntax*, 157–196. New York: Academic Press.

Bresnan, Joan. 1990. Levels of representation in locative inversion: A comparison of English and Chicheŵa. Unpublished manuscript, Stanford University and Xerox PARC.

Bresnan, Joan. 1994. Locative inversion and the architecture of Universal Grammar. *Language* 70, 72–131.

Bresnan, Joan, and Jonni Kanerva. 1989. Locative inversion in Chicheŵa: A case study of factorization in grammar. *Linguistic Inquiry* 20, 1–50.

Bresnan, Joan, and Tatiana Nikitina. 2003. On the gradience of the dative alternation. Unpublished manuscript, Stanford University. http://www-lfg.stanford.edu/bresnan/new-dative.pdf.

Broekhuis, Hans, Evelien Keizer, and Marcel den Dikken. 2003. Nouns and noun phrases. *Modern Grammar of Dutch Occasional Papers* 4. Tilburg University.

Browning, Marguerite. 1987. *Null Operator Constructions*. Unpublished doctoral dissertation, MIT.

Bruening, Benjamin. 2001. QR obeys Superiority: Frozen scope and ACD. *Linguistic Inquiry* 32, 233–273.

Burzio, Luigi. 1986. *Italian Syntax*. Dordrecht: Reidel.

Campbell, Richard. 1997. Specificity operators in SpecDP. *Studia Linguistica* 50, 161–188.

Cardinaletti, Anna, and Maria-Teresa Guasti. 1992. Epistemic small clauses and null subjects. Paper presented at ESCOL 1991.

Carlson, Greg, and Tom Roeper. 1980. Morphology and subcategorization: Case and the unmarked complex verb. In Teun Hoekstra, Harry van der Hulst, and Michael Moortgat, eds., *Lexical grammar*, 123–164. Dordrecht: Foris.

Carnie, Andrew. 1995. *Non-verbal Predication and Head Movement*. Unpublished doctoral dissertation, MIT.

Carrier, Jill, and Janet Randall. 1992. The argument structure and syntactic structure of resultatives. *Linguistic Inquiry* 23, 173–234.

Casillas Martínez, Luis. 2001. A surface-based account of agreement in Spanish and French N_1/A de N_2 affective constructions. Unpublished manuscript, Stanford University.

Caspel, P. van. 1970. Een schat van een (niet meer zo jong) kind. *De Nieuwe Taalgids* 63, 280–287.

Cheng, Lisa. 1986. *de* in Mandarin. *Canadian Journal of Linguistics* 31, 313–399.

Cheng, Lisa. 1997a. Marking modification in Cantonese and Mandarin. Unpublished manuscript, UCI and HIL/Leiden.

Cheng, Lisa. 1997b. On possession in Cantonese, Mandarin and Taiwanese. Paper presented at ICCL 6, University of Leiden.

Chomsky, Noam. [1955] 1975. *The Logical Structure of Linguistic Theory*. New York: Plenum Press.

Chomsky, Noam. 1981. *Lectures on Government and Binding*. Dordrecht: Foris.

Chomsky, Noam. 1985. *Knowlege of Language: Its Nature, Origin, and Use*. New York: Praeger.

Chomsky, Noam. 1986. *Barriers*. Cambridge, MA: MIT Press.

Chomsky, Noam. 1995. *The Minimalist Program*. Cambridge, MA: MIT Press.

Chomsky, Noam. 2000. Minimalist inquiries: The framework. In Roger Martin, David Michaels, and Juan Uriagereka, eds., *Step by Step: Essays on Minimalist Syntax in Honor of Howard Lasnik*, 89–115. Cambridge, MA: MIT Press.

Chomsky, Noam. 2001. Derivation by phase. In Michael Kenstowicz, ed., *Ken Hale: A Life in Language*, 1–52. Cambridge, MA: MIT Press.

Churchward, C. Maxwell. 1940. *Rotuman Grammar and Dictionary*. Sydney: Methodist Church of Australia. (Reissued in 1978 by AMS Press, New York.)

Chvany, C. 1975. *On the Syntax of BE-Sentences in Russian*. Cambridge, MA: Slavic Publishers.

Cinque, Guglielmo. 1990. *Types of A'-Dependencies*. Cambridge, MA: MIT Press.

Cinque, Guglielmo. 1999. *Adverbs and Functional Heads*. Oxford: Oxford University Press.

Clifton, E. 1969. The English pseudo-cleft. Unpublished manuscript.

Collins, Chris. 1997. *Local Economy*. Cambridge, MA: MIT Press.

Collins, Chris. 2003. The internal structure of vP in Juǀ'hoan and ǂHoan. *Studia Linguistica* 57, 1–25.

Coopmans, Peter. 1989. Where stylistic and syntactic processes meet: Locative inversion in English. *Language* 65, 728–751.

Corver, Norbert. 2003. On the syntax of *You(r) idiot!* Unpublished manuscript, Utrecht University.

Culicover, Peter. 1993. Evidence against ECP accounts of the *that-t* effect. *Linguistic Inquiry* 24, 557–561.

Culicover, Peter, and Robert Levine. 2001. Stylistic inversion and the *that-t* effect: A reconsideration. *Natural Language and Linguistic Theory* 19, 283–310.

Curme, G. O. 1931. *A Grammar of the English Language*, Vol. 3: *Syntax*. Boston: Heath.

Dalgish, Gerard. 1976. *The Morphophonemics of the Olutsootso Dialect of (Olu)Luyia*. Unpublished doctoral dissertation, University of Illinois at Urbana-Champaign.

Dalgish, Gerard. 2002. Bantu locatives and grammatical relations. Paper presented at the CUNY Syntax Supper Special Mini-Workshop on Locative Inversion, CUNY Graduate Center, May 14, 2002.

Davidson, Donald. 1975. The logical form of action sentences. In Donald Davidson and Gilbert Harman, eds., *The Logic of Grammar*, 235–245. Encino, CA: Dickenson.

Déchaine, Rose-Marie. 1993. *Predicates across Categories: Towards a Category-Neutral Syntax*. Unpublished doctoral dissertation, University of Massachusetts, Amherst.

Declerck, Renaat. 1988. *Studies on Copular Sentences, Clefts and Pseudoclefts*. Dordrecht: Foris/Leuven: Leuven University Press.

Delsing, Lars-Olof. 1993. *The Internal Structure of Noun Phrases in the Scandinavian Languages*. Unpublished doctoral dissertation, University of Lund.

Dik, Simon. 1983. Auxiliary and copula *be* in a Functional Grammar of English. In F. Heny and B. Richards, eds., *Linguistic Categories: Auxiliaries and Related Puzzles*, vol. 2, 121–143. Dordrecht: Reidel.

Dikken, Marcel den. 1987. Secundaire predicatie en de analyse van small clauses. *GLOT* 10, 1–28.

Dikken, Marcel den. 1991. Particles and the dative alternation. In John van Lit, René Mulder, and Rint Sybesma, eds., *Proceedings of the Second Leiden Conference for Junior Linguists*, 71–86. Leiden: University of Leiden.

Dikken, Marcel den. 1994. Predicate Inversion and minimality. In Reineke Bok-Bennema and Crit Cremers, eds., *Linguistics in the Netherlands 1994*, 1–12. Amsterdam: John Benjamins.

Dikken, Marcel den. 1995a. Copulas. Paper presented at GLOW Tromsø; unpublished manuscript, Vrije Universiteit Amsterdam/HIL.

Dikken, Marcel den. 1995b. Extraposition as intraposition, and the syntax of English tag questions. Unpublished manuscript, Vrije Universiteit Amsterdam/HIL.

Dikken, Marcel den. 1995c. *Particles: On the Syntax of Verb-Particle, Triadic and Causative Constructions*. Oxford: Oxford University Press.

Dikken, Marcel den. 1996. How external is the external argument? Unpublished manuscript, Vrije Universiteit Amsterdam/HIL.

Dikken, Marcel den. 1998a. Appraising *The Raising of Predicates*. *Linguistische Berichte* 174, 246–263.

Dikken, Marcel den. 1998b. Predicate Inversion in DP. In A. Alexiadou and C. Wilder, eds., *Possessors, Predicates and Movement in the Determiner Phrase*, 177–214. Amsterdam: John Benjamins.

Dikken, Marcel den. 1999. On the structural representation of possession and agreement: The case of (anti-)agreement in Hungarian possessed nominal phrases. In I. Kenesei, ed., *Crossing boundaries: Theoretical advances in Central and Eastern European languages*, 137–178. Amsterdam: John Benjamins.

Dikken, Marcel den. 2002. "Pluringulars," pronouns and quirky agreement. *The Linguistic Review* 18, 19–41.

Dikken, Marcel den. 2003a. On the morphosyntax of *wh*-movement. In Cédric Boeckx and Kleanthes Grohmann, eds., *Multiple Wh-Fronting*. Amsterdam: John Benjamins.

Dikken, Marcel den. 2003b. *The Syntax of the Noun Phrase in Rotuman*. Munich: LINCOM Europa Academic Publishers.

Dikken, Marcel den. 2005. Specificational copular sentences and pseudoclefts. In Martin Everaert and Henk van Riemsdijk, eds., *The Blackwell Companion to Syntax (Syncom)*. Oxford: Blackwell.

Dikken, Marcel den, and Anikó Lipták. 1997. *Csoda egy nyelv*—Nominal-internal predication in Hungarian. In Jane Coerts and Helen de Hoop, eds., *Linguistics in the Netherlands 1997*, 61–72. Amsterdam: John Benjamins.

Dikken, Marcel den, and Ana Longenecker. 2004. Relating the predicate to its subject. Unpublished manuscript, CUNY Graduate Center; abstract in *GLOW Newsletter* 52, 36–37.

Dikken, Marcel den, André Meinunger, and Chris Wilder. 2000. Pseudoclefts and ellipsis. *Studia Linguistica* 54, 41–89.

Dikken, Marcel den, and Alma Næss. 1993. Case dependencies: The case of Predicate Inversion. *The Linguistic Review* 10, 303–336.

Dikken, Marcel den, and Pornsiri Singhapreecha. 2004. Complex noun phrases and linkers. *Syntax* 7, 1–54.

Dixon, Bob. 1994. *Ergativity*. Cambridge: Cambridge University Press.

Doetjes, Jenny, and Johan Rooryck. 2001. Generalizing over quantitative and qualitative constructions. Unpublished manuscript, University of Leiden.

Doherty, Cathal. 1996. Clausal structure and the Modern Irish copula. *Natural Language and Linguistic Theory* 14, 1–46.

Doron, Edit. 1983. *Verbless Predicates in Hebrew*. Unpublished doctoral dissertation, University of Texas at Austin.

É. Kiss, Katalin. 1987. *Configurationality in Hungarian*. Budapest: Akadémiai Kiadó/Dordrecht: Reidel.

É. Kiss, Katalin. 1994. Genericity, predication and focus. In Zoltán Bánréti, ed., *Papers in the Theory of Grammar*. Budapest: Hungarian Academy of Sciences.

É. Kiss, Katalin, ed. 1995. *Discourse Configurational Languages*. Oxford: Oxford University Press.

É. Kiss, Katalin. 2002. *The Syntax of Hungarian*. Cambridge: Cambridge University Press.

Elbourne, Paul. 1999. Some correlations between semantic plurality and quantifier scope. In *NELS 29 Proceedings*. Amherst, MA: GLSA.

Emonds, Joseph. 1976. *A Transformational Approach to English Syntax*. New York: Academic Press.

Emonds, Joseph. 1985. *A Unified Theory of Syntactic Categories*. Dordrecht: Foris.

Eskenázi, A. 1967. Quelques remarques sur le type *ce fripon de valet* et sur certaines fonctions syntaxiques de la préposition *de*. *Le français moderne* 35, 184–200.

Español-Echevarría, Manuel. 1997. Definiteness patterns in *A/N of a N* constructions and DP-internal XP movement. In *Proceedings of the 8th Student Conference in Linguistics*, 145–169. MIT Working Papers in Linguistics 31. Cambridge, MA: MIT Department of Linguistics and Philosophy.

Español-Echevarría, Manuel. 1998. *N/A of a N* DP's: Predicate raising and subject licensing. In Armin Schwegler, Bernard Tranel, and Myriam Uribe-Etxebarria, eds., *Romance Linguistics: Theoretical Perspectives*, 67–80. Amsterdam: John Benjamins.

Everaert, Martin. 1992. Nogmaals: *Een schat van een kind*. In H. Bennis and J. W. de Vries, eds., *De binnenbouw van het Nederlands: Een bundel artikelen voor Piet Paardekooper*, 45–54. Dordrecht: ICG Printing.

Ferrazzano, Lisa Reisig. 2002. *Ci*. Paper presented at the CUNY Syntax Supper; unpublished manuscript, CUNY Graduate Center.

Fiengo, Robert. 2002. Talking, topics, types, and tokens, with some thoughts about anaphora. Unpublished manuscript, CUNY Graduate Center/Queens College.

Fiengo, Robert, and Robert May. 1994. *Indices and Identity*. Cambridge, MA: MIT Press.

Franks, Steven, and Asya Pereltsvaig. 2004. Functional categories in the nominal domain. In Olga Arnaudova, Wayles Browne, Maria Luisa Rivero, and Danijela Stojanovic, eds., *Proceedings of FASL 12*, 109–128. Ann Arbor: Michigan Slavic Publications.

Freeze, Ray. 1992. Existentials and other locatives. *Language* 68, 553–595.

Frege, Gottlob. 1879. *Begriffsschrift. Eine der arithmetischen nachgebildete Formelsprache des reinen Denkens*. Halle a. S.: Verlag von Louis Nebert. (Translated as *Concept Script: A Formal Language of Pure Thought Modelled upon that of Arithmetic*, by S. Bauer-Mengelberg, in Jean van Heijenoort, ed., *From Frege to Gödel: A Source Book in Mathematical Logic*, 1879–1931, Cambridge, MA: Harvard University Press, 1967.)

Friedeman, Marc-Ariel. 1992. On the D-structure position of subjects in French. In Sjef Barbiers, Marcel den Dikken, and Claartje Levelt, eds., *Proceedings of the Third Leiden Conference for Junior Linguists*, 155–168. Leiden: University of Leiden.

Fukui, Naoki, and Margaret Speas. 1986. Specifiers and projection. *MIT Working Papers in Linguistics* 8, 128–172.

Gaatone, David. 1988. Cette coquine de construction: Remarques sur les trois structures affectives du français. *Travaux de linguistique (Gand)* 17, 159–176.

Geist, Ljudmila. 1999. Russisch *byt'* ('sein') als funktionale und/oder lexikalische Kategorie. *ZAS Papers in Linguistics* 14, 1–39.

Gérard, Josselyne. 1978. Mon ostie de ... *Cahiers de linguistique* 8.

Giorgi, Alessandra, and Giuseppe Longobardi. 1991. *The Syntax of Noun Phrases: Configuration, Parameters and Empty Categories*. Cambridge: Cambridge University Press.

Giusti, G. 1997. The categorial status of determiners. In L. Haegeman, ed., *The New Comparative Syntax*. London: Longman.

Givón, Talmy. 1973. Opacity and reference in language: An inquiry into the roles of modalities. In J. P. Kimball, ed., *Syntax and Semantics 2*. New York: Seminar Press.

Groat, Erich, and John O'Neil. 1996. Spell-out at the LF interface. In Höskuldur Thráinsson, Samuel D. Epstein, C. Jan-Wouter Zwart, and Werner Abraham, eds., *Minimal Ideas*. Amsterdam: John Benjamins.

Grohmann, Kleanthes. 2003. *Prolific Domains: On the Anti-locality of Movement Dependencies*. Amsterdam: John Benjamins.

Groot, Albert Willem de. 1949. *Structurele syntaxis*. Den Haag: Servire.

Guasti, Maria-Teresa. 1993. *Causative and Perception Verbs*. Turin: Rosenberg & Sellier.

Guéron, Jacqueline. 1980. The syntax and semantics of PP-extraposition. *Linguistic Inquiry* 11, 637–678.

Guéron, Jacqueline. 1990. Particles, prepositions, and verbs. In Joan Mascaró and Marina Nespor, eds., *Grammar in Progress*, 153–166. Dordrecht: Foris.

Guéron, Jacqueline. 1992. Types syntaxiques et types sémantiques: La phrase copulative comme *palimpseste*. *Revue québécoise de linguistique* 22, 77–115.

Guéron, Jacqueline. 1994. Beyond predication: The inverse copula construction in English. In Guglielmo Cinque, Jan Koster, Jean-Yves Pollock, Luigi Rizzi, and

Raffaella Zanuttini, eds., *Paths towards Universal Grammar*. Washington, DC: Georgetown University Press.

Guéron, Jacqueline. 2001. Review of Alain Rouveret, ed., *Être et avoir: Syntaxe, sémantique, typologie*, Presses Universitaires de Vincennes (1998). *Lingua* 111, 131–155.

Guéron, Jacqueline. 2003. On tense and aspect. Unpublished manuscript, Université de Paris III–Sorbonne Nouvelle.

Guéron, Jacqueline, and Teun Hoekstra. 1993. The temporal interpretation of predication. In Anna Cardinaletti and Maria-Teresa Guasti, eds., *Small Clauses*, 77–108. *Syntax and Semantics* 28. New York: Academic Press.

Hale, Kenneth, and Samuel Jay Keyser. 1993. On argument structure and the lexical expression of syntactic relations. In Kenneth Hale and Samuel Jay Keyser, eds., *The View from Building 20*, 53–104. Cambridge, MA: MIT Press.

Halevy, Rivka. 2000. Developments in the status and functioning of the "separated construct" in contemporary Hebrew. *Leshonenu* 63, 61–80. (In Hebrew.)

Halliday, M. A. K. 1967. Notes on transitivity and theme in English, Part 2. *Journal of Linguistics* 3, 199–244.

Halliday, M. A. K. 1968. Notes on transitivity and theme in English, Part 3. *Journal of Linguistics* 4, 179–215.

Harris, Roy, and Talbot Taylor. 1997. *Landmarks of Linguistic Thought I: The Western Tradition from Socrates to Saussure*. 2nd ed. London: Routledge.

Heggie, Lorie. 1988. *The Syntax of Copular Structures*. Unpublished doctoral dissertation, University of Southern California.

Heim, Irene, and Angelika Kratzer. 1998. *Semantics in Generative Grammar*. Oxford: Blackwell.

Hertog, Cornelis Herman den. 1903. *Nederlandse spraakkunst*. (3rd ed., introduced and edited by H. Hulshoff, 1972–1973.) Amsterdam.

Hetzron, Robert. 1971. Presentative function and presentative movement. *Studies in African Linguistics*, supplement 2, 79–105.

Heycock, Caroline. 1991. *Layers of Predication: The Non-lexical Syntax of Clauses*. Doctoral dissertation, University of Pennsylvania. (Published version: New York: Garland, 1994.)

Heycock, Caroline. 1994. The internal structure of small clauses. *Proceedings of NELS 25*, 223–238. Amherst, MA: GLSA.

Heycock, Caroline. 1995. Asymmetries in reconstruction. *Linguistic Inquiry* 26, 547–570.

Heycock, Caroline. 1998a. Is this the solution or is the solution this? Review of *The Raising of Predicates* by Andrea Moro. *GLOT International* 3(4), 16–19.

Heycock, Caroline. 1998b. Predication and identity: A moving target. Unpublished manuscript, University of Edinburgh.

Heycock, Caroline, and Anthony Kroch. 1999. Pseudocleft connectedness: Implications for the LF interface level. *Linguistic Inquiry* 30, 365–397.

Higginbotham, James. 1985. On semantics. *Linguistic Inquiry* 16, 547–593.

Higginbotham, James. 1987. Indefiniteness and predication. In E. Reuland and A. ter Meulen, eds., *The Representation of (In)definiteness*, 43–70. Cambridge, MA: MIT Press.

Higgins, Roger. 1979. *The Pseudo-Cleft Construction in English*. New York: Garland.

Hoekstra, Teun. 1988. Small clause results. *Lingua* 74, 101–139.

Hoekstra, Teun. 1996. The active-passive configuration. In Anna Maria di Sciullo, ed., *Configurations: Essays on Structure and Interpretation*, 41–51. Somerville, MA: Cascadilla Press.

Hoekstra, Teun. 1999. Parallels between nominal and verbal projections. In David Adger, Susan Pintzuk, Bernadette Plunkett, and George Tsoulas, eds., *Specifiers: Minimalist Approaches*, 163–187. Oxford: Oxford University Press.

Hoekstra, Teun, Harry van der Hulst, and Frans van der Putten. 1988. Struktuurparadoxen bestaan niet. *Spektator* 17, 300–316. (English version in Teun Hoekstra, *Arguments and Structure: Studies on the Architecture of the Sentence*, 219–240. Berlin: Mouton de Gruyter, 2004.)

Hoekstra, Teun, and René Mulder. 1990. Unergatives as copular verbs: Locational and existential predication. *The Linguistic Review* 7, 1–79.

Hornstein, Norbert. 1994. An argument for minimalism: The case of antecedent-contained deletion. *Linguistic Inquiry* 25, 455–480.

Hornstein, Norbert. 1995. *Logical Form*. Oxford: Blackwell.

Hornstein, Norbert, and David Lightfoot. 1987. Predication and PRO. *Language* 63, 23–52.

Horvath, Julia. 2000. Interfaces vs. the computational system in the syntax of focus. In Hans Bennis, Martin Everaert, and Eric Reuland, eds., *Interface Strategies*. Amsterdam: Koninklijke Nederlandse Akademie van Wetenschappen.

Huang, C.-T. James. 1993. Reconstruction and the structure of VP: Some theoretical consequences. *Linguistic Inquiry* 24, 103–138.

Huddleston, Rodney. 1971. *The Sentence in Written English*. Cambridge: Cambridge University Press.

Hulk, Aafke. 1996. L'«autre» *de*: Une tête quantificationelle? *Langue française* 109, 44–59.

Hulk, Aafke, and Christine Tellier. 1999. Conflictual agreement in Romance nominals. In J.-Marc Authier, Barbara Bullock, and Lisa Reed, eds., *Formal Perspectives on Romance Linguistics*. Amsterdam: John Benjamins.

Hulk, Aafke, and Christine Tellier. 2000. Mismatches: Agreement in qualitative constructions. *Probus* 12, 33–65.

Hulk, Aafke, and Els Verheugd. 1994. Accord et opérateurs nuls dans les projections adjectivales. *Revue Québécoise de linguistique* 23, 17–46.

Huot, H. 1981. *Constructions infinitives du français: Le subordonnant DE.* Geneva: Librairie Droz.

Iatridou, Sabine, and Anthony Kroch. 1992. The licensing of CP-recursion and its relevance to the Germanic verb-second phenomenon. *Working Papers in Scandinavian Syntax* 50, 1–25.

Jespersen, Otto. 1924. *The Philosophy of Grammar.* London: Allen & Unwin.

Jespersen, Otto. 1961. *A Modern English Grammar on Historical Principles.* London: Allen & Unwin/Copenhagen: Munksgaard.

Johannessen, Janne Bondi. 1998. *Coordination.* Oxford: Oxford University Press.

Johnson, Kyle. 1991. Object positions. *Natural Language and Linguistic Theory* 9, 577–636.

Kamp, Hans. 1975. Two theories about adjectives. In Edward Keenan, ed., *Formal Semantics of Natural Language*, 123–154. Cambridge: Cambridge University Press.

Kayne, Richard. 1975. *French Syntax: The Transformational Cycle.* Cambridge, MA: MIT Press.

Kayne, Richard. 1984. *Connectedness and Binary Branching.* Dordrecht: Foris.

Kayne, Richard. 1985. Principles of particle constructions. In Jacqueline Guéron and Hans-Georg Obenauer, eds., *Grammatical Representation*, 101–140. Dordrecht: Foris.

Kayne, Richard. 1989. Null subjects and clitic climbing. In Osvaldo Jaeggli and Kenneth Safir, eds., *The Null Subject Parameter*, 239–261. Dordrecht: Kluwer.

Kayne, Richard. 1993. Toward a modular theory of auxiliary selection. *Studia Linguistica* 47, 3–31.

Kayne, Richard. 1994. *The Antisymmetry of Syntax.* Cambridge, MA: MIT Press.

Kayne, Richard. 1998. Overt versus covert movement. *Syntax* 1, 128–191.

Kayne, Richard. 2002a. On some prepositions that look DP-internal: English *of* and French *de*. Unpublished manuscript, New York University.

Kayne, Richard. 2002b. On the syntax of quantity in English. Unpublished manuscript, New York University.

Kayne, Richard. 2003. Some notes on comparative syntax, with special reference to English and French. Unpublished manuscript, New York University.

Kennedy, Chris. 1997. Antecedent-contained deletion and the syntax of quantification. *Linguistic Inquiry* 28, 662–688.

Kennedy, Chris, and Jason Merchant. 2000. Attributive comparative deletion. *Natural Language and Linguistic Theory* 18, 89–146.

Klein, Maarten. 1977. *Appositionele constructies in het Nederlands.* Unpublished doctoral dissertation, University of Nijmegen.

Kondrashova, Natalya. 1996. *The Syntax of Existential Quantification*. Unpublished doctoral dissertation, University of Wisconsin–Madison.

Koopman, Hilda, and Dominique Sportiche. 1990. The position of subjects. *Lingua* 85, 211–258.

Koster, Jan. 2000. Extraposition as parallel construal. Unpublished manuscript, University of Groningen.

Kratzer, Angelika. 1988. Stage-level and individual-level predicates. In Emmon Bach, Angelika Kratzer, and Barbara Partee, eds., *Papers on Quantification*. NSF Report, grant BNS 8719999, University of Massachusetts, Amherst.

Kratzer, Angelika. 1995. Stage-level and individual-level predicates. In Gregory Carlson and Francis Jeffry Pelletier, eds., *The Generic Book*, 109–137. Chicago: University of Chicago Press.

Kratzer, Angelika. 1996. Severing the external argument from its verb. In Johan Rooryck and Laurie Zaring, eds., *Phrase Structure and the Lexicon*, 109–137. Dordrecht: Kluwer.

Kuno, Susumu. 1971. The position of locatives in existential sentences. *Linguistic Inquiry* 2, 333–378.

Kupferman, Lucien. 1981. *Il y a une place de libre*: Study of a construction. *Linguistics* 18, 821–848.

Kupferman, Lucien. 1994a. Une assignation de cas assez exceptionelle. *Linguisticae Investigationes* 8, 151–175.

Kupferman, Lucien. 1994b. Typologie des constructions en *de*-adjectif. *Travaux de Linguistique et de Philologie* 32, 85–95.

Kuroda, Shige-Yuki. 1988. Whether we agree or not. In William Poser, ed., *Japanese Syntax: Papers from the Second International Workshop on Japanese Syntax*. Stanford, CA: CSLI.

Lagae, V. 1994. *La prédication interne au groupe nominal: Les constructions du type «il y en a une de libre»*. Unpublished doctoral dissertation, Katholieke Universiteit Leuven.

Lapesa, Rafael. 1962. Sobre las construcciones *el diablo del tori, el bueno de Minaya, ¡Ay de mí!, ¡Pobre de Juan!, Por malos de pecados*. *Filología* 8, 169–184.

Larrivée, Pierre. 1994. Quelques hypothèses sur les structures syntaxique et sémantique de *ce fripon de valet*. *Revue québécoise de linguistique* 23.

Larson, Richard. 1988. On the double object construction. *Linguistic Inquiry* 19, 335–391.

Larson, Richard. 1998. Events and modification in nominals. In D. Strolovitch and A. Lawson, eds., *Proceedings from Semantics and Linguistic Theory (SALT) VIII*. Ithaca, NY: Cornell University.

Larson, Richard, and Robert May. 1990. Antecedent containment or vacuous movement: Reply to Baltin. *Linguistic Inquiry* 21, 103–122.

Lasnik, Howard. 1999. *Minimalist Analysis*. Oxford: Blackwell.

Lasnik, Howard. 2001. Subjects, objects, and the EPP. In William D. Davies and Stanley Dubinsky, eds., *Objects and Other Subjects: Grammatical Functions, Functional Categories, and Configurationality*, 103–121. Dordrecht: Kluwer.

Lasnik, Howard, and Mamoru Saito. 1990. *Move α*. Cambridge, MA: MIT Press.

Lasnik, Howard, and Mamoru Saito. 1991. On the subject of infinitives. *CLS* 27, 324–343. (Reprinted with minor revisions in Howard Lasnik, *Minimalist Analysis*. Oxford: Blackwell, 1999.)

Léard, Jean-Marcel. 1997. Structures qualitatives et quantitatives: Sacres et jurons en Québécois et en Français. In Pierre Larrivée, ed., *La structuration conceptuelle du langage*, 127–147. Leuven: Peeters.

Leu, Thomas. 2003. *What for* a movement is this? Unpublished manuscript, New York University.

Leu, Thomas. 2004. *What for* properties are odd? Paper presented at the 19th Comparative Germanic Syntax Workshop; unpublished manuscript, New York University.

Longenecker, Ana. 2002. An analysis of the Spanish *N of a N* construction "el tonto del médico." Unpublished manuscript, CUNY Graduate Center.

Longobardi, Giuseppe. 1994. Reference and proper names: A theory of N-movement in syntax and Logical Form. *Linguistic Inquiry* 25, 609–665.

Lødrup, Helge. 1991. The Norwegian pseudopassive in lexical theory. *Working Papers in Scandinavian Syntax* 47, 118–129.

Lyons, John. 1977. *Semantics*. Cambridge: Cambridge University Press.

Malchukov, Andrej. 2004. *Dependency reversal in noun-attributive constructions: Towards a typology*. Munich: LINCOM Europa.

Manzini, M. Rita. 1980. On control. Unpublished manuscript, MIT.

Manzini, M. Rita. 1983. *Restructuring and Reanalysis*. Unpublished doctoral dissertation, MIT.

Marantz, Alec. 1997. No escape from syntax: Don't try morphological analysis in the privacy of your own lexicon. In Alexis Dimitriadis, Laura Siegel, Clarissa Surek-Clark, and Alexander Williams, eds., *University of Pennsylvania Working Papers in Linguistics* 4, 201–225.

Massam, Diane. 2001. On predication and the status of subjects in Niuean. In William D. Davies and Stanley Dubinsky, eds., *Objects and Other Subjects: Grammatical Functions, Functional Categories, and Configurationality*, 225–246. Dordrecht: Kluwer.

Matushansky, Ora. 2002. A beauty of a construction. Paper presented at the 21st West Coast Conference on Formal Linguistics, University of California, Santa Cruz, April 5–7, 2002.

May, Robert. 1985. *Logical Form*. Cambridge, MA: MIT Press.

McCawley, James. 1988. *The Syntactic Phenomena of English*. 2 vols. Chicago: University of Chicago Press.

McConvell, Patrick. 1988. To *be* or double *be*: Current change in the English copula. *Australian Journal of Linguistics* 8, 287–305.

Mikkelsen, Line. 2002a. Reanalyzing the definiteness effect: Evidence from Danish. *Working Papers in Scandinavian Syntax* 69, 1–75.

Mikkelsen, Line. 2002b. Specification is not inverted predication. In Masako Hirotani, ed., *Proceedings of NELS 32*, 403–422. University of Massachusetts, Amherst: GLSA.

Mill, John Stuart. 1856. *A System of Logic*. 4th ed., vol. 1. London: John W. Parker and Son.

Milner, Jacques. 1978. *De la syntaxe à l'interprétation: Quantités, insultes, exclamations*. Paris: Editions du Seuil.

Milner, Jean-Claude. 1973. Un processus de dislocation qualitative. Chapter 2 of *Arguments linguistiques*. Paris: Maison Mame.

Montague, Richard. 1973. The proper treatment of quantification in ordinary English. In K. Hintikka, J. Moravcsik, and P. Suppes, eds., *Approaches to Natural Language*, 221–242. Dordrecht: Reidel.

Moore, G. E. 1903. *Principia Ethica*. Cambridge: Cambridge University Press.

Moro, Andrea. 1988. Per una teoria unificata delle frasi copulari. *Rivista di grammatica generativa* 13, 81–110.

Moro, Andrea. 1990. *There*-raising: Principles across levels. Paper presented at GLOW Cambridge.

Moro, Andrea. 1991. The raising of predicates: Copula, expletives and existence. *MIT Working Papers in Linguistics* 15. Cambridge, MA: MIT.

Moro, Andrea. 1993. *I predicati nominali e la struttura della frase*. Padova: Unipress.

Moro, Andrea. 1997. *The Raising of Predicates: Predicative Noun Phrases and the Theory of Clause Structure*. Cambridge: Cambridge University Press.

Moro, Andrea. 2000. *Dynamic Antisymmetry*. Cambridge, MA: MIT Press.

Mulder, René. 1992. *The Aspectual Nature of Syntactic Complementation*. Unpublished doctoral dissertation, University of Leiden/HIL.

Mulder, René, and Marcel den Dikken. 1992. Tough parasitic gaps. In K. Broderick, ed., *Proceedings of NELS 22*. Amherst, MA: GLSA.

Napoli, Donna Jo. 1989. *Predication Theory: A Case Study for Indexing Theory*. Cambridge: Cambridge University Press.

Neeleman, Ad. 1994. *Complex Predicates*. Unpublished doctoral dissertation, University of Utrecht.

Nichols, Johanna. 1992. *Language Diversity in Space and Time*. Chicago: University of Chicago Press.

Noailly–Le Bihan, Michèle. 1984. Enigme en syntaxe. *Lingvisticae Investigationes* 8, 105–116.

Obenauer, Hans-Georg. 1994. *Aspects de la syntaxe A-barre*. Thèse de doctorat d'État, Université de Paris 8.

Oehrle, Richard. 1976. *The Grammatical Status of the English Dative Alternation*. Unpublished doctoral dissertation, MIT.

Paardekooper, Piet. 1956. Een schat van een kind. *De Nieuwe Taalgids* 49, 93–99.

Padučeva, E., and V. Uspenskij. 1979. Podležaščee ili skazyemoe? (Semantičeskij kriterij različenija podležaščego i skazyemogo v binominativnyx predloženijax.) *Izvestija Akademii Nauk SSSR, Serija Literatury i Jazyka* 38(4), Moscow, 349–360.

Panagiotidis, Phoevos. 2003. Empty nouns. *Natural Language and Linguistic Theory* 21, 381–432.

Partee, Barbara. 2000. Copula inversion puzzles in English and Russian. In Kiyomi Kusumoto and Elisabeth Villalta, eds., *Issues in Semantics*. UMOP 23, 183–208.

Pekelder, J. 1994. Genuscongruentieverschijnselen in de kwalitatieve binominale NP. Unpublished manuscript, Université de Paris Sorbonne.

Penhallurick, John. 1984. Full-verb inversion in English. *Australian Journal of Linguistics* 4, 33–56.

Pereltsvaig, Asya. 2001. *On the Nature of Intra-clausal Relations: A Study of Copular Sentences in Russian and Italian*. Unpublished doctoral dissertation, McGill University, Montréal.

Pereltsvaig, Asya. 2004. Semitic nominals: Rehabilitating the head movement approach. Unpublished manuscript, Yale University.

Pesetsky, David. 1989. Language-particular processes and the Earliness Principle. Paper presented at the 12th GLOW Colloquium, Utrecht, April 5, 1989; abstract in *GLOW Newsletter*.

Pesetsky, David. 1998. Some optimality principles of sentence pronunciation. In Pilar Barbosa, Danny Fox, Paul Hagstrom, Martha McGinnis, and David Pesetsky, eds., *Is the Best Good Enough? Optimality and Competition in Syntax*, 337–383. Cambridge, MA: MIT Press and MITWPL.

Pinto, Manuela. 1997. *Licensing and Interpretation of Inverted Subjects in Italian*. Unpublished doctoral dissertation, University of Utrecht.

Postal, Paul. 1969. On so-called "pronouns" in English. In F. Dinneen, ed., *19th Monograph on Languages and Linguistics*. Washington, DC: Georgetown University Press; reprinted in David Reibel and Sanford Schane, eds., *Modern Studies in English*, 201–224. Englewood Cliffs, NJ: Prentice-Hall, 1969.

Postal, Paul. 1994. Parasitic and pseudo-parasitic gaps. *Linguistic Inquiry* 25, 63–117.

Postal, Paul. 2004. *Skeptical Linguistic Essays*. Oxford: Oxford University Press.

Postma, Gertjan. 1994. The indefinite reading of WH. In Reineke Bok-Bennema and Crit Cremers, eds., *Linguistics in the Netherlands 1994*, 187–198. Amsterdam: John Benjamins.

Postma, Gertjan. 1995a. Zero semantics—The semantic encoding of quantificational meaning. In Marcel den Dikken and Kees Hengeveld, eds., *Linguistics in the Netherlands 1995*, 175–190. Amsterdam: John Benjamins.

Postma, Gertjan. 1995b. *Zero Semantics: A Study of the Syntactic Conception of Quantificational Meaning*. Unpublished doctoral dissertation, University of Leiden/HIL.

Postma, Gertjan. 1996. De negatieve polariteit van het syntactische GHE-partikel in het Middelnederlands. Unpublished manuscript, University of Leiden/HIL.

Progovac, Ljiljana. 2003. Structure for coordination. In Lisa Cheng and Rint Sybesma, eds., *The Second GLOT International State-of-the-Article Book*, 241–287. Berlin: Mouton de Gruyter.

Pustet, Regina. 2003. *Copulas: Universals in the Categorization of the Lexicon*. Oxford: Oxford University Press.

Quirk, Randolph, Sidney Greenbraum, Geoffrey Leech, and Jan Svartvik. 1985. *A Comprehensive Grammar of the English Language*. London: Longman.

Rapoport, Tova. 1987. *Copular, Nominal and Small Clauses: A Study of Israeli Hebrew*. Unpublished doctoral dissertation, MIT.

Regula, M. 1972. Encore une fois *ce fripon de valet*. *Revue de linguistique romane* 26, 107–111.

Reinhart, Tanya, and Eric Reuland. 1993. Reflexivity. *Linguistic Inquiry* 24, 657–720.

Reuland, Eric. 1983. Governing *-ing*. *Linguistic Inquiry* 14, 101–136.

Richards, Norvin. 1997. *What Moves Where When in Which Language?* Unpublished doctoral dissertation, MIT.

Riemsdijk, Henk van. 1990. Functional prepositions. In Harm Pinkster and Inge Genee, eds., *Unity in Diversity*, 229–241. Dordrecht: Foris.

Ritter, Elizabeth, and Sara Rosen. 1993. Deriving causation. *Natural Language and Linguistic Theory* 11, 519–555.

Rizzi, Luigi. 1982. *Issues in Italian Syntax*. Dordrecht: Foris.

Rizzi, Luigi. 1986. Null objects in Italian and the theory of *pro*. *Linguistic Inquiry* 17, 501–557.

Rizzi, Luigi. 1990. *Relativized Minimality*. Cambridge, MA: MIT Press.

Rizzi, Luigi. 1997. The fine structure of the left periphery. In Liliane Haegeman, ed., *Elements of Grammar: Handbook of Generative Syntax*, 281–337. Dordrecht: Kluwer.

Roberts, Ian. 1987. *The Representation of Implicit and Dethematized Subjects*. Dordrecht: Foris.

Rochemont, Michael. 1986. *Focus in Generative Grammar*. Amsterdam: John Benjamins.

Rochemont, Michael, and Peter Culicover. 1990. *English Focus Constructions and the Theory of Grammar*. Cambridge: Cambridge University Press.

Roeper, Tom. 1983. Implicit arguments and the head-complement relation. *Linguistic Inquiry* 18, 267–310.

Rooth, Mats. 1985. *Association with Focus.* Unpublished doctoral dissertation, University of Massachusetts, Amherst.

Rosen, Sara. 1989. *Argument Structure and Complex Predicates.* Unpublished doctoral dissertation, Brandeis University.

Ross, John Robert. 1972. Act. In G. Harman and D. Davidson, eds., *Semantics of Natural Language*, 70–126. Dordrecht: Reidel.

Ross, John Robert. 1997. The source of pseudo-cleft sentences. Handout of a talk given at the University of Pennsylvania.

Ross, John Robert. 1999. That is the question. Handout of a talk given at Humboldt University, Berlin.

Ross, John Robert. 2000. The frozenness of pseudo-clefts. Unpublished manuscript, University of North Texas.

Rothstein, Susan. 1983. *The Syntactic Forms of Predication.* Doctoral dissertation, MIT; distributed by IULC in 1985.

Rothstein, Susan. 2000. *Predicates and Their Subjects.* Studies in Linguistics and Philosophy 74. Dordrecht: Kluwer.

Rouveret, Alain. 1996. *Bod* in the present tense and in other tenses. In Robert Borsley and Ian Roberts, eds., *The Syntax of the Celtic Languages*, 125–170. Cambridge: Cambridge University Press.

Royen, Gerlach. 1947–1954. *Buigingsverschijnselen in het Nederlands.* Amsterdam: Noord-Hollandsche.

Russell, Bertrand. 1903. *The Principles of Mathematics.* London: Allen & Unwin.

Ruwet, Nicolas. 1982. *Grammaire des insultes et autres études.* Paris: Editions du Seuil.

Safir, Kenneth. 1985. *Syntactic Chains.* Cambridge: Cambridge University Press.

Safir, Kenneth, and Tim Stowell. 1988. Binominal *each. Proceedings of the North East Linguistic Society* 18, 426–450.

Sauerland, Uli. 2003. Intermediate adjunction with A-movement. *Linguistic Inquiry* 34, 308–314.

Schlenker, Philippe. 2003. Clausal equations (A note on the connectivity problem). *Natural Language and Linguistic Theory* 21, 157–214.

Scholten, Christina. 1988. *Principles of Universal Grammar and the Auxiliary Verb Phenomenon.* Unpublished doctoral dissertation, University of Maryland.

Selkirk, Elizabeth. 1995. Sentence prosody: Intonation, stress, and phrasing. In John Goldsmith, ed., *The Handbook of Phonological Theory*, 550–569. Oxford: Blackwell.

Seuren, Pieter. 1985. *Discourse Semantics.* Oxford: Blackwell.

Seuren, Pieter. 1998. *Western Linguistics: An historical introduction.* Oxford: Blackwell.

Shaked, Amit. 2001. Predicate Inversion in Hebrew complex noun phrases: The *N of a N* construction. Unpublished manuscript, CUNY Graduate Center.

Siegel, Muffy. 1976. *Capturing the Adjective*. Unpublished doctoral dissertation, University of Massachusetts, Amherst.

Simpson, Andrew. 2001. Definiteness agreement and the Chinese DP. *Language and Linguistics* 2, 125–156.

Simpson, Andrew. 2002. On the status of "modifying" DE and the structure of the Chinese DP. In Sze-Wing Tang and Luther Liu Chen-Sheng, eds., *On the Formal Way to Chinese Languages*. Stanford, CA: CSLI.

Singhapreecha, Pornsiri. 2001. Thai classifiers and the structure of complex Thai nominals. In B. K. T'sou, O. O. Y. Kwong, and T. B. Lai, eds., *Proceedings of the 15th Pacific Asia Conference on Language, Information and Computation*, 259–270. Hong Kong: Language Information Sciences Research Centre, City University of Hong Kong.

Sleeman, Petra. 1996. *Licensing Empty Nouns in French*. Unpublished doctoral dissertation, University of Utrecht.

Smith, Michael. 1999. From instrumental to irrealis: Motivating some grammaticalized senses of the Russian instrumental. In Katarzyna Dziwirek, Herbert Coats, and Cynthia Vakareliyska, eds., *Annual Workshop on Formal Approaches to Slavic Linguistics*, 413–433. Ann Arbor: Michigan Slavic Publishers.

Starke, Michal. 1995. On the format of small clauses. In Anna Cardinaletti and Maria-Teresa Guasti, eds., *Small Clauses: Syntax and Semantics* 28, 237–269. New York: Academic Press.

Stenshoel, Eric. 2004. Are all particles created equal? Paper presented at the 19th Comparative Germanic Syntax Workshop; unpublished manuscript, CUNY Graduate Center.

Stowell, Tim. 1981. *Origins of Phrase Structure*. Unpublished doctoral dissertation, MIT.

Stowell, Tim. 1983. Subjects across categories. *The Linguistic Review* 2, 285–312.

Sugita, Mamori. 2001. Set-theoretic commutativity of noun phrases in Predicate Inversion constructions. Unpublished manuscript, CUNY Graduate Center.

Suñer, Avelina. 1990. *La predicación secundaria en español*. Unpublished doctoral dissertation, Universitat Autònoma de Barcelona.

Suñer, Avelina. 1999. La aposición y otras relaciones de predicación en el sintagma nominal. In Ignacio Bosque and Violeta Demonte, eds., *Gramática descriptiva de la lengua española*. Madrid: Espasa.

Svenonius, Peter. 1996. The Optionality of Particle Shift. *Working Papers in Scandinavian Syntax* 57, 47–75.

Swart, Henriette de, Yoad Winter, and Joost Zwarts. 2005. Realizations and capacities: Optional articles in Dutch predicate nominals. Unpublished manuscript, Utrecht University, Technion Haifa, and Radboud University.

Szabó, Zoltán. 2001. Adjectives in context. In R. Harnish and I. Kenesei, eds., *Perspectives on Semantics, Pragmatics, and Discourse*, 119–146. Amsterdam: John Benjamins.

Szabolcsi, Anna. 1983. The possessor that ran away from home. *The Linguistic Review* 3, 89–102.

Szabolcsi, Anna. 1994. The noun phrase. In Ferenc Kiefer and Katalin É. Kiss, eds., *The Syntax of Hungarian. Syntax and Semantics* 27. New York: Academic Press.

Szekely, Rachel. 2002. Agreement in Italian "N_1 *di* N_2" constructions. Unpublished manuscript, CUNY Graduate Center.

Szendrői, Kriszta. 2003. A stress-based approach to the syntax of Hungarian focus. *The Linguistic Review* 20, 37–78.

Takano, Yuji. 2003. How antisymmetric is syntax? *Linguistic Inquiry* 34, 516–526.

Tang, C.-C. J. 1983. On the deletion of *de* in Chinese: Studies in possessive and modifying phrases. Unpublished manuscript, National Taiwan Normal University.

Tang, C.-C. J. 1993. Chinese *de* and English *'s*. *The Bulletin of the Institute of History and Philology*, Academica Sinica, Taiwan, vol. 63, 733–757.

Taraldsen, Knut Tarald. 1979. Remarks on some central problems of Norwegian syntax. *Nordic Journal of Linguistics* 2, 23–54.

Thomas, J. 1970. Syntagmes du type *ce fripon de valet, le filet de sa mémoire, l'ennui de la plaine. Le français moderne* 38, 312–439.

Toorn, Maarten van den. 1966. Bedoelen en verstaan: De aard van het syntactisch verband. *De Nieuwe Taalgids* 59, 29–35.

Torrego, Esther. 1985. On empty categories in nominals. Unpublished manuscript, University of Massachusetts, Boston.

Troseth, Erika. 2004. Negative inversion and degree inversion in the English DP. Paper presented at GURT 2004; posted on *Linguistics in the Big Apple*, at http://web.gc.cuny.edu/Linguistics/liba/papers/troseth_LIBA.pdf.

Tutescu, Mariana. 1969. Le type nominal *ce fripon de valet. Revue de linguistique romane* 33, 299–316.

Ueno, Yoshio. 2005. A note on the structure of Predicate Phrase + *be* + *that*-CP. *Linguistic Inquiry* 36, 155–160.

Vendler, Zeno. 1967. *Linguistics in Philosophy*. Ithaca, NY: Cornell University Press.

Vergnaud, Jean-Roger. 1974. *French relative clauses*. Unpublished doctoral dissertation, MIT.

Verheugd, Els. 1990. *Subject Arguments and Predicate Nominals: A Study of French Copular Sentences with Two NPs*. Amsterdam: Rodopi.

Vinka, Mikael. 1999. On Swedish verb particle constructions. Unpublished manuscript, McGill University, Montréal.

Vries, Mark de. 2002. *The Syntax of Relativization*. Unpublished doctoral dissertation, University of Amsterdam.

Whelpton, Matthew. 1995. *The Syntax and Semantics of Infinitives of Result in English*. Unpublished doctoral dissertation, Trinity College, Oxford University.

Whitman, John. 2004. *There* constructions. Paper presented at the Susumu Fest, CUNY Graduate Center, May 17, 2004.

Wierzbicka, Anna. 1980. *The Case for Surface Case*. Ann Arbor, MI: Karoma.

Williams, Edwin. 1975. Small clauses in English. In J. Kimball, ed., *Syntax and Semantics*, vol. 4. New York: Academic Press.

Williams, Edwin. 1980. Predication. *Linguistic Inquiry* 11, 203–238.

Williams, Edwin. 1987. Implicit arguments, the binding theory, and control. *Natural Language and Linguistic Theory* 5, 151–180.

Wit, Petra de. 1997. *Genitive Case and Genitive Constructions*. Unpublished doctoral dissertation, University of Utrecht.

Zamparelli, Roberto. 2000. *Layers in the Determiner Phrase*. New York: Garland.

Zaring, Laurie. 1996. Two "be" or not two "be": Identity, predication and the Welsh copula. *Linguistics and Philosophy* 19, 103–142.

Index

à, 44, 45–47, 147, 238, 293n25, 305n72. *See also* Preposition, as RELATOR; RELATOR

Aarts, B., 16, 34, 77, 166, 167, 174, 175, 181, 182, 187, 207, 213, 215, 216, 235, 256n27, 287n1, 288n1, 289n8, 290n12, 295n32, 304n68, 306n74

Abney, S., 162, 213, 215, 236, 246, 287n1

Abraham, W., 207, 208, 214, 288n1, 289n9, 298–299n46, 304n65, 305n71, 306n75

Absolutive. *See* Case, absolutive

Accusative. *See* Case, accusative

Ackrill, J., 8

Active/passive diathesis alternation, 43, 258n39, 259n40, 259n42, 261n46. *See also* Passive

Adger, D., 69, 70, 75, 251n2, 266nn11–13, 267n16, 269n24

Adjective/Adjectival, 5, 7, 13, 29, 31–33, 35–37, 43, 48–50, 55, 91, 210, 211, 222, 223, 224, 229, 231–235, 240, 241, 247, 254n12, 256n26, 257n28, 257n32, 259n42, 261n48, 262n51, 264n4, 266n10, 289n8, 289n10, 291n19, 292n21, 297n39, 298nn44–45, 303n63, 304n67, 306n76, 307n83
  attributive, 30, 36, 55, 211, 257n28, 257n32, 298n45, 304n67
  intersective, 31, 32
  modification. *See* Modification, adjectival
  modifier. *See* Modifier, adjectival
  nonintersective, 31, 32
  noun, 289n8
  predicate. *See* Predicate, adjectival
  predication. *See* Predication, adjectival

Adjunct(ion), 18, 27, 38, 40, 51, 54, 114, 123, 128, 134, 241, 242, 252n7, 253n12, 254n12, 272n2, 282nn49–50
  to arguments, 252n7
  head, 114
  intermediate, 54, 123, 252n7, 282n49, 282n50
  to meaningless categories, 123, 282n50
  right-, 40, 51, 241, 242, 272n2
  and topicalization. *See* Topicalization, adjunction approach to

Adverb(ial), 7, 13, 29–32, 38–43, 46, 53, 54, 60, 128, 147, 241, 242, 247, 256n25, 258nn35–36, 263n58, 272n2, 273n4, 283n56, 283n58, 285n70, 298n45
  interpretation/reading (of attributive modifier), 30, 31
  manner, 30, 31, 39, 272n2, 273n4
  modification. *See* Modification, adverbial
  modifier. *See* Modifier, adverbial
  negative, 128, 283n56
  predicate. *See* Predicate, adverbial
  predication. *See* Predication, adverbial
  quantificational, 41
  scope. *See* Modification, adverbial
  suffix *-ly*, 30, 31, 256n26
  temporal, 46, 60

Åfarli, T., 283n60

African American Vernacular English. *See* English

Agent, 14, 43, 44, 260n43
  implicit (in passives), 260n43. *See also by*-phrase

Agentive (interpretation of) noun phrase. *See* Noun phrase, agentive (interpretation of)

Agree, 44, 47, 53, 54, 112, 113, 117–119, 191, 202, 203, 256n26, 259n42, 261n47, 262n56, 263n57, 301n58. *See also* Agreement

Agreement, 69, 96, 97, 106, 117–119, 121, 129, 154, 156, 158, 160, 169, 180, 185, 190–192, 201–204, 211, 218, 221, 222, 228, 254n15, 261n49, 263n57, 274n13, 275n14, 277n27, 277n29, 278n34, 280nn43–44, 288n1, 294n31, 295n33, 296nn36–38, 296–297n39, 298n43, 306n79. *See also* Agree; Disagreement

Agreement (cont.)
case, 261n49
as a category or relationship, 254n15
in Copular Inversion constructions, 96, 97,
117, 118, 154, 156, 158, 274n13, 275n14,
280n43
definiteness, 201, 204
gender, 185, 211, 228, 294n31, 295n33,
297n39
index, 288, 295n33, 297n39
locative, 106, 277n29
in ("beheaded") Locative Inversion
constructions, 118, 119, 158, 277n27,
278n34
number, 69, 96, 169, 190–192, 274n13,
275n14, 277n27, 280n43, 294n31,
296n36, 296n38, 296–297n39, 298n43
participle, 263n57
in/with QBNPs, 185, 190–192, 201–204,
211, 228, 288n1, 294n31, 295n33,
296nn36–38, 296–297n39
semantic, 228, 295n33
Spec-Head, 202
subject-predicate, 180, 190, 202
Aissen, J., 284n62
Akmajian, A., 73, 267n15
Alexiadou, A., 53
als, 2, 174, 175, 224, 291n91. *See also*
Preposition, as RELATOR; RELATOR
Alternative realization, 278n31
American English. *See* English, American
A-movement. *See* Move(ment), A-
A′-movement/extraction. *See* Move(ment),
A′-
Anagnostopoulou, E., 53
Andrews, A., 258n35
Animacy, 286n81
Antecedent-Contained Deletion (ACD),
136–142, 284n65, 285n67, 285n69
and A-movement, 284n65, 285n69
and extraposition, 139, 140, 142, 285n67,
285n69
Antipassive, 262n56. *See also* Passive;
Ergative, languages
Antisymmetry, 12, 17, 40, 59, 91, 233,
264n5, 309n100
dynamic, 91, 264n5
Antonyi, P., x
Aoun, Y., 133
Applicative, 106, 107, 277n28
Appositive, 288n2
Argument, 9, 10, 13, 14, 17–21, 25, 28, 35,
49, 46, 87, 103, 252n7, 254nn12–13,
257n32, 260n43, 261n47, 267n15,
268n21, 278n36
co-, 19

external, 10, 14, 18–20, 25, 56, 254n12,
254n13, 260n43, 261n47, 278n36
internal, 10, 14, 35, 56, 257n32
structure, 87
Aristotle, 7, 8, 10, 25, 27, 144, 267n15
Arnauld, A., 11, 12
Article, 34, 70, 159, 163–166, 168–172,
175–177, 179, 181–186, 191–193, 196–
199, 201–212, 214–217, 225, 226, 246,
264n6, 269n24, 288n4, 290n14, 293n25,
294n27, 294nn29–31, 295n32, 298n42,
298–299n46, 300n52, 301n54, 301nn56–
57, 302n60, 302n62, 304n66, 305n69,
307n87, 308n96, 309n97
definite, 70, 159, 164, 181, 182, 198, 199,
201–206, 208, 212, 222, 246, 269n24,
288n4, 293n25, 298n42, 300n52, 301n56,
301n57, 302n62, 305n69
indefinite, 34, 163, 165, 168–176, 179,
181–185, 191–193, 197, 201, 205–210,
215–217, 225, 226, 246, 264n6, 269n24,
288n4, 294n27, 294nn29–31, 295n32,
298–299n46, 301n54, 304n66, 305n69,
307n87, 308n96
negative, 172, 183, 184, 294n30, 302n60
"spurious," 171, 175, 176, 179, 183, 184,
192, 198, 201, 204–209, 212, 215, 217,
225, 226, 246, 290n14, 294n29, 300n52,
302n60, 304n66, 305n69, 307n87
definite, 198, 204, 206, 208, 212, 246,
300n52
indefinite, 171, 175, 176, 179, 183, 184,
192, 201, 205, 207, 209, 215, 217, 225,
226, 246, 290n14, 294n29, 300n52,
302n60, 304n66, 307n87
null/zero allomorph of, 304n66, 305n69
as, 2, 34, 36, 37, 62–64, 77, 78, 84, 147,
162, 165–168, 170, 172, 173, 176, 179,
180, 187, 188, 216, 245, 252n5, 256n23,
257n31, 266n10, 273n3, 289n6, 291n19,
292n22. *See also* Preposition, as
RELATOR; RELATOR
Asp(ect), 53, 147, 148, 150, 152, 216, 218,
251n1, 259n42, 262n52, 282n50, 285n71
as LINKER, 147, 148, 150
null, 148
particle. *See* Particle, aspectual
Asymmetry/asymmetrical, 3, 7, 8, 13–15,
17, 41, 42, 55–57, 65, 66, 71, 75, 80,
124, 247, 249
c-command. *See* C-command
Asyndetic coordination. *See* Coordination
Attribute, 35, 36, 50, 51, 262n51
Attributive, 30, 36, 55, 162–173, 175–177,
179, 182–184, 186–188, 196–199, 202–
212, 216, 229, 232, 235, 237, 245,

257n28, 257n32, 262n51, 264n4, 288n2,
    288–289n6, 289n8, 289n12, 290nn13–
    14, 294n27, 295n33, 296n37, 298n45,
    299–300n48, 300n52, 300–301n53,
    301nn54–55, 302nn60–61, 304n67,
    306n74, 306n79, 307n80, 310n101
adjective. *See* Adjective/Adjectival,
    attributive
interpretation, 50, 262n51, 288n2, 289n6,
    290nn13–14, 300n52, 300–301n53,
    307n80
modification. *See* Modification, attributive
modifier. *See* Modifier, attributive
QBNP. *See* Qualitative Binominal Noun
    Phrase (QBNP), attributive
Augment. *See* Pronominal, augment
Austin, F., 181, 182
Autonymous 2-marking. *See* Theta (2-)
    marking, autonymous
Azoulay-Vicente, A., 229, 232, 306n75

Bailyn, J., 16, 252n5, 266n11
Baker, M., 14, 106, 107, 179, 251n1,
    258n40, 259n40, 260n43, 277n28,
    292n22, 309n98
Baltin, M., 139, 142, 287n83
Barbiers, S., 40
Bare. *See under* Copular, sentence;
    Infinitive; Noun phrase; Predicate,
    nominal; Qualitative Binominal Noun
    Phrase (QBNP); Small clause; VP
Barrier, 18, 123, 253n12, 259n42, 282n49
  minimality, 18, 253n12
be, 1, 2, 12, 29, 32, 33, 35, 37, 39, 44, 45,
    49, 52, 61–63, 71, 72, 78, 85, 90, 92, 93,
    143–146, 148, 153, 154, 164, 165, 167,
    168, 177, 184, 186, 212, 218, 244,
    265n7, 265n8, 267n15, 269n24, 270n27,
    271n29, 287n84, 292n22, 306n77. *See
    also* Copula; LINKER; RELATOR
"doubling," 265n8, 271n29. *See also*
    Copula, doubling
"equative," 71, 72, 267n15
eventive, 265n7
/have alternation, 292n22. *See also have*
identity-, 270n27
and multiplicity, 71, 72, 218, 265n8,
    267n15
obligatoriness/omissibility of, 92, 93, 143–
    146, 148, 153, 154, 177, 244, 287n84
as (transitive) verb, 71, 267n15
Belletti, A., 51
Bennis, H., x, 2, 170, 171, 174–177, 188,
    190, 204, 206, 207, 215, 223, 225, 226,
    229, 236, 264n6, 265n6, 288n1, 294n29,
    296n36, 298n43, 299n48, 304n66,

305nn69–70, 305n73, 307n82, 307n84,
    307n87, 309n97
Benveniste, É., 44, 239, 258n39
Berg, T., 274n13
Bernstein, J., 198, 309n99
Binding, 18, 19, 66, 124, 128, 129, 130, 141,
    154–156, 243, 260n43, 278n37
A'-, 130
Principle A, 19, 128, 129, 260n43
Principle C, 66, 129, 141
of variable (pronoun), 124, 154–156
Birner, B., 82, 153, 274n7
Blom, A., 2, 78, 79, 271n31, 271n32
Bobaljik, J., 134
Boeckx, C., 279n37
Bolinger, D., 236, 267n15
Bonet, E., 51
Borer, H., 22
Borroff, M., 309n97
Bowers, J., 15, 16, 19, 34, 55, 71, 77, 175,
    251n2, 252n5, 256n27
Branigan, P., 283n56
Braver, C., 306n76
Bresnan, J., 82, 86, 87, 98, 100, 101, 106,
    130, 272n1, 272n2, 273nn4–5, 280n43,
    282n52, 284n62, 286n74, 286n77
British English. *See* English, British
Broekhuis, H., 191, 288n2, 294n30, 296n36,
    296n39, 306n79
Browning, M., 255n19
Bruening, B., 133–137
Burmese, 256n22
Burzio, L., 51
by(-phrase), 43, 44, 61, 84, 85, 147, 258–
    259n40, 260n43, 261n46, 262n52. *See
    also* Preposition, as RELATOR; RELATOR

Campbell, R., 153, 257n29
Cardinaletti, A., 254n15
Carlson, G., 107
Carnie, A., 269n23
Carrier, J., 58
Cartography, 27, 40, 55
Case, 22–24, 29, 44, 45, 47–49, 52, 66, 67,
    117–119, 121, 207, 214, 252n5, 256n21,
    260n43, 261nn46–47, 261n49, 262n55,
    263nn56–57, 266n10, 277n27, 278n31,
    278n36, 280nn43–44, 305n71, 305n72
absolutive, 263n56
accusative, 23, 44, 45, 47, 52, 69, 117,
    261n47
as default (English), 117, 280n43
agreement. *See* Agreement, case
checking, 24, 29, 44, 47, 48, 52, 118,
    256n21, 261n46, 262n55, 263nn56–57,
    278n36, 280nn43–44

Case (cont.)
dative, 207, 214, 266n10, 278n31, 305n71
on predicate, 266n10
default, 117, 214, 280n43
ergative, 263n56
feature, 22–24, 29, 44, 47, 52, 118,
256n21, 261n49, 262n55, 280nn43–44
genitive, 181, 214, 215, 220, 305n72. *See
also* Saxon genitive
instrumental, 66, 67, 260n43
on predicate, 66, 67
-licensing. *See* Licensing, Case-marker as
RELATOR, 67
marking, 47, 252n5, 260n43, 305n72
exceptional (ECM), 45, 46, 98, 140, 149,
287n84. *See also* Causative, ECM;
Predicate, Inversion
nominative, 44, 52, 66, 67, 117, 118, 207,
214, 218, 221, 252n5, 256n21, 263n56,
277n27
as default (German), 214
on predicate, 66, 67
relative, 263n56
Casillas Martínez, L., 200, 228, 288n1,
291n20, 292n21, 295n33, 297n39,
305n72, 308n96
Caspel, P. van, 207, 287n1
Catalan, 293n25
Category, 9, 11, 15, 20–24, 29, 40, 62, 64,
111, 131, 147, 148, 151, 152, 198,
251nn1–2, 253n8, 254n15, 255n18,
255n20, 257n30, 258n36, 259n42,
261n48, 262n50, 282n50, 309n98
blocking, 259n42
empty/null, 257n30, 262n50
functional, 11, 15, 20–24, 29, 40, 62, 64,
147, 148, 151, 152, 251n1, 251n2,
254n15
lexical, 9, 15, 23, 29, 147, 255n18, 258n36,
261n48
movement. *See* Move(ment), category
"nonsubstantive," 23
Causative, 18, 23, 45–47, 50, 53, 60,
259n41, 261nn46–47, 262n52, 264n3
ECM, 45, 46
ergative *vs.* unergative-based, 261n47
faire-infinitive, 45, 47, 50, 60, 261n46,
261n47
faire-par, 261n46, 262n52, 264n3
C-command, 7, 12, 13, 41, 42, 66, 116, 124,
127–129, 155, 277–278n29, 283n58
asymmetrical, 7, 41, 42, 124
domain (of subject), 128, 129
immediate, 13
mutual, 12, 66

Celtic, 68–70, 72, 75, 76, 79, 266n11,
269n24
Checking. *See under* Case; Domain;
Feature
Cheng, L., 240
Chichewa, 87, 106, 107, 118, 130, 131,
278n34, 284n62, 285n72
Chinese. *See* Mandarin Chinese
Chomsky, N., x, 2, 5, 16–20, 22, 23, 25, 44,
45, 55, 58, 65, 100, 109, 110, 112–116,
124, 131, 134, 151, 152, 209, 243,
252n3, 252n7, 253–254n12, 254n13,
254n15, 255n17, 255n19, 258n36,
259n42, 278n36, 279n37, 279n39,
279n42, 282n49, 286n76
Church Slavonic, 265n8
Churchward, C. M., 25
Chvany, C., 267n15
Cinque, G., 27, 40–42, 55, 101, 130, 147,
211, 258n35, 258n38, 276n22
Cleft construction, 69, 70, 75, 130, 249. *See
also* Pseudocleft construction
it-cleft, 69
Clifton, E., 157
Clitic, 227, 228, 259n40, 261n47, 262n55,
263n57, 268n21, 308n89
-case alternation, 261n47
-doubling, 259n40
inversion. *See* Inversion, subject clitic
pro-predicate. *See* Pro-predicate, *lo*
Coindexation, 67, 102, 123, 124, 141,
282n51
Collins, C., 111, 251n1, 278n35
Comment, 10, 25–28, 157, 158, 270–
271n29. *See also* Topic, -Comment
structure
Comparative QBNP. *See* Qualitative
Binominal Noun Phrase (QBNP),
comparative
Complementizer, 54, 126, 177, 181, 227,
261n3, 280n43. *See also for*; *of*
Complete Functional Complex (CFC), 112
Compound, 163, 173, 258n34, 292n32,
304n67, 306n80
N-N root, 163, 173, 258n34, 306n80
Configuration(ality), 4, 12, 14–16, 22, 23,
29, 43, 55, 57, 59, 89, 124, 125, 247,
261n46
of predication. *See* Predication,
configuration(al)
Construct state, 221, 222
Coopmans, P., 100, 131, 309n98
Coordination, 16, 17, 55, 129, 139, 253n8,
267–268n18, 283n57, 294–295n32
asyndetic, 129, 139, 283n57

in QBNPs, 294–295n32
structure of, 16, 17, 55
Copula, 1, 2, 4, 11, 12, 17, 39, 44, 49, 52,
    62, 63, 68, 71, 72, 75, 76, 87, 90–94, 97,
    123, 143–148, 150, 152, 153, 164, 166,
    168, 169, 171, 172, 177, 178, 203, 205,
    206, 208, 209, 211–213, 216, 217, 221,
    237, 239, 244, 246, 248, 265n8, 266n11,
    267nn14–15, 268n19, 268n22, 270–
    271n29, 287n84, 292n22, 296n34,
    297n39, 305n69, 305n72, 306nn75–76,
    309n99. *See also be*; *de*; *di*; LINKER; *of*;
    RELATOR; *šel*; *thîi*; *van*
  "defective," 68, 75, 266n11
  doubling, 270–271n29. *See also be,*
    "doubling"
  as lexical/2-role assigning element, 71,
    76
  nominal, 4, 164, 168, 169, 171, 172, 177,
    178, 203, 205, 206, 208, 209, 211–213,
    216, 217, 221, 237, 239, 246, 248,
    296n34, 305n69, 305n72, 309n99. *See
    also de*; *di*; *of*; *šel*; *thîi*; *van*, Dutch
  transitive, 71
Copular. *See also* Copula
  element, 2, 4, 11, 44, 116, 143, 151, 152,
    168, 177, 216–218, 221, 245, 246, 248,
    249, 269n25
  Inversion, 4, 58, 81–83, 85–87, 90–92, 98,
    99, 108, 110–112, 116, 117, 121–123,
    126, 132, 135, 137–139, 143, 145, 146,
    150–156, 158, 177, 180, 195, 231, 244,
    248, 249, 261n49, 272n1, 274n5, 276n21,
    280n43, 282n50, 282n53, 299n47
  and agreement. *See* Agreement, in
    Copular Inversion constructions
  sentence, 1–4, 8, 12, 29, 30, 34, 56, 62–80,
    84, 90–98, 126, 132, 137, 139–141, 144,
    152, 153, 156–161, 169, 174, 179, 189,
    190, 192, 197, 218–221, 230–232, 247–
    249, 266n11, 267nn14–15, 267nn17–18,
    268nn20–21, 269nn23–25, 270n28, 270–
    271n29, 271n32, 274nn8–9, 274n12,
    275nn14–15, 280n43, 281n47, 282n51,
    285n68, 287n84, 289n8, 291n20, 298n40,
    308n92
  "bare," 62, 64–70, 80, 247
  canonical, 3, 58, 78, 90, 139–141, 159,
    219, 230, 231, 247
  defective, 266
  equative, 70–80, 84, 91, 92, 94, 96, 144,
    247, 267n18, 268nn220–21, 269n23,
    274n9, 282n51
  identificational, 77, 78, 247, 274n8, 270–
    271n29

inverse/inverted, 1–3, 58, 68, 71, 72, 78,
    79, 84, 90, 92, 94–97, 126, 132, 137,
    140, 141, 144, 153, 156–158, 160, 189,
    219, 221, 230, 231, 247, 267n14, 267n17,
    274n9, 274n12, 275n15, 280n43, 281n47,
    285n68, 287n84, 308n92
  predicational, 67, 77–80, 94, 152, 218,
    271n29
  specificational, 71, 72, 75–80, 84, 91, 92,
    95–97, 153, 219, 220, 226n11, 267n14,
    269nn23–25, 270–271n29, 271n32,
    275nn14–15
  typology, 56, 58, 77–79, 92, 153, 247,
    267n15, 270n28
Corver, N., x, 2, 170, 171, 174–177, 188,
    190, 204, 206, 207, 215, 223, 225, 226,
    229, 236, 264n6, 265n6, 288n1, 294n29,
    296n36, 298n43, 299n48, 304n66,
    305n69, 305n70, 305nn72–73, 307n82,
    307n84, 307n87, 309n97
Crossover, 124, 263n58, 272n1, 272n2,
    273n4, 273n5, 275n16, 275n18, 275n19,
    283n55
Culicover, P., 54, 101
Curme, G. O., 182

Daalder, S., 2, 78, 79, 271n31, 271n32
Dalgish, G., 105
Danish, 119, 120, 272n2, 281n46, 305n72
Dative, 45, 47, 50, 102, 107–109, 119, 121–
    123, 133, 207, 214, 215, 238, 239, 248,
    266n10, 278n31, 285–286n74, 297n39,
    305n71, 305n72
  alternation, 107, 133, 239. *See also* Dative,
    Shift
  case. *See* Case, dative
  construction. *See* Prepositional dative
    construction
  ethical, 297n39
  morphology and the licensing of null P,
    278n31
  PP, 107–109, 238, 239, 309n98
    as predicate, 107–109, 238, 239, 309n98.
    See also Predicate, prepositional
  preposition. *See* Preposition, dative
  Shift, 102, 107, 108, 119, 121–123, 248,
    285–286n74. *See also* Double-object
    construction
Davidson, D., 256n25
de. *See also* Copula, nominal; LINKER;
    Preposition, as LINKER/RELATOR;
    RELATOR
  in Dutch. *See* Article, definite
  in French, 185, 209, 228–239, 289n8,
    305n69, 305n72, 306n75

de (cont.)
  in Mandarin Chinese, 240–245, 310n105
  in Spanish, 174, 180, 191, 199–205, 209,
    211, 235, 302nn62–63
Déchaine, R. -M., 14, 15, 147
Declerck, R., 92, 96, 230, 247, 267n15,
    269n23, 270n29, 271n32, 274n7, 274n13
Default case. *See* Case, default
Definite
  article. *See* Article, definite
  noun phrase. *See* Noun phrase, definite
  predicate nominal. *See* Predicate, nominal
Definiteness
  agreement. *See* Agreement, definiteness
  feature, 202, 203, 205, 206, 302n62
Degree, 185, 227, 228, 292n21, 295n33,
    297n39
  high, 227
  modifier. *See* Modifier, degree
  "pure." *See* Qualitative Binominal Noun
    Phrase (QBNP), "pure degree"
Delsing, L. -O., 304n66
Demonstrative, 183, 185, 191, 193, 196,
    198–202, 205, 206, 212, 220, 233,
    269n24, 294n27, 296–297n39, 300n49,
    300–301n53, 301nn55–56, 301n58,
    302nn62–63, 303n64, 306n79, 308n96
  DemP, 233, 301n55, 301n56
Derivationalism *vs.* Representationalism,
    109
Determiner, 32, 33, 168, 180, 181, 183, 185,
    186, 198, 201, 215, 236, 291n20, 293n25,
    294n27, 294n31, 295n32, 296n34,
    301n54, 301n58, 303n64. *See also*
    Article
  null, 168, 199
di, 163, 199, 204, 205, 207, 209, 283n59,
    288n6, 301n54. *See also* Copula,
    nominal; LINKER; Preposition, as
    LINKER/RELATOR; RELATOR
Diathesis. *See* Active/passive diathesis
    alternation
Dik, S., 267n15
Dikken, M. den, ix, 1, 2, 4, 21, 26, 32, 53,
    56, 73, 96, 103, 104, 107, 111, 116, 119,
    120, 122, 124, 127, 143, 145, 146, 148,
    156, 157, 165, 170, 171, 174–177, 188,
    190–192, 194, 195, 204, 206, 207, 215,
    223, 225, 226, 229, 231, 232, 235, 236,
    238, 239, 254n15, 255n19, 256n22,
    259n42, 261nn46–47, 262n52, 263n2,
    264–265n6, 271n29, 271n31, 274n13,
    275n17, 277n25, 277nn27–28, 278nn30–
    31, 281n48, 284n63, 287n83, 287–
    288n1, 288n2, 292n22, 294nn29–30,
    296n36, 296n39, 298n43, 298n45,

299nn47–48, 304n66, 305n69, 305n73,
    306n79, 307n82, 307n84, 307n87,
    308nn90–91, 308n94, 309n97, 309n99,
    309n100, 310n103
Directional(ity), 3, 4, 12–15, 43, 55, 56, 60,
    61, 247. *See also* Predication,
    directionality of
Disagreement, 96, 190, 296n36, 298n43. *See
    also* Agreement
Dissimilation, 169
Ditransitive. *See* Triadic
Dixon, B., 262n56
Doetjes, J., 162, 177, 185, 196, 199, 227,
    228, 288n1, 289n8, 292n23, 294–
    295n32, 295n33, 297n39, 300n49,
    301n58, 306n79
Doherty, C., 69, 266nn11–12
Domain, 2, 5, 12, 16, 29, 113–115, 152,
    252n3, 277n27, 278n37, 279n40, 279n42,
    286n76
  binding, 278n37. *See also* Binding
  c-command. *See* C-command, domain (of
    subject)
  checking, 277n27
  -extending head movement. *See*
    Move(ment), head
  minimal, 5, 12, 114–116, 252n3, 279n40,
    279n42
  of a head-movement chain, 114, 279n40,
    279n42
Doron, E., 218
Double-object construction, 107, 108, 119,
    120, 133, 136, 238, 281n48, 284n63,
    286n74. *See also* Applicative;
    Prepositional dative construction;
    Triadic construction
Dummy, 44, 265n7. *See also* Expletive
do, 265n7
Dutch, 2, 4, 96, 97, 119, 168–171, 174, 175,
    181, 183, 188–194, 196–198, 204–207,
    210–212, 215, 223–227, 236, 246, 264–
    265n6, 271n31, 274n12, 275n14, 280n43,
    287n1, 288n2, 289n11, 290n14, 291n19,
    293n25, 294n30, 296nn36–37, 297n39,
    298n41, 299n46, 300n52, 302n59,
    304nn66–67, 305n70, 306n79, 307n87

É. Kiss, K., 125, 126, 192, 195, 217, 266n10
Economy, 28, 110–112, 150, 151, 206, 225,
    265n8
  global *vs.* local, 111
ECM. *See* Case, marking
ECP, 109, 123, 252n7, 253n12, 259n42
Elbourne, P., 188
Embedding, 53, 60, 64, 86, 94, 95, 115, 117,
    125, 126, 128, 129, 146, 150, 151, 154–

158, 160, 165, 166, 168, 172, 194, 198,
202, 216, 235, 264n4, 273n5, 274n12,
280n43, 283n58, 286n80, 287nn83–84,
292n22, 298n45
in DP, 168, 172, 198, 202, 216, 235
in nonbridge contexts, 154–157, 286n80
in NumP, 165, 166
Emonds, J., 153, 272n1, 278n31, 286n77,
287n83
English, 2, 4, 13, 16, 24, 26, 37, 45, 52, 53,
62, 69–71, 73, 82, 87, 88, 94, 96, 98,
100, 102–106, 108, 109, 117–120, 126,
131, 132, 150, 163, 168, 169, 174, 175,
181, 183, 187–190, 192–194, 197, 198,
200, 206–209, 212, 213, 216–218, 220,
221, 226, 231, 234, 236–39, 244–46,
252n5, 256n23, 258n34, 259n42, 260n43,
261n46, 265nn6–8, 266n10, 267n14,
270n26, 270n29, 272n2, 275n14, 276n23,
277nn26–27, 280n43, 281nn45–46,
284n62, 285n74, 286n75, 288nn3–4,
289n7, 289nn10–11, 289–290n12,
290n13, 290n15, 291n19, 293n25,
294n27, 294nn29–30, 295n32, 296nn36–
38, 298nn40–41, 299n46, 299–300n48,
300–301n53, 302n61, 304n66, 304n68,
305n72, 306n76, 307n80, 307n83,
307n86, 309n99, 309–310n101
-A vs. -B, 119, 120
African American Vernacular, 290n15
American, 187, 213, 236, 293n25, 300n48,
300n54
British, 119, 120, 182, 188, 189, 213,
281n45, 289n7, 290n12, 293n25, 296n36,
300n48, 300–301n53
nineteenth-century, 290n15
Old, 291n19
EPP, 44, 48, 52, 53, 112, 118–120, 152,
255n17, 263n57, 279n41, 282n49
Equative
copular sentence. See Copular, sentence
predicate. See Predicate, equative
Equidistance, 2, 112, 114–117, 149, 152,
161, 178
Ergative. See also Causative, ergative vs.
unergative-based; Inversion, Free
case. See Case, ergative
languages, 262–263n56
Eskenázi, A., 287n1
Eskimo, 262–263n56
Español-Echevarría, M., 165, 174, 179, 180,
185, 199, 201–203, 206, 235, 288n1,
288–289n6, 290n13, 291n17, 292nn20–
21, 293n25, 300nn51–52, 300n54,
301n57, 302nn61–63, 308n96
Everaert, M., 183, 213, 215, 287n1

Exclamative, 168, 208, 222–229, 248,
297n39, 298n44, 304n66, 307n85,
309n97
was (für)-, 208, 304n66
wat-, 223–226, 307n85
wh-, 5, 222–229, 248, 309n97
Expletive, 15, 88, 102, 267n15, 272n2,
284n62. See also Dummy; Transitive,
expletive construction
Extraction, 18, 27, 54, 71–75, 81, 83–86,
92–94, 99, 100, 103, 104, 107, 108, 121–
126, 130, 131, 134, 135, 139, 141, 143,
151, 161, 194, 195, 213, 220, 251n1,
252n2, 252n7, 253n11, 254n12, 258n35,
258n38, 263n57, 267n18, 268n18,
268n21, 273n3, 273n5, 274n11, 275n17,
276n20, 277n24, 281n74, 282n49,
282n53, 299n47. See also Move(ment)
A'-. See Move(ment), A'-
across-the-board, 268n18
of fronted PP (in Locative Inversion
construction), 273n5
long-distance, 18, 86, 101, 124, 254n12
of postcopular/postverbal subject, 71–74,
83–86, 104, 121–124, 135, 141, 143,
194, 195, 213, 277n24, 281n74, 299n47.
See also Subject, postcopular/postverbal
of PP secondary predicate, 104
of precopular noun phrase, 125, 126
restrictions, 81, 84, 86, 92–94, 126
sub-, 27, 100, 122, 123, 282n53
from focus, 282n53
from postcopular/postverbal subject, 122,
123, 134, 135, 139, 194, 195, 213
from subject, 27, 100
from topic, 27, 100
wh-. See wh-, extraction
Extraposition, 127, 139, 140, 142, 213,
258n35, 283n56, 283n57, 285n67,
285n69
and ACD. See Antecedent-Contained
Deletion (ACD)
and base-generation/movement, 127, 130,
139, 142, 283n57
of heavy noun phrases. See Heavy NP
Shift
of relative clause. See Relative clause,
extraposition
string-vacuous, 140
Event, 14, 30–32, 41, 42, 44, 46, 53,
258n38, 260n43, 265n7
caused/causativized, 46
control, 260n43
-related reading, 31
role (E-role), 31, 32, 41, 265n7
variable, 32

faire-infinitive (causative). *See* Causative,
   faire-infinitive
faire-par (causative). *See* Causative, *faire
   par*
Feature, 22–24, 29, 44, 47, 48, 52, 53, 54,
   63, 65, 66, 89, 111, 114, 115, 117–119,
   129, 131, 169, 180, 190, 202, 203, 205,
   206, 209, 210, 212, 218, 221, 225,
   256n21, 256n26, 259nn41–42, 261n49,
   262n55, 265n7, 266n9, 277n27, 277n29,
   279n41, 280nn43–44, 282n49, 302n62.
   See also Case; Definiteness; Focus;
   Gender; Move(ment); Negative; Phi-/N-
   feature; T(ense); *wh*-checking
   "by proxy," 280n43
 content as prerequisite for moving
   RELATOR head, 209, 210, 212
 movement, 279n41. *See also* Move(ment)
 semantic, 266n9
 uninterpretable, 24, 48, 52, 54
Ferrazzano, L., 260n44
Fiengo, R., 66, 89, 141, 284n66
Focalization, 7, 28, 247, 275n19. *See also*
   Focus
Focus, 16, 28, 29, 51, 52, 70, 82, 83, 85,
   87–90, 124–126, 131, 151, 157, 230,
   247, 262n54, 269n25, 270n29, 272n2,
   275n19, 276n20, 285n68, 291n18
 feature, 89
 head, 28
 identificational/exhaustive, 82, 125
 intonation, 82, 88, 272n2
 movement, 29, 89, 124, 125, 276n20
  long-distance, 124, 125
 narrow, 82, 83, 262n54
 particle, 28, 29
 presentational, 82, 87, 88
 projection, 82, 83, 85
 as trigger for inversion, 87–90, 291n18
 wide, 51, 52, 262n54
for, 35–39, 48, 49, 62–64, 77, 78, 84, 85,
   147, 162, 170, 187, 188, 216, 245,
   252n5, 256n23, 257n32, 261n49, 262n51,
   264n4, 266n10, 273n3, 280n43, 289n6,
   302n61. *See also* Preposition, as
   RELATOR; RELATOR
 as infinitival complementizer, 261n49,
   280n43
Franks, S., 252n5
Free
 Inversion. *See* Inversion, Free
 Relative. *See* Relative clause, free
 state, 221, 222
Freeze, R., 292n22
Freezing (effect), 48, 83
Frege, G., 7–10

French, 45–47, 76, 147, 185, 206, 226–232,
   234–241, 261n47, 287n1, 289n8, 291–
   292n20, 293n25, 294n26, 294–295n32,
   295n33, 297n39, 300–301n53, 305n69,
   305n72, 306n79
 Old, 294n26
 Québécois, 287n1, 289n8, 293n25, 305n72
Friedeman, M. -A., 51
Fukui, N., 18
Function, 9, 17, 38, 49, 63, 82, 87, 89, 125,
   126, 131, 257n29, 264n4, 283n54
 -argument structure, 9
 pragmatic, 89, 125, 126, 131, 283n54. *See
   also* Focus; Topic
 from predicates (properties) to predicates
   (properties), 38, 49, 63, 257n29, 264n4
Functional, 7, 10–12, 15, 16, 20–24, 26–29,
   34, 40, 54–57, 62, 64, 76, 77, 80, 87,
   105, 111, 113, 115, 116, 120, 139, 147,
   148, 150–152, 175, 178, 179, 195, 209,
   211, 226, 240, 245, 251nn1–2, 254n15,
   255nn17–18, 256n27, 260nn45–46,
   264–265n6, 267n15, 269n24, 288n4,
   293n24
 category. *See* Category, functional
 connective, 12
 element, 15, 24, 55, 120, 226, 240
 Grammar, 267n15
 head. *See* Head, functional
 structure, 3, 7, 24, 28, 56, 62, 260n45,
   260n46
  of small clause. *See* Small clause, and
  functional structure

Gaatone, D., 287n1
Gaelic, 68, 75, 76, 266n12, 266–267n13,
   267n16, 269nn24–25
 Irish, 68, 269n25
 Scottish, 68, 75, 76, 266n12, 266–267n13,
   267n16, 269nn24–25
Geist, L., 266n11
Gender, 180, 185, 211, 218, 226, 294n31,
   295n33, 297n39, 301n58, 303n64,
   304n66, 306n79
 agreement. *See* Agreement, gender
 feature, 180, 218
 mismatch, 180
Genitive. *See* Case, genitive; *see also*
   Partitive genitive
Gérard, J., 287n1, 289n8
German, 119, 207–210, 212, 214, 215,
   278n31, 298–299n46, 303n64, 305n71
 Swiss, 303n64
Gerund, 280n43
Giorgi, A., 51
Giusti, G., 198

Givón, T., 271n32
Greed, 152
Groat, E., 134
Grohmann, K., 256n23, 279n37
Groot, A. W. de, 287n1
Guasti, M. T., 51, 60, 254n15
Guéron, J., x, 79, 82, 88, 97, 126, 147,
    259n42, 274n7, 275n15, 282n52, 282n53,
    286n81

Hale, K., 14, 19–21, 254n13, 259n42
Halevy, R., 306n78
Halliday, M. A. K., 267n15, 271n32
Harris, R., 12
have, 36, 37, 44, 45, 258n41, 292n22
  as *be* + P, 44, 292n22
  -perfect, 45, 259n41. *See also* Perfect
Head, 2, 4, 7, 10, 15, 16, 19, 20–23, 26–28,
    31, 33–36, 38, 40, 41, 44–46, 48, 50, 52,
    53, 55–57, 62, 64, 70, 72, 75–77, 80, 81,
    84, 93, 97, 98, 102, 104, 105, 109, 110,
    113–121, 139, 145–152, 161, 164, 166,
    168, 169, 171, 172, 175, 176, 178–181,
    184, 190, 191, 194, 195, 198, 199, 201–
    206, 208–213, 218, 220, 221, 225, 226,
    229, 233, 238, 241–246, 248, 249,
    252n3, 254n15, 255n17, 256n27, 257n29,
    257n32, 259–260n42, 262n52, 264–
    265n6, 268n20, 271n29, 278n34,
    279nn40–41, 279n42, 282n49, 283n57,
    285n70, 286n76, 288n4, 292nn21–22,
    300n51, 301n56, 306n74, 306n79,
    308n88, 309n97, 309n100, 310nn104–
    105
  adjunction. *See* Adjunct(ion)
  colon, 283n57. *See also* Coordination,
    asyndetic
  of compound, 292n21
  empty/null, 4, 93, 97, 98, 102, 110, 120,
    152, 172, 178–180, 198, 248, 292nn21–
    22, 300n51. *See also* Predicate, empty-
    headed
  Final Filter, 257n32
  functional, 2, 4, 7, 15, 16, 22, 26–28, 34,
    56, 57, 62, 64, 76, 77, 80, 105, 113, 115,
    116, 139, 147, 148, 150, 152, 175, 178,
    179, 195, 209, 245, 248, 249, 254n15,
    255n17, 256n27, 264–265n6, 269n24,
    288n4
  of small clause. *See* Small clause,
    functional head of
  lexical, 20–22, 35, 41, 116
  and 2-role assignment, 20, 21
  minimal domain of. *See* Domain, minimal
  movement. *See* Move(ment), head
  Movement Constraint (HMC), 109

of phase, 113–115, 118, 149, 282n49. *See
    also* Phase
  -raising analysis of relative clauses. *See*
    Relative clause, head-raising analysis of
  of relative clause. *See* Relative clause,
    head
  semantic, 34, 184, 306n79
Heavy NP Shift, 127–130, 139, 140, 143,
    272–273n2, 273n5, 275n16, 275n18,
    283n55, 283nn57–58, 285n67
  and base-generation, 127, 130, 283n57
Hebrew, 217–221, 267n15, 269n24,
    306nn78–79. *See also* Construct state;
    Free, state; *šel*
Heggie, L., 2, 73, 78, 156, 158, 267n15,
    268n20, 272n1, 282nn52–53, 287n84
Heim, I., 134
Hertog, C. H. den, 79
Hestvik, A., 283n60
Hetzron, R., 82
Heycock, C., xi, 2, 12, 15, 19, 72, 73, 79,
    84, 91, 92, 94, 124–126, 132, 137–139,
    144–146, 153–156, 159, 177, 195,
    268n19, 268n20, 272n1, 281n47, 283n59,
    285nn70–71, 286n77, 286n80, 298nn45–
    46
Higginbotham, J., 35, 36, 50, 51, 257n32,
    262n51, 267n15
Higgins, F. R., 73, 77, 80, 82, 91, 92, 94,
    153, 157, 247, 267n15, 269nn22–23,
    270n29, 271n32, 274n8
HMC. *See* Head, Movement Constraint
    (HMC)
Hoekstra, T., xi, 2, 21, 30, 58, 84, 122, 123,
    147, 153, 254n15, 258n39, 259n42,
    272n1, 273n2, 286n77, 307n81
Hornstein, N., 136–138, 254n15, 284n65,
    285n69
Horvath, J., 88, 89, 274n6
Huang, C. T. -J., 18
Huddleston, R., 267n15
Hulk, A., 164, 165, 206, 227–231, 287–
    288n1, 289n8, 290n14, 295n33, 297n39,
    300–301n53, 301n58
Hulst, H. van der, 30
Hungarian, 88, 89, 124, 125, 191, 192, 194–
    196, 217, 218, 221, 222, 231, 235, 236,
    261n49, 266n10, 274n6, 298nn40–41,
    303n63, 306n77, 309n99
Huot, H., 229
Hyperonym, 79, 271n32
Hypokeimenon (subject), 8, 25, 27
Hyponym, 79, 271n32

Iatridou, S., 286n82
Icelandic, 119, 278n31

Idiom, 262n54, 277n42
Incorporation, 44, 45, 106, 107, 148, 179,
    238, 262n55, 277n28, 278n34, 285n72,
    291n19, 292n22
  of A, 291n19
  and "morphological licensing," 179
  of N, 262n55
  of null predicate head, 179, 292n22
  of P, 44, 106, 107, 238, 277n28, 278n34,
    285n72, 292n22
  of V, 45
Indefinite
  article. *See* Article
  noun phrase. *See* Noun phrase
  wat-, 223, 224
Index, 66, 109, 124, 228. *See also*
    Coindexation
  agreement. *See* Agreement, index
  referential (as feature), 66
Infinite regress, 136, 139–142, 284n65,
    285n69. *See also* Antecedent-Contained
    Deletion (ACD)
Infinitive, 45, 47, 50, 52, 60, 61, 86, 98, 99,
    138, 143, 255n19, 255n20, 261nn46–47,
    283n58
  bare/naked, 61, 255n20
  faire- (causative). *See* Causative, *faire-*
    infinitive
  InfP, 260n45
Information structure, 82, 87, 89, 90, 125,
    217, 230, 231, 237, 258n38, 272n2,
    275n19, 308n92. *See also* Focus, Topic
Instrumental. *See* Case, instrumental
Internal Subject Hypothesis. *See* LP-
    Internal Subject Hypothesis
Interrogative, 4, 71, 222–224, 226, 227, 248
  wat voor, 223, 225, 226, 236
  wh-, 4, 222, 248
Intersection/Intersective, 17, 23, 30, 31, 32,
    55, 65, 253n9, 287n85
  adjective. *See* Adjective/Adjectival,
    intersective
  interpretation/reading, 30–32
  relationship, 17
  set. *See* Set, intersection
Inversion, 10, 11, 37, 49, 50, 51, 55, 57, 58,
    60, 72–74, 78, 80–165, 175, 177–180,
    185, 186, 195, 196, 198, 205, 209, 210,
    218, 220–222, 226–228, 230, 231, 233–
    246, 252n4, 256n22, 261n49, 262n53,
    264n5, 264–265n6, 268–269n22, 270–
    271n29, 271n32, 272n1, 272–273n2,
    273n4, 273–274n5, 275n7, 275nn16–19,
    276n21, 276nn22–23, 277n25, 277n27,
    278nn32–35, 279n38, 280n43, 282n50,
    282nn52–53, 283n55, 284nn62–63,

    285nn72–73, 285–286n74, 286n75,
    286n79, 286n81, 287nn84–85, 292n22,
    299n47, 307n81, 307n86, 308n89,
    309n97, 310n104
  Copular. *See* Copular, Inversion
  Free, 51, 60, 262n53, 263n57
    with ergative/unaccusative verb, 263n57
  Locative. *See* Locative, Inversion
  Predicate. *See* Predicate, Inversion
  subject-aux(iliary), 99, 155–158, 160,
    286n81, 287n84, 307n86
  subject clitic, 227, 228, 308n89. *See also*
    Clitic
Irish Gaelic. *See* Gaelic
Italian, 50–53, 60–62, 96, 163, 164, 198,
    199, 201, 204, 206–208, 212, 260n44,
    262n54, 263n57, 268n21, 280n43,
    283n59, 288n3, 288n6, 293n25, 295n33,
    296n36, 297n39, 298n42, 300n52,
    301n54, 303n63

Jespersen, O., 79, 267n15, 305n72
Johannessen, J., 17
Johnson, K., 58, 258–259n40, 260n43

Kamp, H., 38, 49, 63, 257n29
Kanerva, J., 106, 130, 282n52
Kategoroúmenon (grammatical predicate),
    8, 25
Kayne, R., x, 17, 28, 40, 45, 51, 58, 59, 90,
    107, 127, 157, 165, 177, 181–183, 185,
    198, 214, 215, 227, 233, 235, 239,
    260n45, 277n29, 284n61, 287n1, 292n22,
    293n24, 301n54, 309n97, 309n100
Keizer, M. E., 191, 288n2, 294n30, 296n36,
    296n39, 306n79
Kennedy, C., 284n65, 285n69
Keyser, S. J., 14, 19–21, 254n13, 259n42
Kinande, 251n1
Klein, M., 287n1
Kondrashova, N., 265n7, 265n8, 267n15,
    269n24
Koopman, H., 18, 51
Koster, J., 129, 139, 283n57
Kratzer, A., 19, 134, 265n7
Kroch, A., 71, 72, 79, 84, 92, 94, 125, 126,
    132, 137–139, 144, 155, 268nn19–20,
    272n1, 283n59, 286n82
Kuno, S., 132
Kupferman, L., 229
Kuroda, S. -Y., 18

Lagae, V., 229, 230
Lancelot, C., 11, 12
Lapesa, R., 287n1, 294n26
Larrivée, P., 287n1

Larson, R., 19, 20, 30–32, 133, 137,
   254n13, 257n28
Larsonian VP-shell structure. *See* VP, -shell
   structure
Lasnik, H., 27, 100, 283n58
Last Resort, 111, 119, 148, 149
Latin, 8, 143, 259n42, 291n19, 305n72
LCA. *See* Linear Correspondence Axiom
   (LCA)
Léard, J. -M., 287n1, 289n8
Learnability, 59
Lepschy, G., 163
Leu, T., 303n64, 304n66, 307n87
Levine, R., 101, 272nn1–2, 273nn4–5,
   275n16, 275nn18–19, 283n55
Lexical
  category. *See* Category, lexical
  head. *See* Head, lexical
  meaning, 288–289n6
  selection. *See* Selection, lexical
Li, Y. -H. A., 133
Licensing, 29, 45, 46, 49, 61, 75, 81, 92, 93,
   96–98, 102, 109, 110, 112, 127–130,
   151, 152, 157, 178–180, 210, 211,
   252n7, 253n12, 276nn21–22, 278n29,
   278n33, 283n56, 292n22, 304n66,
   309n97
  Case-, 49
  content, 93, 102, 179, 276n21
  formal, 75, 93, 102, 179, 276n21
  morphological, 179, 292n22. *See also*
   Incorporation
  polarity item. *See* Polarity Item
  by. T, 45, 46
  trace, 252n7, 253n12, 278n33. *See also*
   ECP
Light verb (*v*). *See* Verb, light (*v*)
Lightfoot, D., 254n15
like, 30, 31, 33, 35, 36, 62–64, 77, 174–180,
   216, 245, 252n5, 256–257n27, 266n10,
   291n19, 292n22. *See also* Preposition, as
   RELATOR; RELATOR
Linear Correspondence Axiom (LCA), 51,
   59, 90, 277n29
LINKER, 1, 2, 4, 25, 26, 80–82, 111, 116,
   117, 123, 143, 145–154, 161, 164, 177–
   179, 184, 186, 194, 198, 202, 203, 205,
   209, 210, 212, 216, 218, 220, 221, 226,
   230, 231, 233–237, 240–242, 244, 245–
   249, 251n1, 256n22, 265n6, 271n29,
   279n42, 282n50, 308n88, 308n93,
   310n104
  null, 147, 148, 150, 152, 193. *See also*
   Asp(ect), as LINKER
  prepositional. *See* Preposition, as LINKER
Lipták, A., x, 191–193, 231, 235, 287n1

Litotes, 171, 184, 290n15, 291n16
L-marking, 123, 258n42
Locality, 1, 2, 5, 11, 12, 45, 81, 87, 111,
   112, 116, 143, 152, 278nn32–33
  of movement. *See* Move(ment), locality of
  of predication. *See* Predication, locality of
Locative
  agreement. *See* Agreement, locative
  Inversion, 82, 83, 86–89, 98–111, 118,
   119, 121–123, 130–135, 148–151, 158,
   238, 248, 264n6, 272n1, 272–273n2,
   273nn4–5, 275nn16–17, 275n19,
   276nn21–23, 277n25, 277n27, 278nn33–
   35, 280n43, 282nn52–53, 283n55,
   284n62, 285nn72–73, 285–286n74
  and agreement. *See* Agreement, in
   ("beheaded") Locative Inversion
   constructions
  "beheaded," 102–110, 118, 119, 121, 122,
   132–135, 148–151, 248, 276n23,
   277n25, 277n27, 278nn33–34, 284n62,
   285nn72–73, 285–286n74
  in raising constructions, 86, 273n4
  and *that-t* effects, 273n5. *See also that-t*
   effect
  suffix, 106, 107, 109, 277n28, 278n34,
   278n35
Long-distance extraction. *See* Extraction,
   long-distance
Longenecker, A., x, 53, 199, 203, 261nn46–
   47, 262n52, 295n33, 297n39, 300n52,
   308n96
Longobardi, G., 51, 294n28
Lødrup, H., 103, 283n60, 284n62
LP-Internal Subject Hypothesis, 17–19,
   253n10, 254n12
Luhya, 105–107, 109, 118, 277nn27–28,
   278nn34–35, 285n72
Lyons, J., 79

Mandarin Chinese, 240–245, 256n22
Manner adverb(ial). *See* Adverb(ial),
   manner
Manzini, M. R., 18, 260n43
Marantz, A., 255n20
Massam, D., 286n75
Matushansky, O., 37, 188, 288n1, 296n38,
   298n40, 306n76, 308n95
May, R., 66, 134, 137, 141
McCawley, J., 289n8
McConvell, P., 271n29
Meinunger, A., x, 73, 146, 147, 271n29,
   287n83
Metaphor(ical), 172, 173
Mikkelsen, L., 82, 272n2, 284n62
Mill, J. S., 267n15

Milner, J., 162, 173, 229, 230, 232, 287n1,
291n20, 294n32, 306n75
Milner, J. -C., 287n1
Minimal
domain. *See* Domain, minimal
Link Condition (MLC), 116
Minimality, 18, 111, 116, 253–254n12
barrier. *See* Barrier, minimality
Relativized, 116
Modification, 7, 29, 30, 36, 38, 39, 41, 43,
46, 53, 71, 79, 94, 108, 210, 212, 229,
241, 242, 247, 298nn44–45, 304n68
adjectival, 7, 29, 30, 36, 210, 211, 247,
298n44, 304n68
adverbial, 7, 29, 30, 38, 39, 41, 43, 46, 53,
241, 242, 247, 298n45
temporal, 46
scope of, 39, 41, 42, 53
attributive, 229, 310n101
by nonrestrictive relative clause, 71, 79,
94. *See also* Relative clause,
nonrestrictive
particle. *See* Particle, modification
Modifier, 30–32, 40–42, 54, 55, 128, 129,
180, 185, 197, 200, 210, 211, 229, 231,
257n28, 258n35, 285n70, 289n8, 292n21,
296n38, 298n45, 306n74
adjectival, 31, 210, 211, 257n28
adverbial, 31, 40–42, 54, 55, 147, 258n35,
285n70, 298n45
attributive, 30, 197, 211, 306n74
degree, 292n21
-NPI. *See* Polarity item, negative
phrase, 306n74
predicate, 30, 32, 257n28
temporal, 129
Montague, R., 267n15
Moro, A., xi, 1–3, 62, 64–66, 69–72, 78,
80, 84, 90, 91, 96, 121–123, 132, 135,
143, 144, 195, 223, 229, 247, 251n2,
254n15, 260n44, 264n5, 266n9, 267n15,
268n21, 272n1, 273n2, 278n37, 280n43,
281n47, 283n59, 285n70
Morphological licensing. *See* Licensing,
morphological
Move(ment), 1, 2, 4, 18, 28, 39, 40, 41, 48,
57, 78, 81–83, 86–90, 97, 98, 100, 102–
105, 108–112, 114–117, 119–122, 125,
127–130, 134, 136, 137, 139, 140, 142,
144, 145, 147, 150–152, 154–156, 161,
172, 177, 178, 181, 185, 186, 203, 209,
212, 218, 224–226, 229, 232–234, 236–
238, 241, 243, 248, 249, 251n1, 252n4,
252n7, 254n12, 254n16, 255n19, 256n23,
258n36, 258n38, 259n42, 262n54,
263n57, 263n1, 264n6, 273n4, 273–

274n5, 276n20, 278n33, 279nn40–42,
282n49, 283n58, 284n61, 284n65,
285n69, 286n76, 301n55, 307n81,
308n94, 309n100, 310n104. *See also*
ECP; Extraction; *that*-trace effect; *wh*-,
extraction
A-, 1, 4, 48, 57, 81, 82, 86, 87, 97, 98, 102,
104, 105, 109, 116, 117, 119, 121, 129,
144, 151, 155, 156, 218, 238, 248,
273n4, 273–274n5, 282n49, 283n58,
284n65, 285n69
A'-, 74, 83–86, 92–94, 103, 107, 108, 121,
123, 124, 126, 131, 139, 151, 177, 181,
220, 224–226, 236, 252n2, 262n54,
267n18, 273n3, 273n5, 282n49, 309n100
category, 111, 131
at LF, 131
feature, 111, 131
focus. *See* Focus, movement
head, 2, 114, 115, 116, 145, 147, 150–152,
178, 203, 209, 212, 229, 249, 259n42,
279n40, 279n42, 286n76
domain-extending, 2, 115, 116, 152
phase-extending, 145, 147, 150–152, 178,
203, 212, 249
in syntax or at PF, 286n76
LF-, 130, 131, 134, 136, 137, 139
locality of, 81, 87, 111, 112, 116, 143, 152,
248, 249
long-distance. *See* Extraction, long-
distance
NP-, 120
of postcopular/postverbal subject. *See*
Extraction, of postcopular/postverbal
subject
QP-. *See* Quantifier, Raising (QR)
P-, 264n6, 278n33. *See also* Incorporation,
of P
PP-, 264n6
remnant, 28, 40, 104, 105, 107, 108, 127,
128, 148, 149, 233, 234, 237, 239, 241,
258n36, 284n61, 308n94, 310n104
rightward, 40, 127, 128
string-vacuous, 100, 140
successive-cyclic, 109, 125, 254n16,
276n20
topic. *See* Topicalization
tough-, 15, 255n19
verb. *See* Verb
VP-. *See* VP, -fronting
wh-. *See wh*-, extraction
Mulder, R., 2, 21, 84, 122, 123, 153,
254n15, 255n19, 272n1, 273n2, 286n77

Næss, A., x, 103, 104, 122, 124, 148, 264n6,
275n17, 277n25, 277n27

Napoli, D. J., 48, 162–164, 166, 187, 199,
204, 208, 213, 215, 244, 247, 258n34,
287n1, 288nn2–3, 288n6, 289n7,
294n27, 295n33, 296n36, 297n39,
300n48, 300–301n53, 301n54, 302n61,
303n63, 310n104
Neeleman, A., 58
Negation, 46, 60, 71, 171, 172, 184, 197,
284n62, 294n30
 contrastive, 172, 284n62
Negative, 127–129, 159, 172, 174, 183, 184,
228, 274n13, 283n56
 adverbial. *See* Adverb(ial), negative
 evaluation, 174, 228
 feature, 129
 indefinite article. *See* Article, indefinite
 polarity item. *See* Polarity item, negative
  (NPI)
 QBNP. *See* Qualitative Binominal Noun
  Phrase (QBNP), negative
 QP. *See* Quantifier, negative
Nichols, J., 262n56
Nikitina, T., 286n74
Niuean, 286n75
Noailly-Le Bihan, M., 287n1, 293n25,
305n72
N of a N construction. *See* Qualitative
 Binominal Noun Phrase (QBNP)
Nom de qualité, 162, 173
Nominal. *See* Noun phrase
Nominalization, 307n81
Nominative. *See* Case
Nondirectionality of predication. *See*
 Predication
Nonintersective
 adjective. *See* Adjective/Adjectival
 interpretation/reading, 31, 32
Norwegian, 103–106, 118–122, 132, 149,
151, 264n6, 275n17, 277nn26–27,
278n33, 281n46, 284n62, 285n74
Noun-complement clause, 241, 243, 244,
310n104
Noun phrase, 2, 5, 33, 34, 37, 54, 55, 66–
74, 79, 80, 82–85, 90, 91, 94–97, 103,
104, 107, 119, 126–130, 132, 134–136,
139, 140, 142–144, 154–156, 158–160,
162–170, 172–177, 180, 181, 183, 184,
186, 188–218, 220–231, 233, 234, 236–
243, 245, 246, 248, 249, 251n1, 256n22,
257n29, 257nn31–32, 264–265n6,
267n13, 268n21, 270–271n29, 272n32,
273n3, 273n5, 274n11, 274n13, 275n18,
277n27, 281n46, 282n50, 283n56,
286nn80–81, 287n85, 287n1, 288nn2–4,
289n6, 289n8, 291n17, 292n21, 293n24,
295n33, 296n37, 297n39, 298n42,

298n45, 298–299n46, 299n47, 299–
300n48, 300n52, 300–301n53, 301n54,
301n56, 302n61, 302n63, 304n66,
305n73, 306n79, 307n85, 308n89,
309n100, 310n103
 agentive (interpretation of), 167
 argumental, 103. *See also* Argument
 bare, 33, 34, 37, 54, 164–169, 186, 197,
  206, 207, 210–212, 216, 257n31, 291n17,
  299n46, 300n52, 300–301n53, 303n64,
  308n93
 complex, 70, 80, 162, 163, 180, 202, 223,
  224, 228, 229, 233, 236, 245, 258n34,
  288n4, 293n24, 297n39, 302n61, 306n79,
  307n85, 308n89
 definite, 68, 70, 91, 94, 152, 153, 159
 heavy. *See* Heavy NP Shift
 indefinite, 67, 82, 91, 152, 153
 objective (interpretation of), 167
 possessed/possessive, 5, 80, 214, 215, 220–
  222, 236–239, 241, 248, 293n24, 302n63
 postcopular. *See* Subject, postcopular
 postverbal. *See* Subject, postverbal
 precopular, 74, 91, 94–97, 126, 156, 158,
  160, 196–199, 203, 287n80, 288n3,
  289n8, 296n37, 305n73
 predicative. *See* Predicate, nominal
 qualitative binominal. *See* Qualitative
  Binominal Noun Phrase (QBNP)
 quantified. *See* Quantifier
 referential, 71, 94
 relativized. *See* Relative clause
 specific, 257n29, 274n11
 size, 169, 186, 193–198, 204, 243
 subject. *See* Subject
Null. *See also under* Asp(ect); Determiner;
  Relative clause; LINKER; Num(ber);
  Operator; Particle; Preposition;
  Pronominal, augment; Pronoun; Pro-
  predicate; RELATOR; Resumptive
 allomorph, 238, 304n66, 305n69
 of "spurious" article. *See* Article,
  "spurious"
 of dative P. *See* Preposition, dative
 noun, 180, 292n21
Num(ber), 69, 169, 171, 179, 184, 187–198,
 210, 211, 225, 226, 254n15, 288n4,
 294n31, 296nn36–37, 298n43, 307n85
 agreement. *See* Agreement
 null, 211
 in QBNPs, 187–198, 294n31, 296nn36–37,
  298n43, 307n85
NumP, 165, 166, 168, 172, 186, 187, 190–
 199, 204, 210–212, 243, 245, 288n4,
 291n17, 299n48, 302n63
Numeration, 111, 302n59

Obenauer, H., 227, 228
Objective (interpretation of) noun phrase.
    See Noun phrase, objective
    (interpretation of)
Oehrle, R., 107, 108
of, 26, 80, 162–164, 166–179, 181–184, 186,
    197, 198, 212–217, 220, 236, 237, 239,
    245, 246, 248. *See also* Copula,
    nominal; LINKER; Preposition, as
    LINKER/RELATOR; RELATOR
  as complementizer, 177, 181
Old French. *See* French
O'Neil, J., 134
one-Replacement, 299–300n48
Operator, 15, 124, 243, 255n19, 257n29,
    268n20, 308n89, 310n101
  empty/null, 15, 255n19, 257n29, 268n20,
    310n101
  logical (∩), 17
  specificity. *See* Specificity

Paardekooper, P. C., 287n1
Padučeva, E., 267n15
Pair-list interpretation, 131
Panagiotidis, Ph., 292n21
Partee, B., 82, 267n15
Parasitic gap, 128–130
Participle, 44, 52, 53, 61, 259n42, 263n47
  agreement. *See* Agreement, participle
Particle, 28, 29, 104, 107–109, 119, 120,
    125, 147, 148, 261n49, 279n30, 281n46,
    281n48, 297n39, 307n82
  aspectual, 147, 148
  case, 261n49. *See also* Case
  construction, 104
  discourse, 297n39, 307n82
  focus. *See* Focus, particle
  modification, 107, 108
   in double object construction, 107
  null/zero, 120
  as phase head, 120, 281n46
  placement, 104, 281n46
Partitive genitive, 181, 182
Passive, 8, 43, 44, 50, 52, 53, 61, 103, 119,
    120, 258n39, 258–259n40, 259n42,
    260n43, 260n45, 261n46, 262–263n56,
    264n3, 277n25, 283n73. *See also* Active/
    passive diathesis alternation; *by*-phrase;
    Participle; Pseudopassive
  double-object, 119, 120
  in ergative languages. *See* Ergative,
    languages
  morpheme, 258n40, 260n43
Pekelder, J., 293n25
Penhallurick, J., 82

Pereltsvaig, A., 62, 64–67, 80, 252n5,
    266n9, 266n11, 282n51, 291n15, 293n25,
    306n78
Perfect, 43, 45, 259n41
Pesetsky, D., 134, 258n35, 287n83
Phase, 5, 112–118, 120, 121, 123, 145, 147,
    149, 150–152, 161, 178, 203, 212, 249,
    259–260n42, 279n37, 281n46, 282n49,
    286n76, 301n58
  edge, 113, 117, 118, 259–260n42
  extension, 115–117, 123, 145, 147, 150–
    152, 178, 203, 212, 249. *See also*
    Move(ment), head
  head. *See* Head, of phase
  Impenetrability Condition (PIC), 113,
    115
  propositional, 113, 259n42
  PrtP as. *See* Particle, as phase head
  small clause as, 112–115, 259–260n42,
    279n37. *See also* Small clause
Phi-/N-feature, 29, 118, 129, 266n9,
    280n44. *See also* Gender; Num(ber)
Pied-piping, 89, 134, 136, 142, 233
  at LF, 134, 136, 142
Pinto, M., 262n54, 262n55
Polarity item, 128, 129, 157, 194, 196,
    274n13, 283n56, 298n45
  licensing, 128, 129, 157, 283n56
  negative (NPI), 194, 196, 298n45
  as modifier, 298n45
Portuguese, 235, 293n25
Possessed/possessive noun phrase. *See*
    Noun phrase, possessed/possessive
Possession, 26, 249
Postal, P., 129, 281n45
Postma, G., 223, 291n19
Postcopular subject. *See* Subject,
    postcopular
Postverbal subject. *See* Subject, postverbal
Predicate, 1–5, 7–23, 25–34, 36–39, 42, 43,
    45, 47–64, 66–73, 75, 76, 78–87, 90–
    102, 104, 105, 107–119, 121–124, 126,
    127, 131, 132, 134, 135, 140, 142–156,
    158–169, 171, 172, 175–181, 183–186,
    188, 190–202, 204, 205, 209–211, 216–
    218, 220–222, 224–233, 235–249,
    251nn1–2, 252nn4–6, 252–253n7,
    253n9, 254nn12–13, 254n15, 255n19,
    256n22, 256nn25–26, 257nn27–30,
    258n36, 261n46, 261n49, 262n51, 263n1,
    264nn4–5, 264–265n6, 265nn7–8,
    266n10, 267n14, 267n17, 268n21, 268–
    269n22, 269n24, 270–271n29, 271–
    272n32, 273nn2–3, 274n7, 275n17,
    276nn21–22, 278n32, 278n34, 279nn37–

38, 280nn42–43, 281n47, 282n50,
  284n63, 286n75, 287n85, 288n3,
  289nn8–9, 289n11, 291n20, 292n22,
  296n36, 296n38, 297n39, 298n40,
  298n43, 300n51, 306n77, 307n81,
  307n83, 307n87, 308nn94–95, 309n98,
  310n101, 310n104
adjectival, 33, 36, 37, 48–50, 91, 235, 241,
  256n26, 262n51, 266n10. *See also*
  Predication, adjectival
  and Copular Inversion, 91
adverbial, 30, 53, 256n25, 258n36. *See also*
  Predication, adverbial
-complement (structure), 4, 13, 43, 45, 47–
  50, 54–56, 61, 80, 161, 162, 172, 176,
  181, 210, 224, 232, 241, 242, 245, 248,
  249, 263n1, 273n3, 292n22, 310n101
empty-headed, 92, 98, 102, 109, 110, 120,
  151, 154, 178–180, 198, 292n21, 292n22,
  300n51
equative, 72. *See also be*
fronting, 18, 98, 104–106, 160
grammatical, 8, 10, 25. *See also*
  Kategoroúmenon
head, 10, 18, 22, 28, 98, 102, 109, 113–
  118, 121, 145, 149–152, 178–180, 248,
  249, 292n22
Inversion, 1–5, 10, 11, 37, 49, 50, 55, 57,
  72–74, 78, 80, 81–87, 90, 92, 94, 95, 98,
  99, 102, 105, 107, 109–113, 116–118,
  121, 122, 124, 126, 127, 131–135, 142,
  143, 145–152, 154, 156, 160–162, 164,
  175, 177–180, 185, 186, 195, 196, 198,
  205, 209, 210, 218, 220–222, 226, 230,
  231, 233, 235–249, 252n4, 264n5, 264–
  265n6, 270–271n29, 273n2, 274n7,
  275n17, 278n32, 279n38, 284n63,
  286n75, 287n85, 292n22, 307n81,
  310n104
  and ECM, 98, 140, 149. *See also* Case,
  marking
linking, 12, 13, 43
logical, 8, 10, 25. *See also Symbebekós*
nominal, 19, 32–34, 36, 37, 39, 48–50, 63,
  66, 82, 85, 90, 91, 94, 99, 111, 124, 140,
  152, 153, 159, 160, 162, 163, 168, 171,
  172, 173, 175, 177, 180, 183–186, 188,
  190, 191, 193, 196, 197, 199–202, 204,
  210, 211, 216–218, 220, 221, 235, 244,
  252n5, 254n15, 257n30, 262n51, 264n4,
  264n6, 266n10, 268–269n22, 273n3,
  280n43, 281n47, 282n50, 289n11,
  296n38, 298n40, 298n43, 300n51. *See*
  also Predication, nominal
  bare, 37, 197, 210, 289n11

definite, 94, 153
specific-indefinite, 153
prepositional, 48–50, 98–110, 118–122,
  148, 149, 158, 236–241. *See also*
  Predication, prepositional
primary, 34, 54. *See also* Predication,
  primary
pro-. *See* Pro-predicate
pronominal, 269n24. *See also* Pro-
  predicate
secondary, 21, 22, 54, 58, 59, 104, 147. *See*
  also Predication, secondary
semantic, 7, 9, 11, 14, 15, 17, 23, 29, 31,
  32, 36, 38
-specifier (structure), 4, 13, 36, 43, 45, 47–
  50, 54, 56, 57, 61, 84–86, 161, 162, 165,
  166, 172, 179, 188, 205, 211, 232, 241,
  242, 245, 248, 249, 252n4, 257n29,
  261n46, 263n1, 273n3, 310n101
stage-level, 265n7
syntactic, 7, 11
Visibility Principle, 147
Predication, 1–5, 7, 8, 10–18, 20–27, 29–
  31, 33, 35–38, 40, 41, 43, 45, 47, 48, 50,
  53–65, 67, 69, 77–80, 82, 84–86, 124,
  141, 147, 161, 162, 164, 165, 175, 183,
  188, 192, 199, 202, 222, 223, 229, 236,
  239–249, 251n1, 252n4, 253nn9–10,
  254n14, 255nn18–19, 255n20, 256n22,
  257n30, 258n39, 259n41, 261n46,
  261n48, 263n1, 264nn4–5, 268n22,
  282n50, 288n3, 304n66, 306n77, 307n83,
  308n95, 309n98, 309nn100–101,
  310n103, 310n105
adjectival, 13, 29, 222, 229–236, 240, 247,
  264n4. *See also* Predicate, adjectival
adverbial, 13, 29, 53, 54. *See also*
  Predicate, adverbial
alternation, 14, 15, 43, 45, 259n41
configuration(al), 4, 11, 12, 14, 16, 22, 23,
  29, 43, 55, 57, 261n46. *See also*
  Configuration(ality)
canonical/straight, 13, 56, 57, 61, 124,
  264n4, 292n22, 307n83
directionality of, 12–14, 247. *See also*
  Predication, nondirectionality of
inverse/inverted, 57, 82, 141, 252n4,
  256n22, 263n1, 282n50
locality of, 11, 12, 45
nominal, 13, 26, 36, 37, 261n48, 264n4.
  See also Predicate, nominal
nondirectionality of, 4, 12–15, 43, 55, 56,
  162, 165, 247–249
prepositional, 36, 261n48. *See also*
  Predicate, prepositional

Predication (cont.)
  primary, 47, 48, 53, 54, 56, 58, 60, 61, 86,
    247, 264n4. *See also* Predicate, primary
  reverse, 13, 33, 35–38, 41, 47, 48, 50, 51,
    54, 56, 57, 61, 84, 85, 188, 245, 252n4,
    259n41, 261n48, 263n1, 264n4
  secondary, 22, 56, 58–60, 247. *See also*
    Predicate, secondary
  straight. *See* Predication, canonical/
    straight
Preposition, 16, 36, 44, 46–50, 52, 53, 85,
    103, 104, 106–109, 111, 133, 141, 147,
    168, 175, 176, 212–214, 238–240,
    252n4, 258n33, 260n44, 261n46, 261n49,
    264n6, 276n22, 277nn28–29, 278n31,
    278n33, 278n34, 280n44, 282n49,
    285n72, 285n74, 288n6, 292n22, 305n72,
    309n98
  as complementizer, 213
  dative, 45, 47, 50, 107, 119, 238–240, 238,
    239, 278n31, 285n74, 305n72
  null/zero allomorph of, 238
  incorporation. *See* Incorporation
  as LINKER, 176, 177. *See also de*; *di*; *of*;
    van, Dutch
  as a monadic category, 309n98
  null, 107, 119, 238, 278n31, 285n74
  as RELATOR, 16, 44, 46–48, 50, 52, 53, 84,
    147, 175, 252n4, 258n33, 261n46,
    261n49. *See also à*; *as*; *by*(-phrase);
    Case, dative; *for*; *like*; *of*; *van*, Dutch
  stranding, 104, 264n6
Prepositional dative construction, 108, 133,
    238. *See also* Double-object
    construction; Triadic
pro, 93, 96, 102, 127, 129, 130, 260n43,
    292n21. *See also* Pro-predicate
  -drop, 96
  licensing (content/formal). *See* Licensing
PRO, 257n29, 260n43
Progovac, L., 17
Pronominal
  augment, 68–70, 75, 76, 269n24, 269n25
    null, 75, 76. *See also pro*
  predicate. *See* Predicate, pronominal
  clitic. *See* Clitic
Pronoun, 129, 218, 219, 223, 269n24,
    280n43, 283n58, 292n21, 305n72
  null, 129
Proper name, 182, 183, 293–294n26,
    294n27, 294n29
Property, 8, 10, 14, 17, 23, 32, 56, 63, 162–
    164, 170, 172, 185, 257n29, 264n4,
    269n22, 301n54
  EPP-. *See* EPP
Proposition, 11, 12, 30, 31, 259n42

Pro-predicate, 70, 72, 73, 75, 80, 92, 95, 98,
    100–102, 112, 151, 158, 160, 268n21,
    271n29, 276n21, 276n22, 278n34
  it, 70, 72
  lo, 268n21
  null, 72, 75, 95, 100, 112, 151, 158, 160,
    271n29
Pseudocleft construction, 73–76, 79, 94, 96,
    97, 137, 156–158, 160, 249, 268n20,
    268n22, 270n26, 270–271n29, 275n14,
    310n101. *See also* Cleft construction
  predicational, 268–269n22, 270n26
  specificational, 73–76, 79, 94, 96, 97, 137,
    156–159, 268n20, 268n22, 270n26, 270–
    271n29, 275n14, 287n84, 310n101
  Type A, 156–159
  Type B, 73, 156–159, 287n84, 310n101
Pseudopassive, 103, 277n25. *See also*
    Passive; Locative, Inversion,
    "beheaded"
Pustet, R., 270n28
Putten, F. van der, 30

Qualitative Binominal Noun Phrase
    (QBNP), 4, 162–222, 225, 227, 229, 234,
    242, 243, 245, 246, 248, 287n1, 287n1–
    306n79, 307n87, 308n95, 309n97
  attributive, 162–173, 175–177, 179, 182–
    184, 186–188, 196–199, 202–212, 216,
    245, 248, 288n6, 289n8, 289n12, 290n13,
    290n14, 294n27, 295n33, 296n37, 299–
    300n48, 300n52, 300–301n53, 301nn54–
    55, 302nn60–61, 306n74, 306n79
  "bare"/*of*-less, 164, 168, 173, 197, 198,
    212, 216, 289n12, 294n27, 300n48
  comparative, 162–165, 167, 170–186, 189–
    199, 202–206, 208–210, 212, 216–221,
    225, 245, 246, 248, 290n14, 293n26,
    294nn30–31, 295n33, 296n37, 297n39,
    298n44, 299nn46–48, 300n49, 300nn51–
    52, 300–301n53, 301n54, 301n55,
    302n60, 304n66, 306n76, 306n78,
    306n79
  and coordination. *See* Coordination, in
    QBNPs
  negative, 172, 183, 197
  "pure degree," 185, 228, 295n33, 297n39
Quantification, 124, 131, 132, 186, 194,
    204, 213, 229, 237, 243, 245, 291n19,
    296n34. *See also* Quantifier
  vacuous, 124
Quantifier, 127, 131–139, 142, 155, 159,
    177, 181, 186, 188, 190, 193–196, 227,
    243, 284n61, 284n65, 284n70, 295n32,
    310n102. *See also* Quantification
  floating, 285n70

negative, 127, 159. *See also* Qualitative
  Binonimal Noun Phrase (QBNP),
  negative
numeral, 188, 190, 194, 195, 243, 310n102
  pure, 132, 194–196
Raising (QR), 133–137, 139, 142, 284n61
  as pied-piping, 134–136, 142
  as Q—raising, 134–136, 142
  restrictions on postcopular/postverbal
    subjects, 131–135, 186
  scope (ambiguity/interaction), 131–138,
    142, 284n65
Québécois. *See* French
Question-answer pair, 157
Quirk, R., 288n5

Ramchand, G., 69, 70, 251n2, 266nn11–13,
  267n16, 269n24
Randall, J., 58
Rapoport, T., 218, 219, 267n15
Regula, M., 287n1
Reinhart, T., 19, 279n37
Relative clause, 5, 26, 69, 71, 72–75, 79, 80,
    89, 92–98, 136, 139–142, 157–160, 223,
    241–243, 248, 249, 267n17, 268nn20–
    21, 272n32, 275n19, 276n21, 281n47,
    285n67, 287n84, 301n54, 301n57,
    302n63, 309n100, 309–310n101,
    310n102, 310nn104–105
  extraposition, 139, 285n67, 285n69
  free, 72–75, 79, 80, 92–98, 157–160,
    267n17, 268n20, 268n21, 272n32,
    276n21, 287n84
    reduced, 72–75, 79, 92–98, 158–160,
    267n17, 268n20, 268n21, 272n32,
    276n21
  head, 26, 93, 97, 152, 242, 268n20,
    309n100
    null, 93, 97, 152
  head-raising analysis of, 309n100
  nonrestrictive, 71, 79, 94, 268n21, 281n47
Relativized Minimality. *See* Minimality
RELATOR, 1–4, 7, 11–17, 22–57, 59–64, 67,
    69, 72, 73, 77, 79, 80, 84–86, 92, 95, 98,
    100, 105–107, 109–120, 123, 124, 127,
    143, 145, 147–152, 158, 161, 164–168,
    171, 172, 175–181, 184, 186, 198, 202–
    206, 208–212, 216, 218, 224, 225, 231,
    233, 238, 241, 242, 244–249, 251nn1–2,
    252nn5–6, 253n7, 255n18, 255n20,
    256nn22–23, 256n26, 257n29, 257n31,
    260n43, 260n45, 261nn46–47, 261n49,
    262nn51–52, 263n56, 264nn3–4, 265n8,
    266n10, 269n24, 273n3, 278n33, 278n36,
    279–280n42, 291n19, 292n22, 304n66,
    307n83, 308n93

as an abstraction, 11, 12, 15, 251n2,
  252n6, 255n18
empty/null *vs.* overt, 49, 63, 64, 167, 206,
  · 209, 212, 225, 249, 260n43
prepositional. *See* Preposition, as
  RELATOR
Remnant movement. *See* Move(ment),
  remnant
Restructuring, 258n34, 283n58
Resumptive, 101, 276n22
Reuland, E., 19, 279n37, 280n43
Rhêma/Rheme, 8, 10, 27
Richards, N., 134
Riemsdijk, H. van, 120
Rightward movement. *See* Move(ment),
  rightward
Ritter, E., 146
Rizzi, L., 27, 51, 93, 102, 256n24
Roberts, I., 258–259n40, 260n43
Rochemont, M., 272n1, 280n43
Roeper, T., 107, 260n43
Rooryck, J., 162, 177, 185, 196, 199, 227,
  228, 288n1, 289n8, 292n23, 294–
  295n32, 295n33, 297n39, 300n49,
  301n58, 306n79
Rooth, M., 27
Rosen, S., 51, 146
Ross, J. R., 157, 287n84
Rothstein, S., 12–14, 21, 247, 253n7,
  256n25, 267n15, 309n98
Rotuman, 25, 26, 256n22, 310n103
Rouveret, A., 76, 269n25
Royen, G., 287n1
Rubin, E., 266n11
Rudnitskaya, E., x
Russell, B., 267n15
Russian, 66, 68, 252n5, 261n49, 265n8,
  266nn10–11, 269n24, 306n76
  Northwestern dialects, 265n8
Ruwet, N., 174, 287n1

Safir, K., 267n15, 287n1
Saito, M., 27, 100, 283n58
Sauerland, U., 282n49
Saxon genitive, 309n99
Scandinavian, 276n23, 281n46
  Mainland, 281n46
Schlenker, P., 157
Scholten, C., 267n15
Scope. *See under* Modification; Quantifier
Scottish Gaelic. *See* Gaelic
šel, 219–222. *See also* Copula, nominal;
  LINKER
Selection, 64, 256n24, 289n9
  lexical, 64
Selkirk, E., 82

Semantics, 7, 9, 11, 14, 15, 17, 23, 29, 31, 32, 36, 38, 67, 131, 141, 144, 159, 163, 178, 185, 196, 199, 253n9, 257n30, 267n15, 268nn19–20, 268n22, 270n26, 289n6, 302n59
  of predication, 7, 9, 11, 14, 15, 17, 23, 29, 31, 32, 36, 38, 253n9
Serbo-Croatian, 306n76
Set, 17, 23, 30, 55, 159, 253n9, 287n85
  intersection, 17, 23, 30, 55, 253n9, 287n85
  strict, 287n85
  identification, 159, 287n85
Seuren, P., 251n1, 267n15
Shaked, A., 219, 306n78, 306n80
Siegel, M., 38, 49, 63, 257n29
Simpson, A., 240, 243, 244, 310n102, 310n105
Singhapreecha, P., x, 223, 229, 232, 233, 256n22, 308nn90–91, 308n94, 309n100
Slavic, 267n15, 269n24, 306n76
Sleeman, P., 292n21
Small clause, 1–4, 7, 17, 18, 22, 26, 34, 38, 56–65, 68–72, 77–80, 90, 91, 93–95, 97, 100, 105, 110–119, 123, 124, 133, 134, 137, 138, 142, 144, 145, 147–152, 158, 164, 167, 168, 172, 175–178, 184, 186, 187, 190, 191, 193, 197, 198, 201, 203, 208, 209, 216, 218, 224, 225, 233, 237–239, 241, 243, 245–249, 251n1, 253n8, 254n12, 254nn14–15, 255n20, 261n48, 264nn4–5, 264–265n6, 268n21, 269n24, 271n32, 272n2, 279n37, 285n70, 292n22, 304n66, 308nn93–95, 310n104
  "bare," 3, 7, 56, 58, 62, 64, 65, 80, 90, 247, 264nn5–6
  functional head of, 2, 34, 116, 147, 148, 150, 175, 245, 264–265n6, 269n24. See also Head, functional
  and functional structure, 22, 34, 56, 62, 77, 80, 113–119, 147–150, 175, 245, 247, 264–265n6
  as phase. See Phase, small clause as
  remnant, 233, 239, 241. See also Move(ment), remnant
  symmetrical, 58, 64, 90, 91, 264n6
Smith, M., 266n11
Spanish, 45, 100, 174, 179, 180, 191, 192, 198–206, 208, 211, 212, 235, 287n1, 291n20, 293n25, 295n33, 297n39, 298n42, 300n49, 300n51, 300–301n53, 301nn56–57, 302n61, 302–303n63, 308–309n96
  Puerto Rican, 291n20
Speas, M., 18
Spec-Head agreement. See Agreement, Spec-Head

Specificational. See under Copular, sentence; Pseudocleft construction
Specificity, 257n29, 259n40, 271n32, 274n11
  Condition, 274n11
  operator, 257n29
Sportiche, D., 18, 51, 285n71
"Spurious" article. See Article, "spurious"
Starke, M., 16
Stenshoel, E., 281n46
Stowell, T., x, 18, 22, 108, 244, 254n12, 267n15, 287n1
String-vacuous. See under Extraposition; Move(ment); Topicalization
Subextraction. See Extraction, sub-
Subjacency, 86, 121, 123, 125, 252n7, 282n53
Subject, 1–5, 7–19, 21–31, 33, 34, 43, 45, 47–52, 54–64, 68–70, 72, 74, 75, 77–81, 83–88, 92–100, 102, 104, 105, 107–124, 126–142, 144, 145, 147–149, 151, 152, 154–158, 160–165, 169, 173, 175, 178–180, 182–184, 186, 188, 190, 191–198, 202, 204, 209, 210, 216–219, 221, 224–228, 230–232, 235, 236, 238, 239, 241–245, 247–249, 251n1, 251n2, 252n6, 253n9, 253n10, 253–254n12, 254n15, 255nn18–20, 256nn21–22, 257n27, 257n29, 258n36, 260n43, 261n46, 261n49, 262nn53–54, 263nn56–58, 263n1, 264n4, 265n6, 265n8, 268n21, 269n25, 270n29, 271n32, 272n2, 273nn4–5, 274n10, 275n16, 275n18, 277n24, 277nn26–27, 279n38, 280nn42–43, 281n47, 284n62, 286n81, 287n84, 296n37, 297n39, 298n43, 301n57, 302n63, 304n66, 307n83, 307n86, 308n89, 308nn92–95, 309n98, 310n104. See also Hypokeímenon (subject)
  -aux(iliary) inversion. See Inversion, subject-aux(iliary)
  clitic inversion. See Inversion, subject clitic
  grammatical, 8, 10, 25
  logical, 8, 10, 25, 27. See also Topic
  LP-internal. See LP-Internal Subject Hypothesis
  postcopular, 67, 68, 79, 82–85, 94–96, 117, 123, 124, 126, 132, 135, 137, 139–142, 154, 155, 188, 190–197, 204, 205, 209–212, 230, 242, 243, 270n29, 280n43, 281n47, 296n37, 298n42, 298n45, 299nn46–47, 299–300n48, 300n52, 301n54, 302n63. See also Subject, postverbal
  extraction/movement of. See Extraction, of postcopular/postverbal subject

and quantification/scope. *See* Quantifier, restrictions on postcopular/postverbal subject
postverbal, 51, 52, 81–83, 85, 87, 99, 104, 111, 117–119, 121–124, 126–127, 130–132, 134–136, 158, 262n53, 262n54, 263n57, 272n2, 273nn4–5, 275n16, 275n18, 277n24, 284n62. *See also* Subject, postcopular
and Antecedent-Contained Deletion (ACD), 136–142. *See also* Antecedent-Contained Deletion (ACD)
extraction/movement of. *See* Extraction, of postcopular/postverbal subject
in Free Inversion, 51, 52, 262n53, 262n54, 263n57. *See also* Inversion, Free
and Heavy NP Shift, 127–130, 272n2, 275n16, 275n18. *See also* Heavy NP Shift
and quantification/scope. *See* Quantifier
and *wh-in-situ*, 130, 131. *See also* *wh*-
-predicate relationship/structure, 3, 8, 10, 11, 26, 31, 48, 54, 56, 58–62, 64, 161, 202, 247, 256n22, 257n27, 261n46, 265n8
thematic, 25
VP-internal. *See* LP-Internal Subject Hypothesis
Sugita, M., 159, 287n85
Suñer, A., 165, 191, 287n1, 291n18, 305n72
Superiority, 134
Superordinate, 79. *See also* Hyperonym; Predicate
Superscriptional, 270n29, 271n32
Svenonius, P., 281n46
Symbebekós (logical predicate), 8, 10, 25
Swart, H. de, 169, 289n10, 304n67
Swedish, 281n46, 304n66
Swiss German. *See* German
Symmetry/symmetrical, 56, 66–68, 70, 80, 265n6. *See also* Asymmetry/asymmetrical
Szabó, Z., 32–34, 257n28, 257n30
Szabolcsi, A., 162, 218, 246, 253n9, 308n87
Szekely, R., 295n33, 296n36, 297n39
Szendrői, K., 89, 274n6

Takano, Y., 127, 128, 258n35, 283n56
Tang, C. -C. J., 240
Taraldsen, T., 103, 283n60
Tautology, 268n20
Taylor, T., 12
T-chain. *See* T(ense), -chain

Tellier, C., 164, 165, 206, 227, 228, 231, 287–288n1, 289n8, 290n14, 295n33, 297n39, 300–301n53, 301n58
T(ense), 15, 16, 23, 24, 28, 29, 44–49, 51–58, 60, 61, 63, 71, 92, 95, 102, 105, 111–113, 117–120, 147, 152, 191, 216–218, 221, 255n20, 256n21, 259nn41–42, 262n53, 262n56, 263nn57–58, 265nn7–8, 267n15, 276n21, 277nn26–27, 277n29, 278n36, 280nn43–44, 306n77
-chain, 147
and EPP, 118. *See also* EPP
feature, 44, 63, 221, 259n41, 259n42
as identifier of *v*, 46, 47
as RELATOR, 16, 23, 24, 28, 51, 53, 54, 255n20, 278n36
-support, 63, 216, 265n7, 265n8
Thai, 229, 232–235, 240, 241, 308n91
that-trace effect, 54, 273n5. *See also* ECP
lifted by adverbials, 54
in Locative Inversion constructions. *See* Locative, Inversion, and *that-t* effects
there-sentence, 273n2
Theta (2-) marking, 35
autonymous, 35
and lexical heads. *See* Head
thîi, 230, 232–235, 241. *See also* Copula, nominal; LINKER
Thomas, J., 287n1
Toorn, M. C. van den, 287n1
Topic, 9, 10, 16, 25–28, 55, 87, 89, 90, 98–102, 122, 125, 126, 135, 156–160, 218, 270–271, 282, 256nn22–23, 270–271n29, 275n19, 275–276n20, 276n21, 282n53. *See also* Topicalization
-Comment structure, 10, 26–28, 157, 158, 270–271n29
hanging, 159, 256n23
head, 27, 55, 271n29
island, 122, 282n53
as logical subject. *See* Subject, logical
marker, 256n22
and movement/base-generation, 101, 102, 122, 135, 156–158
and subextraction, 100
Topicalization, 7, 25, 27, 98–100, 125, 126, 247, 252n7, 256n23, 273n3, 275–276n20, 287n83, 307n86, 309n98. *See also* Topic
adjunction approach to, 27
PP-, 256n23, 309n98. *See also* Locative, Inversion
string-vacuous, 27, 100
VP-. *See* VP, -fronting
Torrego, E., 100
Tortora, C., 309n99

tough-movement. *See* Move(ment), *tough*-
Transitive
  copula. *See* Copula, transitive
  expletive construction (TEC), 272n2
  pseudopassive. *See* Pseudopassive
Triadic, 28, 119
  construction, 28. *See also* Applicative;
    Double-object construction;
    Prepositional dative construction
  predicate, 28
Troseth, E., 258n37, 284n66, 309n97
Tutescu, M., 287n1
Typology, 56, 58, 73, 77–79, 92, 153, 247,
    267n15, 270n28
  of copular sentences. *See* Copular,
    sentence
  language, 270n28

Unergative, 25, 47, 50, 51, 261n47, 262n53,
    263n57, 278n36
Uniformity of Theta-Assignment
    Hypothesis (UTAH), 14, 15
  and the external argument, 14, 15
Uspenskij, V., 267n15

vacuous. *See under* Extraposition;
    Move(ment); Quantification;
    Topicalization
van.
  Dutch, 2, 169–171, 174–176, 183, 188–
    193, 197, 206, 207, 210, 212, 215, 225,
    226, 265n6, 298n41, 308n88. *See also*
    Copula, nominal; LINKER; Preposition,
    as LINKER/RELATOR; RELATOR
  Hungarian ('be'), 217, 306n77. *See also*
    Copula; RELATOR
Vehicle change, 141. *See also* Antecedent-
    Contained Deletion (ACD)
Vendler, Z., 30
Verb. *See also* VP
  causative. *See* Causative
  dynamic, 58
  epistemic, 58
  lexical, 63, 123
    copula as. *See* Copula, as lexical/2-role
    assigning element
  light (*v*), 19, 22–24, 44–47, 52, 55, 112,
    255n17, 255n18, 255n20, 261n47,
    262n55, 282n49. *See also* vP
  generalized, 23, 282n49
  movement/raising, 71, 109, 262n53,
    263n57. *See also* Move(ment)
    and PF, 109
  successive-cyclic, 109
  positional, 58
  Second, 274n12, 280n43

Vergnaud, J. -R., 309n100
Verheugd, E., 78, 229, 230, 247
Vinka, M., 281n46
Voice, 19
*v*P, 112, 251n1, 254n13, 258n36, 282n49.
    See also Verb, light (*v*)
  as phase, 112, 282n49
VP, 14, 18–20, 24, 31, 32, 40–42, 45, 46,
    51–53, 60, 82, 128, 136–142, 252n7,
    253n11, 253–254n12, 254n13, 255nn18–
    20, 258n36, 259–260n42, 260n45,
    261nn46–47, 262n54, 263n57, 272n2,
    284n64, 285n67, 286n75
  as argument of Infl, 252n7
  bare, 45, 259n42
  causativized, 46, 60, 260n45, 261nn46–47.
    See also Causative
  -fronting, 18, 40, 41, 252n2, 252n7. *See
    also* Move(ment)
  gap, 136–142, 284n64. *See also*
    Antecedent-Contained Deletion (ACD)
  -Internal Subject Hypothesis. *See* LP-
    Internal Subject Hypothesis
  reconstructed, 141, 284n64. *See also*
    Antecedent-Contained Deletion
    (ACD)
  remnant, 128. *See also* Move(ment),
    remnant
  root-, 45, 46
  -shell structure, 20, 32, 254n13
  in SpecTP, 52, 53, 286n75
  as 2-governed by Infl, 252n7
Vries, M. de, 283n57

was für-exclamative. *See* Exclamative
was für-interrogative. *See* Interrogative
wat-exclamative. *See* Exclamative
wat-indefinite. *See* Indefinite
wat voor-interrogative. *See* Interrogative
Welsh, 75, 76, 269n25
wh-
  exclamative. *See* Exclamative
  extraction, 71–73, 108, 125, 126, 130, 195,
    277n24, 281n74, 282n49
    in inverse copular sentences, 71, 125, 126,
      281n47
    in equative copular sentences, 71–74
    of postcopular/postverbal subject. *See*
      Extraction, of postcopular/postverbal
      subject
  feature, 89, 131
  in-situ, 130, 131
  interrogative. *See* Interrogative, *wh*-
Whelpton, M., 260n43
Whitman, J., 272n2
Wierzbicka, A., 266n11

Wilder, C., x, 73, 146, 156, 157, 271n29,
    287n83
Williams, E., 10, 12, 17, 58, 59, 260n43
Winter, Y., 169, 289n10, 304n67
Wit, P. de, 288n1

Zamparelli, R., 70, 94
Zaring, L., 76, 267n15, 270n27
Zero allomorph. *See* Null, allomorph
Zwarts, J., 169, 289n10, 304n67